JACOB HARRIS PATTON, A. M., PH. D.

A POPULAR HISTORY
OF
THE PRESBYTERIAN CHURCH
IN THE
UNITED STATES OF AMERICA

BY
JACOB HARRIS PATTON, A.M., Ph. D.
AUTHOR OF
FOUR HUNDRED YEARS OF AMERICAN HISTORY;
NATURAL RESOURCES OF THE UNITED STATES;
POLITICAL ECONOMY FOR AMERICAN YOUTH;
POLITICAL PARTIES IN THE UNITED STATES;
WHICH RELIGION SATISFIES THE WANTS OF
THE SOUL? ETC.

ILLUSTRATED

**Fredonia Books
Amsterdam, The Netherlands**

A Popular History of the Presbyterian Church in the United States of America

by
Jacob Harris Patton

ISBN: 1-4101-0463-X

Copyright © 2004 by Fredonia Books

Reprinted from the 1900 edition

Fredonia Books
Amsterdam, The Netherlands
http://www.fredoniabooks.com

All rights reserved, including the right to reproduce this book, or portions thereof, in any form.

In order to make original editions of historical works available to scholars at an economical price, this facsimile of the original edition of 1900 is reproduced from the best available copy and has been digitally enhanced to improve legibility, but the text remains unaltered to retain historical authenticity.

THE AUTHOR RESPECTFULLY DEDICATES THIS HISTORY

TO THE

MINISTRY, THE ELDERSHIP AND THE PRIVATE MEMBERS

OF THE

PRESBYTERIAN CHURCH.

PREFACE.

This volume is designed to trace concisely but clearly the History and Principles of the Presbyterian Church from the time of Henry VIII. to the close of the General Assembly of 1899. The effort has been to present the facts in such history, and note their influence; meanwhile, to give special attention to the all-important phase of the *inner Christian life* of the Church. In ascertaining the knowledge in respect to the latter subject, attention has been directed, as occasion required, to the lives and labors of leading men in the ministry, as well as laymen, around whom clustered influences for good, that often extended far and wide in their respective communities, and even to the Church at large.

The author has availed himself of highly important and original documents pertaining to the Congregationalists and Presbyterians during the Colonial period. (*See authorities consulted.*)

When preparing his "Four Hundred Years of American History," the attention of the author was often drawn to the influence of the Presbyterian Church during the last half century of the Colonial times and also during the current growth of our national life. This influence was felt upon the domestic and Christian as well as upon the political life of the people. In our country, governed as it is by representatives elected by the people themselves, the moral connection between political and church life is consistent and peculiarly intimate. It therefore comes within the scope of this history to trace the influences, good or bad, of the events and policies, whereby the condition of public affairs has incidentally aided the progress of the Church, and sometimes had a retarding effect, as in the case of war or of financial or industrial disturbances whereby all the citizens were more or less affected.

The rule has been to record only those facts which have

had influence, and to present them in such fulness that the reader may easily see their bearings upon the subject in hand, and also to mould the history into a consecutive narrative, in order that the transition from one subject to another may be easily seen.

The reader will learn from its inner Christian life that it has always been a missionary church; that its principles of religious liberty repudiate absolutely the assumption of civil authorities to interfere in any respect *whatever* in religious affairs, but, on the other hand, to confine themselves strictly to protect the religious rights of *all* the citizens, without reference to matters of their belief.

This volume is written in the hope of inducing intelligent Presbyterians of both sexes, especially the middle-aged and the younger portion, to become familiar with the remarkable history of their own church, in its early trials, and the great leading principles of its church polity, by which the rights of the people—the church members—have ever been recognized and respected, and that while most strenuous in its adherence to the essential doctrines of the Gospel, yet in respect to non-essentials ever liberal.

The illustrations consist of the portraits of some of the Presbyterian worthies who did so much to promote the cause of Christianity by their labors within their own Church. They were the men who, being efficiently supported by brother ministers of lesser note, were enabled, in the latter part of the last century and the first half of this, to lay the foundations of the present benevolent institutions of the Church, which to-day are so grandly exerting influence for good. Many others of these noble men have also been noticed in brief sketches under the title of "Presbyterian Worthies," who, working in unison, though often in different spheres, had the same object in view.

NOTE: At the bottom of each picture are numbers designating the page in the book on which the person's name is mentioned.   J. H. P.

New York City, March, 1900.

THE FOLLOWING AUTHORITIES HAVE BEEN CONSULTED.

Historians of the Presbyterian Church: Rev. Drs. Charles Hodge, Richard Webster, Robert Davidson, Robert Thompson, and Lenord W. Bacon (the last two, VI., XIII. Ch. Hist. Series). Dr. E. H. Gillett, 2 vols., an admirable work, revised in 1864. Prof. Charles A. Briggs, American Presbyterianism, covering the Colonial period. The latter history has the merit of being greatly enriched by the use of *original manuscript documents,* which were "unknown to previous historians" [of the Presbyterian Church], "with the single exception of those" [that were made public] "of the Society for the Propagation of the Gospel in Foreign Parts." (*See p. 94 of this volume.*)

Prof. Briggs, during a sojourn in Great Britain in 1884, availed himself of an opportunity in a dozen or more libraries—secular and ecclesiastical—to search for manuscript reports and documents that pertained to the Congregational and Presbyterian churches in America during the Colonial period. All the documents having a bearing on that subject he had transcribed under careful supervision, and afterward deposited the copies in convenient volumes in the Library of Union Theological Seminary, New York City. Portions of these documents were published for the first time in an Appendix—*pp. I.-CXXII.*—to American Presbyterianism.

Drs. Robert Baird, "Religion in America"; Charles W. Baird, "Huguenot Emigration." Bishop Meade, "Old Churches of Virginia." Benedict, "History of the Baptists." Rev. Drs. Francis Hawks, "Episcopal Church in Virginia and North Carolina"; William H. Foote, "Sketches of Virginia"; Abel Stevens, "History of Methodism"; Sprague's "Annals of the American Pulpit"; "The Briggs Heresy Case," by Dr. John J. McCook, and the other documents pertaining to the same.

CONTENTS.

CHAPTER I.

American Presbyterianism.—Parity of the Ministry.—Elders or Presbyters.—The Bishops.—Paul and Timothy, Commissioners.—The Reformers on Church Government.—Union of Church and State.—The Prelatical Form of Church Government. 1

CHAPTER II.

THE REFORMATION IN ENGLAND.

Magna Charta.—Wycklif and Tyndale's Translations.—Englishmen's Rights.—The People's Voice in Church Government.—Different Forms of Which.—Henry VIII. as Head of the Church.—Progress of the English People.—The Prelatical System.—The Puritan.—Union of Church and State in England.—The Exiles Abroad.—What They Learned. 9

CHAPTER III.

PARITY OF THE MINISTRY OR CLERGY.

Significant Names.—The Term Rector.—The Non-Persecutors.—Partial Responsibility of a Subordinate.—Apostolic Succession. 18

CHAPTER IV.

A PHASE OF THE REFORMATION.

A Religious Force.—Self-Supporting Church.—Its Spirituality Enhanced.—*Jure Divino* Doctrine.—True Relation of the State to the Church. 27

CHAPTER V.

PRESBYTERIANS AND PURITANS IN HENRY VIII.'S REIGN.

PAGE.

Confessions of Faith.—The Two Parties.—The Heroic Age.
—Harmony of Beliefs.—TheXXXIX. Articles. . . 31

CHAPTER VI.

PRESBYTERIANS IN THE REIGNS OF ELIZABETH AND JAMES.

The Formation of a Presbytery.—The Independents Unorganized.—The Primitive Church Self-supporting.—King James—His Character.—James and the General Assembly.—The Influence of the Bishops.—Hopes Disappointed.—Migrations to Ireland.—The Culdee Church.—The Translation of the Bible. 36

CHAPTER VII.

SABBATH DESECRATION—THE SOLEMN LEAGUE AND COVENANT.

The Book of Sports.—Influence of the Sabbath.—The Continental Sabbath.—The Solemn League and Covenant.—Why Were the Bishops Feared?—Effects of Trials and Persecutions.—Presbyterian Household Training. . 46

CHAPTER VIII.

WESTMINSTER CONFESSION—EVENTS CONNECTED THEREWITH.

The Parliamentary Ordinance.—Westminster Assembly.—Directory for Public Worship.—The Members of the Assembly.—Its Character.—Civil Commotions.—Apostolic Succession—Questions Thereon.—Cromwell's Doings.—The New Parliament.—The Divine Right for Church Government.—Plan for a State Church. . . 55

CONTENTS. XI

CHAPTER IX.

MIGRATIONS TO THE COLONIES—CONGREGATIONAL AND PRESBYTERIAN.

PAGE.

Puritans in Virginia.—Policy of the Virginia Company.—Plymouth Colony.—A Presbyterian Church Organized.—Why the Presbyterians were Liberal.—Limited Influence of the Synod.—The Constitution of the Congregational Church.—Migrations of Presbyterians to New York.—Christian Brotherhood Practised.—Statement of Governor Andros.——Influence of the Act of Toleration. . 66

CHAPTER X.

CONTRASTS IN LANDHOLDINGS—CAVALIERS—ELDERS AS WORTHIES.

Royalists.—Berkeley's Prayer.—Why the Enmity of the Clergy.—The Charter for Maryland.—The Liberal Policy.—The Repentant Chaplain.—Presbyterian Elders and Worthies.—Doughty and Hill. 76

CHAPTER XI.

FRANCIS MAKEMIE—PRESBYTERIANISM IN SEVERAL COLONIES.

Francis Makemie.—His Business Talents.—The Memorial Church.—A Stanch Defender of Religious Liberty.—A Presbyterian Church Organized.—Makemie's Trial.—Presbyterianism in New Jersey—In Delaware and Pennsylvania.—In South Carolina.—Missionaries from New England.—A Colony Formed on the Isthmus of Darien. 82

CHAPTER XII.

THE PRESBYTERY OF PHILADELPHIA (1706).

Presbytery Constituted.—The First Missionary Society.—"Heads of Department."—A Society for Propagating the Gospel.—Difficulties and Progress.—Introduction of the Eldership. 91

CHAPTER XIII.

Persecutions and Trials.

A Church and Parsonage Seized.—Bribery and Trickery.—The Case of the *First* Presbyterian Church.—A Law Misapplied. 99

CHAPTER XIV.

Formation of a Synod.

Missionary Funds.—Fraternal Intercourse.—Test and Schism Acts.—William Tennent.—The *First* Log College.—Guarding the Faith.—The Effects of the Adopting Act.—Liberal and Strict Subscription.—Presbyterians in Maine.—Transfer of the Log College.—Princeton College.—The Educational Fund.—The Leading Points of Influence. 107

CHAPTER XV.

Origin of Presbyterianism in Virginia.

Morris' Reading-House.—Persecutions and Petty Annoyances.—The Name Presbyterian.—Further Annoyances. 121

CHAPTER XVI.

The Log Colleges.

The Bible Studied as a Whole.—The Two Academies—Hampden — Sidney. — Augusta Academy. — Theology Taught Separately.—Private Classical Schools.—Schools Beyond the Alleghanies (North).—Germs of Two Colleges—Jefferson and Washington.—Study on Two Lines.—The Religious Influence.—Schools beyond the Alleghanies (South).—Greeneville College. 127

CONTENTS. XIII

CHAPTER XVII.

PRESBYTERIAN SETTLEMENTS IN THE SHENANDOAH VALLEY.

PAGE.

Letters of the Synod and Governor Gooch.—Presbyterians in North Carolina.—Mission of Rev. William Robinson. —Dr. Samuel Davies.—An Incident.—The Presbyterians of Hanover County Specially Hated.—Modes of Levying Church Rates.—The Mecklenburg Declaration.—A Sad History. 137

CHAPTER XVIII.

REVIVALS—DIVISION AND REUNION.

Moravians and Pietists.—Influence of Pietism.—Differences of Opinion.—The Old Side.—New Side.—Division of the Synod.—Zeal for Religion.—The Reunion.—Long Island Churches. 149

CHAPTER XIX.

SEPARATION OF CHURCH AND STATE IN VIRGINIA.

The Half-Way Covenant.—Why the Harsh Intolerance in Virginia.—The Vagrant in Connecticut and New York. —Illiberal Laws in Virginia.—Freedom from Ecclesiastical Clannishness.—Grades of Ministerial Education.— Severe Conflicts.—Efforts to Reform Clerical Morals.— Preachers Appointed by the Crown.—English Church Established.—Influence of an Educated Ministry.—Conflicts in Respect to Salaries.—A Great Principle Established. 159

CHAPTER XX.

SEPARATION OF CHURCH AND STATE—CONTINUED.

The Struggle Begins.—Committee on Religion and Morality. —The Petitions; The Demand as a Right.—Upon Whom Fell the Burden of the Conflict?—The Legislature Met on Its Own Ground.—Objectionable Laws Repealed.—

Prejudices Roused.— Tories.— Whigs.— Quakers.— The General Assessment.—Another Memorial.—Defects in the Law of Repeal.—Security for Religious Rights Demanded.—Protest against Incorporating the Episcopal Church.—General Assessment Again.—Effects of Petitions.—Contests in Respect to Glebes.—A Half-Century of Intolerance Remembered.—An Apology Urged.—Who Began the Movement and Secured the Result.—Religious Freedom and Patriotism.—Influence of the Measure in New England.—Slavery Opposed.—Personal Responsibility Recognized.—Self-Denial and Benevolence.—Influence of the Voluntary Principle.—A Nation's Moral Training. 175

CHAPTER XXI.

THE TROUBLOUS TIMES.

Patriotism.—Pastoral Letter.—The Evil Influence.—The Two Movements.—Kinds of Church Government.—A Comprehensive One.—Discordant and Rival States. . . 198

CHAPTER XXII.

THE GENERAL ASSEMBLY ARRANGED FOR.

Increase of the Church.—Four Synods Organized.—The General Assembly Constituted.—The Address to President Washington; His Reply.—Doctrinal Truths Guarded.— A Christian Patriotism.—*Ex-officio* Members.—Voting by Orders.—Ecclesiastical Despotism. . . . 205

CHAPTER XXIII.

PRESBYTERIAN MOVEMENTS IN THE SOUTH.

The Migrations.—The Three Pioneer Ministers.—Retarding Influences.—The Sabbath Desecrated.—The Surveyor; His News.—The Founding of a Church.—The Planters of the Church in Tennessee.—A Peculiar Type of Infidelity.—The Political Clubs. 214

CHAPTER XXIV.

THE GREAT REVIVAL.

Rev. James McGready.—Irreligious Conditions.—Characteristics of the Revival.—Injurious Divisions.—The Influence of the Revival.—Camp Meetings.—Uneducated Men Licensed to Preach.—Cumberland Presbyterians.—Another Great Revival.—The Counterpart.—The Revival Extends.—The Contrast. 224

CHAPTER XXV.

THE WAY PREPARED FOR THE PLAN OF UNION.

Line of Migration.—Losses and Regains.—Interest in Missions.—Plan of Union Suggested.—Presbyterial Government Preferred.—Why the Churches Prospered.—Why Western New York Prospered.—Result of Christian Effort.—Effects of the Great Revival.—Standing Committees Appointed.—The Sad Interference.—Efforts in Favor of Temperance.—Reports on the Same. . . 235

CHAPTER XXVI.

PRESBYTERIAN WORTHIES.

Taggart, Dana, Morrison.—Blatchford, Nott, Porter.—Rodgers, Perrine, Romeyn, Spring.—Richards, Griffin.—Green, the Alexanders, Miller, Finley.—Janeway, Wilson, Skinner, Ely, Patterson. 246

CHAPTER XXVII.

PRESBYTERIAN WORTHIES—CONTINUED.

Hoge, Rice.—John McMillan.—Porter, Power, Marquis, Dunlap, Ralston.—An Appreciative Estimate.—The Combined Influence. 257

CHAPTER XXVIII.

PROGRESS OF THE CHURCH.

PAGE.

Formation of National Societies.—The Western.—Educational Societies, Their Union.—Duelling.—Opposition to Slavery, Deliverance on.—Francis Herron.—Revivals in the South.—Progress in Religion, How Promoted.—The Migration of a Church.—Prayer Meetings.—Union Meetings.—Drs. James Hall and S. E. McCorkle. . . . 265

CHAPTER XXIX.

PROGRESS OF THE CHURCH—CONTINUED.

Drs. Ingles and Nevens.—Religious Interest in New Jersey.—Increase of the Church in New York State.—Dr. James Carnahan.—Associations and Presbyteries.—Religion West of the Genesee.—Immigration.—Co-operation. 280

CHAPTER XXX.

SETTLEMENTS AND CHURCHES IN THE WEST.

Settlement of Marietta.—Revs. Story, Lindsley, Hughes.—Cincinnati Founded.—The First Church Organized.—Settlements in the Reserve.—Ministers of the Presbytery of Ohio.—Rev. Joseph Badger.—Woman's Self-denying Labors.—Population and Preachers. . . 288

CHAPTER XXXI.

INCREASE OF THE CHURCH.

Accessions from Other Bodies.—Reports on Revivals.—Board of Missions.—The *Ex-officio* Principle Suggested.—Efforts for an Educated Ministry.—Revivals in Colleges.—Theological Seminaries.—Churches in Need of Pastors.—Domestic Missionary Society.—Charleston Association, Its Action.—Psalmody, Intemperance, Sabbath Desecration.—Increasing Interest in Missions.—Deliverance on Slavery. 301

CHAPTER XXXII.

INCREASE OF THE CHURCH—CONTINUED.

Plans for Placing the Bible in Every Family.—Increased Missionary Efforts.—Home Missionary Society Formed.—Influence of the First Address of the Committee.—Eastern Christians Interested. — Destitutions. — The Church in New Orleans and Mobile.—In Huntsville.—In Georgia, Carolinas, Florida.—Church beyond the Mountains. 310

CHAPTER XXXIII.

THEOLOGICAL SEMINARIES.

Auburn Seminary.—Western or Allegheny.—Lane.—Centre of Population.—Religious Condition of the Great Valley.—Seminary at Maryville.—Oakland College.—Union Seminary, Virginia.—President Matthew Brown. . 318

CHAPTER XXXIV.

LOUISIANA PURCHASED.

Indian Missions in the Southwest.—In Georgia.—The Indians Removed.—Individual Influence.—Dr. Charles Coffin.—Dr. Isaac Anderson.—President of Maryville College.—The Migration of a Congregation, James White Stephenson.—Characteristic Zeal.—Gideon Blackburn. 326

CHAPTER XXXV.

NEW ORLEANS—THE TOWNS UP THE RIVER.

The People of New Orleans.—Elias Cornelius.—Sylvester Larned.—Religion in the Towns up the River.—Samuel Royce.—Educational Society.—The American Board.—The Action *ex Officio*. 338

CHAPTER XXXVI.

Numerous Revivals.

Revivals in Ohio, Indiana, and Illinois.—In Kentucky, the Carolinas, and Georgia.—In Virginia.—The Sabbath, Sunday Mails.—The Famous Report on the Same.—Ratio of Representation in the Assembly.—Statistics of the Church. 345

CHAPTER XXXVII.

Societies—Churches—Colleges.

Home Missions.—Organizing Churches.—Father Dickey.—Immigration of Farmers.—The Time of Commissions Limited.—The Church at the Capital of Indiana.—Rev. Isaac Reed.—Number of Churches and Ministers.—Missionaries in Illinois.—Illinois College. 353

CHAPTER XXXVIII.

Relation of Churches to Certain Presbyteries.

Why the Interest in Missouri.—Religious Character of St. Louis.—The Tour of Samuel J. Mills.—Rev. Samuel Giddings.—Rev. Timothy Flint.—Reasons for the Migration.—A Number of Missionaries.—John Matthews.—Missions in Michigan.—Traits of Early Settlers.—Labors of Rev. John Monteith.—Mission at the Straits of St. Mary.—The Reports.—Wives of Missionaries. . 364

CHAPTER XXXIX.

A Change of Policy.

Progress of the Church.—The Awakened Interest.—The Change within Thirty Years.—Areas of Missionary Territory compared.—What Presbyteries Had at Stake.—Church Discipline.—Irresponsibility of Voluntary Societies.—The Assembly's Board, and of Education.—Elements That Caused Friction.—An Important Movement.—Scotch Presbyterians.—The Special Ground Taken. 380

CONTENTS.   XIX

CHAPTER XL.

Unsubstantiated Rumors.

Conflict of Theological Opinions.—New Measures.—Unjust Suspicions.—An Important Rule Adopted.—Ministers Ordained Injudiciously. 392

CHAPTER XLI.

The Trial of Albert Barnes.

The Sermon.—Appeal to the Synod.—The Matter Submitted.—Elective Affinity.—Biblical Notes.—The Second Trial.—The Appeal to the Assembly.—Bible Study Promoted.—The Example Followed.—The Terms of Distinction. 399

CHAPTER XLII.

Trial of Dr. Lyman Beecher.

A Feeling of Unrest.—The Recommendations.—Suspicions Disproved.—Dr. Beecher and Dr. Wilson.—The Charges Not Sustained.—Dr. Wilson Withdraws His Appeal.—Suggestive Considerations.—Abstract Phases of Thought. 408

CHAPTER XLIII.

Measures Leading to the Division.

The New and the Old School.—Conditions on Which Ministers Were Received.—The Charges in the Memorial.—The Protest Not Received.—The Act and Testimony.—Signers and Objectors to the Act.—A Convention Called.—The Effects of the Agitation.—Grievances.—Elective Affinity.—Changes of Opinion.—A Committee of Conference.—Misleading Statements.—Instructions Transcended.—Union Theological Seminary in New York City. 416

CHAPTER XLIV.

The Division of the Church.

PAGE.

Plans Laid for Future Action.—The Philadelphia Convention.—Its Recommendations.—A Special Grievance.—The Assembly of 1837.—Expression of Good Will, Reasons for Action.—An Ominous Vote.—Amicable Division Proposed.—Excision of Synods.—Dealing with Presbyteries.—Board of Missions.—The Protests.—Errors Acted Upon.—The Connecticut Missionary Society.—Sad Statistics.—Difficulties in Attending General Assemblies. —The Action on Slavery.—The Pastoral Circular. . 430

CHAPTER XLV.

The Two Assemblies.

Complaint and Acts of the Convention.—The Assembly of 1838.—The Crisis Had Come.—The Old School Assembly.—The Question of Slavery.—The New School Assembly.—Effort to Effect a Compromise.—The Two Civil Court Trials. 448

CHAPTER XLVI.

The Two Assemblies—Continued.

Synods Dissolved.—Abbreviated Creeds.—*Ad Interim* Committee.—Two Plans for Mission Work.—An Indirect Influence.—Financial Disturbances. 456

CHAPTER XLVII.

The Two Assemblies—Continued.

Protests and Criticisms.—The Adjustments.—The Work of Both Assemblies.—Aloof from Slavery Agitation—Conversions.—Difficulties in Co-operation.—The Secession of Synods.—The American Missionary Association.—The Revival of 1857. 463

CONTENTS.   XXI

CHAPTER XLVIII.

THE TWO ASSEMBLIES—CONTINUED.

PAGE.

A Decided Stand Taken.—A Change in the Mode of Conducting Missions.—The Old School Unhindered.—Emancipation—The Freedmen.—Innovations Attempted.—Triennial Assemblies.—Protests.—Singular Results. . 472

CHAPTER XLIX.

THE REUNION.

Preparing for Reunion.—The Civil War.—Renewed Difficulties.—The Cry for Help.—The Committees on Reunion—the Basis.—Woman's Work.—Proffered Fraternity.—Synods Consolidated.—The Discipline Revised. —Statistics of Spiritual Progress.—The Presbyterial Centennial.—Church Periodical—Seminaries.—Revision Desired. 480

CHAPTER L.

PRESBYTERIAN WORTHIES.

Edward Robinson, Philip Lindsley.—Charles Hodge.—William Adams.—Henry Boynton Smith.—Robert Jefferson Breckinridge.—W. G. T. Shedd.—Daniel Baker.—Henry Little. 493

CHAPTER LI.

TRIAL OF DR. BRIGGS.

The Professorship Founded.—The Outline of Study.—His Inaugural; Action Thereon.—The First Trial by the Presbytery.—The Second Trial Exaustivo.—Reason as an Authority.—The Stress on Reason.—The Pentateuch and Isaiah.—Progressive Sanctification.—The Soul in the Middle State.—Second Probation. 511

CHAPTER LII.

Errors or Discrepancies in the Bible.—The Two Citations.—Prejudices Excited.—Two Classes.—Facts to Be Considered.—A Race Redemption.—The Minute Adopted.—Inerrancy of the Bible.—A New Phase.—The Protest.—The Explanatory Resolution.—Misapprehensions.—A Review.—Comments.—The Outcome.—Second Protest.—Union Seminary Independent. 529

CHAPTER LIII.

Assemblies of 1894-1899.

Case of Professor Smith.—Comparison of Statistics.—Increased Contributions.—The Rule.—Home Missions.—Effects for Good on Two Lines.—An Eventful Period.—The General Assembly of 1899. 545

CHAPTER LIV.

Assemblies of 1898-1899.

Overtures on Triennial Assemblies.—The Assembly of 1899.—Patriots—Citizens and Christians. . . . 551

LIST OF PORTRAITS.

	FACING PAGE
Jacob Harris Patton, A. M., Ph. D.	*Frontispiece*
Rev. Samuel Davies, D. D.	48
Rev. John Rodgers, D. D.	78
Rev. John McMillan, D. D.	108
Rev. Archibald Alexander, D. D.	130
Rev. Eliphalet Nott, D. D.	160
Rev. John Holt Rice, D. D.	186
Rev. Francis Herron, D. D.	216
Rev. Charles Coffin, D. D.	244
Rev. James Carnahan, D. D., LL. D.	282
Rev. Gardiner Spring, D. D.	304
Rev. Philip Lindsley, D. D.	316
Rev. Charles Hodge, D. D.	340
Rev. Lyman Beecher, D. D.	370
Rev. Gideon Blackburn, D. D.	390
Rev. Matthew Brown, D. D., LL. D.	404
Rev. Albert Barnes	416
Rev. Robert J. Breckinridge, D. D., LL. D.	436
Rev. Edward Robinson, D. D., LL. D.	492
Rev. Henry Boynton Smith, D. D., LL. D.	502

A POPULAR HISTORY

OF THE

PRESBYTERIAN CHURCH IN THE UNITED STATES OF AMERICA

I.

To have a clear conception of the principles and organization of the Presbyterian Church in the United States of America, it is essential to trace its origin in Europe, especially its history in Great Britain. From the latter country Presbyterian immigrants introduced into this land that form of church government and internal policy, which, in consequence of distinctive features, has been characterized as *American Presbyterianism.*

This denomination holds and practises the theory of a church government by elders or presbyters—these words being the same in meaning, while from the latter the name is derived. This form of government combines the democratic principle with the representative or republican, inasmuch as the church members elect the elders as their representatives, thus utilizing the wisdom, the influence, and the experience of their best men. It also brings into view two distinct features: one recognizing the *parity* of the ministry or clergy (page 18), the other *the right* of the church members—in political phrase, the people—to have a voice in such government by means of lay representatives or elders of their own choosing.

The main principles in accordance with which the Presbyterian Church in the United States is governed were held and virtually acted upon by the reformed churches on the continent of Europe immediately after the commencement of the Reformation (1517). This may be said of all those who held the *parity* of the ministry: the Huguenots in France, the Church of Holland, the Lutherans in Germany, and the churches in Geneva, Switzerland. The parity of the ministry was in contradistinction to the Roman Catholic hierarchy, or form of priestly rule, and the latter's modification in the Church of England. Thus there was a radical difference in the mode of government between the reformed churches and the latter two. The parity of the clergy or ministry is based on our Lord's positive statement: "One is your Master even Christ; *and ye are brethren.*"

Elders or Presbyters.—Whatever may have been the form of church government among the children of Israel, it is evident from the records thereof that the order of elders played an important part from the earliest times, even when they were in bondage in Egypt. These elders appear to have been heads of families or tribes, their authority being patriarchal or paternal; they were also, it would seem, representatives of the people at large (Ex. iii. 16, 18 and iv. 29–31). This order of rulers, evidently established by Divine authority, was extended and fostered by Moses, and kept up, it may have been, in a modified form during the kingly rule, and while they were captives at Babylon; and after their return to Judea was continued till the time of Christ. During all this time, as incidentally noted in the New Testament, the elders appear to have been associated in the government with the scribes and chief priests, but they were not of either order. The rulers of the synagogue were termed elders, they being elected because of their age—as the name implies—and other qualifications. The title was given to those who conducted the religious services of the synagogue, such as reading the Law, expounding its meaning and prayer. This form of government, naturally, passed over from the Jewish synagogue into the Christian churches that were organized among the converts from that faith, as well as among those from the Gentile world. At this early period of the church the presbyters or elders were "the regular teachers or pastors, preachers and leaders of the congregations—the term presbyter is no doubt of Jewish-Christian origin, a translation of the Hebrew title applied to the rules of the synagogue."

It was very natural that that form of church government should be transferred with modifications growing out of the existing circumstances to the Christian churches composed of Jewish converts, and afterward to those that were organized among the Gentile Christians. The Jewish people looked upon this mode of governing and of giving instruction in their synagogues as having the sanction of Divine authority.

The Bishops.—The word "bishop"—episkopos—(overseer) applies to the official duties of the elders or presbyters, as teachers or pastors of congregations. These terms were used interchangeably, they being synonymous, as when Paul sent from Miletus (Acts xx. 17, 28) to Ephesus and called the presbyters or elders of the church in that city. In his address to them in the 28th verse he says: "Take heed to yourselves and to all the flock in the which the Holy Spirit has made you bishops" —overseers—Greek episkopous. It will be noticed that these terms are in the *plural,* and the connection shows that they apply equally to the same persons—the elders, the presbyters or the bishops, the latter word expressing one phase of the official character of the persons in rule in the churches at Ephesus. These elders or presbyters appear to have been equal in authority, no one superior to another—this is in accordance with the parity of the ministry as announced by our Lord when he said, as has been noted, *"All ye are brethren, I am Master."* In one instance Paul (Phil. i. 1) addresses the saints in Christ Jesus with the bishops and deacons—the plural form again. In this passage he does not use the terms presbyters or elders; these different official designations were used one for the other, as in Acts xx., as just cited. The custom of thus naming the officers in the churches prevailed at that time; and still further, these names being in the plural corroborate the theory that they were thus used because they were in meaning synonymous. Again, in Paul's charge to Titus (Titus ii. 5, 6) to appoint elders (presbyters) he uses the plural. Afterward in the same connection he defines what should be the qualifications of each one of these elders, but in speaking of the individual he uses the singular only. The office of the modern bishop of a diocese or district does not appear to be foreshadowed in these passages. "The office of the early bishops, when they became distinguished from other presbyters, was not at all a roving episcopate. It was a *local* or parochial episcopate or superintendency—as completely so as the office of any Congregational or Presbyterian pastor at the present day." (*Prof. G. P. Fisher.*)

Paul and Timothy's Commissions.—When writing to Timothy (Tim. iv. 14) Paul urges him not to "neglect the gift that is in thee which was given thee by prophecy with the laying on of the hands of the presbytery (presbuteron—the eldership—referring to the ceremony that was used in ordaining or licensing a presbyter to preach the gospel. Paul also relates of himself (Acts xxii. 5) that by order of the *eldership*—perhaps of the Jewish sanhedrim—he was commissioned to go to Damascus on a persecuting errand. It will be noticed that in the case of licensing Timothy, it was not the laying on of the hands of one man as a bishop appointed for the purpose, but of the whole body of presbyters collectively.

The transition in the general mode of government from the Jewish Church into the Christian, was so natural and simple that there was no necessity to give an explanation of the process, hence the mode is mentioned only incidentally as being well known to those living at the time. This mode of government by elders had the Divine sanction in the Jewish Church, God being King and Master.

The Reformers on Church Government.—It was not strange in the great Reformation commencing in 1517, when the prominent leaders became more and more familiar with the system of government that prevailed in the primitive church, as traced incidentally in the accounts given in the gospels and in the epistles or writings of the Apostles. They there learned of the *parity* of the ministry, and that the form of government by elders or representatives of the church members had passed over from the Jewish Church into that of the Christian. And also, that the latter did not depart from the usual form of government, but only separated themselves from their Jewish brethren, inasmuch as they accepted the spiritual truths proclaimed by Jesus in relation to himself and his mission as the Messiah, which truths the Jews rejected. They also learned that when Christian churches were formed among the Gentiles, the Apostles continued the system of church government already existing in the churches in Jerusalem. They learned still further from profane and ecclesiastical history, that in the course of ages, as the result of the union of Church and State, there grew up another form of church government, which was in violation of the principle, "All ye are brethren," and out of which arose a class of superiors in the church known as bishops. Those of the latter who lived in the cities gradually assumed precedence of their fellows living in the suburban districts—they claiming the title of archbishop or metropolitan. The simple and primitive government by presbyters, the representatives of the church members or people, was thus superseded by the unpaternal and unrighteous assumption of these ecclesiastics. This assumption did not end here, but in time culminated in the Papacy and its various grades of church rulers, to the entire exclusion of the lay representatives as found in the primitive church. The true Reformers, therefore, rejected the papal system of government as being unscriptural, and so constituted as to exalt certain men into positions in the church, not by the choice or votes of the church members, but by appointments often made by secular influence. This mode was contrary to the primitive form and to our Lord's fundamental injunction upon his disciples, that they "being brethren," were not to usurp authority over one another. The Reformers universally rejected the papal form of church government, and even characterized its head as the "Anti-Christ," concerning whom, long ages before, prophecy had warned the saints.

The Union of Church and State had been in existence from the age of Constantine—300 A. D.—and was in full vigor in the time of Luther. The impression in that day was that the church in some way ought to be dependent for pecuniary support upon the state, and the latter on that theory assumed to regulate its affairs—both secular and spiritual. Hence, the Lutheran churches, though repudiating such rule, were forced to accept a church government by officers styled "consistories," who were appointed by the several princes then ruling in Germany. The Reformers, however, as they progressed in their knowledge of spiritual truths, as derived from the study of the sacred Scriptures, were led to notice the evil influence that fell upon the spirituality of the church members in consequence of the appointments of ecclesiastical instructors that were made by the secular authorities. Hence the Church of Holland, the Huguenots and the Church of Geneva, with John Calvin leading, virtually repudiated the secular rule, and went back to the spiritual, which prevailed in the primitive church. The latter had no secular pecuniary aid, but was *self-supporting*. Meantime the Jewish ecclesiastical authorities, as well as the heathen Roman government, were both bitterly opposed to the spiritual doctrines of the Christian system.

The Prelatical Form of Government.—In Great Britain there grew up a modified form of church government derived from that of Rome and known as *Prelatical;* the latter has in it the elements of the papacy, but it has hitherto reached only as high as the Archbishop of Canterbury —the primate of *all* England. This system was the direct outgrowth of the union of Church and State—to relate the full history of the process by which this result was attained is beyond the scope of this narrative.

In the prelatical system of church government in England the only element that prevented its culminating in a sort of popedom was that a majority of its clergy or ministers believed and preached the fundament doctrines of the Bible and of the primitive church, in respect to the plan of salvation through the atonement of Christ. Though trammeled by the secular and often irreligious influence of the union of Church and State, the labors of these godly ministers are grand in the field of theology, and have been fraught with untold blessings from that day to this to the English-speaking people of the world. The English people of that day were far better prepared than any other in Europe to receive and appreciate the doctrines of the Bible, because, as we shall see, the knowledge of its truths to a much greater extent had permeated their minds than in the case of the people on the continent. In addition they had clearer conceptions of their civil rights.

II.

THE REFORMATION IN ENGLAND.

The Reformation in England, owing to peculiar circumstances, assumed one phase that was not possible to the same extent on the Continent. That was the intelligent interest and the earnest part which the common people took in the matter. The English, says D'Aubigne, the historian of the Reformation, were better prepared to accept the religious movement under Luther than any other of the nations of Europe, because they had more knowledge than they of the Bible and its truths. They also had more advanced ideas of civil liberty; that knowledge enabled them to see the consistency of the principles held forth in the Bible in connection with the freedom of man.

Magna Charta.—The barons, virtually the representatives of the people, had compelled John—a most tyrannical king—to give them the famous *Magna Charta* in 1215. This document secured to the English people, though after many struggles with arbitrary kings and rulers, what they called "Englishmen's Rights." The first instance, as far as we know, of the Scriptures being given in their own tongue to the English, was the Anglo-Saxon version of 995 A. D. This version had influence, no doubt, in enabling the people to appreciate their individual rights as secured by the great Charta. In the century (1324-1384) following the granting of the latter, appeared John Wyclif, who translated the *Vulgate* into English, and who also boldly proclaimed the doctrine—in contradiction of the assumed authority of the Pope—that the Holy Scriptures were the *only supreme* authority in the church. Saying: "The Holy Spirit teacheth us the sense of Scripture, as Christ opened the Scripture to His Apostles." The English-speaking people in every land ought to recognize the obligations they are under to that remarkable man. He was one of the most learned men of his age; he received from Oxford the degree of Doctor of Divinity with the title of "Evangelical Gospel Doctor," which implies he made the Bible a special study. His translation of it laid the foundation for that well known superiority of Bible knowledge among the English-speaking people, when compared with that of their contemporaries.

His translation was laboriously transcribed by the pen, as printing had not yet been invented. These manuscripts were costly and held by the people as sacred treasures above all price. The Catholic priests did all they could to destroy them, and thus prevent their circulation. These Scriptures with the *Magna Charta* kept the English far in advance of those on the Continent in respect to their ideas of religious and civil liberty. The followers of Wyclif for more than a century after this period continued to preach the same doctrines to the people at large. For such preaching many of them suffered martyrdom. Wyclif was the Morning Star of the Reformation, as he preceded John Huss nearly half a century—Wyclif died in 1384, and Huss perished at the stake in 1415.

Tyndale's Translation of the Bible.—In the following century (1484-1531) William Tyndale, "a hunted man of the people," also translated the Bible into the common language. This version was far in advance of that of Wyclif, derived from the Vulgate alone. Printing was invented by Gutenberg about 1450, and, in consequence, the circulation of the Scriptures among the common people was very much increased. For thus giving the word of God to his countrymen in their own tongue, Tyndale suffered martyrdom on October 6, 1536. His last audible prayer was: "Lord, open the eyes of the King of England." Henry VIII. died eleven years afterward, but he had previously ordered a Bible—Tyndale's translation—to be placed in every church in England, and there fastened to the desk, but free for the people to read for themselves, or have it read to them. In this way the people at large were trained in religious knowledge and also in civil rights.

Englishmen's Rights.—It is not strange that under such training for two centuries or more that the English people demanded and acquired for themselves what they were proud to call "Englishmen's Rights." These "Rights" included civil and religious liberty to an extent at that time nowhere else known; these sentiments gave a great impulse to the principles embodied in the Reformation, when the latter were made known to the people at large, whose minds were thus prepared to accept them. The English reformers, when in search of the mode of government in the primitive church, went to the New Testament, wherein they found that the members of the church had a voice in their religious affairs.

The People Have a Voice in Church Government.—This practical knowledge of civil rights led the English people and their ministers or pastors to institute in accordance with the manner of the primitive church a form of government in which the church members had a voice. This mode is learned only from incidents casually mentioned in the New Testament. For illustration, in Acts, Chapter vi. is given an account of the reasons for the institution of the office of deacon, and also the manner in which deacons were chosen. They were elected by the church members, and as such presented to the Apostles;

"and when they had prayed, they laid their hands on them." The same form or ceremony of the "laying on of hands of the presbyters" is recorded incidentally in Timothy (I. Tim. iv. 14.), when a preacher of the word was commissioned. Here we learn of two classes of officers in the church government—deacons and elders or presbyters. As the Apostles applied rules or ceremonies to suit the exigencies of their times, so did the English Reformers adopt on the same principle a mode of church government that was adapted to their own times, after they had thrown off the authority and mode of the Romish hierarchy.

All the Reformers fell back upon the general principles of church government, which were inferred from the incidental mention of the same in the New Testament. They adopted the government by presbyters—those who were to teach the people, or the ministry or ruling elders, whose duties were to aid in ministering to the spiritual wants of the flock; but both were the servants, in a Christian sense, of the church members.

The government by representatives elected by the church members, under the names of elders or presbyters, obtains in the Reformed churches on the Continent of Europe. They are, however, all in contrast with the Roman Catholic rule, in which the people have no voice, and formerly to a great extent with the prelatical mode that prevails in the Church of England, and also in the Episcopal in the United States. In the latter country, among the descendants of the former class of churches on the Continent, are the Church of Holland's daughter, the Reformed Dutch, the German Reformed, and the Lutheran.

Different Forms of Church Government.—At the time of which we write, in England the voice of the people was much more pronounced than it was on the Continent, owing to their being better trained in civil affairs and the exercise of "Englishmen's rights." In consequence of this influence, the denominations assumed significant names as Congregationalists or Independents—because each church was independent of any sister church—they were practically democratic, as the government of their churches was in the hands of the individual members of the congregation, and who voted direct on all church questions. The Presbyterian system was equally as democratic in principle as the Congregational, since the power was also in the hands of the church members. As a matter of expediency, and to avail themselves of the *services of their best men,* the members of individual churches choose those of their own number whom they deem competent, because of their general knowledge and piety, to represent them in any form that was necessary to good order. These representative laymen are known as elders or presbyters—the latter term was applied only to the minister or pastor. The Presbyterian system is *democratic-republican.*

Henry VIII. as Head of the Church.—Theological discussions arose between the Reformers and the advocates of the Roman Catholic Church, in which the spiritual characteristics and doctrines of the latter were subjected to searching inquiries, as to their consistency with the truths of the Bible. These controversies led to a diligent study of the doctrines found in the word of God, not alone by the learned among the English Reformers, but also by the people themselves, especially those who had access to the sacred volume. The contest became of absorbing interest to all. These religious conflicts continued through the reign of Henry VIII., who, meanwhile, on his own account, had a personal quarrel with the Pope, in which he unceremoniously severed the English Church from the authority of Rome, and had the audacity to place himself at its head. A man of the moral character of Henry was unable to appreciate the religious elements of a Christian church, which he looked upon as so dependent on the State that it could be properly used to promote purely secular ends, as well as his own private designs, though the latter might be immoral in their character. With him the religious phase of the question, of which he had no realizing sense, was of secondary importance, though it was all-important in the eyes of his Christian subjects.

The Progress of the English People.—During these years of trial the Christian people of England were groping their way to a higher plane of religious intelligence and political freedom. The transition from civil liberty to the recognition of the rights of conscience was gradual, but some of its universal reception by that portion of the people who were sufficiently intelligent to take in the whole situation.

These complex ideas gradually penetrated the minds of great numbers of the common people who had access to the word of God. To understand the remarkable progress that was made during these centuries in this direction, we must take into consideration the unusual self-reliance of the people, and the organizing characteristics of the Anglo-Saxon race, which seemed to be specially endowed with a genius for self-government. This element came into play in the organization of the forms of church government that obtained in England. The system of the union of Church and State was antagonistic to this freedom of action exercised by the Puritan ministers of the gospel, and still more to the laity taking part in church government. The spirit of arbitrary rule in the Roman Catholic Church in the time of Henry VIII. was transferred under him to the affairs of the Church of England; though a strong opposition to that domineering spirit was found within the ranks of the sturdy lay members.

Prelatical System.—So great was the desire of the Puritan ministers to promote vital piety among the people themselves, that they looked upon the mode of church government as of secondary consideration when compared with that supreme object. They wished a church stripped of the excrescences and superstitious errors which during the Middle Ages had vitiated the spiritual principles and ordinances of the primitive church. On the other hand, the *prelatical* system established by King Henry and fostered by his daughter, Queen Elizabeth, during her long reign, made the Church and State dependent upon one another. In addition the ground was taken that all, both ministers and people, ought in their worship conform to the mode and ceremonies instituted by the bishops or prelatists. The Puritans looked upon any form of church government, when religious liberty was not infringed, as of secondary importance, and when this arbitrary demand was made at the instigation of the bishops, they preferred to go back for their model of church government to the primitive church, and also to be taught and governed by spiritual teachers and rulers of their own choosing, rather than by those appointed by the secular authorities, often composed of irreligious men.

The Puritan System.—There were differences of opinion among the Puritans in relation to the mode of church government. Some preferred Independency or Congregationalism, and others the presbyterial or representative form, but as the mode was non-essential to the great end they had in view, that of preaching the gospel, these differences interfered but little with their fraternal relations with one another. Afterward, however, when ambitious men, more worldly than humbly pious, endeavored to have the government adopt one or the other to be supported by the State, the uniform fraternal feeling within the ranks of the Puritans was somewhat diminished, as was the case in the time of the troubles incident to the Commonwealth era, more than half a century later.

Origin of the Union of Church and State.—As the church from the time of Constantine (about 300, A. D.) had been in connection with the state, that came to be considered as its normal condition. The Reformers did not at once grasp the many spiritual difficulties that arose from the connection; they had advanced only so far as to discover the injury to spiritual religion in having irreligious men as government officials appointing clergymen to positions in the church. Such officials were usually incompetent to appreciate the spiritual and Christian qualifications that were essential to the correct performance of the duties of the minister or pastor. Thus it was in the Church of England from the time of Henry VIII. forward. The question as to the good or evil effects of the system is not yet settled, neither in England nor in some countries on the Continent, wherein the salaries of certain preachers are paid by the government. From the nature of the case, preachers or bishops thus dependent for their living or position in the church, must be more or less trammeled in their ministrations, though often, perhaps, unconsciously.

The Exiles Abroad—What They Learned.—We cannot go into detail of the struggles of the Puritans—Independents and Presbyterians—for nearly a century in working out the system that they afterward accepted as the best form of church government. Persecution by the prelatical party at different times drove numbers of these ardent men into exile. They went to the Continent, and because of the greater freedom enjoyed there, numbers made their homes for the time in Switzerland. There they learned more clearly concerning the Presbyterian form of government and the scriptural authority for its institution. Through the influence of John Calvin that system had been adopted at Geneva, which city has been characterized as at that time, "The Metropolis of the Reformed faith, which system was consolidated by Calvin." When these exiles returned home after the persecutions relaxed, they wished that simple, yet comprehensive system to be adopted in England.

So little importance did the Puritans attach to the form of church government, which they in one sense deemed non-essential, that they were willing as a compromise that there should be bishops—that is, ministers, placed over a district or diocese, if such bishops were to be responsible to the presbytery, a representative body of the ministers and elders of the church. They contended that a bishop was still a presbyter; no matter how high the position in which his brethren placed him, he was still a presbyter—the highest order in the primitive church. The President of the United States is promoted by his fellow-citizens to be the chief servant of the people, yet he is still a citizen, and on the same principle the minister promoted to be a bishop by his fellow-presbyters is still a presbyter. Even John Knox—that staunch presbyterian—"held episcopacy to be lawful, but not convenient; an allowable form of government, but not the purest or the best." Andrew Melville, another Scotch reformer, "held episcopy to be unlawful—opposed to Scripture—allowable in no circumstances."

III.

The Parity of the Ministry or Clergy.

The parity of the gospel ministry is based on the words of our Lord to his disciples (Matt. xxiii. 8, 10): "One is your Master, even Christ; and *all ye are brethren;*" and apparently to make the statement more emphatic he subjoins: "Neither be ye called masters; for one is your Master, even Christ;" to illustrate still further He adds: "But he that is greatest among you shall be your servant." From these passages it is a clear inference that the parity of the gospel ministry is of divine origin as was the parity among the disciples themselves. The same principle our Lord illustrates again and again. When the *ten* heard of the petition of the two sons of Zebedee (Matt. xx. 20-29) "they were moved with indignation against the two brethren." But the Lord rebukes them by saying: "Whosoever will be great among you, let him be your servant." On another occasion, to rebuke their worldly ambition in "wishing to be greatest in the kingdom of heaven," meaning thereby a temporal one (Matt. xviii. 1-4), he placed in their midst a little child, saying: "Except ye be converted and become as little children, ye shall not enter into the kingdom of heaven." The declaration of our Lord, that ye are brethren; I am your Master, is as strong in its assertion as that made again and again in the old dispensation that Jehovah, alone, was King in Israel.

The phrase "whosoever will be great among you, let him be your minister," can mean nothing more than when the presbyters or ministers choose, because of his fitness, one of their number for some particular office, in which his special ability can be utilized for the benefit of the whole—such an one is honored as their chief servant. He is thus, for the time being, placed in a prominent but temporary position; meanwhile, his status among his fellow presbyters remains the same and is not affected by the highest honors that can be conferred upon him by his brethren. Had this spirit of brotherly equality and the injunction to love one another, together with the application of the Golden Rule, prevailed in the church through the ages, there would have been no opportunity for one man or set of men to usurp authority over the church members and their pastors—in consequence there would have been no Pope nor Archbishop of Canterbury.

Significant Names.—The titles given their preachers or religious teachers by these denominations, who receive the *parity* of the ministry as a truth derived from Holy Scripture, are very significant—such as *minister;* that is, one who ministers to the spiritual wants of the church members; an office held in high honor. The word is derived from the Latin, and means a servant. The word *pastor* is also used, but it applies more fully to a minister in charge of a church or congregation. Pastor is likewise of Latin origin, but it is a perfect translation of its Greek counterpart, which means a shepherd. In the New Testament the word designates the person who takes care of the flock or the members of the church. This form of expression came over from the Old Testament use of the Hebrew word meaning a shepherd, as seen in numerous illustrations in the Psalms and elsewhere.

The terms minister or pastor are designed to designate the kindly offices of those who bear to church members the endearing relation of a religious teacher and adviser; and who is a sympathizer in time of trouble and trials, which may be in the form of spiritual doubts, or of domestic sorrows, that so often cross the paths of the Christian, as well as of those who are not of the fold of Christ.

The Term Rector.—When we come to the *prelatical* form of church government, we find instead of the terms minister or pastor that of *rector*. This word is derived from a Latin verb, signifying *to rule*. It carries with it, therefore, the savor of master as a ruler, and is devoid of the idea of consolation and trust that is associated with the name of minister or pastor. The latter title suggests the kindly care of the real shepherd toward his flock, which sentiment is applied in a figurative sense to the pastor of the members of a church or congregation—his flock. The term shepherd is found in the Old Testament in numerous instances expressing in corresponding figurative language the love of God for his people. Even Homer describes one of his best heroes as the *shepherd* of his people.

The term *rector*, in designating the religious teacher and guide of the membership of a Christian church, is unauthorized in the New Testament in form and in spirit. In spite of this *misnomer*, as to title, we find in our day rectors in the Episcopal Church who are devoted ministers and pastors of the members of their respective charges.

The term minister or pastor is used in the Methodist Episcopal Church; the jurisdiction of their bishops is not limited to dioceses, but pertains to the whole church. They rejected the term presbyter, but retained that of elder, its translation.

The question suggests itself, why did the worthies of the Church of England discard the name minister, as used by our Lord himself, and as used by Paul, for the term rector? History supplies the answer. The word rector as applied in this connection, is the outgrowth of the absolute and arbitrary rule within the Roman Catholic Church, which appeals to priestly authority alone and repudiates the laity having a voice in the government of that church. This arbitrary spirit of the Roman priesthood and method of church government passed over in a somewhat diluted form from that of Rome into the Church of England. In like manner the latter has imitated quite often certain ceremonies of the former. The Church of England's daughter, the Episcopal Church in the United States, when adapting its organization to the new order of things, after the adoption of the Federal Constitution, unfortunately followed the Mother church in retaining the title rector, instead of using terms so expressive and consoling as minister or pastor.

The Non-Persecutors.—It is an interesting question, and worthy of study, why those denominations which held and practised the parity of the ministry never have persecuted their fellow-Christians because of their religious opinions. To this noble class belong the Church of Holland, the Waldenses, Huguenots, the Lutherans on the continent of Europe, while in Great Britain and in her colonies are found in the same category the Independents, the Presbyterians and the Baptists. These denominations have different views on non-essential points, but they all acknowledge that they *are brethren*, according to the Lord's injunction to his disciples.

History records cases of harsh measures against certain persons on a part of a few who held the doctrine of the parity of the ministry, as for illustration in the case of Roger Williams. In the latter instance it was not at all because of his purely religious opinions, but of his political, which the Puritans of Massachusetts thought would destroy all order and government. Roger Williams, though possessing many admirable traits of character, was certainly very eccentric. "He separated himself not only from the English Church, but from all who would not separate from it and from all who would not separate from the latter, and so on, until he could no longer, for conscience' sake, hold fellowship with his wife in family prayers. After long patience the colonial government deemed it necessary to signify to him that if his conscience would not suffer him to keep quiet and refrain from stirring up sedition and embroiling the colony with the English government, he would have to seek freedom for that sort of conscience outside of their jurisdiction, and they put him out accordingly, to the great advantage of both parties and without loss of mutual respect and love." (*Am. Church History Series, Vol. XIII., p. 100, L. W. Bacon.*)

But these cases of harsh measures were sporadic, while the persecutions of the Romish hierarchy and prelates of the Church of England were for religious opinions *alone* and on principle, a bad one to be sure, but nevertheless on principle. The prelates or bishops in colonial times instigated persecutions in the American colonies, more or less annoying, against those whom they characterized "dissenters," until such power was taken away by the adoption of the Constitution of the United States in 1788, which act, established in this land religious liberty on a true and firm basis.

Partial Responsibility of a Subordinate.—Those denominations that reject the parity of the ministry, are more or less wedded to forms in their church services, though it is difficult to find in the mode of worship in the primitive church authority for such forms. There can be no *parity* of the clergy where one minister is a subordinate to another as his superior—his bishop. That bishop is that minister's superior—in a certain sense a master—when the Lord Jesus said: "One is your Master, even Christ; ye are brethren," on an equality, before me and among yourselves. Under such circumstances there exists on the part of the bishop a sense of authority over the *rectors* of his diocese, while on their part there is a sense of inferiority in the presence of their bishop. This sentiment must diminish to an equal degree the sense of individual responsibility on the part of the subordinate rector. Inasmuch as the responsibility that should be rendered to the Master *himself* is diminished by the fact that it is given partially to the bishop. From the nature of the case it must be so; there is no denying the lack of the sense of responsibility, when to do this or that the permission must come from a superior, with whom the ordinary clergyman does not and cannot feel himself recognized in the true sense—a brother in equal standing. This feeling springs spontaneously toward one of their number, who may be consecrated as bishop. The latter is more than *primus inter pares,* for he never lays down his office nor returns to the ranks. On the contrary, among those who hold and practise the parity of the ministry, an officer, it may be a moderator of a synod or president of a congregational association, as soon as his term of office expires he returns to the ranks. Because of the confidence that his brethren repose in him they make him their honored representative servant, and as such they respect the office and its incumbent for the time being, giving diligence to conform to the rules that he is authorized by his peers to enforce, and no further. Ministers or pastors under such conditions realize that their responsibility is to the Master *supreme,* and that it is not divided between that Master and a human superior as a bishop. The sense of this responsibility is a stimulant to the performance of duty to the Lord alone.

The two divine principles the *parity* of the clergy or ministry and the *Golden Rule,* if recognized and applied in the government of the Church, would necessarily free it from the evil of one portion of the ministry domineering over another. Under such conditions there would be no abuse of the Lord's rule, "ye are brethren," nor ecclesiastical tyranny.

Apostolic Succession.—The Presbyterian Church derives the authority for her ministry from the Apostles and they direct from the Master himself. This is an Apostolic succession, but not a *succession of Apostles.* The latter—to whom Paul was admitted, for did he not *see* the Lord?—had special gifts, and they were also able personally to bear witness of His life, His death and resurrection, but these qualifications they could not transmit to successors. They were authorized by the Head of the Church "to ordain elders (presbyters) in every church," to perform the sacred duties of teachers and rulers, and they in turn to ordain similar officers. This was a genuine Apostolic succession, which embraced successive generations of elders or ministers thus set apart to the services of the Church of Christ.

"Presbyterians believe in a succession from the Apostles; in a historic episcopate—not diocesan but pastoral—which runs back through a long line of ordained presbyters to the very men whom the Lord Christ chose to found and organize His Church." (*Presbyterian Doctrine,* by H. Van Dyke, p. 18.) Again: "Presbyterianism recognizes that the pope and the prelates are presbyters, but declines to recognize them as of higher order than presbyters. For presbyters are the genuine bishops of the New Testament, and the true apostolic succession is in the presbyters who have been ordained by the Apostles and their successors from the foundations of the Christian Church until the present time. It has the true apostolic succession in striving after the apostolic faith in its purity, integrity and fulness." (*Am. Pres., p. 82.*)

Humanly speaking it would seem strange that the authority to ordain ministers to the sacred office was left by the Divine Master to the contingencies incident to a line composed of individual men, rather than to the whole body of elders to ordain by "the laying on of the hands of the Presbytery" (I. Tim. iv. 14); all of whose members are equal as brethren, in accordance with the Lord's instructions and admonitions. The former mode may be illustrated by a chain made up of a number of individual links, if one drops out the chain is worthless; the latter, by the cable of a suspension bridge, which is composed of numerous strands of wire. In the one case the lost link is fatal to the whole system; in the other the many strands preclude such fatality

The theory of the Apostolic succession, as held in the Church of England and by a class in the Episcopal Church in the United States, known as High Church, legitimately leads to the denial of the validity of the ordination of the ministry in the other denominations of Christians. This is a remarkable phase of ecclesiastical and arrogant assumption, especially in the face of the fact that these denominations have been marvelously blest by the Master in their efforts to bring sinners to repentance and to the Saviour.

Suppose it were true "that (church) sacraments are valid only when dispensed by episcopally-ordained priests; what should we expect to find? Why, this: that the spiritual life of Christendom should be restricted to Episcopal communions, while beyond their pale, in the Churches of the Reformation, neither Christian faith nor Christian holiness, for the last three hundred years, should have been preserved"—a ministry "holding by the Divine will a monopoly of grace ought to be the bright conspicuous seats (examples) of every virtue and of Christlike service for mankind." Why should not such benign influence also reach the private members of such church and make them, preeminently, models in their self-denial for Christ's sake, and in their utter repudiation of the vanities of the fashionable world? (*Anglican View of the Church, by Dr. J. Oswald Dykes, p. 13.*)

The deliberate opinion of numbers of eminent scholars and clergymen of the Church of England on the extreme view of the "Apostolic succession," and also as to the "post-apostolic origin of the episcopacy," should have great weight with every class of intelligent Protestant laymen. That eminent historian, Dean Milman, characterizes the "historic episcopate" as "the fiction of ecclesiastical vanity and baseless." Archbishop Whately, Bishop Lightfoot, Dr. Hatch, Canon Farrar, Dean Stanley "rob the episcopate of its priority," says the last mentioned. "It is sure that nothing like modern episcopacy existed before the close of the first century. That which was once the Gordian knot of theologians has been untied, not by the sword of persecution, but by the patient unravelment of scholarship."

IV.

A Peculiar Phase of Reform.

The religious movement originating in the Reformation under Luther assumed a peculiar phase in England, owing to the characteristics of the people themselves. This phase was designated Puritanism by its enemies, but it soon commanded the latter's respect by the power of its intense earnestness in efforts to reform the church and to promote a true and inner religious or vital piety in the hearts of the people. We of this later age and of more knowledge and truer interpretation of the Bible, and under the influence of the amenities of a more advanced Christianized civilization, may smile at what we term the crudities of those days. Notwithstanding all that, how grandly those Puritans filled their sphere of duty in their day and generation. Their mode of Christian action was different from the similar religious movements on the Continent, because their presentation of truth came directly home to a people better trained in biblical knowledge and in relation to their civil rights than those of the different nations on the Continent. The people of the latter that came nearest to the Anglo-Saxons in that respect were those who occupied the district of Switzerland, of which Geneva was the principal city.

A Religious Force.—Puritanism as a religious force was antagonistic to the numerous evils that were the outgrowth of a corrupt form of Christianity; and it was so radical in its principles that it wished to strip the church of these excrescences, and go back for a model to the heart-religion of the primitive church. To do which it saw no other way than to stamp out the forms of worship and, in its opinion, superstitious errors that prevailed. It was not satisfied with that gain alone; it wished, as far as possible, to assimilate its mode of church government to that which was instituted by the early church and adapt it to the exigencies of an age far distant, and under far different circumstances. Hence the Puritan would strip off all extraneous ceremonies that had been introduced in the Middle Ages, in order to allure the semi-barbarous peoples of those times by means attractive to the eye. Its inherent force consisted in an ardent, heart-felt, spiritual religion of the primitive type, which recognized the truths of the Bible as paramount to the teachings of men.

Self-Supporting Church—Its Spirituality Enhanced.— It seems strange that the Puritans in going back to early Christianity—before the year 300—for their system of church government, were unable to realize and act upon the historical fact that the church of that period was entirely unconnected with the secular government of the time and was self-supporting. In consequence, it was free to preach the gospel without being interfered with by a secular authority, which claimed a voice in the management of its spiritual affairs on the plea that it paid the salaries of the preachers and also bore other expenses Let us be charitable toward these good men, who were unable at once to grasp the situation in all its bearings. The union of Church and State came down to them—a legacy of the ages—since the question or policy of the disseverence of the two had not even been suggested.

As the union of Church and State had been established for centuries, the Reformers accepted the arrangement as the best for both parties. When they went back to the primitive church as their model in doctrine and church government, they all recognized the *parity* of the ministry, but failed to notice the fact that the primitive church was free from state influence—except as an inimical force for nearly three hundred years. That the state instead of fostering Christianity was its persecutor and bitterest foe, and in almost every form opposed the preaching of the gospel, yet in spite of all this the spirituality of the church grew and the number of its members increased continually, and during those three centuries *the church was self-supporting*. The leading Reformers took for granted that the existing relations between the church and the state was a proper one; and it appears never to have occurred to them that for the church to be freed entirely from secular influence might possibly promote its spirituality and success They did not raise the question whether it was better for the spirituality of the church to be entirely disconnected with the state, and thereby avoid the evils incident to its being used for selfish purposes by ambitious and unchristian men. They never broached the idea of the church going back to the primitive mode of being supported by the voluntary contributions of its own members, rather than for their ministers to draw their salaries from the public treasury.

The Jus Divinum Doctrine.—On the other hand, the question with them was which denomination had a system of church government that had the divine sanction, *jus divinum,* as they termed it. Such denomination would of course be adopted as the State Church. This question was agitated more or less in England for about a century; and it remained to be discussed and settled one hundred and fifty years afterward in the new world. (See p.   .)

The prelatical party had the doubtful advantage after the time of Henry VIII. of being the State Church, and then the Independents under Cromwell, and for a short time the Presbyterians under the supervision of ambitious men. The English Parliament in 1645 wished the divines, who were then in session framing the Westminster Confession of Faith, to give their views on the subject of a *jure divino* form of church government. The mere form of such government is non-essential in itself, and may be also to the progress of the gospel of Christianity. The principles are so comprehensive that the form is but a convenience to suit the people and the age, but not to interfere with the spirituality of the church members themselves.

True Relation of the Church to the State.—It seems that only a very limited number of the Puritans doubted the expediency of the union of Church and State. The exiles, when they returned from the Continent in Elizabeth's reign, brought with them clearer and more decided views on the subject, and which were far in advance of those they formerly held. These advanced opinions were the outgrowth of their intercourse with the reformers on the Continent, especially with John Calvin. To this influence may be traced the clear definition of the relation of the state or magistrate to the church, which was afterward, and for the first time, put forth distinctly by the Westminster Divines (1643-5), nearly all of whom were Presbyterians. Therein it was clearly stated that it was the duty of the state to protect the church in its rights as a religious body, but the church was in no sense to be interfered with in its legitimate functions, nor as such controlled by the state. The church was not to be put under obligations to the secular power, whereby its religious influence could be diminished.

V.

THE PRESBYTERIANS AND PURITANS IN HENRY VIII.'S REIGN.

It is not within the scope of this writing to give an account in detail of the many conflicts that occurred between the two main religious parties—the prelatical and the puritan or presbyterian—during the period commencing with the reign of Henry VIII. and ending with that of Elizabeth—about ninety years. The freedom of thought and its free expression, as involved in the theory of "Englishmen's Rights," led to an almost continuous discussion of theological questions during this period, and to a greater number of religious sects in England than in any other country of Europe. These discussions cleared the theological atmosphere and in the end led to grand results in the way of harmony by means of preparing summaries of doctrine as exponents of the truths of the word of God. These were the harbingers of the formulating in the next century the Westminster Confession, the most elaborate of all, and which has had the greatest number of adherents. It seems to have been a century in which there was manifested an unusual desire to draw up formularies of doctrine.

Confessions of Faith—Among the Puritans, those who held the presbyterial form of church government, were strenuous advocates for formulating creeds of systematic theology deduced from the truths of the Bible. The Presbyterians of Scotland drew up a Confession (1560) the handiwork of John Knox—that man so bold amid eccle-

siastical dangers, and withal remarkable for his ability
and integrity. The Puritan element in the prelatical party
prepared the XXXIX Articles of that church (1563);
and the Presbyterians of Ireland, also, drew up a confession (1615), while among the Reformed on the Continent several creeds were formulated. In this turmoil
of theological discussions the ablest intellects and most
learned men of the time, clerical and laymen, took part.

The Two Parties.—There were at this time two distinct parties among the Christians of England—the Prelatical or Bishops' party, the latter took their inspiration
as to church polity from the Church of Rome, while the
Puritans, which included Presbyterians and Independents
or Congregationalists, derived theirs from the primitive
church. The prelatists, sustained by royalty, kept as near
as possible to the Church of Rome. During these times
many Puritans suffered martyrdom, especially in Bloody
Mary's reign, such as the evangelical Bishops Latimer
and Ridley. Meanwhile great numbers of the Reformers,
on account of these relentless persecutions, fled to the
Continent, and did not return until the commencement of
the reign of Elizabeth. During Bloody Mary's reign of
five years 280 Puritans and Presbyterians were put to
death, *five* of whom were evangelic bishops who were
burned at the stake. Mary was under the control of Roman Catholic priests. Such sufferings tried men's souls,
but during all these years the Puritans in England were
rising to a higher plane of piety and learning, and to a
better appreciation of religious liberty. Many of those
driven into exile went to Geneva and studied in the school
of John Calvin, in which was moulded a consistent system
of theology. They returned still better prepared to enter
into the struggles for the truth. To be sure, during the
reign of Elizabeth but few comparatively of the Reformers suffered death, but their ministers were treated out-

rageously; they and their families were often reduced to beggary by being deprived of their livings, because they conscientiously refused to conform to the Romanizing and arbitrary demands of the Queen's bishops; they were thrown into prisons and treated in a manner more harrowing than death itself. The intelligent laity became more and more incensed at the bishops, while the main body of the common people began to sympathize with the persecuted. But when the time of danger came in the form of attempts at invasion by the Armada, none were more loyal to their Queen and country than these persecuted ministers and their people.

The Heroic Age.—"Puritanism was the great religious force of the seventeenth century; the most powerful influence in British thought and life since the Reformation." In religious affairs "the Puritan era is the heroic age of Great Britain and of America. In it were laid the foundations for all that is noblest and best in subsequent times. * * * This unifying principle has been at work as the most potent force in Anglo-Saxon history; working through many generations of conflict, changing intolerance into toleration." The Puritans emphasized preaching rather than the sacraments and public prayer. When the preachers were silenced in the churches, pious laymen established lectureships, and the work of exposition went on with greater freedom and redoubled energy. * * * By persecution the Puritans were constrained to be great preachers, and they enjoyed the gift and learned the art of free prayer. * * * The preaching of the gospel and the prayer-meeting have been two leading features in all Puritan regions. * * * The non-conforming churches of England, the Presbyterian churches of Scotland, and Puritan churches of America have maintained their preëminence in this respect. The gift of prayer has been bestowed in marvelous richness and efficacy upon these churches." (*Am. Pres., pp. 27, 39.*)

Harmony of Beliefs.—In that day the study of the Holy Scriptures by the English theologians of both parties induced a similarity of views on the essential doctrines of Christianity; such as the inspiration of the Scriptures themselves, which being thus accepted as the word of God, they in consequence became the rule of Christian faith. We have in our own day a parallel case. The facilities for the study of the Bible, especially in the tongues in which it was originally written, have been wonderfully increased within the last hundred years. These aids are in the form of elaborately prepared lexicons and critical commentaries; the results of the unremitting toil of learned and conscientious men; these helps are utilized by students in all the Protestant theological seminaries in the land. It is a remarkable fact, and one that is cheering to the heart of the church, that in the *evangelical* denominations of to-day, the clergymen and the intelligent laity, who thus study the word of God, are more at one in their cordial acceptance of the essential truths of Christianity than ever before.

The XXXIX. Articles.—The Puritan element within the prelatical ranks formulated the XXXIX. Articles of the Church of England (1563). This compendium of scriptural truth has taken its place among the confessions of the Reformed churches. Article VI. says: "Holy Scripture containeth all things necessary to salvation, so that whatever is not read therein, nor may be proved thereby, is not to be required of any man that it should not be believed as an article of faith." John Wyclif, a hundred years before, had proclaimed that: "The Holy Spirit teacheth us the sense of Scripture as Christ opened the Scriptures to his Apostles." Thus the position of the Bible as the Christian's infallible rule of faith and

HENRY VIII.'S REIGN.

practice was set forth by the followers of Wyclif, and to such an extent that the doctrine was familiar to the leading minds among the common people. On the other hand, the bishop or prelatical party "rallied around the Book of Common Prayer" and demanded uniformity to it, but "the Puritans took their stand on the 6th Article of the XXXIX., and contended that the Romish and unscriptural things should be removed from the Prayer Book." There were at this time two classes of bishops, the Romanizing, who, encouraged by royalty, wished to bring the English Church into closer connection with that of Rome, and the Puritan or *evangelical bishops,* who earnestly desired to protect and promote true religion. This evangelical spirit cropped out occasionally among the clergy of the Church of England during the next one hundred and fifty years, and finally burst forth in all its splendor in the times of John and Charles Wesley and George Whitefield

VI.

THE PRESBYTERIANS IN THE REIGNS OF ELIZABETH AND JAMES.

The struggles of the Puritans with the Romanizing bishops of Elizabeth reign were severe, while often the form of persecution was changed. All these outrages of the Bishops were connived at by the wordly, politic and insincere Queen. Some of these friends of religious liberty and truth suffered martyrdom; meanwhile great numbers of their leaders and pastors were fined, imprisoned or driven into exile, because their conscience forbid them to use in their worship the ritual and prayer-book enjoined by the prelatical party, as they looked upon the latter as containing unscriptural expressions and sentiments. The Reformed churches of that day, for the greater part, used in their worship a book containing prayers, the latter custom having passed over from the Romish into the Protestant churches. The Puritans were groping their way and learning the truth from year to year as they progressed in their study of Holy Scripture. They ascertained there were sentiments or doctrines embodied in these prayers that had no scriptural authority, and therefore they wished the book to be *purged* of these objectionable features.

The Formation of a Presbytery.—In Elizabeth's reign it required great diligence to avoid the spies and informers in the interests of the bishops. Toward the end of her reign the Presbyterian element among the Puritans formed secretly an organization out of which grew a

Presbytery, which was constituted in 1572. A book of discipline was drawn up, and after much friendly discussion and revisions, was adopted in 1590. This discipline or Confession was subscribed to by about 500 ministers, residing in different counties in England. To accomplish this much it took nearly twenty years of assiduous care in holding secret meetings. The bishops by means of sneaking spies, having learned of the movement, became greatly alarmed and to suppress such opposition to their mandates renewed their persecutions more vigorously than ever.

The Independents Unorganized.—It is to be noted in this controversy that the Presbyterian element among the Puritans organized presbyteries in opposition to the prelactical powers. The Congregational or Independent element, as individuals, manifested their opposition to the bishops, but they took no measures to organize as churches in having a confession of faith to unite them as a body in order to wield their power in a concentrated form. This was the legitimate result of each church having no organic connection with other churches. The independent mode of church government led to the isolation of the respective churches and tended to limit their influence, because of their being thus restricted. It also had a tendency to engender the selfishness of individual churches, since they had no special means of becoming acquainted with the wants of their brethren, even in the churches of their own order, and consequently there was a lack of sympathy with one another. At this crisis, therefore, they had no organization to oppose the high-handed measures of the bishops, since such organized effort was inconsistent with their mode of church government, but as individuals they were the equals of their Presbyterian brethren in withstanding prelatical assumptions, but their concentrated energies was unutilized, because of the isolation of each church's membership. In the following century the Independents or Congregationalists, under Oliver Cromwell, manifested great strength and energy in an organization that was of a church militant order. That organization was the outcome of the arbitrary and indomitable will of Oliver Cromwell. In spite of the theories of Independency, he forced the Congregationalists into a compact body—but only to disintegrate as soon as the master mind was gone.

The Primitive Church Self-Supporting.—While these troubles were agitating the people of England, similar trials were in progress in Scotland, where the Presbyterian Church was in connection with the state. That form of church government by elders and presbyters had been established in Scotland through the efforts of John Knox and Andrew Melville, in the reign of Mary Queen of Scots.

The union of church and state in that day was deemed essential for the support of the Christian religion. It is remarkable that it did not occur to these good men that the primitive church held itself aloof from any alliance with the Roman government, and was of itself self-supporting. Though the heathen priesthood and the secular authorities of the empire were hostile to the Christian religion, yet it so far prevailed in numbers that at the end of 300 years the government, as a matter of state policy and of its own accord under Constantine, constituted it the state religion by a decree, thus repudiating heathenism. From that day forward the alliance of the church with the secular power has been more or less a retarding influence in the progress of a pure and a spiritual life among the church members; especially may this be said of those who were in any way connected with the court or under royal influence.

King James—His Character.—King James VI. of

Scotland and afterward James I. of England was the son of the unfortunate Mary Queen of Scots and Henry Stuart, Lord Darnley. He began his reign in Scotland in 1577 and in England in 1603. He had been educated by tutors, Presbyterian ministers, who endeavored to train him for the office of a king, and to instruct him in relation to the prominent question of the time—that of religious affairs. These tutors, excellent men and scholars, do not seem to have been very successful; he appears to have had a fine memory for *words alone*. Thus he remembered the precise words or terms in which his instructions were given, but was deficient in the power to assimilate or make as his own mental furniture the ideas they conveyed. Dr. George Buchanan, his principal instructor, when charged with having made him a *mere pedant*, declared "it was the best he could make of him." When freed from his tutors and made king, he took up the rôle of an incessant talker on all occasions; but of mere verbiage, and that uttered indistinctly. His tutors had labored to repress his unbounded conceit, rebuking him sternly rather than flattering his vanity, but now he was unrestrained.

He was a most devout believer in the *divine right* of kings, and appeared to have a notion that as a king he himself could never make a mistake. He thought a king had a divine right to make or unmake laws at his own pleasure, and was bound by no obligation in such matters—it would seem in his case not even to keep his own word. When in Scotland at one time he professed to have a profound belief in the Presbyterian mode of church government and form of worship, and even went so far as to ridicule the mode of worship of the Church of England, which as an imitation of that of Rome he characterized as "an evil said mass."

James and the General Assembly.—James had difficulty

with the Presbyterian General Assembly of Scotland, which was established December 20, 1560, seventeen years before he became king. Episcopacy, at the time, was the state religion, but under the influence of John Knox the nation superseded it by Presbyterianism. In 1578 the revised or Second Book of Discipline became the authorized standard or Confession of Faith of the Church of Scotland. Immediately after James began to lay plans to reinstate Episcopacy. During this struggle numerous Presbyterian ministers and prominent laymen were driven into exile, and as usual the greater part went to Geneva. Finally in 1584 James and his nobles arbitrarily restored Episcopacy, and a servile parliament sanctioned the illegal act of placing the government of the church in the hands of the king. The following year the exiles returned and were more determined than ever to maintain their civil and religious rights, and the whole nation was soon on the verge of rebellion. James was compelled to yield to a compromise, by which a modified Episcopacy was introduced (1586), by which bishops were "to be held responsible to the General Assembly, and to act according to the advice of the synods and presbyteries"—the appointees of James were bishops only in name. Thus the project failed in an inglorious manner.

The Influence of the Bishops.—As soon as James became King of England he fell under the influence of the bishops, who had carried religious matters with a high hand in Elizabeth's reign. They immediately detected his weak points, and flattered him in the most fulsome manner. He abominated the freedom of thought and speech and zeal for religious liberty that characterized the leaders in the Scotch Presbyterian Church. He was not learned and wise, but shrewd as that class of mind— a sort of semi-lunatic—usually is. He saw that the government of the Presbyterian Church, in which the private members had a voice through their best men, the elders, who were chosen as their representatives, was not consistent with his *divine right* as head of the church and King of England. As an indication of his policy he announced his famous axiom: *"No Bishop, no King,"* by which he meant that the bishops would sustain him in his plans to suppress religious freedom. On that principle or basis he henceforth acted as king and head of the established church.

Hopes Disappointed.—When James was about to become King of England the English Puritans expected that, under the circumstances, he being a professed Presbyterian, they would be relieved of the annoyances to which they had been subjected in the reign of Elizabeth. They were, however, doomed to be sorely disappointed. The king put himself under influences that were hostile to true religious liberty. As James claimed the *divine right* for kings, so his leading bishop, Bancroft, claimed the *divine right* for prelacy. The latter charged the Presbyterians of Scotland with following the doctrines taught at Geneva, and at the same time he denounced the English Puritans as being influenced by the Scotch Presbyterians. We have just seen that the attempts of James and his bishops to establish Episcopacy in Scotland had failed, and in that controversy Presbyterianism had triumphed. This was eleven years before James became King of England. He was deeply mortified and greedy for revenge because of this, his defeat.

Notwithstanding these incidents, in order to avert evil, the English Puritans presented to James, when on his way from Scotland to ascend the throne of England, a petition expressing loyalty and asking for relief. This petition was scarcely noticed, though it was signed by nearly one thousand names of ministers and prominent gentlemen. The following year (1604) a conference was summoned and held at Hampton Court. The debate was between the bishops and the Puritans. James himself presiding. Dr. Reynolds, professor in Cambridge, spoke in behalf of the Puritans, and Bishop Bancroft on that of the prelates. The king kept joining in with his usual volubility. The Puritans were dismissed contemptuously and found their interests in a worse condition than they were even under the reign of Elizabeth.

Soon afterward the leading Scotch Presbyterian ministers were invited to London to hold a similar conference. They too were insulted and, in modern phrase, bulldozed by the king and his bishops. James went even so far as to treacherously imprison some of the men whom he had invited to a friendly conference. He seemed to delight in every opportunity to show his ill-feeling toward his own countrymen, especially those who were in favor of free discussion and religious liberty. Numbers of the Scottish Presbyterian ministers as well as of the English Puritans fled the country.

Migrations to Ireland.—Great numbers of the persecuted ministers and their people migrated from England and also from Scotland to Ireland, where they were protected by the evangelical bishops of that island. These immigrants aided in strengthening the Irish Presbyterian Church. The Scotch settled principally in Ulster and the English in Dublin and vicinity. Great numbers of the descendants of these Presbyterians afterward migrated to the American colonies.

James in 1584 attempted, as we have seen, to supersede Presbyterianism in Scotland by establishing Episcopacy but failed, and again in 1592, but without success, as the Presbyterian Church was then put on a national basis but liable to be disturbed at any time by the kings of England under the influence of the bishops. Thus his son, Charles I., about fifty years afterward (1640) made a similar attempt with like success. This uncertain state of affairs in Scotland remained for about sixty years longer, when in 1707 by treaty Scotland and England formed a union, and the Presbyterian became the State Church of Scotland and the Episcopal that of England.

The Culdee Church.—It is here not out of place in this history to compare the claims to antiquity of the Church of Scotland as such with those of the Church of England. The little island of Iona—containing only about four square miles of territory—lies off Mull on the west coast of Scotland. Though so insignificant in size, it ought to have a peculiar interest for American Presbyterians, because through the Church of Scotland they can trace their line of ecclesiastical ancestry back to the "ancient Church of the Culdees," which was founded on this island very near Apostolic times. This church was Apostolic in doctrine, presbyterial in polity, while it repudiated the celibacy of the clergy. It maintained some of the usages of the Greek or Oriental church and "coëquality," that is, the parity of the ministry, and was governed by presbyters. Numerous historical arguments are adduced to prove that the Culdee Church was the outgrowth of the labors of exiles driven by persecution from the Church of Galatia in Asia Minor, to which the Apostle Paul addressed an epistle. The Galatians were of *Celtic* origin, as were the Scots. Tertullian, who lived in the second century A. D., asserts that "Those parts of Britain that were inaccessible to the Romans" (*i. e.*, Scotland) "had become subject to Christ." In those early times the Phœnicians came to Cornwall in Wales to trade for tin. Why could not the persecuted Christians of Galatia come with them to the Scottish Isles and bring the gospel to their kindred, the Celts of Scotland, of Wales and of Ireland?

The greatest interest, however, centers in the college established on *Iona* by that sainted man, Columba, in

A. D. 564, which under his successors was for centuries a training school or theological seminary for Christian missionaries to the heathen round about. *It was not a monastery.* Columba was a Celt and a native of Ireland, of royal lineage, that of the Kings of Ulster. He and his assistants, twelve in number, were imbued with the gospel of Christ, as was the Culdee Church. "Laborious researches of German scholars show that this Scottish church did more to carry a *pure gospel* to all the parts of Great Britain, France, Germany and Switzerland during the sixth, seventh and eighth centuries than all Christendom besides, and with this gospel to diffuse letters and science, industry and civilization." This was accomplished by sending forth from Iona century after century Christian men well trained for the work. These missionaries were called Culdees—a name whose origin is unknown.

In A. D. 607 Augustine, a monk, came from Rome to convert the Saxons, who had succeeded the Romans in the control of England. Long afterward Pope Gregory the Great made a similar but more successful attempt. These Romanists resorted to their usual tactics, and from the twelfth and thirteenth century onward, for four hundred years, popery labored to crush out the Scottish or Culdee Church, but never fully succeeded because witnesses for the truth never failed in that church. When the Reformation under Luther came in 1517 the faithful descendants of the "ancient Culdee Church" were prepared to be with it in sympathy. "The Reformation Church of Scotland was, therefore, simply a reappearance of the old primeval church." Thus we see how the Scottish Church was linked with the Apostolic, and we can trace, also, the links that connected the Church of England with that of Rome. The respective influence of these two origins can be distinctly recognized to-day. (*The Culdee Church, by Dr. T. V. Moore.*)

The Translations of the Bible.—The most efficient influence exerted over the English mind during the times of these religious troubles was undoubtedly the translation of the Bible into their own tongue. It had a great effect in preparing the way for the acceptance of the gospel by the common people. There were made several consecutive versions of the Bible, all, however, based on William Tyndale's translation, who in consequence of making known to his countrymen the word of God in their own tongue, suffered martyrdom.

One version was made (1539-41) in the reign of Henry VIII.; then another known as the Genevan, because made in that city, in 1560; which was followed by a version known as the Bishop's Bible, 1568, and 1572, in Elizabeth's reign, and finally King James's Bible, published in 1611. Thus we see that for nearly three-fourths of a century the preparation of these various versions of the Holy Scriptures occupied the attention of the learned men among the Puritans and the evangelical prelatists. This agitation on the subject attracted attention to the importance of the Holy Scriptures, and had an immense influence on the minds of the common people in leading them to read and study the word of God to a much greater extent than among any other people of Europe.

Another element was quietly at work during these troublous times of discussion and persecution, and that was the devoted attention which these learned men, though differing so much on other questions, gave to the Holy Scriptures by studying them in the originals—Hebrew and Greek—and from time to time preparing revised or better translations.

A POPULAR HISTORY OF
THE PRESBYTERIAN CHURCH.

VII.

SABBATH DESECRATION—SOLEMN LEAGUE AND COVENANT.

James I. issued a programme of amusements for the Sabbath day, known as the 'Book of Sports" (1618). According to his direction, it was drawn up by Bishop Moreton. It gave permission for the violation of the afternoon of the Sabbath day, after the morning services in the church; its open avowal being "to encourage recreations and sports on the Lord's day." Such mode of spending the Sabbath was customary among the Roman Catholic churches on the Continent, as it is for the most part to-day. The object of James was evidently to annoy the Puritans, as he well knew they kept and deemed all hours of the day equally sacred; perhaps his ulterior motive was to find an accusation against them.

Book of Sports.—The "Book of Sports" was directed to be read at the morning service in all the parish churches throughout England, but the evangelical Archbishop Abbot interfered so strenuously that it was read only to a very limited extent. The order therefore remained virtually obsolete for fifteen years, till 1633, when Charles I., at the instigation of Archbishop Laud, revived the "Book of Sports" and ordered it to be read and obeyed. The Romanizing bishops were in favor of the Sabbath being desecrated, while the evangelists exerted their influence in favor of preserving its sanctity. The Puritan pastors, rather than violate God's law by reading the order, gave up their livings in great numbers, and were turned upon the world, many of them penniless.

This conscientious and strenuous struggle of the Puritans—Presbyterians and Independents—to preserve the sanctity of the Sabbath has been fraught with untold blessings to the English-speaking people the world over, and nowhere greater than in the United States. The Puritans may appear in this age to have carried their views of the sanctity of the day to an unnecessary extent, yet that sternness of purpose produced a blessing which they never could have bequeathed if they themselves had been less strict in its observance. Their intense desire to preserve the Sabbath in its integrity led them toward a closer adherence to the Old Testament than to the New. For illustration, they were accustomed to commence the Sabbath on Saturday evening at sunset. This custom had an unhappy influence; since the Sabbath also ended at sunset, its evening was often spent in a manner calculated to fritter away the good impressions that may have been received in the house of worship during the day.

Influence of the Sabbath.—The keeping holy this blessed day has been an all-important agent in preserving the knowledge of God and His worship fresh among the people. How different would have been the religious influences abroad on the Continent of Europe since the Reformation if the reformers, such as Luther, Melanchthon, Zwingli, and even John Calvin, and their various co-workers, had been as strenuous in the defence of the sacredness of the Lord's day as was John Knox in Scotland! Under such circumstances, there would not be in existence what is now known as the *Continental Sabbath*, whose blighting influence is felt in the United States, even among the multitudes of those brought up in Christian families and who travel abroad, especially on the Continent, and who often return home imbued with a spirit indifferent if not absolutely antagonistic to the proper reverence for the sacredness of the fourth commandment. The observance of the Sabbath held the Jewish people fast to Jehovah, the living God, and which observance appeals the more earnestly to Christians, since it is the weekly reminder of the resurrection of the Blessed Saviour.

If a proper Christian observance of the sacredness of the Sabbath had prevailed in France from the times of Calvin and of Beza forward, could that nation have degenerated into infidelity? Could the terrible scenes of the Revolution of 1789 been enacted in its moral and bloody aspects? If the Sabbath had been observed by the reformers on the Continent as strictly as it was in Scotland or even in England, Romanism could not have regained so much of the influence which it had lost because of the Reformation. Neither could the priesthood have virtually deprived the people at large of the Bible. A people thoroughly trained to reverence and to keep that sacred day could never have been seduced again into Romanism, nor to permit *saints' days* to usurp its place and sacredness.

The Sabbath on the Continent.—The question has often been raised, Why did not the Reformers on the Continent have as clear and distinct views of the sacredness of the Sabbath as had Knox and his co-workers? The answer has usually been, that they were so accustomed to the number of *saints' days* in the Roman calendar, and in comparison with which days, especially those devoted to the Virgin Mary, the Lord's day was deemed less sacred. Again, the continental reformers were at the first absorbed in lines of controversy that did not especially involve the observance of the Sabbath. These reformers failed to insist on the practice of spiritual religion with the earnestness of the

REV. SAMUEL DAVIES, D. D.
(130, 140, 141, 168, 171.)

Puritans; hence the proper observance of the Sabbath as sacred time did not appear to them so essential. This lack of appreciation of the Lord's day has been a great hindrance to the advancement of spiritual religion among the common people on the Continent.

Saints' days, on the other hand, never held so much sway in the established church in the British Isles as they did on the Continent, because the mass of the people were better informed in respect to Bible truths, as we have already noted in this narrative. The continental reformers, therefore, had not as good material to act upon as had the English and Scotch divines. The English people, because of their knowledge of the Bible, were too well informed as to the sacredness of the fourth commandment to permit any saints' days to supersede its importance. That commandment required the holy rest of one day in seven, as well as the appropriate duties pertaining to six days of labor. On the contrary, the saints' days in Italy, for instance, sometimes demanded one or two holidays a week, thus diminishing the material progress of the people.

The Solemn League and Covenant.—In our day of religious liberty and civil freedom we can scarcely appreciate the intense interest that the English people themselves had in their church affairs. In this respect they were in contrast with the Protestant nations on the Continent; the latter being hitherto under the heel of the ecclesiastical despotism of the Roman hierarchy, which crushed the earliest aspirations of religious liberty, and therefore they could not attain that intelligent view of the rights of conscience which the English and Scotch people had been acquiring for a century or more.

As a defensive measure and to secure unity among themselves the Scotch entered into a compact known as the "Solemn League and Covenant" (1638). This has been characterized as "an act of consecration on the part of the Scottish people, which as to its essence is one of the noblest transactions of modern times." It was signed by the people with remarkable enthusiasm; with uplifted hands they took an oath to maintain its principles. In England Charles I. under oath signed the league and covenant in order to conciliate the people; but he evidently had no intention to keep his oath.

This document embodied as its main features: "The preservation of the Reformed religion in the Church of Scotland, in doctrine, worship, discipline, and government according to the word of God and the example of the best Reformed churches. . . . That we shall endeavor to bring the churches of God in these three kingdoms to the nearest conjunction and uniformity in religion, confession of faith, form of church government, directory for worship, and catechism."

To sustain these prominent measures the members of the House of Commons and the members of the Westminster Assembly likewise took an oath with uplifted hands in the presence of one another and afterward they individually signed the document. They also vowed "to extirpate popery, prelacy, superstition, heresy and schism, profaneness and whatsoever shall be found to be contrary to sound doctrine and the power of godliness" (1643).

Why Were the Prelates Feared?—It may seem strange that those who had been the victims of persecution so often and in so many forms—from the prison and the stake to being deprived of livings or driven into exile—should express in such strong terms their desire to "*extirpate* popery and prelacy." They simply acted in self-defense. Let it be remembered that both these ecclesiastical parties—Roman Catholic priests and Romanizing prelates—when connected with the government, persistently stimulated the latter to persecute those who wished to worship God in their own way, according to their own conscience. These signers of the League and Covenant intended nothing more by this strong language than by political means—not persecution—to prevent Romanism ruling in the councils of the nation and in the church, and also for the same reason free themselves from the underhand rule of the bishops of the Church of England, who were or might be in the same relation to the government. The Presbyterians and the Independents recognized the *parity of the ministry,* and in consequence among them the tendency was to treat one another as brethren and equal in their calling, while opinions held in respect to nonessentials were not a bar to fraternal intercourse. Neither was it on account of church government, because for the sake of peace and conciliation the Scotch and also the English Presbyterians had consented to a mixed sort of government or compromise in which bishops were recognized, but in Scotland they were held responsible to the General Assembly, while in England the bishops, if responsible to any authority, they were to the king, the assumed head of the church since the time of Henry VIII.

The opposition was to that class of bishops such as Laud and several others, known as Romanizers, who labored secretly and often treacherously during the reigns of the Stuarts to bring the English Church and people under the sway of the Roman hierarchy. This class of bishops persecuted with zeal and apparent delight, while the evangelical bishops, such as Archbishop Ussher and Abbot, and many others, were accustomed to protect those who for conscience' sake could not conform, and they labored also in behalf of the freedom of conscience.

For threatening the "extirpation" of popery and prelacy the bishops had their revenge—though petty. It seems that at their instigation the first Parliament under

Charles II. ordered the Solemn League and Covenant to be burned by the common hangman in the streets of London (May 22, 1661).

The Effect of Trials and Persecutions.—In this concise narrative we have seen the influence that during so many generations trained the Presbyterian leaders and they in turn the people, so that in the refining process induced by trials and persecutions Presbyterianism became "a religious system which is animate with the influences of the Holy Spirit. Christ is present in it as its enthroned Sovereign and Saviour. It is a real Christianity which rejects everything that is not a product of the *Christianity* of Jesus Christ. * * * This principle recognizes the supremacy of the Holy Spirit in the Scriptures, but declines to imprison His divine energy in its external form and letter. Presbyterianism did not reject the authority of the papal church and that of the prelatical church in order to establish the authority of a Presbyterian Church. It made supreme the living word of the living God; it bound itself to the Holy Spirit, who uses the word of God as a means of grace. It recognizes the enthroned Christ as the source of Christianity to every age. The word of God is the 'scepter of His Kingdom,' and divinely called presbyters are his officers, commissioned to govern the church with his authority and in his fear. * * * It has the true Apostolic succession in striving after the Apostolic faith in its purity, integrity and fulness.

"Presbyterianism belongs to the modern age of the world, to the British type of Protestantism; but it is not a departure from the Christianity of the ancient and medieval church. It makes steady progress toward the realization of the ideal of Christianity in the golden age of the Messiah. (*Am. Pres., pp. 5, 8, 11, condensed.*)

Presbyterian Household Training.—We hope this concise sketch of the training of the members of the Presbyterian Church—ministers as well as the laity—in the school of adversity where self-reliance was practically taught, will enable the reader to appreciate more fully the character of the first Presbyterian preachers to this country. The systematic instruction both in religious and secular affairs, given in the families of the Puritans or Presbyterians, had great influence for good. In proportion as the parents were intelligent they desired a still better education for their children than they themselves had enjoyed in their youth. Thus this God-implanted principle in the hearts of parents secured for each succeeding generation of the family a better education than that of the former. This influence has passed on and is felt in Presbyterian families more to-day than ever before. The private members of the church were thus, for the most part, trained in the knowledge of the Scriptures, while after its formulation, as an aid to that study, was used the Westminster Confession of Faith. This was a concise compendium of the doctrines which the ministers and elders and other intelligent laymen, members of that famous assembly, believed to be contained in the word of God. In addition for the benefit of youth the Larger and Shorter Catechism were prepared and made as familiar as household words to the Presbyterian youth of both sexes.

Such were the characteristics of the first Presbyterian ministers that came as preachers to the colonies, out of which grew the United States, and such was the knowledge of sacred things that pervaded the Congregational and Presbyterian households which emigrated thither from the three kingdoms. After they had settled in this new land they did not neglect the religious instruction of their children, but brought them up in an intelligent fear of the Lord, by means of teaching them not merely to read and study the word of God, but likewise to commit to memory, and that understandingly, the catechisms of the church. The sublime doctrines of Christianity were thus stored in the minds of their children to be brought forth and applied as occasion required when manhood and womanhood were attained.

VIII.

THE WESTMINSTER CONFESSION—EVENTS CONNECTED THEREWITH.

As the church was in connection with the government it was conceded that parliament had a right to interfere in its affairs. It is well to bear in mind that in those days the questions, which for the greater part absorbed the attention of parliament, were those pertaining to religious matters, as they had an influence upon the succession to the crown, while the intermeddling with the rights of conscience had been for several generations a prolific source of annoyance and evil to the people at large. The members of the parliaments of that period, as a general rule, were well acquainted with these religious questions, and often because of such qualifications were they chosen.

As already noted, there were in existence at this time, besides minor ones, no less than three prominent Confessions—that of the Presbyterians of Scotland (1560); the XXXIX. Articles of the English Church (1563), and that of the Irish Presbyterian Church (1615). The English Presbyterians, as yet, had not framed a Confession. A sentiment pervaded the minds of the Reformed ministers of the British Isles and of the intelligent laymen of all religious parties—except the Romanizing bishops—that there should be formulated a Confession of Faith for the whole kingdom.

The Ordinance of Parliament.—Meanwhile, the prelatical party, encouraged by the King, Charles I., was continually making encroachments upon the religious rights of the Puritans—the Presbyterians and Independents. To remedy these evils and also to unite all the people in favor of a single Confession of Faith, the latter desired to have summoned "an assembly of divines and learned laymen under the protection of parliament, who should be free in its action from the domination of the prelates." At this time parliament was antagonistic to the king because of his Romanizing policy in respect to the Church of England. A "Grand Remonstrance," drawn up and numerously signed, was presented to the king (1641) in which it was proposed for him to summon such an assembly. Charles refused to sanction a call for such purpose, and afterward (July 1, 1643) issued a proclamation forbidding the meeting of the assembly, which in spite of his opposition had in the meantime been summoned by parliament. Parliament of its own motion issued an ordinance (1643) for a certain number of learned and godly divines to be selected from the religious parties of England, who should take in hand to formulate such a creed or confession. The commissioners to which assembly "were to confer and treat among themselves of matters concerning the liturgy, discipline and government of the Church of England * * * clearing the doctrine of the same from all false aspersions and misconstructions * * * touching the matters aforesaid as shall be most agreeable to the word of God." The assembly was enjoined to report progress regularly to parliament.

The Westminster Assembly.—In accordance with this ordinance the famous assembly met at Westminster in King Henry VII. chapel, July 1, 1643. During a labor continuing for about three years they formulated the well-known Westminster Confession of Faith. This included the Catechisms, larger and shorter, a selection of Scripture proof-texts, and in addition a Directory of Public Worship. Its special merits have made this confession in all respects the most complete work of the kind ever produced. That it has been thus recognized we infer from the length of time, more than two hundred and fifty years, that it has been an authority in the Calvinistic churches of the English Protestant world and the vast numbers of others who have also accepted its interpretation of the word of God. No human work is perfect, but this in its sphere would seem as nearly perfect as men at that time could make it.

The Directory of Public Worship.—The Directory of Public Worship engaged the attention of the assembly nearly six months. When finished it was sent to parliament; that body having approved the work, it was ordered to be observed in the churches (1645). This directory in its spirit was consistent with the principle of toleration in non-essentials as held by the Presbyterian portion of the Puritans, and therefore it left as optional with the churches and ministers whether in public worship they should use written or unwritten prayers. Neither did the framers *intend to impose* that special form of worship upon the churches.

The Members of the Assembly.—The Westminster Assembly was composed of 121 divines, whom the parliament had carefully selected as representatives from all the counties of England and Wales, and also from the Universities of Cambridge and Oxford. There were only ten or twelve Independents or Congregationalists in the assembly. This fact may have been owing to their system of church government, in which each church was accustomed to frame or not its individual confession. Irish Presbyterians were also represented, and so were the *evangelical* bishops of the Church of England and in Ireland. *Ten* nobles represented the House of Lords and *twenty* of their ablest men from the House of Commons —thus recognizing the rights of Christian laymen to take part in the affairs of the church. The great majority, however, were Presbyterians, the number of which was increased by commissioners from the Scotch Church, who were invited to join in formulating a creed or Confession of Faith for the whole kingdom.

The commissioners from the Scotch Church reported from time to time to their General Assembly the proceedings of that of the divines at Westminster, and finally laid before the former the completed Confession of Faith and the catechisms, including also the Directory for Worship. After discussion the General Assembly of the Scotch Church, instead of its own, substituted in all its parts the Confession of Faith formulated by the Westminster divines (1647). Says Hetherington (*Hist. of the Scotch Church, p. 193*): "This, therefore, may be regarded as the assembly by which was completed the second Reformation of the Scottish Church, and the full arrangement of its confession and form of worship and discipline."

The Character of the Assembly and Its Work.—This was a remarkable company of divines: "Such a band of preaching and praying ministers as gathered in the Westminster Assembly the world had never seen before. * * * The main portion of the members was selected, in the nature of the case, from the great body of the ordained ministers of the Church of England, who had long been Puritans and Presbyterians. Never since has England been in the position to secure such another full representation of her Protestantism as the Westminster Assembly afforded. The three great parties which now divide British Protestantism were adequately represented among the learned divines named in the ordinance." (*Am. Pres., p. 62.*) "The Westminster standards are, historically speaking, the final crystallization of the elements of evangelical religion after the conflicts of sixteen hundred years; scientifically speaking, they are the richest and most precise and best guarded statement ever penned of all that enters into evangelical religion, and of all that must be safely guarded if evangelical religion is to persist in the world; and, religiously speaking, they are a notable monument of spiritual religion." (*Prof. Benj. B. Warfield.*)

Civil Commotions.—While the Westminster Assembly was in session England, Scotland and Ireland were disturbed by civil commotions, which resulted in battles between the armies of the opposing parties. These conflicts, occurring principally in England, were owing to the opposition of the English people to the tyrannical acts of Charles I. He quarreled with three successive parliaments from 1625 to 1629; by royal prerogative he in an arbitrary manner dissolved them in turn, because they insisted on redressing the existing civil and ecclesiastical wrongs. For eleven years he ruled in church and state after the manner of an oriental despot; that is, without a parliament or reference to the will of the people. The members of these parliaments for the most part were presbyterian in their religious views, and were identified with the policy of constitutional government and civil liberty. In 1640 a parliament was elected, but it refused to be dissolved by the mandate of the king or to adjourn; hence it is known as the Long Parliament, as it lasted for about twelve years. One of its first acts was to pass a resolution to the effect that it should not be dissolved except with its own consent. This parliament boldly advocated the civil and religious rights of the people, the latter meanwhile becoming more and more in sympathy with its proceedings. They were in process of training for ere long making an end of royal tyranny and prelacy, which were linked together by the king and his Archbishop Laud.

The Question of Apostolic Succession.—Two subjects

during this period agitated the minds of the religious parties in England—that of the *Apostolic succession* or the "regular and uninterrupted transmission of ministerial authority from the Apostles," and the Divine authority for a form of church government.

The Presbyterians claim that "the presbyters are the genuine bishops of the New Testament, and the true Apostolic succession is in the presbyters, who have been ordained by the Apostles and their successors from the foundations of the Christian Church until the present time." This mode of Apostolic succession would of itself seem more rational than to limit it to a single line of individual bishops. The latter would be more liable to be broken by some one dropping out than in the lines of numerous individuals as ministers or presbyters. The instances recorded in the primitive church wherein persons were ordained or set apart to the ministry, the ceremony used was that of the laying on of the hands of the presbytery collectively and not by a single bishop, elder or presbyter. (See I. Tim. iv, and Acts vi. 6; also xiii. 3.)

These officers of the primitive church may be included in three classes, namely: pastors or teachers, elders and deacons. The pastors and teachers engage in the preaching of the word and in the administration of the sacraments; the pastors and the ruling elders, when combined, have judicial power; while the care of the poor belongs to the deacons. (Acts Chap. vi.) Presbyterianism claims that there is no higher order of church officer found in the New Testament than that of teacher or presbyter, as the Greek word translated *bishop,* in every instance, is used synonymously with presbyter or elder. They claim thus to follow as nearly as possible the method of government used in the primitive church, and also that "their ministry is descended from Christ *through* the Apostate

Church of Rome, but not *from* the Apostate Church of Rome." This is on the principle that "the power of God's ordinance depends not on the person that does execute the same, but upon a higher foundation (authority), the institution of Christ." "Ministerial acts are not vitiated nor made null, though they pass through the hands of bad men, but stand good to all intents and purposes to such as receive them aright, by virtue of their office authoritatively derived from the first institution. * * * Our ministry is derived to us from Christ and his Apostles by succession of a ministry continued in the church. We have a lineal succession from Christ and his Apostles; not only a lineal succession, but that which is more and without which the lineal is of no benefit, we have a doctrinal succession also." (*Divine Right of the Gospel-Ministry, 1654, as quoted in Amer. Pres., pp. 2, 3.*)

Cromwell's Doings.—The Presbyterians were in favor of a constitutional government, through which they hoped the people would secure all their rights, civil and religious. The Independents, who during these commotions had rapidly increased in numbers, were extremely radical in their views, both as to the civil government and the prelacy. These characteristics at once attracted multitudes who had been previously neutral or indifferent. Oliver Cromwell was at their head. In 1643 he took command of the army; his marvelous influence inspired his soldiers with religious enthusiasm, though he did not neglect to make them perfect in military drill. After a series of victories in the course of four years Charles fell into Cromwell's hands (Nov. 30, 1648).

The first of Cromwell's measures when he assumed authority was to have expelled from the House of Commons of the Long Parliament the 140 Presbyterian members (Dec. 6, 1648); the remaining members, being Independents, began to legislate for themselves. This remnant is known in history as the *"Rump Parliament."* They at once abolished the House of Lords, then resolved to try Charles for his life (Jan. 1, 1649), and for that purpose named 150 commissioners. On the 20th of the same month the king was brought before this extemporized court. Charles refused to plead, on the ground that the court was illegally constituted; nevertheless he was promptly condemned, and on the 30th of the same month beheaded. Against these high-handed and illegal proceedings the Presbyterians protested, not that they were or could be in sympathy with Charles and Archbishop Laud in their tyrannies and intolerance, but that it was without sanction of law, while to go to such extremes they deemed unnecessary under the circumstances and most unjustifiable.

The New Parliament.—When the Restoration of Charles II. took place, February, 1660, the Presbyterian members of the Long Parliament, who had been illegally expelled by Cromwell, reassembled as a parliament, but at once resolved on a dissolution and on an election of a new House of Commons, thus purposely affording an opportunity for the people to express their opinions by their votes. The new House met on April 25, 1660, and took the oath of the "Solemn League and Covenant." (*See Chap. VII.*)

Charles II., however, adopted as his motto his grandfather James's axiom, "No bishop, no king," and the best that could be done was to institute a compromise, by moderate Presbyterians and moderate Episcopalians, combined in a mixed form of church government.

The Divine Right for Church Government.—The assumption that any form of church government can claim a divine right for the same has plainly no direct sanction in the Scriptures, but is only an inference from the mention, incidentally, of cases involving church government or regulation. Efforts were made by the different religious parties or denominations in those troublous times to prove that each of their respective forms of church government was *jure divino,* or of divine authority. This being the case, it was natural for each to desire to be in connection with the state, and no doubt these good men persuaded themselves that their own church under such circumstances would be in a sphere of greater usefulness.

In accordance with the theory of the times, the Long Parliament took measures that were essential for the support of the church and for its union with the state. In those days, compared with the present, the statesmen and divines were limited in their views of religious liberty and they were unwilling to favor all denominations alike by supporting their respective ministers from the public funds. On the contrary, the policy was to select one denomination and make it the only recipient of state favor or support, and in addition, what was exceedingly unjust, the *unfavored* ones had not only to support their own ministers but share in the expense of the State Church by paying tithes for its benefit. Each denomination wished to prove that its form of government was of *divine* authority, and in such case it had an undoubted claim to be placed in union with the state. How much time was wasted in the discussion of these questions! On them the Scriptures are silent, except only in incidentally mentioning the manner in which the affairs of the primitive church were administered.

Plan for a State Church.—The *politicians* of the Long Parliament were in favor of making the Presbyterian denomination the State Church, as had already been done in Scotland. In accordance with this partiality it passed a bill (Jan. 29, 1648): "For the speedy dividing and settling the several counties of this kingdom into distinct presbyteries and congregational elderships." The Parliament, after conferring with the assembly of divines at Westminster, issued the following order: "That there be forthwith a choice made of elders throughout the kingdom of England and Wales." In these regulations the ratio was instituted of *two elders* to one minister in the meetings of the presbyteries. In this early day we see how careful the Presbyterians were *to secure the rights* of the people or church members. This mode of government was in marked contrast with that of the Romish Church, wherein the private members had no voice, and the same principle was prominent in the Church of England under James and the two Charles, wherein the bishops ruled with a high hand and repudiated the idea that the private members should have a voice in church affairs.

In accordance with the model proposed by the Westminster Confession, the Presbyterian form of church government was to be adapted to England, Wales and Ireland. This organization of the Church of England on a Presbyterian basis similar to that of Scotland was prevented by the interference of Cromwell and the Independents, but owing to the disintegrating principle of the latter's mode of church government this union with the State had but little influence, if any at all. That rule was continued during the Commonwealth, but the Episcopal was restored as the State Church under Charles II. in 1660, after an interval of about twelve years.

It is worthy of note that the theory of the Apostolic succession henceforth became an element in the political world, as with it was associated the *jus divinum* authority of the king. The Romanizing bishops even gave their sanction to this theory in order to strengthen their own influence both in the Church and State. Says Prof. Fisher: "The theory that there can be no church without prelatical bishops was never maintained by Episco-

THE WESTMINSTER CONFESSION. 65

palians in England until the days when a school of theologians, who were at the same time supporters of the tyranny of the Stuarts, brought it forward and used it in the controversy with the Puritans." (*The Validity of Non-Prelatical Ordination, p. 18.*)

IX.

EMIGRATIONS TO THE COLONIES—CONGREGATIONAL AND PRESBYTERIAN.

We have concisely traced the influences that led to the outgrowth of Presbyterianism in the British Isles. We have noted its underlying principles, such as the *parity* of the ministry; a church government by presbyters; if not in so many words, practically the same among the Reformed churches on the Continent and the Bible accepted as the only infallible rule of faith and practice. Their form of church government, in which the church members had a part, was in opposition to the prelatical system, the outgrowth of the arbitrary rule of the Church of Rome. That system, however, suited the kings and queens of England, who impiously assume to be the head of the church, while the genuine Reformers held that Christ, alone, was the head of His Church, as he himself declared to his disciples when he said that he was the Master.

Puritans in Virginia.—We learn incidentally from history that among the English emigrants who came to Virginia (1607), and who founded the first English permanent settlement upon the soil of the present United States, there were Puritan ministers. Some of these, it is probable, were Presbyterians and some were Independents, but as the form of church government was looked upon as non-essential by both parties among the Puritans, we find the terms expressive of either form very seldom used. We learn, however, incidentally that these ministers were not prelatists and did not conform to the rites and ceremonies of the established church. One of them, Alexander Whitaker, whom George Bancroft characterizes as "the self-denying apostle of Virginia," after describing in a letter the religious services on the Sabbath day, remarks incidentally (1614): "Here neither surplice nor subscription"—that is to the church services—"is spoken of."

Some thirty years after this declaration was made (1645) it was "specially ordered that no minister should preach or teach publicly or privately except in conformity to the Church of England; non-conformists were banished." The reader will notice that when this order was issued the Westminster Assembly of Divines was in session, Charles I. was on the throne, and the civil commotions had already commenced which brought him to the block. Nevertheless, prelatical influence at home urged the authorities in Virginia to persecute the non-conformists. The indirect rule of the bishops in that colony was exceedingly intolerant toward the non-conformists or dissenters, and in consequence of these continued persecutions there occurred one hundred and thirty years afterward the severest struggle for religious liberty in American history—which will be noted further on, p. 159—and which resulted in the complete overthrow of the interfering prelatical power in the state. About this time (1643) the Virginia Puritans invited preachers from the Colony of Massachusetts Bay to supply the religious wants of the people, but when they came they were forbidden to preach by the colonial authorities and were also ordered to leave the country. Sir William Berkeley was appointed Governor in 1642, and he held the office for nearly forty years. He is represented as a courtier and "very malignant toward the way of the churches" in New England. He had been instructed to enforce the ceremonies of the Church of England. There had been no religious persecution till 1642, when Berkeley was appointed Governor, and to him belongs the odium of instituting the persecution of these Christians, who would not violate their conscience by conforming in their worship to the prescribed ceremonies of the established church.

The Policy of the Virginia Company.—The sympathy of the original Virginia Company was with the Puritan ministers, and oftentimes when such were deprived of their livings in England because they would not conform to the rules laid down by prelatical authority, the company would aid them in migrating to Virginia. This action roused the anger of James and he arbitrarily revoked the charter of the company (1624). While the charter was in existence Virginia was under Puritan control; not indeed that form of Puritanism which became dominant in New England and ruled Great Britain under the Lord Protector, but the Puritanism of the English Presbyterians, who desired to reform the national church." (*Am. Pres., p. 90.*) The American colonies were added to the bishopric of the Bishop of London, whose duty it was to appoint for them their clergy.

The Puritans had sent ministers as missionaries to the Bermuda or Somers Islands as early as 1612, and numbers of these from time to time migrated to Virginia. Meantime many Puritan ministers and also Puritan families were coming as settlers to the same colony. Among the ministers was Robert Bolton, who preached at Elizabeth City and to the colonists on the eastern shore of the Chesapeake.

The Plymouth Colony.—Thirteen years after the commencement of the colony in Virginia the Pilgrim Fathers landed at Plymouth, Massachusetts (Dec. 22, 1620). Owing to the continual annoyances instigated by the English bishops this congregation had previously sought relief by removing in a body from England to Holland, where they could enjoy religious liberty. Their pastor, John Robinson, went with them as their guide. He was remarkable for his toleration and Christian charity, and with his spirit the entire congregation appear to have been imbued. After a sojourn of several years in Holland they resolved, for valid reasons, to migrate to the new world, and thither the larger portion went. Their beloved pastor was unable to accompany them, but he entrusted the management of the enterprise to their elder, William Brewster. Death prevented Robinson joining his flock in their new homes at Plymouth. (*Patton's Four Hundred Years of American History, I., pp. 93-103.*)

For nearly ten years the congregation was without a pastor. For eighteen years the colony was a pure democracy; the male members voting on every question pertaining to the secular government, while in respect to church matters the form was independent, though in the congregation were many Presbyterians, among whom was Elder Brewster.

A Presbyterian Church Organized.—The founding of a Presbyterian colony on Massachusetts Bay was encouraged by "the Presbyterian leaders in the South of England and also in London." The Rev. John White of Dorchester was a controlling mind in planning the enterprise. So much interest did Christian men take in the project that Arthur Lake, the evangelical Bishop of Bath and Wells, declared "he would go himself but for his age." It was to be a "colonization on a higher principle than the desire of gain." The first instalment of colonists came in 1625, but the perfect organization did not take place till 1629, after a second and quite a large company of immigrants arrived, when a Presbyterian church was fully constituted. Their pastor was Rev. Samuel Skelton, and their teacher Francis Higginson.

Why the Presbyterians Were Liberal.—The Puritans who were presbyterian in their opinions on church government were liberal and looked upon such form of rule merely as expedient. They were extremely anxious that the essential doctrines of the gospel should be held in their purity, and they also wished to promote the cause of Christ and preserve the peace of the church. Thus when occasion required they united with the Congregationalists in the New World, as they had already done in both England and Scotland. On this principle the Presbyterian Churches fraternized with those of the Plymouth colony. Dr. Dexter says: "The early Congregationalism of this country was a Congregationalized Presbyterianism or a Presbyterianized Congregationalism, which had its roots in the one system and its branches in another; which was essentially Genevan (Calvinistic) within the local congregation and essentially other outside of it." (*Congregationalism, p. 463.*) This combination of church organization gradually passed out of existence in the colony and the main body of the churches became Congregational in their form of government, the Presbyterians acquiesced as a matter of expediency and a promoter of peace. Another element had, perhaps, an unconscious influence in after years. That was the success of Cromwell and the Independents in seizing the secular government in England, which action had a marked effect in New England during the Commonwealth (1649-1658) of promoting an increase in the numbers of the churches that adopted the Congregational mode of government. From this influence came the union of Church and State after the Cromwell pattern in Massachusetts, and afterward in Connecticut, and which arrangement remained in force forty years after the Presbyterians had compelled the separation of Church and State in Virginia (1773-1786). The influence of the latter led within a few years to a similar separation in the Carolinas and Georgia.

Limited Influence of the Synod.—There were no pure presbyteries as there are to-day formed in New England on account of the differences of opinion on the subject of church government. The synods, so named, were only used for consultation and advice. They had no power to use discipline; their authority being spiritual and moral. This was consistent with the underlying principle which made each Congregational Church independent and virtually isolated from sister churches.

The Constitution of the Congregational Church.— The first Congregational Church in America was formed in Charlestown on the 30th of July, 1630. Soon afterward, "crossing the Charles River, it became known as the First Church of Boston," and it also became "the seminal center of the ecclesiastical system of Massachusetts." It embodied as one of the principles of Congregationalism: "The equality of the several churches, free from the jurisdiction of ecclesiastical court or bishop; free from the jurisdiction of one church over another, and free from the collective authority of them all." (*Bancroft, vol. i., p. 238, last revision.*)

The members of the Independent or Congregational churches in New England were largely in the majority, and prospered greatly, but in the course of time they unfortunately became somewhat intolerant in respect to other denominations of Christians.

The Presbyterians of New England took much interest in evangelizing the natives. John Eliot, the Apostle to the Indians, was a Presbyterian, and the Presbyterians who settled at Salem made efforts also to send the gospel to the Indians in their vicinity.

Migration of Presbyterians to New York.—In those times of ecclesiastical annoyances, if not harsh persecutions, most of the emigrants from the British Isles to the American colonies came in organized bodies, bringing with them their ministers, as did the Pilgrims to Massachusetts, the Roman Catholics to Maryland and the Friends to Pennsylvania. In only one instance, already noticed, did the Presbyterians attempt this mode, when a Presbyterian congregation emigrated and settled in Massachusetts with Rev. Samuel Skelton as their pastor. In after years during more than a half century such movements of congregations from one colony to another sometimes occurred in order to enjoy more religious liberty, and perhaps for other reasons.

The liberality of the Dutch on the Island of Manhattan and vicinity stands out prominent, and perhaps for this reason more than any other Presbyterian ministers and laymen with their families availed themselves of this liberality and migrated to the colony of New York. The first was Rev. John Young, who had been ordained in the Church of England. He came direct from New England and organized a church at Southhold, Long Island (1640). The second was Abraham Pierson. He was a graduate of Cambridge. His first pastorate was Lynn, Massachusetts; thence he removed to South Hampton, Long Island, and afterward to Branford, Connecticut. From the latter place he migrated with a portion of his church members to Newark, New Jersey, where he organized the first Puritan Church in that state. It was his son of the same name who became President of Yale College in 1692.

Francis Doughty, who had been silenced for non-conformity in England, emigrated to Taunton, Massachusetts. There he maintained the Presbyterian doctrine of infant baptism, but owing to the hostile influence of the Congregational minister he was forced to leave. He and his wife and Richard Smith, a ruling elder, and other adherents came to Newtown, Long Island, but soon after an Indian war broke out, and this small number of Presbyterians with their minister fled to Manhattan for safety. Thus Doughty became the first Presbyterian minister in New Amsterdam (1643). He preached there for five years and was supported by the contributions of his own people and the voluntary gifts of the Dutch who attended his ministry. He afterward went to Virginia, about 1650.

The second Presbyterian minister in New Amsterdam was Richard Denton, though only temporarily. Numbers of the Dutch and French attended on his preaching in a church building that was within the fort, and at different hours of service. During this period and immediately afterward the number of Puritans and Presbyterians increased, so that when New Amsterdam was captured (1664) by the English there were within the bounds of what is now New York six Puritan or Presbyterian ministers and their congregations, much to the credit of the liberality and toleration of the Dutch authorities, Peter Stuyvesant being then the Governor. Here were members of the Church of Holland, Presbyterians and Independents, as well as Jews and Quakers, all living in harmony and as far as history shows each denomination enjoying religious liberty. The Presbyterians and Independents were the more numerous and were looked upon as the more substantial.

Rev. Richard Denton deserves a passing notice. He was a Presbyterian in his views of church polity. He was of a good Yorkshire family and received his education at Cambridge (1623). For seven years he was a pastor in his native land, but because of persecutions he left for America about the year 1630, and for five years he labored at Watertown, Mass., but because of his Presbyterianism he was opposed by certain Congregationalists, and in consequence he removed in 1635 to the valley of the

Connecticut and settled in a place which he named Weathersfield. Meanwhile he preached also at Stamford, but in 1644 we find him at Hempstead, Long Island, where he remained as pastor of the Presbyterian (Christ's) Church for fifteen years, when in 1659 he returned to England. A large number of his church members followed him to Hempstead.

Richard Denton was recognized as a fine scholar. The Dutch pastors of New Amsterdam describe him to be a Presbyterian and "an honest, pious and learned man." Though the regular pastor at Hempstead, Denton occasionally ministered in New Amsterdam in an English Puritan Church, after the Rev. Francis Doughty (1650) left for Virginia.

Christ's First Presbyterian Church at Hempstead recently (October, 1894) celebrated with imposing ceremonies the 250th anniversary of its permanent founding by Richard Denton. "Our claim is not that the Hempstead church is the oldest Protestant and presbyterial in form in the churches in America * * * but that it is the oldest of the denomination which has always been called by the name Presbyterian." (*Souvenir of the 250th Anniversary, etc., p. 20; Am. Pres., p. 102.*)

Christian Brotherhood in Practice.—The beautiful condition mentioned above of Christian brotherhood and mutual toleration was destined to be changed soon, for when the English took possession of the province for the second time (in 1674) almost at once was felt the persecuting spirit of the bishops around the corrupt court of Charles II. Notwithstanding these annoyances for about twenty years afterward Presbyterian and Independent ministers, some with their families and not a few adherents, continued to emigrate from England and Scotland and from the north of Ireland to the colonies of New York and New Jersey. Many of these made their homes on Long Island, which seems to have been to these immigrants a favorite region. Meanwhile many settled in what is now known as Westchester County, as well as on the Isle of Manhattan itself.

Statement of Governor Andross.—In 1678 Edmund Andross, who was Governor under James II., wrote that there were in the province "religions of all sorts; one Church of England, several Presbyterians and Independents, Quakers, Anabaptists of several sects, some Jews, but Presbyterians and Independents most numerous and substantial." During this period we notice the names of nearly thirty ministers who came at different times and settled in many places within the jurisdiction of the New York colony. It would seem that the Presbyterians and Independents increased at even a greater ratio than did their ministry.

Influence of the Act of Toleration.—Until the great Revolution of 1688—when James II. was driven from the throne to give place to William of Orange—the difficulties that arose between the royal governors and the people, both Dutch and Puritan, pertained to civil affairs rather than to religious matters. The Revolution of 1688 had to a certain extent brought toleration to those Christians in England who dissented from the established church, but not to the same class in the colonies, inasmuch as the secular authorities of the latter held that the Act of Toleration did not apply to the colonies. We shall see that after a long and severe struggle it was finally decided in the case of the Colony of Virginia (1748, p. 168) that the act did apply to the colonies.

X.

Contrast in Land-Holdings—The Cavaliers—Elders as Worthies.

In Virginia owing to royal grants of large bodies of land—often whole counties—to court favorites, an effort was made to found a system of landed estates, which in important respects was in contrast with the settlements in the northern colonies. In Virginia these large grants of land rendered the population less in proportion to the extent of territory occupied than in the latter, the result in time was a landed aristocracy modeled somewhat after that of England. This aristocracy was from first to last derelict in its duty toward the general education of the youth of the colony. In Massachusetts, for example, the landed system was in direct contrast, as in the latter the estates in land were comparatively small, while the law, and subsequently the rule in the other New England colonies, was far-reaching in its influence. In accordance with the law the farms were compact and so arranged that one end should jut on a street, on which were placed the dwellings, and they within a specified distance from the meeting-house and the school-room. These two contrasted systems produced in time radical differences in the educational and religious training of the people; for illustration, public or common schools were firmly established in Massachusetts in 1647; and these soon became the heritage of the children throughout New England, and in time in the other free-labor States, while not a common school in the usual sense was in existence south of

Mason and Dixon's line till they were established by the national government after the close of the Civil War. (*Patton's Four Hundred Years of American History. I., p. 124; II., pp. 858, 859.*)

In a community in which all the youth were taught the essential elements of an education there was a better foundation on which to base a Christianized civilization than in one in which the majority of the parents were illiterate, and consequently the children ignorant.

The Royalists.—Another element, that of the Royalists or Cavaliers, prevailed in Virginia and the Carolinas, but nowhere else in the colonies. The Cavaliers or Royalists were all in connection with the Church of England and were fair exponents of the persecuting spirit which that church inherited from the hierarchy of Rome. For this reason we find that after the abrogation of the original charter of the Virginia Company, the dissenters, or those Christians who could not in their conscience conform to the ceremonies of the established church, were at the mercy of the clergy of that church then in the colony. The latter, for the most part, were stimulated by the spirit of the bishops at home, as they were incessantly urging the royal governors, the court and civil authorities to prohibit the dissenting ministers preaching, except under certain harsh conditions. To their honor, be it said, the royal governors—except Sir William Berkeley—were inclined to favor the dissenting ministers in preaching the gospel—we will see in the course of this narrative this fact made manifest. The Colony of Virginia was the only one in which the civil authorities had arbitrary power in church affairs, and it was the only one in which a contest for religious liberty could be made direct with such authorities.

Berkeley's Prayer.—Sir William Berkeley is the author of the now famous words of gratitude and prayer: "I thank God there are no free schools nor printing in the colony; and I hope we will not have them these hundred years; God deliver us from both!" (*Patton's Four Hundred Years, etc., I., pp. 138, 139.*) Such was the predominant influence on the education of the youth of the colony, and whose effects are felt even in our own times.

Why the Enmity of the Clergy?—The Cavaliers looked upon the Presbyterians as inimical to the established church, and therefore to the House of Stuart. In consequence of this feeling the clergy of that church in the colony were bitterly opposed to the Presbyterian ministers that came to Virginia as missionaries. This hostile spirit on the part of these clergy toward all dissenters continued unabated from 1642 to 1786, when, as we shall see, the connection between the State and the Church was severed forever.

The Charter for Maryland.—Sir George Calvert, afterward Lord Baltimore, left the Protestant Church and professed himself a Roman Catholic, which ingratiated him with King Charles I. Calvert desired to found a colony where those of his present faith could flee to avoid persecution. After making a fruitless attempt on the barren territory of Newfoundland, he applied to Charles for a grant of land and the privilege of founding a colony in the fertile and beautiful region north of Virginia. The request was granted, and he obtained a charter and a district of territory, the greater part of which is now included in the present State of Maryland (1632).

The Liberal Policy.—Calvert was prudent and far-seeing; having been trained in his youth as a Protestant, he repudiated intolerance as a policy, and he invited the Puritans who were then being driven out of Virginia by the persecuting Berkeley, to come and share the religious privileges that were enjoyed by the Catholics, for whom, ostensibly, his colony was founded. The latter soon be-

REV. JOHN RODGERS, D. D.
(141, 208, 247, 280.)

CONTRAST IN LAND-HOLDINGS.   79

came the minority, owing to the influx of those thus invited. The colony freed from civil and religious turmoil continued to flourish for years; the privileges of the people were understood; allegiance was acknowledged to the home government, and the rights of the heirs of Lord Baltimore were respected.

The people advanced so far in their ideas of the liberty of thought and free expression that the authorities passed a law (1649) granting perfect toleration to *all Christian sects;* two years previous Rhode Island had granted toleration to *all opinions, infidel as well as Christian.*

The Repentant Chaplain.—Rev. Thomas Harrison was at one time the chaplain of Governor Berkeley. He was a strict conformist and stern opposer of those Christians who did not conform, and he is charged with instigating the Governor to acts of intolerance against the Puritan ministers. Harrison, however, relented in his manner toward the persecuted, and finally became himself an earnest Christian minister or Puritan. The Governor dismissed him from his service as chaplain. He then devoted himself to preaching to a Presbyterian church at Nansemond. He was so much annoyed by petty persecutions that he removed to Boston and thence to England, where in behalf of the church members of Nansemond, he complained to the government of the ill-treatment which they had received at the hands of the Governor. The Council of State was now under Cromwell (1649) and it required Berkeley "to permit the same Mr. Harrison to return to his said congregation and to the exercise of his ministry there." Mr. Harrison, however, did not return to Virginia, but the members of his church in order to avoid further persecutions migrated to Maryland under the leadership of their ruling elder, William Durand. The congregation was invited by Captain William Stone, a Protestant, who was then Governor of the colony for Lord Baltimore. This company of exiles was afterward followed by many families from the vicinity of Nansemond, who thus escaped from the intolerance of Berkeley. Durand was a man of sterling character and influence. This may be inferred from the fact he was appointed secretary of the commission sent from England to reduce Virginia and Maryland to obedience to the parliament.

The Worthy Elder.—Colonel Ninian Beall was well qualified as a Christian and benevolent man to succeed the excellent elder, William Durand. Mr. Beall came to Maryland in 1657; he made his way to success; from a mechanic of limited means he became for the times a man of wealth, owning much land. Enterprising in business he aided the people by introducing needed manufactures, such as a flour mill and a furnace to smelt iron from ore found in the vicinity. In these times of trouble from hostile Indians he took an interest in military affairs, and on occasion commanded a portion of the provincial troops. In recognition of such service the Colonial Assembly gave him a special grant.

In the affairs of the Presbyterian Church on the west shore of the Chesapeake he was an efficient officer, holding as best he could the church members together in the absence of a pastor. "He may lay claim to be called the father of Presbyterianism in Maryland. He was present at its birth, sustained it in its day of weakness and in 1704 gave it a handsome endowment of land at Upper Marlboro, or Patuxent, for a church building." He lived to a great age, 92 years, dying in 1717; he was well acquainted with the ministers who constituted the first presbytery. (P. 92.) He saw a single church grow into a vigorous synod. * * * It is almost certain that he is the 'ancient and comely man, an elder amongst the Presbyterians,' who entertained for some days

Thomas Wilson, the famous Quaker preacher, at his house in 1692"—as noted in the latter's life. (*Early Presbyterianism in Maryland, p. 13.*)

Doughty and Hill.—Rev. Francis Doughty, whom we have seen as the first Presbyterian minister in New Amsterdam, had a difficulty with the Governor, Peter Stuyvesant, in relation to a land grant of which the Governor wished to deprive him, and to avoid the anger of the former Doughty migrated to the Colony of Maryland. For this high-handed measure the Governor was called to an account by the authorities in Holland. (*Am. Pres., p. 101.*) Doughty preached to the exiles from Virginia, and thus he labored until his death, in traveling from place to place as an apostle. The little flocks to whom he ministered in time were organized into churches, which were afterward represented in a presbytery.

Another worthy of this period deserves mention— Matthew Hill. He had been ejected from his living in England because of his non-conformity (1662), and seven years later we find him preaching to the people in Maryland, whom he describes as "a loving and a willing people * * * and not at all fond of the litany or ceremonies." "To Francis Doughty and Matthew Hill, long-forgotten worthies, the Presbyterian Church in the Middle States is indebted for its early planting. They were the pioneers and martyrs in its ministry, and their sufferings and toils were the seed of the church." (*Am. Pres., p. 113.*)

XI.

Francis Makemie—Presbyterianism in Several Colonies.

The most devoted and influential minister in the cause of Presbyterianism in its earlier days in the colonies of Virginia and Maryland was Francis Makemie. He came in 1683 from the north of Ireland. He belonged to that portion of the people denominated Scotch-Irish; that is of Scotch ancestry, but natives of Ireland. There is no record of the names of his parents, and only a reference to the days of his youth. He says of himself that in his fifteenth year, while under the instruction of a pious schoolmaster, he felt the influence of the Holy Spirit in his soul.

He studied in the University of Glasgow and was licensed to preach by the Presbytery of Laggan in Ireland, under whose direction he was sent as a missionary to the Barbadoes or Bermuda Islands, and from there he came to Maryland. He traveled much as an itinerant and preached to the small Presbyterian flocks that were scattered in Virginia and Maryland, especially in the latter. He is said to have been the first dissenting minister that was permitted by the colonial authorities to preach in Virginia; this permission was, perhaps, in consequence of his having a certificate authorizing him to preach in Barbadoes. He is thought to have been the first minister of the Geneva or Calvinistic school that made his residence in this region.

He came thither about forty years after the formulation of the Westminster Confession, in which was a clear statement in respect to the duties of the civil magistrate, as pertaining to religious worship. He was evidently familiar with these principles as put forth in that confession, as he made an application of them in his argument with the colonial authorities, when advocating his right to preach the gospel.

Makemie's Business Talents.—Makemie appears to have been a man of some means, which, says tradition, was derived from the fortune of his wife, who was the daughter of a wealthy colonist of Accomac County, Virginia. He was a successful merchant in the West India trade. When in the colonies he traveled and preached, though his secular affairs often required his absence, but finally he settled down and devoted his whole time to preaching and at his own expense; in that respect adopting the Apostle Paul as his model. Thus he labored from first to last, about twenty-five years. He organized into churches the little groups of Presbyterians of Maryland, many of whose members were exiles from the religious intolerance of Berkeley in Virginia.

It appears that after 1698 Makemie made Snow Hill, on the eastern shore of Maryland, his settled home. The church of which he was pastor was authorized by the Provincial Assembly about 1699. For the reader will remember that in 1692 the Church of England was by law established in Maryland—hence the necessity for a *permit* to have a Presbyterian church. The perfect freedom of religious worship had vanished from Maryland, and now the bishops at home and the clergy in the colony stimulated the civil authorities to interfere with the "dissenters." The Presbyterians felt this influence still further in their being compelled by law to pay taxes to support the clergy of the established church.

The Memorial Church.—A few years since, in 1889,

at Snow Hill was dedicated the "Francis Makemie Memorial Church." Thus after the lapse of nearly two hundred years, Makemie's labors were duly recognized and honored by a thankful generation of Presbyterians. Makemie left no descendants. Says a chronicler of the times: "Numerous parents manifested their respect for his memory by giving his surname to certain of their children and in the last century in that region Makemie was very common as a Christian name."

A Staunch Defender of Religious Liberty.—Francis Makemie was a steadfast and consistent defender of the right to preach the gospel, in which character he often figured. The famous *Toleration Act* was passed in 1689. It afforded religious liberty under certain conditions, but only partially to the dissenters in England, and not even to the same extent in the colonies, as the authorities of the latter, especially in Virginia, assumed that the act did not apply to the colonies, and the Virginia civil officers and courts acted on that principle for more than half a century after the time of which we write, and in fact till compelled by Presbyterian influence to yield the point. (*See p. 168.*) Makemie claimed that the Act of Toleration was in force in the colonies, as well as in England. This opinion he presented with great force in an argument before the Governor and Council in Virginia, and afterward in New York before Lord Cornbury. He demanded in both instances the recognition of the rights of conscience as acknowledged by English law. He claimed it was no crime to preach the gospel to those who desired to hear it.

After the Church of England was established in 1692 Makemie applied under the Toleration Act to the court in Accomac for a license to preach. The court could not deny him, because he used his own *private houses*, of which he had two, as preaching places, and they were protected by the common law, since an "Englishman's house was his castle," and not even the king himself could legally enter it without the owner's permission. Public buildings in Virginia were denied the dissenters for religious worship.

A Presbyterian Church Organized.—Makemie organized a Presbyterian church, which was named Rehoboth, and whose house of worship remains to this day on the Maryland side of the Potomac. In his will he left the house "for the ends and use of a Presbyterian congregation, as if I were personally present, and to their successors forever, and none else, but to such of the same persuasion in matters of religion." Makemie organized a sufficient number of Presbyterian churches, which at his death in 1708 required for their pastoral care three ministers. In all his life he was in advance of many of his own age, and a consistent advocate for civil liberty and equal religious rights, granting in spirit and in act to others the same rights that he demanded for himself.

Thus in this region, so isolated because of its position, it being "a narrow neck of land between the ocean and Chesapeake Bay," and on that portion which belongs to Maryland, originated the mother churches of the Presbyterian denomination in the Middle States. The land of this district was by no means inviting to colonists because of the fertility of its soil, for it was as barren then as it is to-day; but it was in Maryland, where religious liberty, till 1692, was enjoyed, in contrast with its neighbor, Virginia, in which the intolerant Church of England held ecclesiastical sway. Owing to its secluded position, there is, perhaps, no region on the Atlantic slope whose inhabitants in their characteristics have changed so little from those of that early day.

Makemie's Trial in New York.—In this connection we notice an incident that made the name of Makemie known throughout the colonies. He was on his way to Boston, accompanied by John Hampton, a Presbyterian minister. Having stopped at New York, he was invited by the Puritans of the place to preach; the Dutch offering their church edifice for the purpose, but Lord Cornbury, the Governor, forbid its being thus used. Makemie, however, preached in a private house (Jan. 20, 1707). According to the recognized "Englishmen's Rights" and English common law, as the court afterward decided, the citizen who offered his own private dwelling for the purpose of holding a religious service was justified, as well as the preacher. Notwithstanding this fact, for thus preaching Makemie was arrested by order of the Governor a day or two later at Newtown, Long Island, where he was to preach. He had with him a certificate authorizing him to preach in Virginia and also in Barbadoes, but not in New York, and therefore the Governor forbid his preaching in the province. Makemie boldly answered the Governor, saying: "To give bond and security to preach no more in your Excellency's government, if invited and desired by any people, we neither dare nor can do." The result was that Makemie was bound over for trial, which was to take place on June 3, 1707. Having been detained a month or more his friends applied to the Supreme Court on writ of *habeas corpus* and he was released on bail (March 1st, 1707). The case of Hampton, who was also arrested, was not pressed. Makemie returned to New York and stood his trial and was acquitted by the court on the ground that he had complied with the conditions of the Toleration Act. Thus his license to preach in the Barbadoes was held to be valid throughout the queen's dominions. But, strange to say, Makemie was obliged by the court to pay the expenses of the trial, £83 7s. 6d. He was defended by three of the ablest lawyers in the province. The tyrannical action of the dissolute Cornbury roused the entire body of the Puritans and Presbyterians against such injustice and intolerance. Francis Makemie died the following year, 1708. (*Am. Pres., XLIX., App.*) (*See p. 94.*)

Presbyterianism in New Jersey.—We have already alluded to the settlement of Abraham Pierson at Newark and of his son of the same name in East New Jersey (1667-1692). Meantime large numbers of Presbyterians were migrating to the same colony from New England and New York—many from the latter to avoid the petty annoyances of the established church. Puritan or Presbyterian churches were established under their ministers at Elizabethtown and at Woodbridge about 1680. A writer of the time describes the people of this portion of Jersey as follows: "They are mostly New England men," of "several sorts of religion, but few are zealous." In every town there is a meeting-house where they worship publicly every week." Their ministers were supported by the voluntary contributions of the people, there being no law providing for their salaries. From Pilloche in Scotland there came in 1685 more than one hundred exiles, who settled mostly at Woodbridge. With them came their pastor, Rev. George Scott, who with his brethren, Archibald Riddel and John Frazer, had been imprisoned because of their fidelity to Presbyterian principles. Others came also, but in not so large companies. A number of Puritans migrated from Fairfield County, Connecticut, under their pastor, Thomas Bridge, and founded a church at Cohanzy, in what was then called West Jersey. At the close of the year 1699 there were only four fully organized congregations of Puritans or Presbyterians in that colony, and three settled ministers.

Presbyterianism in Delaware and Pennsylvania.—The earliest founding of Presbyterianism in Delaware was under the ministry of Samuel Davis, who had a church and congregation at Lewes in 1692. Davis was probably an Irishman. He supported himself by business pursuits. It appears from their correspondence on the subject, that the ministers of Boston took an interest in sending the gospel to Delaware and to Pennsylvania. They sent Rev. John Wilson to New Castle, Delaware, to minister to the church in that place, and Rev. Benjamin Woodbridge to Philadelphia. The latter bore a letter of introduction from Governor Danforth of Massachusetts to Governor Markham of Pennsylvania, saying: "Our beloved brother, Benjamin Woodbridge, now sent, not to handle such points as are matters of controversies among Protestants, but to preach unto as many of all persuasions as the Lord shall make willing to hear such truths, even as are without controversy, even the great mystery of godliness." (*Am. Pres., p. 125.*) Woodbridge was superseded by Rev. Jedediah Andrews (1698), who served as the pastor of this, the only Presbyterian church in Philadelphia, for many years until his death. He became one of the fathers of the first American classical presbytery—consisting of ministers and elders—in the colonies.

Presbyterianism in South Carolina.—While these migrations were in progress in the northern colonies Presbyterian immigrants were coming into the southern, especially into South Carolina. Owing to civil commotions in Scotland numbers of Scotchmen, who were not in sympathy with the English government, were banished. A company of these, consisting of twenty-two, sailed from Glasgow having with them a minister, William Dunlop. They landed at Port Royal, South Carolina, about 1685 or 1686, and commenced a settlement, but owing to the unwholesomeness of the locality it was soon abandoned.

Their pastor returned to Scotland, where he rose to eminence as principal of the University of Glasgow.

Missionaries Sent—A Colony Formed.—Meantime the attention of the New England Puritans was directed to these southern colonies and they sent thither ministers as missionaries, under whose ministrations a number of churches were established in the colony. An attempt was also made by a trading company to found a colony of Scotch people on the Isthmus of Darien in 1698 or 1699. The General Assembly of Scotland sent to the colony several ministers to preach and act as pastors. Three of these ministers, Alexander Shields, Francis Boreland and Archibald Stobo, instituted the Presbytery of Caledonia, the *first* presbytery in the New World. The germs planted here were not, however, permitted to grow and flourish. For within a few years the colony was broken up through the enmity of French and Spanish and hostile English traders—the home government meanly conniving at the outrage, as it did not wish to cherish a Scottish colony. The majority of the colonists finally migrated to New England, where they were received with great kindness. Of their ministers one died and another returned home, and one—Archibald Stobo and his wife—were on their way to Scotland when the ship was driven by a storm to seek shelter in the harbor of Charleston, S.C. There he was invited to become the pastor of a Presbyterian congregation whose minister, John Cotton, had died recently. He accepted the invitation and spent his life as their pastor and in the promotion of Presbyterianism in that colony. Stobo was a graduate of the University of Edinburgh (1697). There were also a number of other Puritan congregations in the vicinity of Charleston. In one instance the members of one entire church with their pastor, Joseph Lord, removed from Charlestown, Mass., to Dorchester, S. C. It has been estimated

90 A HISTORY OF THE PRESBYTERIAN CHURCH.

that in 1700 there were in the Carolinas several thousands of distinctive Presbyterians, besides those who were Congregationalists.

XII.

The Presbytery of Philadelphia (1706).

There had been no effort at the end of the seventeenth century to constitute a presbytery and form of government for the Presbyterian churches that were scattered along the Atlantic slope from Connecticut to Florida. At this time there had been Presbyterian ministers in the midle colonies for about a quarter of a century, and who labored in the capacity of evangelists or traveling preachers and also as settled pastors. There were some ten or more Presbyterian-Puritan churches in New York and New Jersey; these were of New England origin, while churches of a more decided presbyterial type abounded further south in Pennsylvania, Delaware, Maryland, Virginia and South Carolina.

Among the people of New England the form of church government — presbyterial or congregational — was deemed non-essential, and under these circumstances those who favored the presbyterial form waved their preferences on that point and joined in with the majority, who were Congregationalists, while in the colonies west of Connecticut the Congregationalists, for similar reasons, merged in with the Presbyterians. It often happened that a Presbyterian minister became the pastor of a Congregational church, and as often was it the reverse. This custom has been kept up to the present time; the two denominations agreeing in the essential doctrines of the gospel thus manifested sympathy with one another. A marked good feeling at this period also prevailed between the Presbyterians and the Congregational or Independent Puritans of the British Isles, and naturally this Christian sentiment extended to their brethren in the New World.

The Presbytery Constituted.—The Presbyterians of the Middle colonies, though all from Great Britain, were of different nationalities, as well as their ministers. Scotland, England, Wales and Ireland had their representatives, while especially in New York a liberal and most excellent element was present in the Dutch population. Such were the conditions under which the mother presbytery of the Presbyterian Church in the United States was constituted. "It was not organized by a higher body. It did not seek authority from the General Assembly of the Church of Scotland or from the Synod of Ulster. It organized itself by a voluntary association of ministers. It seems to have taken the Presbytery of Dublin as a model. It was a broad, generous, tolerant spirit which effected this union." The Presbytery of Dublin, whose members were chiefly English Presbyterians, maintained its independence of the Synod of Ulster, although some of the ministers were members of both bodies. "The Presbyterians of the north of Ireland were from Scotland, as those of the south were from England. The northern Presbyterians were zealous for the Scotch presbytery, but the southern were suspicious of its claims for jurisdiction." (*Am. Pres., p. 133.*)

There were present seven ministers; they met at Freehold, New Jersey, in 1706. This appears from the minutes to have been the second meeting, the record of the first one having been lost with the first page of the minutes, and it is presumed that the presbytery was really formed in 1705. Four of the ministers present were settled pastors, and three were missionaries or itinerants. Their respective charges were far separated, and great must have been the difficulties of traveling on account of the badness of the roads; the Indians were even yet on the borders of the settlements. Francis Makemie was pastor at Snow Hill, Maryland—whom tradition says was the moderator. John Wilson at New Castle, and Samuel Davis at Lewes, Delaware, and Jedediah Andrews at Philadelphia. The others, John Hampton, an Irishman; Nathaniel Taylor, probably an Englishman, and George Macnish, a Scotchman. At this time Archibald Stobo, a Scotchman, was pastor of a Presbyterian Church at Charleston, South Carolina. Four years after the formation of the presbytery (1710) Macnish became the pastor of a Presbyterian church at Jamaica, Long Island, which put itself under the care of the presbytery of Philadelphia—the name assumed by that body. Macnish soon became the stalwart leader of the Puritans and Presbyterians in the Province of New York, and by his Scotch pluck and perseverance triumphed over those who wished to trample upon the rights of the dissenters.

Francis Makemie wrote in respect to the presbytery: "Our design is to meet yearly, and oftener if necessary, to consult the most proper means for advancing religion and propagating Christianity in our various stations." "The American Presbyterian Church began historically at the bottom, and only by degrees did it rise into the magnificent system which we now behold. It was not a reconstruction of an old papal system into a new Presbyterian system, as in Scotland. It was a free and natural growth in accordance with the preferences of the congregations themselves. American Presbyterianism was born and nurtured and reached its maturity in freedom. It developed naturally in acordance with the circumstances of the country. * * * It was the external struggle against injustice and tyranny, and the internal struggle with narrowness, intolerance and bigotry, that made Presbyterianism in America the champion of civil and religious liberty." (*Amer. Pres., pp. 131, 289.*)

The First Missionary Society.—An earnest and effective effort was made on the part of the Presbyterians and Congregationalists in London and the vicinity to promote the interests of the Protestant churches at home and abroad—meaning the American colonies. They formed an organization in 1691, July 1, entitled "Heads of Department," in order to facilitate their work; they also established a fund by liberal contributions for two purposes: one to aid feeble congregations, the other to assist in training ministers to supply such churches. This is the first effort on record of the formation of a gospel missionary association and educational society. The movement "was designed to rally the Presbyterian and Independent churches of Great Britain and her colonies against prelacy and popery." The latter two were the inveterate and irrepressible antagonists of the doctrines and preaching of the ministers of the former.

Society for Propagating the Gospel in Foreign Parts.—The establishment of the association, "Heads of Department," no doubt suggested the formation of the "Society for the Propagation of the Gospel in Foreign Parts," and which was formed and chartered in London ten years later, in 1701. The latter was instituted in accordance with the desire and plan of Dr. Thomas Bray, who after the Church of England was by law established in Maryland in 1692, was appointed by King William "Ecclesiastical Commissioner" for the American colonies. He devoted himself with untiring energy to make the Church of England supersede all others in America. This new society had the sanction of the archbishops, bishops and members of the nobility and leading clergy of England, many of whom became *corporate* members. Dr. Bray urged that the society should send no less than forty

Protestant missionaries (churchmen) to the American colonies. To attain the supremacy in the latter, the society had the advantage of abundant funds, while its hopes of success were cherished by the persecuting principles involved in the rule of the English bishops. The former liberal spirit of the government of Maryland, now vanished. Meanwhile the respective governors became the tools of the illiberal hierarchy in England. Against such odds in addition to the opposition of the civil and military authorities, the Presbyterians as well as other dissenters had to contend, but in the end they triumphed. The exceptionally bad character of many of the clergymen sent out by the Bishop of London, especially to Virginia and Maryland, neutralized nearly all the efforts of Dr. Bray by means of that society to propagate Episcopacy. In truth, these men were recommended to the good Bishop of London by the civil authorities. John Talbot, an English churchman and chaplain in the navy, and who traveled in the colonies for two years in the interests of the society, in speaking of the situation, wrote: "We want a great many good ministers (Church of England) here in America, but we had better have none at all than such scandalous beasts as some make themselves—not only the worst of ministers, but of men." (*See p. 169.*) Then he assigns as a reason that: "Those we have to deal with are a sharp and inquisitive people; they are not satisfied with one doctor's opinion, but (we) must have something that is authentic, if we hope to prevail with them." (*Gillet, I., p. 22.*)

Difficulties and Progress.—The formation of the presbytery appears to have given an impulse to the cause, especialy in the middle colonies. Numerous difficulties had, however, to be overcome, the principal being the want of ministers and the means to support them, the church members were but ill-supplied with this world's goods, though they were benevolent to the best of their ability. In contrast with this was "the Society for the Propagation of the Gospel in Foreign Parts." It was sending so many Church of England missionaries that within a few years all the Episcopal clergy in the colonies north of Virginia were sent out by that society. They were supplied with abundant funds; were encouraged by the home government and the influence of the chaplains and the English officers of the army and the navy who were on duty in the colonies. It was made a special point to resist New England influence, giving as a reason why the society should send missionaries lest "Presbyterian ministers from New England would swarm into these countries (Middle colonies) and prevent the increase of the church." Thus wrote a beneficiary of the society.

There was at this time remarkable harmony and charity among the ministers and the Presbyterian-Puritan Church members in respect to evangelical doctrines. They were Calvinists and received the Westminster Confession as the embodiment of gospel truth. There were, no doubt, tacit differences of opinion in respect to the form of church government, but that non-essential dogma was relegated to the background. Each Presbyterian minister and missionary was absorbed in preaching the gospel and in performing his pastoral duties, new churches were increasing faster than they could be supplied with preachers and pastors. In order to obtain the latter an extensive correspondence was kept up with the Presbyterians of England, Scotland and Ireland, and also with the prominent ministers of New England, who sympathized deeply with the churches in the Middle colonies.

Notwithstanding these many difficulties there prevailed a quiet and continuous progress in the influence of the gospel. The churches increased in number, but were separated more or less by distance. This condition made it somewhat difficult for all the ministers to attend the regular meetings of the presbytery, and at the end of about ten years from its formation it was deemed wise to divide it into three, that of Philadelphia, the original, New Castle and Snow Hill—afterward absorbed in that of New Castle. Some time afterward, through the influence of Macnish, then pastor at Jamaica, and the recommendation of presbytery, the Presbytery of Long Island was constituted—afterward named New York (1738). It may be remarked in this connection that all the ministers that served these churches were thoroughly educated men; they were graduates of either Scotch or English universities, and had availed themselves of the best theological training of the times.

The Introduction of the Eldership.—The successive meetings of presbytery led to the recognition of the lack of representation in it of the church members. In order that their rights might be represented the custom of sending an elder or lay commissioner with the pastor was introduced. At first the meeting of presbytery was composed of ministers alone, and they consulted in relation to the best interests of the cause of Christ. In 1710 for the first time we find recorded in the minutes that an elder sat in the presbytery as the representative of his church in the absence of the pastor. We have already noticed that the rights and interests of the church members were recognized by the presbyteries in England. Experience taught lessons, and in 1714, as it had hitherto been only advisory in its disciplinary action, the presbytery took measures to have the records of the church sessions presented to it for revision. This was not an absolute demand, but was put in the form of a request, and the design was to preserve order and keep in constant touch with the churches. Numbers complied with the request, but others declined. The lack of compliance with this judicious request was owing, very probably, to the Congregational proclivities of a portion of the church members, who were in favor of the latter form of church government. With them the oversight proposed by the presbytery may have been looked upon as infringing the system of each individual church being independent of every other one. Those churches which adopted the eldership designed thereby to utilize their most competent men in the government of individual churches as well as to be their representatives in the judicial uses of the church. Presbytery previous to this time had not exercised discipline to much extent, if at all, beyond being advisory. They could pass an indirect censure only on a delinquent by striking his name from the roll of members. Time and experience afforded the necessity of its having more extensive authority in the line of discipline over the churches, and yet in compliance with the American idea that it should be with the consent of the governed.

XIII.

PERSECUTIONS AND TRIALS.

It is unfortunate that the history of the many persecutions and trials of the founders of the Presbyterian Church in the Middle colonies, especially in New York and Virginia, is so little known to the Presbyterian general reader. We can go only partially into detail in respect to these outrages, yet we will give an instance or two that may serve as specimens of the spirit that inspired the bishops of the Church of England wherever it acquired power by being established in any of the colonies. In the motherland the *Romanizing* bishops at that time were the powers behind the throne in ecclesiastical affairs, and in the colonies where that church was established they indirectly stimulated the civil authorities to acts of tyranny toward those who were dissenters—a contemptuous term applied about this time to those who *dissented* from the assumptions of the Church of England.

A Church and Parsonage Seized.—In the town of Jamaica, Long Island, years before the Church of England was established in the colony, the inhabitants—Presbyterians—Puritans for the most part—voluntarily subscribed the funds and built a church and a parsonage. In 1702 there were in the village of Jamaica more than one hundred and fifty families, mostly from New England. These people were characterized by a writer of the time as being "exemplary for all Christian knowledge and goodness." They had a pious and excellent minister,

Mr. John Hubbard, who, with his congregation, was dispossessed of their church building (1705). This outrage was committed by order of the Governor of the colony, the "infamous Lord Cornbury," who, according to George Bancroft, "joined the worst form of arrogance to intellectual imbecility." Lord Cornbury, in the following manner, placed in charge of this church building John Bartow, a Church of England missionary. On a certain Sabbath Mr. Hubbard preached in the forenoon, but before he arrived to conduct the usual services of the afternoon Bartow slipped into the church, and with a few to respond, began reading the litany. Presently Mr. Hubbard came; he did not interfere, but retired and announced to his congregation that he would preach under a tree in the neighboring orchard, which he did. Meanwhile Barton, having finished his reading, locked the door of the church and gave the key to the sheriff. The owners of the church applied for the key, but the sheriff refused to give it up. For this high-handed measure of demanding the key, and asserting their rights to their own property, Mr. Hubbard and the chief men of his congregation were summoned before Governor Cornbury in New York, who upbraided them, and forbade Hubbard preaching in the church.

It happened that during this year an epidemic of sickness prevailed in the colony, and Cornbury asked Mr. Hubbard, in an apparently friendly manner, for the use of the parsonage as a hospital, as it was accidentally unoccupied. When the sickness disappeared, Cornbury refused to give back the parsonage, but issued a warrant without legal authority to the sheriff to dispossess Mr. Hubbard, and to give it to the Church of England minister whom the Governor had put in charge; and the latter, strange to say, under the circumstances, forthwith occupied the parsonage. In addition, the land belonging to the parsonage was also seized and divided into lots and sold for the benefit of the established church. The case of Makemie and that of the seizure of the Presbyterian church at Jamaica, L. I., are two of the outrages committed by Cornbury—they speak for themselves. He has been recently eulogized in a church history on the ground that "he was noted for his ardent churchmanship." Some eight years afterward (1710) Rev. George Macnish became a Presbyterian pastor in Jamaica. Lord Cornbury had disappeared, and another Governor—Robert Hunter—was in his stead. Macnish entered at once upon a suit in the civil court to have the property restored to the rightful owners, and by his indefatigable exertions and Scotch pluck, he succeeded, in 1727, but only after a contest lasting a number of years. The righteousness of this decision was recognized by all except the Episcopal clergy, with the renegade Vesey—of whom more presently—at their head; the latter appealed to the Bishop of London.

Bribery and Trickery.—A similar instance of such church charity occurred in New York itself. Governor Fletcher gave permission to build a church edifice by voluntary contributions among the people at large. The funds were forthcoming, and the building was finished. It was the first of the edifices belonging to the present *Trinity* in New York City, thus afterward named. At that time there were scarcely any churchmen or their families in the town, except the officers belonging to the army or the civil authorities, and the officers of the navy when occasionally in the harbor. It was understood and conceded that the new church building virtually belonged to the Presbyterian-Puritans, since nearly all the funds were contributed by them. In accordance with this view the Governor made no objection to the wardens or vestrymen inviting a Presbyterian minister to become the pastor.

They called the Rev. William Vesey of Hempstead, Long Island, to become that pastor (1695). Vesey was a native of Braintree, Massachusetts, a graduate of Harvard, and had been trained under the supervision of Increase Mather, with whom he was a favorite. Through the influence of the latter, Vesey was sent to "strengthen the Puritans in New York." He became, therefore, the first pastor of this new church, thus erected almost entirely by the contributions of those who had no sympathy with the Church of England in its mode of government and forms of worship. There was at this time only one clergyman of the established church in New York—the chaplain in the fort. What we have seen Cornbury secure by tyranny and violence, we shall see Fletcher attain by virtual bribery and trickery. Let an address to the then Bishop of London, that was sent a few years afterward (1714) by Church of England men living then in the Province of New York, tell the story. It says: "He [Increase Mather] spared no pains and care to spread the warmest of his emissaries [Presbyterian-Puritan ministers] through this province, but Governor Fletcher, who saw into this design, took off Mr. Vesey by an invitation to this living *and a promise to advance his stipend considerably*, and to recommend him for holy orders to your Lordship's predecessor, all of which was performed accordingly, and Mr. Vesey returned from England in priest's orders."— (*Am. Presbyterian, p. 147; Doc. Hist. N. Y. III., p. 438.*) Vesey was ordained by the Bishop of London Aug. 2, 1697. On his return he was, by an arbitrary order of the Governor, installed *as rector of Trinity Church*. This church building was owned, to all intents and purposes, by the Presbyterian congregation, who as such had called Vesey to become their pastor, but now a system of worship was instituted within it that the congregation did not recognize as Scriptural. The Presbyterians were helpless;

this was the only church in the town where religious services were held in the English language. "Vesey was maintained by a tax levied on all the inhabitants of the city."

Soon after his usurpation Vesey became a most virulent and unrelenting foe to his former associates and ecclesiastical friends. Under his leadership *Trinity Church* from this time forward took the front rank in its persecution of the dissenters, in every available form of petty annoyances too numerous to mention in this narrative. It has been urged as an apology that Vesey may have been influenced by the views of the moderate Presbyterians of England, who at that time, for the sake of peace, perhaps, preferred the Episcopal to the Congregational mode of church government, and in accordance with that view he wished to combine in a single church organization the many Presbyterians with the comparatively few Episcopalians. Had this been his motive, he would have been conciliatory in his policy, but instead he was extremely arrogant and hostile toward the Presbyterians and the other dissenters, his former friends and patronizers.

Rev. James Anderson, the first pastor of the First Presbyterian Church in New York City, in a letter dated Dec. 3, 1717, says in relation to Vesey: "One (minister) was called from New England, who, after he had preached some time here, having a prospect and a promise of more money than what he had among dissenters, went to Old England, took orders from the Bishop of London, and came back here as minister of the established Church of England. Here he yet is, has done, and still is doing what he can to ruin the dissenting interest."—(*Am. Pres., pp., LXXVII-VIII. App.*)

Another Illustration.—Afterward the Presbyterians erected, about 1719, a church in Wall Street, then as now known as the *First Presbyterian Church*. The vestry of *Trinity* induced the civil authorities to refuse them a charter or deed for the lot on which the church building was to stand. In consequence of this intolerant opposition, arrangements were made by which the charter and deed were vested in the General Assembly of the Church of Scotland, and the latter, when the persecuting power of the established church was annihilated by the War of Independence, transferred the charter and the deed to their legitimate owner—the First Presbyterian Church of New York City.

A Law Misapplied.—In accordance with the views of the times, the Assembly of the Colony of New York in 1693 passed an act that was similar in character to previous ones for the purpose of supporting the gospel. "There can be no doubt that it was the intention of the Assembly to provide for the maintenance of the dissenting clergy. Such had been the manifest tendency of the previous legislation on the subject. All the members of the Assembly, but one, were dissenters, while the Church of England was hardly known in the Province." * * * "In fact it [the law] was arbitrarily and illegally wrested from its true bearing, and made to answer the purpose of the English Church party, which was a very small minority of the people who were affected by the operation of the law."—(*Dr. G. H. Moore, Hist. Mag., 1867, p. 328.*) Says an authority: "There was no face of the Church of England here till about 1693." Some years later another writer stated that the number of the Church of England members in the population of the province was *one in seven*. The dissenters had at their own expense erected, as far as we know, every church edifice in the province.

The obvious intention of the act of 1693 was wrested by Governor Fletcher, whom George Bancroft characterizes as "a covetous and passionate man," to apply *only* to the clergy of the Church of England. To enforce this false interpretation against the Presbyterian-Puritan congregations of the province, the Governor often seized their church buildings and placed in them Episcopal clergy, under the plea that the latter belonged to the established church. "It was under this act [1693], and this interpretation of it, that Trinity Church was established in 1697." (*Hist. of Episcopal Church, p. 166.*) The struggle and turmoil lasted for many years, even till the Revolution. We have given these historic facts as examples of the persecuting spirit which prevailed in that church in the colony of New York, while the case in that of Virginia was even more outrageous.

The hostility of the Church of England, especially toward the Presbyterians, as manifested by the civil authorities, continued long after their intrusion into the Trinity church building. This animosity does not appear openly against the Dutch Christians, but only toward the English-speaking people who were dissenters. The Presbyterians, after enduring for some years these petty tyrannies, retired from *Trinity* and met together and worshiped in private houses, until finally they erected a place of worship for themselves in Wall Street, as already noted. This inveterate hostility extended so far that traveling Presbyterian ministers, who happened to pass through the Province of New York, were liable to be arrested by the civil authorities if they dared to preach without a license. The triumphant vindication of Makemie, in spite of the brutal opposition of Governor Cornbury, had not been forgotten; for obvious reasons the clergy of the established church feared the Presbyterian ministers, because of their learning and their love for and promotion of genuine religious liberty.

The ecclesiastics of the home church desired greatly to appoint bishops on American soil, but that project was frustrated by the united efforts of the Congregationalists and Presbyterians. This unrelenting persecution retarded the progress of the Presbyterians in those colonies wherein the Church of England was established. The fine scholarship and Christian zeal of their ministers, with the co-operation of intelligent and pious church members, at the end of many years of labor and toil triumphed grandly.

XIV.

THE FORMATION OF THE SYNOD.

The presbyteries had now grown to four from one, and had extended their jurisdiction over the churches scattered along the Atlantic coast from Eastern Long Island to Virginia. It was thought expedient to constitute a synod, in order to unite all these churches and presbyteries in closer bonds of fellowship, and thus promote the cause of Christ under the form of American Presbyterianism. The synod thus constituted was named Philadelphia, and was composed of four presbyteries—Philadelphia, New Castle, Snowhill, and Long Island, afterward New York.

Missionary Funds.—Almost the first act of the newly created synod was to take measures to establish a "fund for pious uses" (1717). This was in answer to the cry for ministers that was coming up from congregations recently founded. The creation of this fund was the original of all the schemes to supply the means for carrying on the home missionary enterprises in the American Presbyterian Church that have grown to such large proportions in our time, and are pressing on to still greater triumphs. This fund was afterward substantially increased by contributions of the benevolent in the Presbyterian Churches in Scotland and in England. Collections were made in those churches, and the amount secured was, in the aggregate, £3,652 10s. It was thought expedient to invest a portion of this amount in merchandise or goods, which were brought to the colonies and sold at a good profit. In the same line the kindly disposed merchants made donations in goods. It is stated that "The merchants were at great pains and did great service in the matter, and were so generous as to transmit the goods free of freight" (1719).

Fraternal Intercourse.—The traditions of the Presbyterian Church are, and always have been, in favor of much and genuine fraternal intercourse among its members. One of the means which it has used in accomplishing this grand result is in having frequent meetings of its church judicatures; more than usual in number, when compared with those of other denominations. The meeting together so often has had, among other desirable effects, that of eliciting sympathy between the members of the different churches in the various sections of the country, and thus promoting a Christianized sentiment of brotherly love. Accordingly, as the number of the churches increased and were scattered in the land, new presbyteries were organized, and as the members desired still more intercourse with one another, since they met only with brethren of their respective presbyteries, they formed a synod which should bear a similar relationship to the presbyteries as that of the latter to the churches. The synod was also constituted in the same ratio as the presbytery—each minister was accompanied by an elder from the church or churches of which he was pastor; in this manner were the rights of the members of the church recognized and respected. All the ministers belonging to the synod were required to meet in session once in each year. This mode of government prevailed for about seventy years; that is, from 1717 to 1788, when the General Assembly was organized—the latter being a representative body, but drawing its delegates not from the synods but directly from the presbyteries, they being nearer the people or church members.

REV. JOHN MCMILLAN, D. D.
(133, 233, 258, 282, 324.)

THE FORMATION OF THE SYNOD.

For a number of years after the formation of the first synod, the increase of the churches was great, and they were much extended along the Atlantic slope, south of Connecticut, while the number of the presbyteries also increased in proportion. It was found that, owing to the distances and difficulties of travel, a great many ministers and elders were unable to attend regularly all the meetings of the synod. To obviate this inconvenience it was decided (1724) to make the synod a sort of representative body—that was done by the presbyteries sending half their number of members in alternate years. It was also arranged that every third year there should be a full attendance of all the members.

The Test and Schism Acts.—After the formation of the synod the progress of the church was much more rapid; numbers of Presbyterians migrated to the colony of New Jersey from New England and New York, and with them came many able and learned men from the British Isles. Scotch-Irish Presbyterians came in great numbers from the north of Ireland; it is estimated in all more than twenty thousand in the course of a few years. By what was called the *"Test Act,"* Presbyterians in Ireland were excluded "from all public offices, honors and employments." The animating spirit of these intolerant laws may be inferred from the fact that "The bishops introduced clauses into their leases forbidding the erection of meeting-houses [for Dissenters] on any part of their estates, and induced many landlords to follow their example." Another law, evidently the outgrowth of the same influence, was passed in 1714, which was called the "Schism Act," its design being to blot out the Presbyterian Church in Ireland. It was estimated that four-fifths of the Protestant inhabitants of the province of Ulster at that time were Presbyterians. This did not prevent outrages of a revolting character being inflicted upon them, when their prominent men were "summoned before the courts on the charge of living in fornication with their own wives, because they had not been married with a ring by an Episcopal rector." (*Church Hist. Series, Vol. VI., p. 54.*)

Froude, in his *History of Ireland* (*pp. 11, 131, 143*) says of the Presbyterians: "Vexed with suits in the ecclesiastical courts, forbidden to educate their children in their own faith, treated as dangerous in a state which but for them would have had no existence, the most earnest of them at length abandoned the unthankful service. If they intended to live as freemen, speaking no lies, and professing openly the creed of the Reformation, they must seek a country where the long arm of prelacy was still too short to reach them. But for Anglican bishops there would have been no Puritan exiles."

Under these circumstances that isle lost thousands upon thousands of its more intelligent citizens, with their families and their pastors. Here commenced a great emigration of Protestants, especially from the northern portion of that island, to America, which continued for forty years, and by which the Presbyterian Church, especially in the Middle colonies, was greatly enlarged and strengthened.

The leading Irish Presbyterians, in an address to the new Lord Lieutenant, Duke of Shrewsbury (1713), announced that they had thoughts of transplanting themselves into America, saying "that we may there in the wilderness enjoy, by the blessing of God, that ease and quiet of our consciences, persons and families which is denied us in our native country." (*Am. Pres., p. 185.*)

William Tennent.—Numbers of these prominent but virtually exiled ministers came to New England, but it appears that the majority of them sought their homes in New Jersey and Pennsylvania. The grandest accession to Presbyterianism from the Episcopal Church was when William Tennent in 1716 came from that church in Ireland and connected himself with the synod of Philadelphia. He was a native of Ireland, of English-Irish descent, and a graduate of the University of Edinburgh (1695). He gave his reasons in full to the synod why he made the change. Tennent settled first in Westchester County, New York, preaching for eight years "with wondrous zeal in the towns of the county."

The First Log College.—At this period, with but few exceptions of graduates of Yale and Harvard, the ministers of the Presbyterian Church were foreigners. This fact suggested to Tennent the importance of the church training for its service some of the native youth. About 1727 Tennent removed from Bedford, New York, to Neshaminy, in the vicinity of Philadelphia, and there he commenced to teach young men the classics and theology in a cabin builded of logs cut from the primitive forest—hence the name *Log College,* and which has become famous as the forerunner of a number of Presbyterian colleges in the Union. "Tennent had the rare gift of attracting to himself youth of worth and genius, imbuing them with his healthful spirit, and sending them forth sound in the faith, blameless in life, burning with zeal, and unsurpassed as instructive, impressive, and successful preachers." (*Webster, p. 367.*)

The enterprise, having no ecclesiastical connection, was entirely private in its character, but its design was to supply the wants of the colonists in respect to a *biblically* trained ministery. This was the first Presbyterian theological school in America. These young men found in Mr. Tennent a teacher thoroughly instructed in the theological and classical studies of the times, and, in addition, one who was imbued with an ardent piety that found vent in preaching a gospel drawn directly from the truths of the word of God itself. This mode of preaching was followed by his pupils, and was adapted to the spiritual wants of those who heard them. The latter were well-to-do, honest and industrious, almost every head of a family owning his farm or plot of ground on which stood his home. These young ministers were taught to be practical; they could preach from a well-arranged pulpit, in a private dwelling, in a school-house, or under the shade of the trees. This school furnished the best education outside of Yale and Harvard, in New England, and of William and Mary in Virginia. Says one in speaking of Mr. Tennent's students: "They were didactic, exhortory, plain, impassioned, often vehement; they used the strong doctrines of the Scriptures as facts for illustration or weapons to subdue the heart; they were fearless of man in the cause of God."

Guarding the Faith.—During the first quarter of the eighteenth century the Presbyterian Church in the British Isles was greatly agitated in respect to diversities of opinion among its younger ministers on certain theological questions. This could be affirmed especially of the churches of Scotland and Ireland; notably in the former was the case of Dr. John Simson, professor of Divinity in the University of Glasgow, who had been, also, the theological instructor of numbers of the Irish Presbyterian ministry. Professor Simson was brought to trial and charged with teaching Socinianism and Arminianism. He disclaimed the charge, and stated that "he was endeavoring to meet the semi-Arianism of the time by better statements of the orthodox doctrines." His explanation appears to have had influence in his trial, for the General Assembly sustained him, and so did the liberal party in the church, both in England and Ireland. There is no doubt, however, that numbers of the students under his care were in sympathy with the doctrinal views which Professor Simson endeavored to refute.

Meanwhile, rumors of these deviations from the Confession of Faith had reached the Presbyterian ministers in the Middle colonies, and they, certainly, had reasons for their anxiety on the subject. In consequence the church was much agitated during a portion of the existence of the first synod (1717-1729). The occasion of this excitement did not originate within the synod itself, but abroad, where a laxity in respect to evangelical doctrines had prevailed to a large extent among the ministers of the Presbyterian Churches in Scotland and Ireland. Some of these held "Arminian and Pelagian errors," and it was known that a number of ministers holding these views had already migrated to the colonies, and others were about to follow; the latter in all probability would wish to unite in this country with the same church. It therefore became a question as to the most efficient mode of guarding against the intrusion into the churches of ministers holding these objectionable views. After the subject had been under discussion in various forms for some years—because at first the members were far from being unanimous as to the best means of warding off the impending evil—the synod finally united upon a plan, which was as follows: "We do, therefore, agree that all the ministers of this synod, or that shall hereafter be admitted into this synod, shall declare their agreement in, and approbation of, the Confession of Faith, with the Larger and Shorter Catechisms of the Assembly of Divines at Westminster, as being in all the essential and necessary articles good forms of sound words and systems of Christian doctrine, and do also adopt the said Confession and Catechisms as the Confession of our Faith." (*Gillett, vol. i., p. 55.*) This was the "ADOPTING ACT" of 1729. The presbyteries were also enjoined to require their licentiates to subscribe the same Confession, etc.

The Effects of the Adopting Act.—This Adopting Act was far-reaching and conciliatory in its influence. It was a compromise between the parties which demanded a sort of cast-iron subscription to every word or form of expression in the Confession of Faith instead of the liberal view as expressed in the phrase, *"the essential and necessary articles."* The latter has been characterized as the *pivot* of the history of the Presbyterian Church in the United States.

"By the Adopting Act American Presbyterianism steered safely through the troubled waters that split the Irish and English Presbyterians into two irreconcilable parties. * * * It was designed to adapt the best Presbyterian models to American soil, and not strive to force Scotch, Irish, Welsh, or English types of Presbyterianism upon the country." (*Am. Pres., p. 221.*)

"By these cautious enactments"—*The Adopting Act, etc.*—"American Presbyterianism was saved from the danger of lapsing into Congregationalism, and at the same time secured a flexibility of development very necessary in a new country, without sacrificing its historic connection with the Presbyterianism of Britain." (*Presbyterian Churches—Their Power in Modern Christendom. By Dr. J. N. Ogilvie, p. 104. Edition of 1896.*)

Liberal and Strict Subscription.—It was very unfortunate for the peace and the spiritual advancement of the church that the Adopting Act was not cordially acquiesced in at once by all parties. Within a few years after the Act (1729) became a rule in the church, certain members of the Presbytery of New Castle virtually disregarded the liberal principles of that act in its requiring the Westminster Confession to be received by ministers and candidates for the ministry, "as being in all the essential and necessary articles good forms of sound works and systems of Christian doctrine." Instead of this judicious view of the subject, the Presbyteries of New Castle and Donegal—an offshoot of the latter—introduced an irritating rule or order, by requiring of their members and candidates in respect to the Confession, "a strict interpretation and verbal subscription." That is, every phrase or expression in the Confession must be *adopted* word for word. This requisition virtually demanded for a human and fallible compilation of religious doctrine the same allegiance that ought to be given to the inspired word of God.

The prime mover and persistent advocate of this measure was Rev. John Thomson, a Scotchman, who is characterized as "a narrow and opinionated man, who became the father of discord and mischief in the American Presbyterian Church." Through his influence his presbytery acted in "defiance of Presbyterian law and practice." Against this "strict subscription" Jonathan Dickinson protested that "it might shut the door of the church communion against many serious and excellent servants of Christ who conscientiously scruple it, yet it is never like to detect hypocrites nor keep concealed heretics out of the church." Such, indeed, had recently been the experience of the synod of Philadelphia. The latter had received Rev. Samuel Hemphill, who came with credentials from a presbytery in Ireland, and who had in the presence of the synod subscribed to the Westminster Confession, and that without scruple. Yet he was found to be unsound in his belief and unprincipled in action, a preacher of other men's sermons—in fine, a heretic and a hypocrite. For a time he completely deceived the synod; at length he was brought to trial and dismissed the ministry.

The agitation in respect to "strict subscription"—though the principles of the Adopting Act finally prevailed—disturbed the harmony of the church for many years and retarded very much its spiritual progress. This is not the only instance in the history of the Presbyterian Church wherein a few "opinionated" men, who were *confident they were right,* when their peers thought differently, have injured the cause of religion.

"Strict subscription" became, also, a question among the Presbyterian ministers and elders in South Carolina. One portion, while strongly in favor of the right of private judgment, was equally as strenuous in not imposing their own interpretations upon their brethren; to do which, they deemed a wrong. The other portion were deeply and justly alarmed at the rumors concerning the progress that certain errors were making in the ranks of the Presbyterian ministers in the British Isles. No doubt many of these errorists would come to the colonies and the ministers of foreign birth, especially, were in favor of guarding the truth by requiring "strict subscription" to the Confession of Faith. The outcome of the agitation was a division; the ministers from New England separated and labored apart from those from Scotland and Ireland. In time the various apprehensions were removed and harmony prevailed once more.

Presbyterians in Maine.—About 1715 or '16 Rev. James MacGregorie migrated from Ireland, and with his flock settled at Londonderry, New Hampshire, while another Presbyterian company afterward formed a settlement on Casco Bay, Maine. These Presbyterians became so numerous that in 1729 the Presbytery of Londonderry was constituted. The Rev. Le Mercier, the pastor of the Huguenot Church in Boston, connected himself with this presbytery. In 1730 Samuel Rutherford arrived with his flock from Ireland, which also found homes in Maine. To these Presbyterian colonists, others were joined in the course of years. All these ministers appear to have been

THE FORMATION OF THE SYNOD.

true adherents of the Westminster Confession and Catechisms.

The Transfer of the Log College.—The young ministers from the Log College continued to be zealous in their missionary labors, and were rewarded by a remarkable and extensive revival, whose influence was felt for a number of years. The institution was thus of immense service to the cause of Christ in training a large number of godly and efficient ministers, though it did not fill all the requirements that were involved in a college fully adapted to the needs of the American Presbyterian Church.

Mr. William Tennent, Sr., died in 1746, and left no one competent to take his place. This was made the occasion of transforming the primitive Log College into a more extensive and imposing institution of learning. Through the efforts of Rev. Jonathan Dickinson, a charter (1747) was obtained for a college from Governor Hamilton of New Jersey. Trustees were elected, and Dickinson was chosen President. The Log College in spirit was transferred from Neshaminy to the President's house in Elizabethtown. It was a great loss to the college that Dickinson died in the first year of his presidency. "No better man could have been found to lay the foundation of Presbyterian higher education in America. He was head and shoulders above his brethren in the ministry in intellectual and moral endowments—the recognized leader in all the crises of the church." (*Am. Pres., p. 306.*) He was a native of Massachusetts and a graduate of Yale (1706) College. Three years later he became pastor at Elizabethtown, New Jersey, and by his commanding talents and conservative spirit he became the great representative of American Presbyterianism of the Colonial period, the symbol of all that was noble and generous in the Presbyterian Church." In the midst of the doctrinal discussions that arose within the church he wrote numerous pamphlets and published sermons. His *"Five Points of Calvinism"* had great influence at the time. The contents of the essay were: Eternal Election, Original Sin, Grace in Conversion, Justification by Faith, Saints' Perseverance.

The Rev. Aaron Burr was chosen to succeed Dickinson, and the following year the college, under a new charter from Governor Belcher—an ardent friend of the institution—was removed to Newark. This college was designed to be pre-eminently a center of education for the Middle colonies. The design was to establish a college where "Those of every religious denomination may have free and equal liberty and advantage of education, any different sentiments in religion notwithstanding." The treatment which the sainted David Brainerd received from the faculty of Yale, and, in addition, the latter's unconcealed hostility to the revival of religion under Jonathan Edwards and his compeers, justly alienated the once good will of the revivalists among the ministers of the New Side.

Princeton College.—The infant college now appealed for aid to the Presbyterians of Scotland, England and Ireland. For this purpose the Synod of New York sent as their agents Rev. Samuel Davies and Gilbert Tennent. They secured more than four thousand pounds. Thus "the Presbyterians of Great Britain showed their sympathy with the broad and tolerant Presbyterians of the synod of New York, rather than the narrow and intolerant Presbyterians of the synod of Philadelphia. * * * The mother of American Presbyterian colleges was planted on the basis of the pledges of Samuel Davies and Gilbert Tennent as to the terms of subscription in accordance with the original Adopting Act (1729). The college was therefore pledged and consecrated to a broad, generous and liberal Presbyterianism." (*Am. Pres., p. 309.*)

The institution, under the name of the College of New Jersey, was removed to Princeton in 1755. The citizens of the town, having "given 200 acres of woodland and ten acres of cleared land." A college building—named Nassau Hall—the gift of other benefactors—was erected, and which for some years was the largest college structure in the United States. The first class, numbering six, was graduated in 1755. Princeton claims that *twenty-five* colleges in the Union indirectly owe their existence to the exertions of her graduates.

The Educational Fund.—About this time a fund of £357 4s. 6d. was given to aid young men in the College of New Jersey who were studying for the ministry. This fund became the nucleus of what has since grown to be the great system of scholarships now existing in Presbyterian colleges and theological seminaries. Associations of this kind and the contributions they give to the object clearly evidence the interest that Presbyterian Church members—male and female—have in an educated ministry for their church.

Princeton College never received aid from the State; it has always been supported by the contributions of Christian liberality.

The Leading Points of Influence.—We cannot in this concise history go into detail as to the names of the many ministers who came from Scotland, Ireland and England, nor locate the numerous churches and congregations which they served. We give the leading points of influence, in order that the reader may have a conception of the great religious movement in the middle colonies that was attended with such grand results. All these ministers from abroad were educated men and impressed their influence upon the communities wherein they labored.

It is to be noted, however, that the theologians of that day confined themselves almost exclusively to the study of the Bible in the original tongues, as well as in the English version. We recognize as correct their clear interpretation of that sacred book in all that pertains to the way of salvation. They received very little aid from the commentaries of men *specially* learned in the exposition of the sacred volume, which in our day has thrown on the subject so much light, and which has been derived from so many and diverse sources. They studied the book itself, collating passage with passage, thus making the inspired word its own interpreter on the great themes of Christian belief. Their scholarship, in consequence, was not broad and diverse, as that of the theologians of our day while the people to whom they preached were on a corresponding low plane of general intelligence:— thus the preachers and people were suited to one another. These theologians, as a rule, were well versed in sacred knowledge derived from the Bible itself, and in the Latin and Greek classics—but of science how little they knew! The sciences were then in their infancy—and the most advanced classes in the colleges were far inferior in scientific scholarship to the young men and women of to-day in our high schools and academies.

CHAPTER XV.

ORIGIN OF PRESBYTERIANISM IN VIRGINIA

In our narrative, though somewhat out of the order of time, we will now tell the story of the origin of Presbyterianism in Hanover County, Virginia. In a rural district in that county some fifty or sixty miles from Williamsburg, then the seat of government of the colony, originated a movement that resulted in establishing Presbyterianism independently of outside influence.

The inhabitants of this isolated neighborhood were of English ancestry, and no doubt had an idea of "Englishmen's rights." "They were of true English descent, and in connection with the established church. . . . None of the Scotch-Irish had emigrated to Hanover, and these people were descended from members of the English Church" (Foote's "Sketches of Virginia," pp. 120, 123). "Traces of the Scotch-Irish were found in Virginia in the latter part of the seventeenth century." Five counties are named in which these *traces* were found, but Hanover is not thus mentioned. "The first migration from Ulster (Ireland) to Pennsylvania was from 1717 to 1750." "The great migration of Scotch-Irish landed at New Castle and made their way northward or westward" ("The Scotch-Irish," vol. i., p. 119; vol. ii., p. 179).

The colonists in Hanover County were ministered to by the clergy of the established church; its incumbents, with few exceptions, were not of a high order of scholarship or of piety (*see pp. 168-169*). Four gentlemen, heads of families, of the more intelligent among the people became dissatisfied with what was preached by the incumbent of their parish church. This movement is supposed to have commenced about 1720, and though unknown to the outside world it continued for many years, a Mr. Samuel Morris becoming almost unconsciously the leader in the cause. These parishioners believed that their incumbent did not preach the Gospel according to the principles laid down in their Bibles, and they thought it more edifying for them not to attend the parish church on the Sabbath, but remain at home and read the Scriptures and other religious books with their families. In this matter they were conscientious; but it is remarkable that they did not act in concert, though each individual had come to the same conclusion as to his duty under the circumstances. They only learned the views of one another when they were arraigned before the civil magistrate and fined for not attending the parish church. After they had learned the opinions of one another, they held a conference and agreed, instead of going to the parish church, to meet alternately at each other's houses, and with their families spend the usual time of the church service in reading the Scriptures and in prayer. One of the party had Martin Luther's commentary on the epistle to the Galatians; this they read also. Another gentleman had met with a few leaves of "Boston's Fourfold State," and being struck by the sentiments therein expressed, sent to England for the book. This was also read. To these books was added a copy of George Whitefield's sermons. They had heard of his preaching in Williamsburg.

Morris' Reading-House.—The work went on for years, and the meetings soon became crowded, because of the interest taken by the people in the subject, since they found the doctrines in the books that were read to be in accordance with the Scriptures, the spirit of the Gospel and the experience of Christians. The multitudes, and often from quite a distance, attending their meetings became so great that no private house could contain them, and necessity demanded the building of a "meeting-house." This was known as Morris' Reading-House; the same name was applied to the others afterward erected. These people had virtually separated from the establishment. It was in every sense a spontaneous movement, which had its origin in the plain inconsistency with Bible truths and with the spirit of the Gospel, of the lives and characters and the preaching of the clergy, who were the incumbents in the various parishes.

They did not assume a name; they organized no church; no dissenting minister had visited them; of such they appear to have had no special knowledge. They were isolated from the rest of the colony, and must have arrived at their opinions on religious truths from simply reading the word of God and books that explained that word.

Persecutions and Annoyances.—Meantime they were continually harassed by the colonial authorities, who as usual were instigated by the clergy. The latter were greatly scandalized that a rebuke to their way of preaching and manner of living should spring up spontaneously among their own parishioners, and they and illiberal laymen in the vestries determined to put down the movement by a series of persecutions and petty annoyances. But those poor Bible readers were loyal to their government and to their own consciences, and they promptly paid from week to week the fines imposed upon them for not attending the parish church and quietly went on with their reading and praying.

Their being called upon so often to explain to the magistrates of the county why they did not attend the parish church, and in consequence were fined, attracted the attention of the governor and council at Williamsburg. The latter had the supreme control of the relations between the dissenters and the established church. The prominent leaders in this innovation were therefore required to appear before the governor and Council and defend themselves in respect to the charges that were preferred against them by the clergy and the civil authorities of the county, and also, in accordance with the Toleration Act, to state by what name they were to be designated. In respect to the latter requirement, they were very much at a loss what to do. They knew of the Quakers, but had not sufficient sympathy with them to take their name; they had learned of Luther from his commentary, and they thought they might be Lutherans—of Presbyterians they had not even heard.

The Name Presbyterian.—Those who were summoned —as noted above—set out from their homes to meet on a certain day the governor and council and defend themselves as best they could. On the way one of the number lodged for the night at a farmhouse, and was detained there the following day because of a severe rain-storm. He took from a shelf a book that appeared to have been little used, as it was covered with dust. He commenced to read, and to his astonishment found therein his views of the Gospel better expressed than he could himself, and in addition there were the texts of Scripture on which these truths were based. He had never before seen or heard of that book, and he wished to purchase it, but the owner presented it to him. When the delegation met in Williamsburg, they conferred together over the book, and all agreed that it expressed their religious views. When they came before the lieutenant-governor, Sir William Gooch, he made inquiry as to their religious views, and also as to the name of their sect. Handing him the book, they made answer that it contained their religious views. The governor examined it, and being a Scotchman by descent, he at once recognized it as the Confession of Faith of the Presbyterian Church of Scotland, and he exclaimed "Why, you are Presbyterians!" They accepted the name. The governor appears to have been much impressed by the earnestness and candor of the men, and he "dismissed them with a gentle caution not to excite any disturbance in his majesty's colony, nor by irregularities disturb the good order of society in their parish."

Further Annoyances.—They were not, however, permitted to pursue their way unmolested, as some time afterward accusations of disorderly conduct were brought against Mr. Morris and some of his friends in Hanover County, inasmuch as they did not attend the parish church, though they regularly paid the fines imposed upon them. This fact by no means conciliated the clergy and the illiberal churchmen, who wished to inflict a severer punishment. The charges were so pressed by these parties that they induced the king's attorney to have the persons thus accused indicted by the grand jury. In consequence, the latter were forced at great expense of time and money to attend the civil court at Williamsburg, some forty or sixty miles distant. After much delay and inconvenience to the accused the charges were proved to be utterly false, and the men were acquitted by the jury. They were, notwithstanding this fact, most unjustly compelled by the court to pay the costs of the prosecution, as was the case in the trial of Rev. Francis Makemie in New York (*p. 86*).

In about a half-century later we find the Presbyterians of Hanover County looming in a remarkable manner as intelligent and stanch advocates for civil and religious liberty.

XVI.

The Log Colleges.

There is no characteristic of the Presbyterian Church more pronounced than its uniform and ardent zeal in behalf of an educated ministry. We therefore think it proper, though anticipating a few events, to devote one chapter to its earlier efforts in that direction—see, also, page 111 for an account of the first Log College. The above fact has always been recognized by the church members and their pastors, while the former, by the faithful labors of the latter, have been placed on so high a plane of Scriptural knowledge that they demand preachers who are competent to teach. Pious Presbyterian parents during successive generations have been familiar with the contents of the Bible itself, and the Westminster Confession and the Catechism and the proof-texts on which the doctrines contained therein are based. In these truths, with the aid of their pastors, they trained their children; meanwhile carefully observing and sanctifying the Sabbath. In this manner a knowledge of the essential doctrines of the Christian system had become interwoven with the religious consciousness of their children, who in turn taught their own, and thus the work went on. This mode of instructing the youth of Christian parents was a custom among the Puritans, whether Congregationalist or Presbyterian. Church members thus trained are quick to discern in a preacher his spirituality and his adherence to the sacred truths with which they themselves are familiar.

The Bible Studied as a Whole.—One effective stimulant to the acquisition of biblical knowledge is found in taking the Bible in all its parts, since this mode of instruction gives clearer views of the symmetry of the truths of the word of God than can possibly be obtained by studying the Scriptures in isolated portions for certain days in the year, as in prayer-books or litanies. The latter mode must have a cramping effect upon the progress of religious and biblical knowledge among the private members of the church.

The Two Academies.—The Presbytery of Hanover, amid its conflict in relation to the separation of Church and State in Virginia, recognized the necessity of founding schools to educate young men for the ministry. The College of William and Mary at Williamsburg was under the control of the established church. That of itself was an objection, but a still greater one was in the prevalence in the college of deistical influences. Two academies were projected by the presbytery; one was located in Prince Edward County, the other in the valley. The former became Hampden-Sidney College.

Over Hampden-Sidney College Dr. Samuel Stanhope Smith presided for a number of years, till called (1798) to the higher position as President of Princeton. He was one of the remarkable men of the period. A Pennsylvanian by birth, the son of Dr. Robert Smith of Pequa, Lancaster County; his mother, a remarkably talented woman, a sister of the two Blairs, Samuel and John—both famous teachers and preachers in the Presbyterian Church of that day. He graduated from Princeton with high honor, was for a time assistant teacher for his father, then tutor in Princeton. Meantime he studied theology and was licensed to preach (1773) by the Presbytery of New Castle. As a preacher he reminded the people of the eloquent Samuel Davies, whose fame was not limited to Virginia. Among the trustees of Hampden-Sidney were Patrick Henry and James Madison.

In 1749 Hanover Presbytery established also Augusta Academy in what is now Rockbridge County. This school was placed under the care of Rev. William Graham. The latter was a graduate of Princeton (1775), a son of a Pennsylvania farmer, in his youth inured to the dangers and hardships of frontier life; a bright intellect, he managed to secure a superior education, which he consecrated to the cause of learning and religion. Under Dr. Graham in this institution was trained Rev. Dr. Archibald Alexander, afterwards so long Professor of Theology in Princeton Seminary. The Revolutionary War, of course, interfered with the academy; its name was changed to Liberty Hall in 1776; and it was chartered as a college (1782) under that significant name. Afterward George Washington endowed it, for the times, with a large amount, and in gratitude the trustees changed the name to Washington (1812)—it is now known as Washington and Lee University. The last name was adopted in 1871.

Theology Taught Separately.—Dr. Graham resigned the Presidency but turned his attention specially to giving instruction in theology to a number of students. The synod of Virginia, recognizing the importance of the movement, and, no doubt, influenced by the Presbytery of Hanover, which, in its contest with the intolerant civil authorities of Virginia, had been trained to have far-reaching views, added a theological department to Liberty Hall. This was the first theological seminary in the United States established in connection with a college. This department was opened for the reception of students in 1794; two years afterward Professor Graham resigned. The loss was so serious that the seminary languished and finally passed out of existence.

The Private Classical Schools.—The Log College of Mr. Tennent (*see p. 111*) was imitated in its plan of study by other private schools. Rev. Samuel Finley, afterward President of Princeton College, established a noted one at Nottingham, Chester County, Pennsylvania. Here were educated, besides a number of ministers, Governor Martin of North Carolina, Dr. Benjamin Rush, a celebrated physician of the times, Governor Henry of Maryland. Among the clergymen were Rev. Drs. Alexander McWhorter and James Waddel. The blind preacher graphically described by William Wirt. The Rev. Samuel Blair, also, founded a classical and theological school at Fagg's Manor, likewise in Chester County, about the year 1743. At this school were educated for the greater part a number of eminent men, such as Rev. Samuel Davies, afterward President of Princeton College; John Rodgers, long a pastor of the historic Brick Presbyterian Church in the City of New York; James Finley, who migrated to Western Pennsylvania and was for many years pastor of the churches of Rehoboth and Round Hill, in the Forks of Yough, and who afterward had private students in theology, and many others.

A classical school modeled on the same plan was in 1743 established at New London, Pennsylvania. It was, however, under the care of the Synod of Philadelphia, and was to be supported by contributions from the congregations. The ministers donated a number of books to the college library. The enterprise on the whole was not successful, as the attention of the students was turned in another direction—toward Princeton.

When the union took place of the Synods of New York and Philadelphia (1758) Nassau Hall or Princeton became the favorite of the united synod. The latter soon overshadowed all these classical schools as its curriculum of study was so much more varied and extensive than

REV. ARCHIBALD ALEXANDER, D. D.
(129, 250, 337.)

could be obtained in the former. In consequence, to Princeton went the majority of the Presbyterian students in their preparation for the ministry.

Schools beyond the Alleghanies.—The same spirit in relation to an educated ministry crossed the Alleghanies into Western Pennsylvania, with the Presbyterian emigrants from New Jersey, Eastern Pennsylvania, Maryland and Virginia. It is worthy of note the facilities at that time for crossing the Alleghany Mountains into the fertile valley of the Ohio were limited to two military roads—the one made by Braddock (1755), which commenced at where Cumberland, Maryland, now stands, and the other made by General Forbes (1758), up the Susquehanna and the Juniata rivers and thence across the mountains. Multitudes of immigrants, the great majority of whom belonged to the different branches of the Presbyterian family, began to pour into that region after peace was assured by France in 1763, ceding Canada to England. The prosperity of these various settlements was unprecedented. We find in that region, within twenty or twenty-five years after the great migration began, a number of private classical and theological schools, each having a limited number of young men as pupils, many of whom were studying for the sacred office. These students, in connection with their classical and literary studies, took up also the study of the Bible in its original tongues and the Westminster Confession. In consequence of this arrangement at the end of their academic course they were equally if not better scholars in theology than in the classics and sciences. This accounts for the historic fact that so many of these students, when examined by the presbyteries, were found prepared and as such were licensed to preach. Oftentimes others, after finishing the prescribed course of study in these schools, devoted a time, usually not defined as to length, in the special study of theology and pastoral duties under the supervision of some pastor. Thus was tacitly recognized the importance of such students having special instruction under competent professors in the science of theology itself, and the influence of this fact led finally to the establishment of Presbyterian theological seminaries—the first in the Union.

The Germs of Two Colleges.—One of these schools, under the care of Rev. Thaddeus Dod, was the germ of Washington College, chartered in 1806. This log schoolhouse was erected in 1781 by the spontaneous efforts of the Presbyterian settlers in the neighborhood. The latter are said to have brought with them their "New Jersey and New England tastes," and in consequence, in point of zeal, for the promotion of education, were in advance of most of the other settlers.

Rev. Joseph Smith was born in 1736 and graduated from Princeton in 1764, and five years later we find him pastor of a church, Lower Brandywine. Here he labored nine years then migrated to Western Pennsylvania and became pastor of two congregations—Buffalo and Cross Creek. Here he remained till his almost premature death, at the age of fifty-six, after twelve years of unwonted success. A revival commenced soon after he entered upon his pastorate and continued to the end of his earthly career. "In the pulpit and out of it his power was wonderful * * * his manner had a strange power that was indescribable. His mind had been disciplined by classical and collegiate drilling, but in the earnest glow of his eloquence he spurned 'scholarly reasoning and cautious logic' as an eagle would a ladder by which to climb."

In 1785 he established a classical school for training young men ultimately for the ministry. He had no separate building and his self-denying wife gave up her kitchen for a school-room. Here commenced the studies of three remarkable men: James McGready, Joseph Patterson and Samuel Porter. They afterward studied theology under the care of Dr. McMillan,

The school of that region which far excelled all others in its influence was established by Rev. John McMillan, D.D., at his residence about two miles from the village of Canonsburg. The original building was composed of round logs taken from the forest in the vicinity. McMillan was a graduate of Princeton and when about to set out for his work beyond the mountains (1776) Dr. Robert Smith of Pequa, his theological instructor, urged him "to look out some pious young men and educate them for the ministry."

In this log college were educated numbers of young men who became missionaries and pastors in that region, while others entered upon different professions. The school was afterward removed to Canonsburg and eventually became Jefferson College, chartered in 1802.

The private members of the Presbyterian churches in this region have always been ardent supporters of an educated ministry. The self-denial of Mrs. Smith was an illustration of the devotion of the women of those primitive times. The indigent but worthy young men who were studying for the sacred office were most cordially aided to eke out their support by the ladies of the several congregations. All at that time wore homespun, or clothes of domestic manufacture. For instance, to aid the students the women often made clothes of domestic linen made from the flax of their clearings, and which was colored by being boiled with new-mown grass. For winter wear flannel, made from domestic wool, which was carded, then spun and woven and fulled to an extent and dyed by means of being boiled amid bark of trees of walnut, perhaps, more than any other, the color thus produced was a light yellow. This "homespun" was used by all in those early days. Tradition tells how Mrs. John McMillan was a faithful and persevering helpmeet for her husband in his labors in relieving him of many corroding cares, and how she sympathized with the young theologians who were his students, and with what motherly care she watched over them in respect to their temporal wants, and by her never-failing faith and practical wisdom cheered them in their paths of duty.

After the removal of Dr. McMillan's school to Canonsburg it was known by the more dignified title—the Academy. The greater part of its necessary expenses was borne by the members of the churches in the country round about. The women, as usual, were preëminently diligent in their way to aid the institution. One form of their raising money for the purpose was to *"knit woolen socks,* which found a ready sale in the stores in Pittsburg." (*President Matthew Brown.*)

Study on Two Lines.—In these schools the young men were taught the classics in connection with theology; in the latter the principal text-books were the Holy Scriptures in their original languages. Many of these students afterward became the missionaries and pastors for the Presbyterian churches scattered through the region watered by the Monongahela, the Allegheny, the Upper Ohio and their tributaries. As Presbyterian immigrants from east of the mountains came flocking in, churches and preaching stations increased in number, and to supply their wants with greater facility the Presbytery of Ohio was set off from that of Redstone in 1793. This was done in accordance with that most influential custom incident to the presbyterian form of church government, namely, that of promoting a frequent and fraternal intercourse among its ministers and elders, as they meet from time to time in the church judicatures; in such meetings of their representatives the private members of the church take an intelligent interest.

Schools Further South beyond the Alleghanies.—A similar spirit in respect to education animated the pioneers of Presbyterianism in the South, who crossed the same mountains into East Tennessee and thence to Kentucky. Rev. Samuel Doak, a graduate of Princeton and also a student of theology under the direction of Dr. Robert Smith at Pequa, was licensed to preach by the Presbytery of Hanover in 1777. He went as a missionary to the settlements on the Holston, and took up his residence in its valley, and there in order to eke out his salary he cultivated his own farm. He was ever diligent in preaching and laboring in the settlements in that region. He also erected a *log-house* and established a classical and theological school, the library for which was carried across the Alleghanies on pack-horses. This school became Washington College in 1795. This was the *first* chartered college in the Valley of the Mississippi; Jefferson, in Western Pennsylvania, was seven years younger. Dr. Doak presided over Washington College for twenty-three years. He then removed to the vicinity of Greeneville, Greene County, where he established another classical school, which was named Tusculum Academy—that title was changed to college when it was incorporated by the legislature; and finally it was united with Greeneville College (1868) and is now known as Greeneville and Tusculum College. "Few men in the history of the church were better fitted by wisdom, sagacity, energy and learning to lay the foundations of social and religious institutions than Dr. Doak." (*Gillett, I., p. 427.*)

Hezekiah Balch.—In 1785 Hezekiah Balch came into East Tennessee. He was a graduate of Princeton in 1762 and had been a classical teacher and student of theology. He was licensed to preach by the Presbytery of New

Castle, and finally migrated to East Tennessee. There he labored in preaching and teaching for more than twenty years. His influence was also exerted in establishing Greeneville College.

Three ministers in this region, Samuel Carrick, Charles Cummings and Hezekiah Balch, and others, overtured the Synod of Philadelphia to be formed into a presbytery. In answer to this request the Presbytery of Abington was set off from that of Hanover and constituted in 1785. Within its jurisdiction was included the territory now occupied by the States of Tennessee and Kentucky. This was the *second* presbytery organized in the valley of the Mississippi, that of Redstone being the older by four years.

It is an interesting fact that there were at this same period two centers of Presbyterian influence west of the Alleghanies, and on the eastern edge of the great and marvelously fertile valley of the Mississippi. The settlements on the headstreams of the Tennessee and the adjacent regions, and those on the headstreams of the Ohio, were almost due north and south, while between them was virtually an unbroken wilderness of nearly four hundred miles. We shall see in the course of this history, when the necessity and opportunity came, with what zeal these Presbyterians labored to send the gospel to the destitute settlements that were afterward founded within the valley of the Mississippi.

XVII.

PRESBYTERIAN SETTLEMENTS IN THE SHENANDOAH VALLEY.

During this period of which we have been writing movements in founding settlements were going on in the Shenandoah valley of Virginia. The first migration thither was led by Joist Hite in 1732. Nearly, if not all of these settlements were made by the emigration of Presbyterians from New Jersey, Pennsylvania and Maryland; to these in after years were added Quakers and Germans from the same states. These migrations came principally from the northern portion of the great valley known as the Cumberland in Pennsylvania and Maryland, the Shenandoah in Virginia, and still further south, as the Tennessee. This continuous valley extends nearly one thousand miles along the depression east of the Alleghanies and west of the Blue Ridge in Virginia, and the corresponding highlands in the other States.

The Letters of the Synod and of the Governor.—The Synod of Philadelphia (1738), on the request of John Caldwell—the maternal grandfather of the famous statesman, John Caldwell Calhoun of South Carolina—sent a commission of two of its members to wait on Lieutenant Governor Gooch at Williamsburg, Virginia. Mr. Caldwell wished to lead a colony from Pennsylvania to homes in the valley of the Shenandoah, and the object of the commission was to obtain a permit for this company to migrate to "the back-parts" of his colony. The members of the synod state in their petition that they are of "the persuasion of the Church of Scotland * * * that those of their profession in Europe have been remarkable for their inviolable attachment to the House of Hanover, and to our gracious King George (II.), and we doubt not but these our brethren will carry the same loyal principles to the most distant settlements where their lot may be cast."

The following year the governor sent an autograph letter to the moderator of the synod, in which after some preliminary remarks he said: "You may be assured that no interruption shall be given to any minister of your profession who shall come among them (the settlers), so as they conform themselves to the rules prescribed by the Act of Toleration in England, by taking the oaths thereby, and registering the place of their meeting, and behave themselves peaceably toward the government." We shall see in this narrative how this promise was kept. (*See p. 146.*) The governor was willing that these settlements should be made in that region, so distant from those on the tide-water, since they served as a protection against the incursions of the Indians.

Presbyterians in North Carolina.—In course of time these Presbyterians found their way into the fertile regions further south in North Carolina, in the County of Mechlinberg and in the valley of the Catawba. Numbers of them also crossed over the Blue Ridge and settled in the adjacent portion of Virginia, and there took part half a century later in a remarkable struggle for religious liberty. Afterward many others passed over the Alleghanies into what is now Kentucky and Tennessee, carrying with them as household books the Bible, the Westminster Confession and its Catechisms.

These settlements having increased in number, applied to the Synod of Philadelphia to send them Presbyterian ministers. In 1719 Rev. Daniel Magill traveled among them as an evangelist and labored for several months in the region and organized a church in the vicinity of where now stands the town of Martinsburg. Some years later (1732) another church was organized at Opeckon, a few miles south of the site of the present city of Winchester. The tide of newcomers continued to flow on for many years. Meanwhile other churches were constituted and the cry for help came up again and again to the synod for more ministers, who might serve as settled pastors when the people became able to support a stated ministry. The Rev. James Gelston, a member of the Presbytery of Donegal, became pastor (1737) at Opeckon. Meantime itinerants were visiting these scattered and feeble churches, but which in the course of years became strong enough to support pastors. The valley, so beautiful in its natural features, the fertility of its soil and the healthfulness of the climate, attracted settlers in large numbers. The Rev. John Blair, afterward famed for his talents and his success as a preacher, itinerated throughout the entire region for two years (1745-6).

The Mission of William Robinson.—The Presbyterians in Hanover County, who still continued to worship in the "reading houses" (*p. 122*), heard of these churches and preachers of their own persuasion in the valley of Virginia, and they too sent a deputation to the Presbytery of New Castle to obtain a minister. The presbytery in response sent the Rev. William Robinson, who as an evangelist had been laboring among the churches in the valley during the previous winter. Robinson was the son of a wealthy English Quaker, who migrated when a youth to the colonies. On July 6, 1743, Robinson preached to a large audience the first Presbyterian sermon ever heard in Hanover County. On the following day the congregation was greatly increased in number, and so continued for four days—the length of time that he could remain with them. Many were awakened and some were converted, and all were deeply impressed. The people manifested their gratitude by offering to pay him liberally for his services, but he absolutely refused to receive any compensation. But they were not to be baffled. They found means to slip the silver into his saddlebags, and when he came to handle them he noticed their unusual weight and on investigation he found the money. "It is your gift," said he, "and there is a providence in it. I know a worthy young man who is struggling under pecuniary difficulties in his studying for the ministry. I will give him the money, and perhaps he may yet come and preach for you. As soon as he is licensed we will send him to visit you; it may be that you may now, by your liberality, be educating a minister for yourselves." Four years later that young man—Samuel Davies—(1747) came to Hanover to the same people and remained for twenty-two years their pastor till called by the church to higher and more responsible positions. He has been characterized on good authority as one of "the greatest divines the American Presbyterian Church has produced"—certainly of the colonial period.

Dr. Samuel Davies.—This remarkable man deserves a passing notice. Of Welsh extraction, born in 1723 in the colony of Delaware, his father a farmer of moderate worldly means and of a devout character, his mother of superior mental endowments and very ardent in her religious convictions. Like Hannah of old, she consecrated her son to the Lord, and for that reason named him Samuel. Davies was the most noted man in the church of that period, not merely as an eloquent and devotedly pious and successful preacher, but as a grand organizer and of great influence among the people and his ministerial brethren because of his mental power and symmetry of character. He traveled much in the colonies and was listened

SETTLEMENTS IN THE SHENANDOAH VALLEY. 141

to by sympathetic multitudes. The congregations to which he ministered in Virginia were some fifteen or twenty miles apart, because the colonial authorities under the influence of the clergy and the illiberal vestries would not permit any more dissenting meeting-houses to be built, notwithstanding the wants of the people. The people in great numbers and often from long distances flocked to hear him preach. He was not only well versed in Christian scholarship, as his theology was drawn directly from the principles of the Bible, but he was at home in the laws of England in respect to the established church and the proper interpretation and intent of the famous partially liberal Act of Toleration enacted in 1690.

In his younger days especially Davies was in very delicate health, and he seemed moved as in the presence of death when he preached, which he often did after a night of pain and sleeplessness. He was afterward President of Princeton College, and to raise funds in whose behalf he was sent to England. On one occasion in returning to Hanover from a meeting of the Synod of New York (1748), to which he belonged as a member of New Castle Presbytery, he brought with him a young man—John Rodgers—just licensed to preach. Forty years afterward (*p. 208*) Rodgers took part in the formation of the General Assembly (1788), at which time he was also pastor of the *Brick Presbyterian* Church in New York City. On his way Rodgers dared preach somewhere without the formality of a license from the Virginia authorities, which he intended to obtain at Williamsburg. His application was flatly refused by the council—all churchmen— though it appears Governor Gooch favored giving the young man a license. Rodgers had dared in the presence of the council to assert his inherent right as a minister to preach the gospel.

An Incident.—We give place to an incident connected

with this refusal of a license to preach. A clergyman of the establishment who learned of the preaching of Rodgers, rode some forty or fifty miles to make a charge against the young man before the Governor and Council for thus preaching and to urge his exemplary punishment. When he presented himself before Governor Gooch he met an unexpected reception. The latter's indignation burst forth; said he: "I am surprised at you! You profess to be a minister of Jesus Christ, and you come and complain of a man and wish me to punish him for preaching His gospel! For shame, sir! Go home and mind your own duty. For such a piece of conduct you deserve to have your gown torn from your shoulders."

The Presbyterians of Hanover Specially Hated.—This council undertook to discuss, if not decide, how many meeting-houses the dissenters should have. That council —all churchmen—was particularly hostile to the Presbyterians of Hanover County, and especially so because they were *not immigrants* from the other colonies, but were *resident laymen* of the established church, and had of their own accord, as a matter of Christian duty, refused to attend the services of the church for reasons already stated (Section XV.), and this before they had learned of such a denomination as the Presbyterians.

The council argued that the Act of Toleration might apply to the Presbyterians that lived west of the Blue Ridge, because with the permission of the Governor they had come thither from Pennsylvania, New Jersey and Maryland, but *not* to those who, on religious grounds, had withdrawn from the established church and thus created a schism and became *dissenters* of the most offensive character. This was virtually the opinion of Peyton Randolph, the king's attorney, and the most bitter lay opponent of the Presbyterians in Hanover County. (*See p. 168.*)

The Two Modes of Levying Church Rates.—In this connection it may be noted that the Cavaliers of Virginia and the majority of the congregational portion of the Puritans of Massachusetts and Connecticut, virtually agreed in deeming it essential that the church should be in connection with the state, in order that the latter might be properly supported. The Congregationalists did not impose fines for non-attendance at church, as did the Churchmen of Virginia; they required only that the taxes which were levied upon the citizens of the town for the general support of the gospel should be paid. "It was the law in both Connecticut and Massachusetts that assessments levied on the town for the support of the ministry, the members or attendants of the Church of England, were at liberty to pay over their assessments to the support of the resident Episcopal minister if there was one in the town" (1727). All the inhabitants were taxed alike, but an exception was made in favor of the Church of England and its members that they "should not be charged with the erection of Congregational meeting-houses" (*Ch. Hist. Series, Vol. III., pp. 234, 235*). What a contrast this mode was with that of the Church of England when it had the power, as in the colonies of New York and Virginia. In the latter *all* the tithes collected from dissenters were demanded for the use of the established church. On the contrary, the Presbyterian element among the Puritans repudiated, absolutely, the right of the *civil authorities* to interfere in religious affairs at all, except so far as to protect all persons and all denominations in their rights, civil and religious. In order to avoid giving the civil magistrate an excuse for such interference, they proposed that the Christians or church members should themselves bear in full the expenses of supporting their own ministers and all the liabilities incurred by the church in respect to money matters. There is not an instance on record wherein the

Presbyterians when free and untrammeled by outside political influence ever did otherwise than support their own church, and accorded the same freedom in religious matters to others which they demanded for themselves.

The Mecklenburg Declaration.—In connection with these movements we anticipate, in point of time, an incident. The migrations of Presbyterians continued to press along the Shenandoah Valley and finally they diverged to the southeast, and crossing the Blue Ridge found homes in the valleys of the Catawba and the Yadkin, as well as in the region between these rivers. This immigration was greatly increased in 1755 because of hostile Indian incursions that occurred after the defeat of General Braddock. The nominal center of the settlements thus formed appears to have been in Mecklenburg County.

To this region came the Rev. Alexander Craighead in 1758; he had been licensed by the Donegal Presbytery in 1734. Though eccentric in some of his peculiar characteristics, he was an ardent advocate of religious and civil liberty. He was also a warm friend of George Whitefield and noted for the spirituality of his preaching and the many revivals which sealed his ministry. He had, likewise, experienced the ecclesiastical tyranny of the established church in Virginia, and when he migrated to North Carolina he enjoyed the freedom of speech and exercised it with great zeal. For more than twenty years as a settled pastor and often as a missionary in the adjacent region he preached the gospel and also proclaimed the opinion that religious freedom could be obtained only in independence of the British crown.

To these settlements in a course of years was also a large influx of emigrants from the north of Ireland—Scotch-Irish—if we may judge from the names of their descendants; some came direct from the port of Charleston, S. C., and others direct from Philadelphia and the

Delaware. These Scotch-Irish Presbyterians were characterized as having "the impulsiveness of the Irishman with the dogged resolution of the Covenanter."

All the Presbyterian ministers and elders, and indeed the male church members in this region, were intelligent and pronounced advocates of religious freedom. In the Mecklenburg County convention they were specially prominent in influence and in numbers. When that convention was in session in May, 1775, a courier arrived and gave information in respect to what was transpiring in the North. The conflicts at Concord and Lexington had already taken place: "Finally with indignation the delegates resolved to throw off the authority of the king and parliament." Ephraim Brevard, "trained in the college at Princeton," and afterward a martyr in the cause, embodied their sentiments in resolutions, which declared: "All laws and commissions confirmed by or derived from the authority of the king and parliament to be annulled and vacated." They were practical men, and they also resolved to take measures to maintain their rights. (*Four Hundred Years, etc., p. 366, and pp. 523-526.*)

This declaration of the convention was an earnest of what followed in after years when the War of the Revolution was in progress. The battle of King's Mountain, which in its influence had a similar effect upon the success of Cornwallis that the battle of Bennington had on that of Burgoyne, was fought mostly by Presbyterians. The leaders in that battle—Cols. Sevier, Shelby, and Campbell—were Presbyterian elders, while the patriots under their commands were for the most part Presbyterians. Gen. Daniel Morgan, who commanded at the battle of "The Cowpens," was a Presbyterian elder, and so was Gen. Pickens of South Carolina. General Francis Marion, of Huguenot descent, was also a Presbyterian.

Lord Cornwallis characterized the region around Charlotte, which was settled by the Scotch-Irish, as a "hornet's nest."

A Sad History.—It may not be in vain in this connection for the author to yield to the temptation and notice the pathetic appeal for aid in respect to education and gospel work that comes to the members of the Presbyterian Church of to-day from the descendants of those patriotic Presbyterians—the rank and file—who, especially in this region, sustained their elders as leaders on the battlefields of the Revolution. Their elders were prominent in the patriotic movements of the times, and two of them, Cols. Sevier and Shelby, were afterward governors of their respective States, Tennessee and Kentucky. It is evident the inhabitants of the mountainous regions of North Carolina and those of the adjacent States, for the most part, are the descendants of the Scotch-Irish Presbyterians, who were the rank and file of the armies just mentioned. This fact is a clear inference from their family names, and besides there was no other people from whom they could have descended. These men were intelligent for the times; they understood and appreciated the principles of civil and religious liberty, for which they hazarded their lives. But alas! for nearly a century a cloud of illiteracy and corresponding ignorance has hung over their descendants. How has this calamity been brought about?

Within four years after the first inauguration of George Washington as President of the United States, Eli Whitney invented the cotton gin (1793); in consequence slave labor became more valuable. The owners of slaves, as this value increased, began to covet the fertile fields of the small farmers, who did not own slaves, but cultivated their lands by their own labor. Prejudices grew up that made the situation of the small farmers intolerable, they being treated as an inferior class by the slave-owners and their families. The lines were strictly drawn in society. Those who earned a livelihood by their own labor were stigmatized as "poor whites" or "white trash," and otherwise annoyed. Though industrious and honest, the small farmers were, virtually, forced to sell their farms in the fertile lowlands and retire to less fertile hills and mountains. Thus the desirable districts of these States were gradually absorbed in large plantations and devoted to the cultivation of cotton and tobacco by slave labor.

These outrages did not end here; the lawmakers were all owners of slaves; no other class ever went to Congress or even to the legislature of any slave-labor State. The only political privilege permitted the non-slave owner to exercise was to vote for the nominees of the slave oligarchy. The latter forbid under severe penalties the teaching of slaves to read and write! What a contrast! Heathen Rome did not deny her slaves the privilege of becoming educated. The legislatures of the slave-labor States never made provision for common schools, as was the case in the free-labor States. The slave-owners were able to educate their families by means of private instruction or by sending them to colleges or seminaries, usually in the Northern States. How sadly different was the case of these "mountaineers." The parents were poor and unable to educate their children, the latter appear in respect to that advantage to have degenerated from generation to generation.

It is equally sad to note that during this period there seems to have been less effort on the part of Presbyterians to follow these poor mountaineers with the gospel than to bring it in its fulness to the people living in the valleys. The result was the mountaineers in course of time became alienated from the church of their fathers, as they were ministered to by good men, though comparatively uneducated as preachers and of different faiths.

When the slave oligarchy in 1861 made an attempt to break up the Union, these mountaineers, with the liberty-loving spirit of their Revolutionary fathers, rallied to defend the integrity of the nation. Let wealthy Americans who value the preservation of the Union, in gratitude aid in giving the children of these loyal patriots educational institutions, which to-day they need and desire so much.

XVIII.

PIETISTS—REVIVALS—DIVISION AND REUNION.

In the first quarter of the eighteenth century "a new religious force burst forth, simultaneously, in different parts of Great Britain and her colonies." It appeared as though the minds of the people in these far-separated places were prepared to receive an impulse toward a pure and heartfelt religion. These movements were at first virtually independent of one another and for a time local in their influence. They were the outgrowth of the phase of religion characterized by the Puritans as "vital piety." The latter were too much influenced by the Old Testament in proportion to the New Testament. They did not apprehend sufficiently the different stages in divine doctrine and morals; but they were faithful to the word of God as they understood it. They desired above all things to be conformed to God's will; and so they resisted conforming to the prelates' will. Their ideal was a holy life in communion with God. This was the noble aspiration of Puritanism which has made British and American society the most ethical and upright, the most manly and godly society the world has yet seen."

Moravians and Pietists.—In the British Isles the leaders in the movement which began about 1738 or 1739 were the brothers, John and Charles Wesley, while intimately with them was associated George Whitefield, so famous for his pulpit eloquence. The Wesleys "were guided by the Moravians into the light and to the adoption of those principles, doctrines and methods which have been the characteristic features of Methodism. * * * Methodism is a revival of Puritanism; it is a genuine development of British Christianity; and yet it was influenced very largely by the pietism of the Continent of Europe. But pietism owed its origin to the impulses of Puritanism in the seventeenth century. * * * Puritanism gave the Reformed churches of Holland and Germany the Covenant theology which became native to the soil * * * and that form of vital, experimental and practical religion became a potent influence in pietism. * * * It was an appropriate international and historical recompense that the Continent should receive British Puritanism and transform it into pietism, and that subsequently Great Britain and her colonies should receive the pietism of the Continent and transform it into Methodism." (*Amer. Pres., pp. 54, 55, 239.*)

Influence of Pietism.—The Rev. Jacob Frelinghuysen, ancestor of the Jersey family of that name, who came from Holland, settled at Raritan, near New Brunswick, New Jersey, and there became pastor of a Dutch Reformed Church in 1720. Here with great zeal he labored for twenty-seven years, and the result was repeated revivals during his pastorate. He was thoroughly imbued with the principles of the pietists who sought to vitalize the piety of the Protestant churches of Germany. He had been educated under the care of eminent pietists in his native land. George Whitefield represents him in his journal as the originator of a series of revivals, saying: "He is a worthy old soldier of Jesus Christ and was the beginner of the great work which I trust the Lord is carrying on in these parts." "Frelinghuysen insisted upon the necessity of regeneration and the practice of piety in order to participate in the Lord's Supper." The same doctrine and conditions were, also, insisted upon by Jonathan Edwards in the great revival at Northampton, Massachusetts (1735).

Frelinghuysen "was systematic, energetic and industrious in his ministerial and pastoral duties. * * * He was the first pastor of the Reformed (Dutch) Church who began to train young men for the ministry."

Differences of Opinion.—After agreeing upon the Adopting Act the synod continued to prosper. During twelve years (1729-1741) more than forty ministers were added to its number; of these, a few had been trained in the American church, but nearly one-half were from Scotland and north of Ireland. Near the close of this period a new element of discord intervened. Differences of opinion were prevalent and had their respective influence. Some of these pertained to the establishment of schools for the instruction in theology of candidates for the ministry, and also in respect to the manner of preaching the gospel; one phase of the latter grew out of the great revival that commenced in 1735 under Jonathan Edwards at Northampton, Massachusetts, and whose influence extended to the Middle colonies (*Patton's Four Hundred Years, etc., pp. 266-268*). Among the leading preachers in the latter were the Tennents—the father and four sons—of whom the more prominent was Gilbert, but they all preached with power and their labors were greatly blest. They were aided also by the celebrated George Whitefield, then on his preaching tours through the colonies. Many members of the synod did not approve the manner of the revivalists, nor certain measures which they introduced, neither did they seem to be in full sympathy with the revival itself; there were, perhaps, as many others who looked upon the work as having the blessing of the Head of the Church.

Two phases of complaint were specially obnoxious: one, the habit of the revivalists preaching when uninvited by the pastor within the bounds of the latter's parish—the answer was the people heard them gladly. The other, the censorious spirit which characterized the conservative ministers as unconverted; for this assertion the ground seems to have been that they did not fully coincide with the measures of the revivalists.

The Old Side—The New Side.—These unfortunate difficulties obtruded themselves, and a few good men were indiscreet, while others were harsh in their judgments. The opponents of the work were characterized as holding "a dead orthodoxy," while it was admitted that the revivalists were equally orthodox, though they were spiritually alive and vividly imbued with zeal for the salvation of men—the latter's style of preaching being exceedingly impressive. The steady conservatives who were opposed to any innovations in the usual routine manner of preaching, were known as the "Old Side," and the fervid revivalists as the "New Side." Thus the agitation continued for several years; meanwhile much bitterness was evolved, and also an immense amount of good in spite of the disturbing elements by which many good men were carried beyond their usual Christian demeanor.

The Division of the Synod.—These differences of opinion and practice finally resulted in the division of the synod, inasmuch as the "New Side" or New Brunswick party and their sympathizers withdrew, thus causing the division. The moderate and conservative in both "Sides" mourned this result.

"The New Brunswick party were zealous for what they regarded as vital evangelical truth, and, in the over-earnestness of their purpose, forgot charity and discretion. * * * The others, indignant under a sense of wrong, were forced to appeal to the authority of the common standards and the rules of the synod, which their brethren had too much disregarded. Thus one party appealed

PIETISTS—REVIVALS—DIVISION AND REUNION.

to the word of God, the other to the Confession of Faith. One, zealous for the truth, fell the victim of its theories; the other, resolute for order, could see only the letter of the constitution." The two synods were therefore constituted (1741)—the "Old Side," known as the Philadelphia, and the "New Side," as that of New York; though the latter did not take form till four years later, when it was duly organized by union with the New Brunswick Presbytery (*Drs. Gillett and Hodge*).

Illiberal Sentiments.—An incident illustrates the spirit that prevailed within the ranks of the Old Side during the earlier years of this division. The Presbyterians of the valley and also of Hanover County, Virginia, applied in 1744 to the New Side, the Presbytery of New Brunswick, for preachers, and the latter sent them two evangelists, William Robinson and William Dean, both graduates of Log College. They traveled through the region and preached with great success, multitudes flocking to hear them. A representative of the Old Side, Rev. John Craig, took offense at the preaching of the evangelists, and he appealed to Governor Gooch *in such terms* that the latter was induced to urge the grand jury of the colony to indict the evangelists. In his somewhat lengthy charge he characterized these ministers as *"false teachers* under the pretended influence of *new light and such like fanatical* knowledge that would lead the innocent and ignorant people into all kinds of delusion."

Mr. Craig acted only as an individual. Strange as it may seem, the Old Side Synod of Philadelphia the following year sent to the Governor a letter of fulsome flattery and of thanks for this persecuting action, saying in part: "It gives us the greatest pleasure that we can assure your honor those persons never belonged to our body, but were missionaries sent out by some who by reason of their divisive and uncharitable doctrines and practices were in May, 1741, excluded from our synod." This letter was signed by the moderator of the synod, Rev. Robert Cathcart. (*Records of Synod, p. 185—quoted; Am. Pres., p. 295*). (*See p. 161.*) During the following thirteen years there gradually came in a more liberal spirit.

Says Dr. Robert M. Patterson, page. 19 of his *American Presbyterianism* (Edition 1896): "The Old Side made orthodoxy their shibboleth; insisted more on intellectual qualifications and high education in the ministry; were stricter in presbyterial order; the New Side placed more stress on experimental religion, vital piety in the ministry, and was more tolerant of departures from ecclesiastical strictness. At the root both were right; in practical conduct and mutual intercourse both were wrong. The church has long accepted the essential points for which each contended."

Zeal for Religion.—The period of the division—seventeen years (1741-1758)—was characterized by an increase of religious influence, especially on the part of the New Side, who continued their fervent mode of preaching, and which was followed by great increase of communicants in the church, and also in the number of young men who became students and eventually devoted themselves to the ministry. In the course of these years such accessions were more than fourfold when compared with that of the Old Side. The New York Synod exhibited great zeal in supplying destitute fields within its bounds, and in consequence the friends of the revival sympathized with them deeply. The Old Side, meanwhile, labored under almost insurmountable difficulties. Their lack of interest in the revivals, if not their direct opposition, deprived them of the sympathy of great numbers of ardent Christians within their own ranks, who, perhaps, were there from location rather than choice. Both parties established schools for training candidates for the sacred office, as already noted; out of one of these grew Princeton College, and, subsequently, the Theological Seminary.

The Reunion.—During these seventeen years continued efforts were made by many in both parties to bring about a reunion, as the cause of religion and brotherly love was deeply injured by the contention, which on the part of some did not partake to a large extent of the spirit of the Sermon on the Mount nor of the Golden Rule. But these asperities were gradually worn away by the attrition of Christian love and forbearance practiced by the prudent in both parties, till the way was prepared for a more stable union of the synods than had ever existed before. At length the leading minds of the majority in both parties were fully prepared to unite the synods, and thus heal the breach in the church. During the seventeen years of the separation there had been no virtual deviation on either side from the doctrinal principles on which the *Adopting Act* was based thirty years before, and they could now unite consistently. The first article of the basis of the union reads: "Both synods having always approved and received the Westminster Confession of Faith and Larger and Shorter Catechisms as an orthodox and excellent system of Christian doctrine, founded on the word of God, we do still receive the same as the confession of our faith." After a number of minor details in relation to some of the presbyteries were arranged, the union was completed (1758).

"At the time of reunion the church consisted of ninety-eight ministers, two hundred congregations, many preaching stations and ten thousand communicants."

Comparative Failure and Success.—These unfortunate differences of opinions did not end here, as the reader in the course of this narrative will meet more than once with antagonisms in the workings of church affairs that were not harmonious with spiritual progress.

The terms Old Side and New Side were used, as we have seen, to designate two phases of religious thought and action; the one lacking sympathy with the progressive evangelical work of the time, and the other, in marked contrast, an ardent promoter of such work. Both parties were orthodox; though the one seemed to be spiritually in a comatose state, while the other appeared to be spiritually vitalized.

Immediately after the division antagonistic feeling, especially on the part of the Old Side, was intensely bitter and manifested itself again and again; but it gradually passed away with the removal or death of *ten* of the prime movers. In consequence, in *seventeen* years the Old Side Synod of Philadelphia gained only *four* in number of its members—originally twenty-six—though fourteen new ones were in the meantime added to it. Of the latter "not a single one was a graduate of an American college."

The New Side Synod of New York meanwhile increased in numbers, both of church members and ministers; of the latter it had at first only *twenty*. That number rose to seventy-two; it had lost eight by death. The majority of these ministers were graduates either of Yale or Princeton.

Long Island Churches.—A spontaneous movement of far-reaching influence was at this time in progress in the colony of New York. The pastors of a number of Congregational churches on Long Island had from observation "become convinced that the presbyterian form of government was better adapted for promoting order and discipline in the churches than the congregational." A number of ministers in Suffolk County held a conference at Southampton April 8, 1747, for the purpose of "concerting measures for the promotion of the Great Redeemer's kingdom, especially within their own bounds." After much prayer for direction, they adopted "the Westminster Confession of Faith, the Catechisms, Directory for Worship and Discipline." Then they organized themselves into "the Presbytery of Suffolk," and appointed their moderator, Rev. Ebenezer Prime, and Rev. Samuel Buel to attend the Synod of New York and request that their newly formed presbytery be received into fellowship with that body. The delegates were cordially received and their presbytery was taken under the care of the synod. Soon afterward, for the most part, the other Congregational churches on the island united with the Presbyterian Church. (*The Prime Family, pp. 28, 29.*)

The Two Records.—The "Old Side" Synod of Philadelphia put itself on record as inimical to the revivals that had been in progress for a year or two in Virginia and even further south, under the auspices of the "New Side" Synod of New York. The latter took measures in 1744 and years succeeding at the earnest request of the Presbyterians of that region to send *devoted* ministers to preach for them. The result was revivals of religion, not only in Virginia, but in North Carolina, laid a firm foundation for Presbyterianism in these two colonies.

There was quite a discrepancy in the progress of the two "Sides," especially toward the latter portion of the seventeen years of the separation. At first the Old Side in some respects had greatly the advantage, though it failed lamentably in its lack of interest in the revivals then in progress, and which had grown out of the measures and preaching of Jonathan Edwards and the Tennents and George Whitefield. "The Old Side had the prestige of the historic succession and the possession of the funds of the church, * * * they made no adequate provision for training a native ministry; they reacted into a barren ecclesiasticism and traditional formalism; they set themselves in opposition to the active forces of the age, and they accordingly found it as difficult to secure fresh supplies of ministers as to enlarge their churches by converts."

Rev. Elisha Spencer, a Presbyterian pastor at Jamaica, L. I., in a letter dated Nov. 3, 1759, the year after the reunion, states that the whole number of dissenting ministers in the Middle colonies was one hundred and forty-three, while there were only sixteen Church of England ministers in the colonies of New York, New Jersey and Pennsylvania. "It is clear that in the middle of the eighteenth century the three latter colonies were overwhelmingly Presbyterian." (*Amer. Pres., pp. 294-296; 313-316.*)

XIX.

THE SEPARATION OF CHURCH AND STATE IN VIRGINIA.

The history of this contest deserves special notice, as it was the most severe struggle in the annals of the American Presbyterian Church in behalf of religious freedom; for during the eventful period of the Revolution it was the only phase of its history outside the usual routine of its regular church duties.

In a relation so intimate as that of the union of Church and State, it is not strange that in former times civil magistrates should have had a sense of responsibility not only pertaining to the people's temporal affairs, but also in respect to the salvation of their souls. In regard to the latter phase of their duties, though unable to define it clearly, it is evident that in the performance of their official acts in matters relating to the people and the church, they were more or less influenced by a sense of this responsibility. Here is the germ from which has sprung, and often honestly, much of the interference of temporal rulers with church affairs. On the other hand, those who willingly or otherwise contributed aid in the form of taxes to the support of the church, wished to have a share in the advantages of its ordinances; and, though they might not be Christians in a Scriptural sense, and could not fully comprehend their relationship to a *church spiritual,* they deemed themselves entitled to the privilege of participating in its rites, including that of the Lord's Supper. Thus, even in the present day, where there is a union of Church and State, in such relation that the former receives pecuniary aid from the latter, we see a great laxity in the admission of persons to that sacred ordinance. Much more in former times, if there were any advantages to be gained in coming to the communion table, this class wished to secure them, since they paid their share of the expense. This was a natural, though a groveling view of the question, and the more intelligent of the unconverted had evidently misgivings on the subject, and, not being satisfied with their own moral condition, partook of the communion with a confused sense, that it might in some way benefit them spiritually.

The Half-way Covenant.—The influences that in process of time brought about the separation of Church and State in this country may be traced to the preaching of Jonathan Edwards and to the principles developed in his controversy in respect to what was termed the "Half-way Covenant," by which persons making no pretension to being Christians in a *spiritual sense* were admitted, among other church privileges, to the communion. This custom grew out of the union of Church and State more than from any other cause. The objections of Edwards were based on moral and spiritual grounds alone; arguing that none but the *regenerate or converted* had a right to come to the Lord's table. In time this truth permeated the minds of religious people, but more effectually, it would seem, the Presbyterians than the Congregationalists; having its share of influence on the separation of Church and State in Virginia, nearly forty years before a similar effect was produced in New England. This phase of the subject for obvious reasons was scarcely noticed in the debates in the legislature during the struggle in Virginia, though in that controversy the undercurrent of this sentiment influenced the minds of the religious people outside the State or Episcopal Church, and strengthened their opposition to such laxity in the admission of persons to

REV. ELIPHALET NOTT, D. D.
(238, 247, 269, 305, 441.)

church privileges, which custom they believed to be injurious to pure spiritual religion.

In his early ministry Jonathan Edwards was the pastor of a Presbyterian church in New York City, and he seems to have been partial to the form of church government practised in that denomination; and, also, he agreed with their views on the non-interference of the civil magistrate with spiritual affairs. He afterward expressed his opinion of the form of church rule then prevalent in New England, saying: "I have long been out of conceit of our unsettled, independent, confused way of church government in this land." On assuming the presidency of Princeton College he connected himself with the Presbyterians.

Up to the time of Edwards there seems to have been little doubt as to the advantage to both parties of the union of Church and State; the prevailing sentiment being that the former could not be supported without the aid of the latter. The idea of sustaining the church by the voluntary contributions of its own friends had found lodgment only in the minds of the advanced few. We see prominent among the arguments used in behalf of this alliance that the church ought to be supported by the secular power, on the ground of the general well-being of society, as its influence would promote in the community honesty, industry and material interests as well as good morals. Under the influence of the preaching of Edwards the indefinable responsibility once attributed to the civil magistrate in relation to spiritual matters was seen to be unscriptural, and instead that responsibility was shown to belong to the individuals alone.

Why the Harsh Intolerance in Virginia.—It is proper to notice why the contest in Virginia partook so much of bitterness, and why the "dissenters" were treated so harshly in that colony. We can thereby divine why these outrages, continuing for nearly a century, produced their legitimate results in the final retribution which came upon the established church, when it retained only its church buildings, while its rectories and glebes were sold under the sheriff's hammer for the benefit of that public from whom originally nearly all the funds to purchase them had been extorted in the form of taxes or tithes. The Church of England was established by law in the colonies of New York, Virginia and the Carolinas about 1692. In the first, the royal governors were the most intolerant toward "dissenters," while the churchmen, or its adherents, were more indifferent on the subject. Perhaps they were somewhat influenced by their surroundings—the tolerant spirit of the Dutch residents—and, moreover, the Episcopal element in that colony did not comprise, it is said, more than one-seventh of the population. In the latter three, on the contrary, intolerance was instigated for the greater part by the clergy and lay churchmen, the governors being disposed to connive at the exercise of religious freedom; that is, they were not very energetic in enforcing the illiberal laws on that subject. Why the churchmen of Virginia were so in contrast with those of New York may be accounted for, since great numbers of Royalists—Cavaliers—in the times of the troubles preceding and during the Commonwealth fled to Virginia, where they were cordially welcomed. They afterward gave tone to Virginian society by diffusing their sentiments of loyalty to the king and to the church, which so ardently espoused his cause; they looked upon the "dissenters" as enemies to both.

The "Vagrants" in Connecticut and New York.—In those days the spirit of intolerance was not found in the established church nor in royal governors alone, as it was the natural outgrowth of the union of Church and State and the misdirected zeal of secular rulers. In 1742 the Connecticut legislature passed a law forbidding a minister preaching in any parish except the one over which he had special charge, unless by invitation of the settled minister or a majority of the congregation. Ministers not residents of the colony thus preaching were to be arrested as *common vagrants.* Under the latter law Rev. Samuel Finley, afterward President of Princeton College, and others were driven from the colony, being characterized as "strolling preachers that were most disorderly." These *vagrants* were Presbyterian clergymen, and no doubt such high-handed measures roused in them an antagonism to the union of Church and State. In consequence of these proceedings and the experience of Presbyterians in the colony of New York, this antagonism spread among that class of Christians in the Middle colonies and further south.

The Presbyterians had been specially annoyed in their earlier days when struggling for existence as a religious denomination, both in New York and Virginia, by the intolerance of the Church of England. They associated the state as the immediate power behind the persecution; though the latter, as it was well known, was frequently urged to this course of action by the clergy of the establishment. "For many years," says a chronicler of the times, "in New York, Maryland, Virginia and South Carolina, the growth of the Presbyterian Church was checked by persecution and intolerance."

Illiberal Laws in Virginia.—The laws were grievous and illiberal in Virginia—more severe than in any other colony. The established churches were built at the public expense in each county town, or where there was a court-house, thus occupying the positions of influence, and the "sects," or "dissenters," as they were contemptuously called by self-complacent churchmen, were compelled to locate their church buildings elsewhere. For three-fourths of a century rigid laws had been enforced against those who did not conform. It is said that until the commencement of the Revolution there was not a Presbyterian or Baptist church building in a village in Virginia, yet the ministers of the former denomination were by far the most learned of any class of preachers in the colony. The rule of the presbyteries of that church was then, as it is to-day, to license only those to preach who have been classically and theologically educated, unless under extraordinary circumstances.

Though "dissenters" were permitted to have church buildings only outside the towns, and even to have these, unless under annoying restrictions, they were sometimes denied, they were, however, *graciously* warned by the civil authorities to "take the oaths enjoined and to register the places of their meetings, and behave themselves peaceably toward the government." This discourteous language was used in respect to those Presbyterians who, among other reasons, in order to avoid the annoyances to which they would be subjected in the eastern portion of Virginia, migrated from Pennsylvania to the back part of that colony and settled in the fertile valleys of the Shenandoah and other streams west of the Blue Ridge. As long as these settlers served as a protection against hostile Indians they were unmolested, and were permitted to have meeting-houses where they pleased. In time Germans and Quakers, also from Pennsylvania, and for the same reasons, perhaps, migrated thither; thus increasing the number of the inhabitants as well as the thrift of the several communities. When these settlements had grown in population and prospered, the establishment wished to occupy the ground, and accordingly the colonial authorities compelled these "backwoods dissenters" to pay taxes in order to build edifices for the established church, and to support incumbents when there were very few of that denomination in the region. The first settlers here possessed remarkable worldly as well as church-militant qualities; they being for the most part Scotch and Scotch-Irish. These characteristics developed themselves when the attempt was made to carry this law into effect.

Freedom from Ecclesiastical Clannishness.—The Presbyterians did not come as a body to this country to form isolated settlements, as did the Puritans in New England, the Dutch in New York, the Quakers in Pennsylvania and the Roman Catholics in Maryland. When persecuted in England, they preferred, rather than emigrate in a body, "to struggle for liberty at home; a struggle which eventually was crowned with success" (*Dr. Charles Hodge, pp. 19, 20*). This may account for the fact that they were so free from a clannish ecclesiasticism; though strong in their opinions, they fell in with the religious people of the colonies and promoted the cause without arrogating to themselves any special preëminence. They held that Jesus Christ had established a form of government for the church "distinct from the civil authority." When parliament, in accordance with "the English idea that the church of any denomination was the creation of the state," abolished Episcopacy and established Presbyterianism, the latter church, as such, had nothing to do with that action; and, on the same principle, they were opposed *to any interference whatever in spiritual matters by the civil magistrate.* "When the arbitrary measures of Charles I. drove the English nation into rebellion, the partisans of the Court were Episcopalians; the opposite party was, or became in the main, Presbyterian" (*Dr. Hodge, p. 23*). These were their traditions, and, true to their influence, the Presbyterians harmonized with the other denominations in the colonies in the effort of spreading the gospel, irrespective of the patronage or opposition of the civil authorities.

Grades of Ministerial Education.—In the earlier days of Virginia the College of William and Mary was established ostensibly "to educate a domestic succession of Church of England ministers," as well as to teach the children of the Indians. But for nearly a half-century preceding the time of which we write, the education of native clergymen was rather discouraged than otherwise. There was, in truth, no special inducement for pious young men to qualify themselves for the sacred office, as so many of the ministers in the established church in the colony were from England. The latter were appointed by the home government and the Bishop of London, to whose diocese the colonies were assigned, and who ordained them, as there was no bishop in America till after the Revolution.

Meanwhile, the "dissenters," and notably the Presbyterians, were making strenuous efforts to educate young men for the sacred office. Early in the eighteenth century the latter established schools to educate young men for the ministry, and persistently refused to license any to preach who had not a classical and theological training, knowing that the influence of an educated ministry must ever be beneficial. In 1748 it was proposed in the Synod of New York and Philadelphia—then the highest judicature in the church—to relax the demands for the classical, literary and theological qualifications of candidates for the ministry. This proposition was voted down by a large majority. Instead of diminishing the time assigned for such preparation, the synod, as if to be emphatic, added another year to the prescribed course of study for their theological students. This same spirit influences the Presbyterians of to-day as much as it did those of nearly one hundred and fifty years ago. They now excel all others in the number of their theological seminaries and in the richness of their endowments. This strictness in demanding a thoroughly educated ministry has had a marked effect in raising the plane of general intelligence among the private members of their denomination.

Says Benedict in his history of the Baptists of that day in Virginia: "Their preachers were without learning, without patronage, generally very poor, plain in their dress, unrefined in their manners, and awkward in their address." Dr. Foote, when writing of the same period in his sketches of Virginia (p. 375) says: Though generally without education, "the zealous Baptist ministers, with all the energy of excited spirits inflamed by their contemplation of divine truth and visions of the spiritual world," preached and labored, and by their fervid exhortations, multitudes were brought to believe and be saved. Dr. Robert Baird, in his *"Religion in America,"* makes a similar statement, both as to their education and their zeal. The ministers of this denomination, especially in the earlier portion of the eighteenth century, suffered more in Virginia from harsh treatment than the other preachers. Their comparative lack of education may have been the occasion of their being treated so contemptuously by the establishment and the civil authorities. Oftentimes, when imprisoned for proclaiming the Gospel in their way, they preached to the sympathizing people from the grated windows of the jails in which they were confined. Let their unflinching Christian zeal and self-denial be honored and emulated!

Severe Conflicts—The Act of Toleration.—Previous to the time of which we write occurred many struggles between the dissenters and the civil authorities, because of the intolerance of the latter. These controversies continued for more than a third of a century, and, by eliciting discussion, prepared the minds of intelligent people for the grand result—the separation of Church and State. In Hanover County—"the birthplace of Presbyterianism in

Eastern Virginia"—were several churches of that denomination, and here labored and preached the celebrated Samuel Davies. (See XV.) His ministrations were interfered with by the Governor and Council, they being urged on by the clergy of the establishment. On one occasion the matter came before the General Court, when Davies argued with great force and eloquence in opposition to Peyton Randolph, the king's attorney. Davies contended that the English "Act of Toleration" applied to the relief of dissenters in Virginia as well as to the same class in England. He won, by his eloquence and learned arguments in favor of religious freedom, the admiration of the better portion of his opponents, who complimented him by saying he "was a good lawyer spoiled." The Presbyterian ministers in Virginia, as well as elsewhere, were careful to conform to the requirements of the Toleration Act, in obtaining licenses before they began to preach. It is worthy of note that not one charge, in this respect, of improper conduct on the part of their ministers was ever even intimated against them by their bitterest enemies—the clergy and vestrymen of the established church. The Presbyterians determined to test the question further, and when Davies afterward went to England to solicit funds for Princeton College they authorized him to bring the case before the King in Council. He did so, and obtained the decision that the Act of Toleration did apply to the colony of Virginia (1748). In consequence of this decision, the General Court of the colony permitted the Presbyterians to establish three new places for preaching. These church buildings were twelve or fifteen miles apart. Under the circumstances this concession was an immense gain, and it was obtained by the perseverance and learning of the ministers belonging to the Hanover Presbytery. The other denominations—Baptists and Quakers—were deeply interested and did all they could to promote the cause of religious toleration by petitions, but the Presbyterians had the boldness to demand religious freedom as a *natural right*, and to argue the question before the civil courts, or with the legislature, and, after a long struggle, secured the ultimate result in the separation of Church and State. This was the legitimate effect of their being able to enforce their own arguments and refute those of their opponents.

Efforts to Reform Clerical Morals.—In no country where the union of Church and State existed, did the civil authorities ever appear to have clear conceptions of that religious liberty which arises from the spiritual condition of man. The magistrates, from their official acts, seem to have had only a dim perception of that all-important qualification of a preacher of the gospel—a change of heart, or to be a Christian. It is not unreasonable to suppose the main cause of this has been that they, themselves, for the greater part, were, individually, strangers to spiritual religion. No matter how pure in their private life, and evangelical in doctrine preachers were, these essential qualifications were oftentimes unrecognized by the secular rulers in appointing them to parishes. The prevalence of these deficiencies was one of the objections alleged against the clergy of the established church in Virginia at a much earlier period than that of which we write. Sir William Berkeley—that staunch churchman—complained, nearly a century before the final struggle began, when writing of the clergy, that "as of all commodities so of this—the worst are sent us—and we have few that we can boast of." The legislature of Virginia found it necessary to prescribe by law certain *negative* qualifications of a minister of the established church. "He was not to give himself to excess in drinking or riot, and spending his time idly by day or night; but to hear or read the Holy Scriptures, catechise the children and visit the sick." A writer states that "many clergymen of profligate lives had found a home in these unfortunate colonies, and found impunity in crime from the want of a power able to correct them." These evils were so glaring, that it was assumed that those sent to the colonies as clergymen were not exemplary Christians, and the evil was not limited to Virginia, as it was enjoined that "on the arrival of any ship in the waters of Maryland, the nearest clergyman [of the church] was to make inquiry whether any minister was on board, and, if so, what his demeanor had been upon the voyage." The clergy themselves complain (1755) that "so few from the two Universities (Oxford and Cambridge) came to the colony," and that "so many who are a disgrace to the ministry find opportunities to fill parishes" (*Dr. Hawks, Vol. I., p. 117, and Vol. II., pp. 80-101*). At a still later day it was charged that "these gentlemen clergy spent much of their time fox-hunting and aping the sports of the aristocracy at home, and in company with the more dissolute of their parishioners." Says Bishop Meade (*Vol. I., p. 10*): "It is a well-established fact, that some who were discarded from the English church yet obtained livings in Virginia." As these ministers were appointed by the civil government, their theological education and their moral worth were not scrutinized as they should have been. These deficiencies had much influence in forming a sentiment by no means favorable to the clergy of the establishment in the minds of the truly religious, not only among "dissenters," but among the same class of churchmen themselves; and a tacit protest existed against a system that permitted men of such character to enter upon the sacred office. It must not be inferred from these statements that there were no excellent Christian men in the establishment, who labored faithfully in their parochial duties; especially could this be said of the native-born.

It has been charged that on the part of the "dissenters" there was an unwarranted hostility toward the establishment. The Presbyterians found no fault with the doctrines of the Church of England as set forth in her Articles, nor did they with her mode of worship or government, as her own members preferred. They demanded for themselves the same religious privileges that they were willing to concede to other denominations, but they denied most emphatically the right of a legislature to interfere, in any manner whatever, with "the spiritual concerns of religion." Said the Rev. Samuel Davies: "Had the doctrines of the Gospel been solemnly and faithfully preached in the established church, I am persuaded there would have been few 'dissenters' in these parts of Virginia, for their first (main) objections were not against her peculiar rites and ceremonies, and much less against her excellent Articles."

Preachers Appointed by the Crown.—It was a grievance of which intelligent Christian churchmen themselves complained, that their preachers were appointed by the Crown without reference to the wishes of the people of the parish. In Virginia and Maryland the vestries might present or recommend a preacher who had not been thus appointed, but even then the governor had the *absolute* right of inducting or putting him in actual possession. Under the more liberal system of the union of Church and State in Massachusetts and Connecticut, the churches were built where needed and the money raised from the whole people of the town or district, who voted the amount and taxed themselves to pay it. The minister was chosen by the members of the church, and in consequence he was acceptable to the majority, and, if not, he could be changed for another; but, as a general rule, he remained for life or during a long pastorate. This was quite in contrast with the arbitrary system that obtained in Virginia and Maryland.

The English Church Established — When? — The Church of England was established in Maryland by the act of King William in 1692, and in North Carolina fifteen years later; the population being composed of "Presbyterians, Independents, Quakers, and other evil-disposed persons." This, it was said, was accomplished by a legislature illegally chosen. The taxes imposed in consequence roused a bitter feeling in the minds of the "dissenters," who by the same legislature were deprived of many of their civil rights; the latter were not recovered until the close of the Revolution. The same church was established in South Carolina in 1704 by a majority of one vote in the legislature, while two-thirds of the population were "dissenters." Meanwhile it had been established in the colony of New York (1693), and was supported by taxes from all the people in proportion to their wealth, though seven-tenths of them were not in sympathy with the favored denomination. In New Jersey special favor was asked for the Church of England, but was never fully granted, and in this anomalous condition it remained till the Revolution. There was never any union of Church and State in Pennsylvania. This freedom from annoyance may account somewhat for the rapid progress made in the growth of Presbyterianism in these two colonies.

Influence of an Educated Ministry.—The comparatively superior education of the Presbyterian ministers gave them a commanding influence in New Jersey and Pennsylvania as well as in Virginia and in the Carolinas. Their zeal and name were identified with the movements leading to more religious freedom, particularly during the period from the close of the French war (1763) till the commencement of the Revolution. For years they had been ardently inculcating these principles in the back counties of Virginia and North Carolina, and, in the end, prepared the minds of their hearers to issue the famed Mecklenburg Declaration (May 11, 1775). In the convention which issued it were several Presbyterian ministers and elders. This influence had already been recognized in England, and the threat was often made by the "church party" that "bishops should be settled in America in spite of all the Presbyterian opposition." The objections of the latter, as often explained, were not against bishops in their spiritual character, but in the temporal power inherent in an established church, as then existing in England and Virginia and the Carolinas. They believed that civil and religious liberty should go hand in hand, but saw the reverse of this in "Lords spiritual" being supported to a great extent by the hard earnings of those who did not sympathize with the ritual and doctrines of the established church.

Conflicts in Respect to Salaries.—During this period there were frequent contentions between the Virginia assembly and the clergy of the establishment in respect to the latter's salaries and their payment. This unseemly contest alienated more or less the public sympathy from the latter. A law of Maryland demanded a poll-tax of "forty pounds of tobaccc" for the benefit of the clergy, but did not specify the quality of the article in which it was to be paid. Many of the planters manifested their view of the justice of the law by furnishing the full weight, but of a villainous quality of tobacco. One of these contests in Virginia was the famous "Parson's case," 1763, in which Patrick Henry performed a part so important.

A Great Principle Established.—In the earlier colonial days the "dissenters" contented themselves with protesting against the infringement of their rights as citizens and the burdens imposed upon them in the form of tithes or taxes by the colonial authorities, oftentimes, as they believed, at the instigation of the clergy of the established church. The Presbyterians, Baptists, and Quakers all chafed under this tyranny, that compelled them to aid in supporting a church whose system they did not approve. These annoyances—many of them by no means petty—led finally to one of the most interesting episodes in our history; the struggle to separate Church and State in Virginia. This contest really lasted about twelve years, from 1773 to 1786, covering more than the entire period of the war of the Revolution, and within two years of the adoption of the constitution of the United States. Owing to the stirring times of which it was contemporary, this remarkable movement has been overshadowed and has not received the attention which its importance deserves. *To establish the principle of supporting the gospel by the voluntary contributions cf its own friends, was as unique in sustaining the church as two years afterward was the anomaly in history of founding a republic composed of States independent in the administration of their own affairs, and yet under a united national government. In each case it was the application of great principles, and both have been equally successful.*

XX.

SEPARATION OF CHURCH AND STATE CONTINUED.

The Struggle Begins—The Memorial.—This contest assumed tangible form in October, 1776, though three years before the Presbytery of Hanover began the agitation in respect to church privileges or religious rights by appointing commissioners to lay the matter before the Virginia Assembly, but "nothing was done in the assembly that year to remedy the disabilities of 'dissenters.'" The commissioners took action on the subject during the two following years, but with a similar result. The Presbyterians were thus the first in taking measures to secure the separation of Church and State, nor did they desist till the end was accomplished twelve years afterward.

When the Declaration of Independence was made, the ground was changed, and, at the first meeting of the Presbytery of Hanover—which was organized in 1755— after July 4, 1776, that body memorialized the legislature or House of Assembly to dissolve the union of Church and State, and thus leave the support of the gospel to its own friends. This memorial discussed the principles on which they demanded the separation. Their arguments were not successfully controverted, and their cogency in the end compelled the assembly to comply with the demand. The memorial showed that such union conflicted with the Declaration of Rights, on which, as the Magna Charta of the commonwealth, all the privileges and rights of the people, both civil and religious, depend; that in the frontier counties in the valley of the Shenandoah, in which region were very few Episcopalians to aid in bearing the expense, those not in communion with the establishment were compelled by law to bear heavy burdens in building church edifices and rectories, purchasing glebes, and in supporting the established clergy. As *all* the colonists were now engaged in a contest with the mother country on account of infringements of their rights, it was inconsistent that *all* the people should not be protected in the freedom of conscience. They expected their representatives in the house of assembly to remove every species of religious and civil bondage. They argued that this oppression retarded immigration to Virginia, and also the progress of the arts and sciences of the State and of its manufactures. In proof of this statement they instanced the rapid growth and improvement of the Northern colonies compared with Virginia, and at the same time directing the attention of the assembly to the many advantages of soil and climate of the latter, yet men refused to migrate to a colony where they could not enjoy the rights of conscience.

They argued that the gospel asked the support of only its own adherents, and did not in that respect need the secular aid; that Christianity would prevail and flourish by its own merits under an all-prevailing Providence. They did not ask ecclesiastical establishments for themselves, nor did they think them desirable for others, as such must of necessity be partial, and in the main injurious to the people at large. They demanded that every law that countenanced religious domination should be immediately repealed; that every religious sect should be protected in the full exercise of its mode of worship; that all invidious distinctions in respect to religious denominations should be abolished, and every person be free to support any one he chose by his voluntary gifts. Such were the sentiments the Presbytery of Hanover advanced on the subject of religious freedom; their arguments cover the whole ground, enunciating the principles held and practiced to-day as truisms throughout the Union.

Committee on Religion and Morality.—With other petitions on the subject, this memorial was referred to a committee on religion and morality; of this committee Thomas Jefferson was chairman. As evidence of the difficulties with which the memorialists had to contend, and how little the members of that assembly appreciated their true relation to the preachers of the gospel, may be cited the following resolution passed November 19, 1776, "That provision should be made for the continuing the succession of the clergy [of the establishment] and for superintending their conduct" (*Randall's "Life of Jefferson," Vol. I., p. 205*). This resolution, designed to forestall or control action on the subject, was passed after the petitions and memorial had been received and referred by the assembly to the committee, and on which the latter had not yet reported.

The Petitions—The Demand as a Right.—The year before (1775) the Baptists petitioned the assembly, "That they might be allowed to worship God in their own way without interruption; to maintain their own ministers separate from others, and to be married and buried without paying the clergy of other denominations"—meaning of the establishment (*Dr. Baird, p. 219*). The Quakers also petitioned to the same effect. The Presbyterians took higher ground; that it was their *right* to do this. They did not ask for a similar permission, but, on the contrary, demanded that *an end be put to the assumption of any such authority in the legislature by dissolving the union of Church and State*. The struggle did not soon end. The Episcopalians presented counter-memorials and so did the Methodists, who in that day deemed themselves in a measure allied to the Church of England, and

were known as the Wesleyan connection. When the
Revolutionary contest began great numbers of the Church
of England clergymen, who had come from England,
went back to that country and left their parishes vacant.
These parishes in large numbers were filled by Methodist
ministers; the latter falling heir in a measure to the
emoluments of the parishes. The Methodists maintained
that the State violated its pledges given in the early days
of the colony to the established church, and that its claims
were in the form of a vested right. In truth they never
were "dissenters;" on the contrary, their sympathies and
church interests were with the establishment; while their
ministers in Virginia, during this struggle, were for the
most part Englishmen. These were sent first (about
1770) by the London conference, America being constituted on that occasion as the *fiftieth* circuit. (*Dr. Stevens' "Hist. of Methodism," Vol. I., p. 442.*)

Upon Whom Fell the Burden of the Conflict.—The
brunt of this conflict fell upon the ministers and laymen of
the Presbyterian Church. As preachers and exhorters the
Baptists were very successful, but it required better-
educated men to cope with the lawyers and statesmen in
the Virginia assembly, and to repel the arguments for the
continuance of the union of Church and State. "The Baptists," says Dr. Hawks, "though not to be outdone in
zeal, were far surpassed in ability by the Presbyterians.
The latter's ablest memorials came from the Presbytery
of Hanover" (*Vol. I., p. 140*). To sustain their views the
church advocates pointed to the history of such union as
existing from Constantine onward, while the prospective
good effects of a separation were at best only a con-
jecture, as the experiment had never been tried, while the
arguments in respect to the injurious moral influence of
appointing improper men rectors of parishes, had but little
influence with the legislature.

The attempt to support the ordinances of the gospel by voluntary contributions of its own well-wishers, appeared to the members of the assembly visionary in the extreme, especially as the "dissenters" in comparison were poor indeed. The wealthy land and slaveholders belonged almost entirely to the established church, and from this class a large majority of the members of the legislature were chosen. "The establishment," says Jefferson, "was truly of the religion of the rich, the dissenting sects being entirely composed of the less wealthy people." And again, "Although two-thirds of our citizens were "dissenters," a majority of the legislature were churchmen." "Among these, however, were some reasonable and liberal men, who enabled us on some points to obtain feeble majorities." "A majority of the inhabitants were obliged by law to pay contributions to support the pastors of the minority. This unrighteous compulsion was grievously felt during the royal government when there was no hope for relief."

The Legislature Met on Its Own Ground.—The advocates of the system in the assembly were met on their own ground by Presbyterian clergymen, who, by their superior knowledge of the subject in all its bearings, won their cause, and the influence of that example banished the system of the union of Church and State from the land. One of the positions honestly taken by good men, was that injury would be done the cause of religion; they assumed that unless aided by the State the church would languish and fail because of insufficient support. On the contrary, the opponents of the system argued that the true friends of a pure gospel would, as a matter of duty, support the church; and moreover, there would not be so much inducement for those who were not governed by the genuine principles of religion to connect themselves with the church—this would be a great gain. The arguments for the continuance of the system had greater weight then than they would have to-day, since the results of voluntary contributions for the support of the gospel and its ordinances have proved their fallacy; as well as the remarkable development of the principle of *personal responsibility* in its influence upon individual Christians in making them more benevolent and more zealous in aiding the cause of religion. This principle now pervades the minds of American Christians to an extent impossible under a system of the union of Church and State, where the responsibility of supporting the gospel is shared between its friends and the world at large, or State.

Objectionable Laws Partially Repealed.—On the 5th of of December, 1776, an act was passed by the assembly which repealed the laws making it an offence to hold any particular religious opinions, and also removing the penalties inflicted upon those who did not attend the service of the established church or worshiped elsewhere. This act, though imperfect, in some respects, virtually dissolved the union between Church and State, by repealing all former laws relating to that union; it also exempted "dissenters" from contributing to the support of that church, but left the latter in possession of all the wealth it had acquired by taxation in the past—this wealth consisted mostly in glebes, parsonages, and church edifices.

The following is the text of the bill: *"We the general assembly do enact:* That no man shall be compelled to frequent or support any religious worship, place, or ministry whatsoever, nor shall be enforced, restrained, molested, or burthened in his body or goods, nor shall otherwise suffer on account of his religious opinions or belief; but that all men shall be free to profess, and by argument to maintain, their opinions in matters of religion, and that the same shall in no wise diminish, enlarge, or affect their civil capacities."

In relation to minor points the contest continued, and the bill for the separation did not go fully into effect till ten years afterward (1786); Jefferson was a member of the assembly in 1776, and chairman of the committee when this partial repeal was made. During the two years following many memorials or petitions were presented by both parties to the assembly; some of these asked for a general assessment or tax for the benefit of all denominations, and some in opposition; while other petitioners stepped back a century and asked that the "sectaries" be prohibited from holding meetings, and none but "licensed preachers" (meaning of the establishment) be permitted to conduct public worship.

Prejudices Roused—Tories—Whigs—Quakers.—After the commencement of the war of the Revolution a strong prejudice was roused against the established clergy, as the great majority of them were ardent loyalists, or "Tories;" the Presbyterians and Baptists were even more ardently "Whigs"—their ministers preached with great zeal the doctrine of resistance to tyrants. The Quakers were, for the greater part, from principle opposed to war in any form, and thus they were often misjudged as to their motives. Under the circumstances, which we of to-day cannot fully appreciate, it was not strange that so many of the clergy were Tories; the traditions of that church were in favor of royalty, and, moreover, a large majority were Englishmen by birth. Unfortunately they influenced their parishioners almost as much in favor of royalty as the dissenting pastors did their flocks in favor of liberty.

The General Assessment—Another Memorial.—The advocates for the union of Church and State did not relax their efforts to retain the secular advantages which the establishment had already, but earnestly contended to secure emoluments, however small. First the attempt was made to have a general assessment of taxes to support all the denominations alike. The Baptists and Quakers as well as the Presbyterians opposed this system; the latter especially, on the ground that aid for the gospel in that form was *injurious* to spiritual religion. Accordingly the Presbytery of Hanover came forward with another of their well-reasoned memorials (1778); and after courteously thanking the assembly for what they had done in repealing some of the offensive and illiberal laws, they proceeded to oppose the "plan of a general assessment." They argued that the only proper object of civil government was to promote the happiness of the people by protecting them as citizens in their rights; to restrain the vicious by wholesome laws and encourage the virtuous by the same means; that the obligations which men owe their Creator are not a proper subject of human legislation, and the worship of God according to the dictates of conscience was an inalienable right. "Neither does the Church of Christ stand in need of a *general assessment* for its support; and most certain we are persuaded that it would be no advantage, but an injury to the society to which we belong; and we believe that Christ has ordained a complete system of laws for the government of His Kingdom, so we are persuaded that by His providence He will support its final consummation." This memorial was also seconded by the urgent protests of the Baptists; the result was that the following year the proposed plan of general assessment was abandoned for the time being. We, to-day, take for granted the principles here enunciated, they having been so thoroughly discussed, while experience has as clearly proved their soundness and utility. These Christian men were fully convinced that the effect of the union of Church and State was, for many reasons, injurious to spiritual religion. Many of these legislators, though they talked so learnedly, were unable to appreciate the question in its spiritual bearings, and for that reason alone the authors of these memorials never urged the arguments derived from this phase of the subject, but judiciously waived them, although they were so convincing to themselves, and to the church members whom they represented.

Defects in the Act of Repeal.—It was only in general terms that the law of December, 1776, dissolved the union of Church and State, and the clergy of the former "still retained the glebes—the lands belonging to the parishes—and also claimed the right of performing marriage ceremonies with the accustomed fees." Therefore the assembly found it necessary (1780) to enact: "That it shall and may be lawful for any minister of any society or congregation of Christians to celebrate the rites of matrimony, and such marriage, as well as those hereafter celebrated by dissenting ministers, shall be and are hereby declared good and valid in law." Yet under this law the Episcopal clergy were, *ex officio,* authorized to celebrate marriages throughout the State, while the ministers of other denominations had to obtain a *license,* and in addition, were limited to certain districts or counties. In answer to this insulting legislation, the Presbytery of Hanover came forward with a carefully prepared argument covering the whole ground of controversy, in which the wrong of the law in relation to performing the rites of matrimony was thoroughly discussed and shown. In due time the law was so modified as to be virtually repealed.

Security of Religious Rights Demanded.—The Presbytery also complained that "the security or religious rights was left to the precarious fate of common law, instead of *being made a fundamental part of our constitution as it ought to be."* They likewise complained that the Episcopal Church was the only one incorporated and could hold property, while all other denominations "were obliged to trust to the precarious fidelity of trustees chosen for the purpose," and they, asking nothing for themselves, demanded that these inequalities in the treatment of Christian denominations should be removed. The assembly continued from year to year to suspend *Church levies;* this policy necessitated continual watchfulness on the part of the "dissenters," till in the latter part of 1779 these levies were abolished; but this action was not acquiesced in sincerely, for after the return of peace the Virginia Assembly again attempted legislation (1784) on the subject; the intention now being to incorporate "all societies of the Christian religion, which may apply for the same." The reason for this apparent liberality cropped out when to the bill was added an amendment authorizing a *general assessment* "to establish a provision for the teachers of the Christian religion." The Hanover Presbytery took measures to oppose this renewal of that project; but meanwhile, though secretly, its friends had been so active that it was apprehended it would pass in spite of all their efforts in opposition. The question was now in a new form, and in it was a temptation. As all would receive aid from the public funds, and the experiment of voluntary support might possibly result in failure, it was not strange that a few Presbyterian ministers for a time wavered, but in the end they came back with still greater force to their former convictions of the truth, that the ordinances of the gospel ought to be supported as a matter of Christian duty by its own adherents, who should in this action be free and untrammeled by any secular or legislative influence whatever.

Protest against Incorporating the Episcopal Church. —Consistent with the original movement was another. A bill was brought forward in the assembly to incorporate the "Protestant Episcopal Church"—the name assumed after the close of the Revolution. This measure was designed to secure to that church the absolute ownership of all the glebe-lands and the buildings thereon erected—all obtained at the public expense by taxation. The persistent Presbytery of Hanover appeared again before the legislature in opposition to this revived measure with its still more objectionable features. The celebrated Dr. John Blair Smith, who at one time was inclined to favor the "general assessment," was heard at the bar of the house in an exhaustive argument in opposition to the enactment of the bill. He continued his address for three days; in which the whole subject was so thoroughly discussed and the evil effects of the proposed law were so clearly pointed out that the scheme was abandoned forever.

The General Assessment Again.—The presbytery took high ground, saying: "We hope that no attempt will be made to point out articles of faith, or to settle modes of worship, or to interfere in the internal government of religious communities, *or to render the ministers of religion independent of the will of the people whom they serve.*" Again, that body protested (August, 1785) against "the incorporation of the Protestant Episcopal Church," so far as to secure to that church "properties procured at the expense of the whole community." The truth is, that in this controversy, lasting for nine years, the assembly having a majority of its members churchmen, did not keep faith with their opponents outside that denomination. From their point of view they thought the ordinances of the gospel would be unsupported and Christianity crippled in its influence. They had never fully realized as individuals their *personal responsibility* in the duty of supporting the gospel, as the "dissenters" had done during the many years in which the latter, as a matter of conscience, sustained their own ministers and the ordinances of the gospel, while at the same time, paying, in the form of arbitrary taxes, their share in supporting a church establishment, whose ritual and form of government they deemed "unscriptural." It is strange that the self-respect and Christian manhood of the churchmen of that day did not induce them to decline receiving money thus wrung from their neighbors, whom they were pleased to characterize as "dissenters." Some of the best minds among the Virginia statesmen were in favor of the "general assessment," such as Patrick Henry, who thought an assessment "should be made for some form of worship or other"; Edmund Pendleton—"an honest man, but zealous churchman," whom Jefferson characterized as, "taken all in all, the ablest man in debate he had ever met," and Richard Henry Lee, who wrote that "avarice is accomplishing the destruction of religion for want of a legal obligation to contribute something to its support," and even George Washington wrote to George Mason (1785), "that he was not much alarmed at the thought of making people pay toward the support of that which they profess." On the other hand, the assessment was opposed by James Madison and George Mason (the intimate friend of Washington), and others—Jefferson being abroad at that time as minister to France. In 1799 all laws made for the benefit of religious societies were repealed, and in 1801 "the '*glebes*,' as soon as vacated by existing incumbents, were ordered to be sold by the overseers of the poor."

The Effects of Petitions and Arguments.—We would not detract one iota from the merit of the Baptists and the Quakers in this struggle, but from the nature of the case—as they presented only petitions and protests—their efforts were not as influential as the Presbyterians, who, from their position on a higher plane of education, both ministers and laity were able to meet their opponents in open debate or by written arguments well put; thus they became the controlling force in bringing about the reform.

Rev. John Holt Rice, D. D.
(257, 258, 323, 394.)

The latter never wavered in their determination to secure the desired end, but, amid discouragements and false faith, they calmly persevered in refuting the arguments of their opponents, and, in the end, winning to their sentiments the more enlightened and liberal-minded churchmen, not only in the assembly, but in the State.

Contest in Respect to the Glebes.—The question of the glebes, which grew out of the repealing act, was also strongly contested, and deserves a passing notice. It was argued that the glebes should be retained by the Episcopal Church, as some of the funds applied in their purchase had been donations. On the other hand, it was contended that the glebes and parsonages were public property, bought almost entirely by funds raised by unjust taxation—the donations being a very small portion of the whole amount. Moreover, the established church had had, up to that time, the exclusive use of the funds thus raised, the advantages of which use far overbalanced the loss of these limited donations, even if they could be separated from the common fund; and in addition it retained its church buildings, though erected by means of moneys derived from taxes imposed upon the whole community. It was suggested that the churchmen were mostly wealthy land and slaveholders, and it was much easier for them, by voluntary contributions, to sustain their own church than for the other denominations of Christians.

On the subject of selling the glebes for the benefit of the whole people, the Baptists were more strenuous than any of the other "dissenters." Says Dr. Hawks: "There was a bitterness of hatred in this denomination (Baptist) toward the establishment, which far surpassed that of all other religious communities in the colony; and it was always prompt to avail itself of every prejudice which religious or political zeal could excite against the church." (*Vol. I., p. 121.*) One reason of this hostile feeling may have been that the Baptists had been persecuted more than the other denominations, and in more degrading forms. The remembrance of these outrages came down from generation to generation, and roused a feeling that was closely allied to righteous indignation. The Presbyterians appear to have viewed the dissolving of the union of Church and State as the all-important question at issue, and when that was accomplished they looked upon that of church property as secondary. In accordance with this general sentiment of rejecting secular aid in any form, the Presbytery of Hanover refused incorporation for their denomination, as had been granted the Episcopal Church, on the ground that it was contrary to their views of propriety, and, from principle, they declined any advantage to be thus obtained. The assembly reconsidered its action, and finally (1787) repealed the law incorporating the Episcopal Church.

A Half Century of Intolerance Remembered.—The Presbyterians also remembered that their church members and ministers had labored for more than a half century under disabilities caused by the intolerance more or less instigated by the Church of England; that in the colony of New York ministers of their denomination had been imprisoned and otherwise maltreated. Notably was this the case of Rev. Francis Makemie, who, when on a visit to that colony from Maryland, was sent to jail by the Governor—Lord Cornbury—because he dared preach in a private house when every hall or church building had been denied him by the same authority; that at the instigation of the "rector and church wardens of Trinity Church," they were not permitted to have a "charter of incorporation for their then only church building, but were compelled to resort to the General Assembly of the Church of Scotland (1730), in whose name as legal trustees the building and land belonging to "the First Presbyterian

Church" was held till the Revolution changed the order of things. They had met the same hostile feeling in Virginia, and in a still more repugnant form. Yet in the famous memorial presented by the Presbytery of Hanover to the Virginia Assembly (October, 1776), and in the many which followed, no bitterness was expressed, but, on the contrary, reasoning on the injurious effects of the union of Church and State, on religious freedom, on the spread of the gospel and its pure and holy influence on the minds of the people.

An Apology Urged.—It is often urged by way of apology that these intolerant proceedings were characteristic of the times; but why were not churchmen as liberal as the "dissenters?" The latter did not interfere with the Church of England in its ordinances; they never were the aggressors; but, as best they could, only defended themselves from the assaults of the former. The truth is, this self-complacent age, though thus apologizing, is scarcely justifiable in assuming to be perfect examples of tolerance in respect to non-essentials in religious matters, when we take into consideration the higher plane on which all denominations of Christians are presumed to stand at the present time in respect to religious freedom. Is not the spirit which to-day manifests itself, sometimes even in evangelical denominations, of virtually *unchurching* those who do not use the same mode as themselves in the rite of baptism, or in ordaining preachers of the word, as *intolerant* in proportion to the light they are presumed to have on the subject of religious liberty, as those who figured so ignobly more than one hundred years ago?

When a Baptist pastor or a rector refuses to give members in good and regular standing in his own church a certificate to that effect, if such members wish to change their church relations to one that is evangelical, but not of the Baptist or Episcopal order, is it strange, if the question arises, wherein does such refusal differ in *spirit* from the instances of intolerance recorded in this narrative?

Who Began the Movement and Secured the Result?—Justice and the truth of history demand that the services of those who accomplished this important result—the separation of Church and State in Virginia—should be recognized. If the statements of certain authors are implicitly received, the inference would be, that Thomas Jefferson originated the measure and carried it to a successful issue. In proof of this theory, they cite the bill he drew up to secure religious freedom, which, as chairman of the committee, he introduced into the legislature. This measure was not brought before the assembly until some weeks after the first memorial of the Presbytery of Hanover was presented to that body, and referred to a special committee (October 11, 1776), "to take into consideration all matters and things relating to religion and morals." Of this committee Jefferson was appointed chairman, and in that capacity he drew up the bill and presented it to the House. There is no historical evidence that he would of his own motion have introduced a bill of that purport, had not petitions and the memorial furnished him an occasion. This memorial was the first to intimate the necessity for the separation of Church and State. The arguments which it contained covered the whole ground of religious freedom; discussing the questions in a manner lucid and terse, leaving nothing more to be added. There is not an idea in Jefferson's preamble and bill that is not expressed or clearly implied in the memorial; the latter is concise and to the point; the former is clothed in easy, flowing terms of generalities; a sort of *theoretical style*—if the term is admissible; a characteristic of the author's manner in treating similar subjects. The *preamble* consists of one sentence, containing fifty-two lines of small print, on an octavo page.

The Presbyterians leading, the "dissenters" were the first in that colony or State to move in this reform; Jefferson joined them, not they him. It is well known, however, that he held liberal, and now deemed correct, views on the general subject of free thought and its free expression, and that the presentation of the memorial gave him an opportunity of which he availed himself to express his sentiments. There is no evidence that he debated the question in the assembly; his influence was exerted privately and by writing. In 1784 he went to France on public business, and the bill which bears his name, when modified by amendments, was passed in 1786—after the lapse of ten years; thus going into full effect through the exertions of George Mason and James Madison, especially the latter, who was an accomplished debater and writer.

During the ten years mentioned the advocates of the union of Church and State in the assembly changed their tactics almost every session, and under different forms sought to gain advantage, however small. These various phases of the contest were counteracted by the persistent efforts of the Presbytery of Hanover. Jefferson, in his *Notes on Virginia,* as quoted by Randall (*Vol. I., p. 204*), charged the Presbyterians with intolerance toward other denominations in the Northern colonies. He made the inexcusable mistake for a man of his position of confounding the Congregationalists with the Presbyterians. He cites no authority for the charge, but he ought to have known that the latter were, and had been, consistent advocates for all to enjoy the same religious freedom which they *demanded* for themselves; and this right, they argued, was derived from a higher authority than that of the civil magistrate. This vital idea was in the first memorial they presented to the assembly, and, moreover, he ought to have borne in mind that even if the Presbyterians wished they had no opportunity to practise intolerance, as they stood aloof—*never desired and never had any control in the civil government of the colonies*. Jefferson, afterward, expressed his gratification that: "All beliefs, whether Christian or Infidel, Jew or Mohammedan, were put on an equality." It does not follow from this statement, as has been charged, that Jefferson held that one system of belief was as worthy of respect as another, but rather that he had in his mind the abstract theory of thought and its free expression.

Religious Freedom and Patriotism.—The Presbyterian Church has ever been on the side of religious freedom and against intolerance. Throughout her entire history, and in all her records, "there is not an act on this great subject that received her sanction, for which she need offer an apology." They were equally as explicit in regard to their patriotism. The synod, their highest court at that time, when in session in Philadelphia, in May, 1775, as patriots declared: "That they did not wish to conceal their sentiments, either as ministers or citizens." Looking forward to a conflict of arms, they say: "That man will fight most bravely who never fights till it is necessary, and who ceases to fight as soon as the necessity is over." This was the position taken and maintained by them throughout the Revolutionary struggle.

Influence of the Measure in New England.—It is interesting to note that the separation of Church and State in Virginia was not without influence, as within a few years afterward, similar results were produced in New York, Maryland and the Carolinas, wherein the Church of England had been established in colonial times. The legislatures of these States dissolved the connection expressly by law, but in New England, where the system was not so arbitrary and unjust, it lingered on an average for forty years longer—Connecticut adopted the voluntary system in 1818 and Massachusetts in 1834.

The adoption of the Church and State system in New England seemed due to the influence of the union with the State of the Independent or Congregational Church in Old England, under the domination of Cromwell. The Congregational Church being in numbers the leading denomination in the colony of Massachusetts, though hitherto self-supporting, was induced to fall into line with the Cromwell theory. It is strange, however, that after we became a nation, the leading minds in both State and Church in that section did not sooner recognize the incongruity of the system with the Constitution of the United States, which repudiates the union of Church and State.

An additional influence with adequate power was needed to change this relation of the Church to the State; that force was in the revivals that pervaded the country (*p. 224*) from A.D. 1800 forward for quite a number of years. "These widespread revivals * * * saved the Church of Christ in America from its low estate and girded it for stupendous tasks that were about to be developed on it. In the glow of this renewed fervor, the churches of New England successfully made the difficult transition from establishment to self-support and to the costly enterprises of aggressive evangelization, into which, in company with other churches to the south and west, they were about to enter." (*Am. Christianity, pp. 244-5.*)

Personal Responsibility Recognized and Strengthened.—An important element of influence—that of personal responsibility in relation to religious duties—was strengthened by this separation, as the church was thus thrown for its support entirely upon its individual members. From the time of Jonathan Edwards forward the *true position of the individual* in regard to personal religion became more fully understood, and the responsibility for the souls of those whom they governed, which we have seen assumed by the civil magistrate, was gradually shifted *from the latter to the individual.* Consistent with this view, evangelical denominations have demanded only one qualification, entitling a person to the privilege of the communion—that of being converted or a Christian. In addition, this sense of responsibility was still further strengthened and made practical when individual members, irrespective of the State, learned to sustain the ordinances of the Church of Christ, and labored to extend the blessings of the gospel; to this principle may be traced that remarkable spirit of benevolence, which, in various forms, has made our times, when compared with the past, the golden age of the world.

Self-Denial and Benevolence.—The "dissenters" in colonial times in their hard discipline acquired the grace of being benevolent. In their zeal for what they believed the truth, they made immense sacrifices; they paid their share not only in supporting a religious establishment with which they had no sympathy, but, in addition, sustained their own church ordinances—thus manifesting a self-denial, which, because of their exertions, American Christians, since that time, have had no occasion to practice. The churchmen of that day were strangers to such self-denial. They had never been in a school where it was taught; nor had they learned the truth of *each one's responsibility* in proportion to his means, to aid in supporting the gospel. In the broadness of liberal sentiments they were far behind the "dissenters," and it became a great blessing to the spirituality of that church when its entire support was thrown upon its own members.

Influence of the Voluntary Principle.—The voluntary principle, based as it is on individual responsibility, has since pervaded the churches of the whole Union, the beneficent effects of which are seen not only in the support of the gospel in all its special relations, and in aiding institutions of learning, but in originating and sustaining the benevolent operations of our day—greater in proportion than ever before—while the whole missionary enterprise in the land, foreign and domestic, may be attributed to the same principle. These "dissenters" were far advanced for the times in the great principles of religious freedom and Christian charity. To them the purity and the free preaching of the gospel was paramount to all other considerations. They held the doctrine, which obtains to-day among the Protestants of the Union, that the Church should not dominate the State, nor the State the Church, but that they should mutually sustain each other —the one by inculcating good morals and obedience to law, and the other by protecting the free preaching of the gospel and the practising of its principles.

A Nation's Moral Training.—It is proper in this history to notice certain events that had influence in moulding the moral character and inner life of the American colonists. After the great Revolution in England of 1688, in consequence of a limited advance made in the Toleration Act toward *genuine* religious liberty, the emigration from the British Isles to the American colonies began to diminish. The condition of the dissenters was made more endurable by that act, as it modified for the better the illiberal rule of the bishops of the Church of England. The act was presumed to apply also to the colonies. In accordance with that view, those Presbyterians who emigrated from the British Isles to America, from 1688 to 1765, did so not specially to avoid persecution, but rather to better their material interests, though no doubt they expected to enjoy more fully religious liberty. A partial exception was in the case of the Presbyterians in the north of Ireland, who suffered much from intolerance. During this period many thousands also came from the Continent of Europe.

After the revocation of the Edict of Nantes (1688) the

exiled Huguenots flocked to America even in larger numbers than ever and found homes in the different colonies, and were everywhere welcomed as worthy citizens. They brought with them their advanced and remarkable skill in the mechanical industries, while they also exerted a Christian influence. In those days they affiliated much with the Presbyterians, though in New York "some of their leading pastors accepted salaries from the 'Society for Propagation of the Gospel,' tendered to them on condition of their accepting the ordination and conforming to the ritual of the English Church."

Great numbers of Germans—Lutherans and German Reformed—began to come about 1684. The latter found homes mostly in Pennsylvania and were also welcomed as a religious, industrious, economical and exemplary people. A colony of nearly 5,000 Germans from the Palatinate settled in 1707 in the valley of the Mohawk; these were followed from time to time by emigrants from the same region; numbers of these, however, afterward migrated to Pennsylvania. They were all desirable citizens. Such were the classes of immigrants during these seventy-seven years. They were all Protestants and in their new homes adhered to their religious views and high-toned moral principles which they derived from their Bibles while cultivating the virtues of industry and frugality.

During this period of seventy-seven years the moral and religious principles of the members of these several denominations composing the colonists had an untrammeled opportunity to permeate the minds of all and freely develop throughout the land. An evidence of that fact is found in the stringent laws in respect to morality which were everywhere enforced. For illustration: the laws in relation to the observance of the Sabbath were as rigid in Virginia under the Cavaliers as they were in New England under the Puritans. That period was as much a training school in morals for the American colonists as were the *forty* years' sojournings of the Children of Israel in the wilderness. The latter were never so much imbued with religion as when at the end of that time they entered the land of Canaan; the same may be said of the American colonists when they entered upon the struggle for independence. The religious tone of the patriots during that contest was remarkable. Witness their trust in the care of the Lord of Hosts, whose aid in their cause they invoked most reverently. This sentiment pervaded the minds of the patriots in every grade of society and in every portion of the land, and manifested itself in the documents issued by their statesmen. These results were the legitimate outgrowth of the Puritan-Presbyterian, scriptural and moral principles which so much imbued the minds of the great majority of the colonists and which *germinal* principles, for three-fourths of a century, had thus an opportunity to develop untrammeled by outside influence. (*Chap. XXIV., Four Hundred Years, etc.*)

XXI.

The Troublous Times.

The prosperity of the church was great during this period of union (1758-1788), but troublous times with the mother country were impending, and when the synod seventeen years later met in Philadelphia on May 17, 1775, blood had already been shed, for just one month before, to a day, the conflicts at Concord and Lexington had taken place. The news had spread throughout the country, producing great excitement and anxiety in the popular mind.

Patriotism—The Pastoral Letter.—The synod, in addition to its ordinary cares and duties which it owed to the churches as such, also realized the dangers that the approaching contest would bring upon their country, and they made known their patriotic sentiments, and in no uncertain tone. They, it seems for the first time, addressed a pastoral letter to the members of the Presbyterian Church throughout the colonies. The spirit of this pastoral was such as to inculcate union among the colonies, and mutual charity and good-will among the different religious denominations, and the promotion of good morals and good government; reformation of manners, personal honesty and humanity on the part of those who might soon be called to the field, as a conflict of arms between the colonies and the mother country seemed inevitable. The synod ordered 500 copies of this pastoral letter to be printed at its own expense, and circulated throughout the churches, from whose pulpits it was read to many thousands. "The Presbyterian Church, by this act of its highest judicature, thus took its stand at Philadelphia by the side of the American (Continental) Congress then in session (in the same city) and its influence was felt in a most decisive manner throughout the bounds of the church."

The Evil Influence.—The Revolutionary War had a lamentably bad effect upon the spirituality of the denominations of Christians among the colonists, and perhaps upon none more than the Presbyterians. To a man they were patriots; their ministers were uniformly among the foremost in advocating the cause of civil as well as religious liberty, and oftentimes they took the lead. As far as we know, nearly all the ministers of the gospel who did not sympathize with the established church in the colonies were Whigs, while the great majority of the rectors of the Episcopal Church were Tories. During the war these incumbents in great numbers left the country and returned to their native England, as they had been appointed by the Bishop of London to livings in those colonies wherein the English church was established.

The political turmoil which so impaired the spiritual condition of the churches began in 1765, when the public mind was so deeply disturbed by the *Stamp Act*. As soon as that was repealed other measures, equally as obnoxious, were either adopted or threatened by parliament, and in consequence the political agitation among the colonists in the form of discussing these affairs was continuous until hostilities commenced. From that time forward the spirituality of the churches was greatly demoralized, in certain vicinities their congregations were scattered and their church buildings desecrated by the British soldierly.

During the entire war the Presbyterians were specially obnoxious to the officers of the British army. Their ministers were often hounded by the minions of the former, the Tories, while prices were set upon their heads by the British military authorities. The vast majority of private members of the Baptist, Congregationalist and Presbyterian churches were Whigs and labored and fought for their country, while the Quakers, because of their being from principle opposed to war in any respect, desired to be neutral, yet in their way they were in the main patriots. The private members of the English church wherever it was established, were nearly all Tories and owing to their church training were opposed to the extension of perfect religious freedom to the *dissenters,* as they contemptuously termed those who differed in their religious views from that church. This could be said of such private members in the States of Virginia, South Carolina and North Carolina. In New England, where Congregationalism and Presbyterianism prevailed, the Tories were comparatively few when compared with the patriots.

The Two Movements.—During the latter part of the hand-to-hand contest between the Virginia Assembly and the Presbytery of Hanover, another important movement was also in progress throughout the entire Presbyterian Church, the discussions in respect to which became more earnest immediately after the close of the Revolution and the signing of the treaty of peace. The question thus agitated was in relation to a plan of church polity that could be adapted to the new order of affairs, which had grown out of the separation from the mother country. These Presbyterian ministers and intelligent laymen took comprehensive views of the situation of their church, which was now free and untrammeled to extend its influence over a continent. It had already crossed the Alleghanies, and in two divisions—one in East Tennessee and Kentucky, the other in Western Pennsylvania—had taken position and founded churches as outposts on the eastern edge of the valley of the Mississippi.

Meanwhile another movement was in progress in respect to the civil or political relations of the States, in which the leading statesmen and intelligent, thinking minds took an absorbing interest. The political question was in what manner the thirteen States could be consolidated into one government, for they were now partially disintegrated, since the resistance to the common enemy, which had held them so long in union, had disappeared, when peace was concluded with England. The lengthy discussions of these questions of government, both in Church and State, no doubt elicited a sympathy that was reciprocal between the leading minds thus engaged; especially can this be said of those statesmen who were members of the churches of the several denominations, while in respect to civil affairs all were deeply interested.

Kinds of Church Governments.—The leading principles of the government of the Presbyterian Church in the United States—though modeled somewhat after that of the same church in Scotland—were from the first republican in form; that is, having the delegates to its judicatures chosen by the people or church members, in order that the former might be truly their representatives. This mode of government was so constituted that it could be adapted to a large or a small number of churches, and also to a large or small number of the members of each church. As a matter of history, it may be noted that the Presbyterian Church established this republican form of government (1705) long before the Declaration of Independence was made, and it has continued virtually unchanged in its application to the present hour. It is clearly seen that this church government is consistent in its principles with our republican institutions—both National and State—that were afterward established.

In contradistinction the mode of church government adopted by the Congregationalists and Baptists was democratic in the extreme, and limited to each church, while the churches themselves were virtually independent of one another in respect to any authorized mode of discipline, or of a uniform confession of faith or doctrine. In accordance with this theory of government, there could be no measures introduced which, in connection with church judicatures, could aid practically in bringing the members of their own churches throughout the entire country into doctrinal and religious sympathy with one another; instead, each church was so much isolated that its influence in consequence was greatly limited. Before the Revolution the Church of England in America was governed by that of the mother country, and almost without reference to the wishes of its church members. Its rectors being appointed by the Bishop of London, under whose jurisdiction the churches of the establishment in the American colonies were placed, and, in addition to this arrangement, the colonial governors had the absolute authority of inducting or not as they pleased these rectors into their sacred office.

The genius for systematic government seems, from the very first, to have imbued the minds of the ministers of the Presbyterian Church, as well as those of its intelligent laymen; the latter always being associated with the former in the exercise of such government. This method assures the individual members of the church that they themselves by means of their representatives—the elders—have a voice in the management of its affairs; such knowledge also enhances their own individual responsibility to aid in promoting the extension of the gospel through the medium of their own church, by means of their personal Christian character and their contributions.

A Comprehensive Church Government.—After the

close of the Revolution and when the States were in their respective governments independent of one another, it would seem the Continental Congress, nominally a legislative body over all, had little influence, as the laws it enacted rose only to the dignity of recommendations. The far-sighted ministers and laymen of the Presbyterian Church saw the necessity for a more comprehensive application of their system of government in order to promote unity of the church throughout the land; at the same time the leading statesmen of the now disintegrated States were devising for them a more compact union, and the formation of a general government in which all should be comprehended. The former foreshadowed the General Assembly of the Presbyterian Church, and the latter the National government of the United States. Both were representative bodies; the delegates to the one were duly authorized to represent the people or church members; to take cognizance of the fundamental doctrines, and a uniform discipline, and all affairs that related to the well-being and prosperity of the whole church, while matters of a local nature were left to the supervision of the minor judicatures; the other to legislate on all affairs foreign and domestic that pertained to the whole Nation, while local matters were intrusted to the care of the individual States.

The church was the first to move in inaugurating this comprehensive system, and as if these men had a prevision of the vastness of the territory occupied to-day by the Presbyterian Church, the plan was so devised that it could be adjusted to all probable exigencies that might occur, and in respect to such adaptation it has been found adequate. Meanwhile the secular or political world was moving on parallel lines in the effort to form a more united government under a constitution.

Discordant and Rival States.—The several States,

though neighboring, were virtually independent of each other, and history records that they were more or less governed by selfish interests, which caused anxiety in intelligent minds, as to whereunto these evils would grow. This spirit of gain was specially manifest in the States that had suitable harbors, and they yielded to the temptation of imposing duties on imported merchandise in such manner as to advance each one's own interests irrespective of the general effect upon their neighbors. This condition of affairs induced the influential men in the several States to take measures for remedying these evils by bringing about a union, thus consolidating them into one government that they might become in fact, as well as in the eyes of the world, a NATION. George Washington said "We must have a government under one constitution; we must treat with other nations as a whole, for we cannot separately." This political agitation continued from the disbandment of the Continental army to the formation of the United States Constitution and its adoption by the people (1783-1788). During this period of four or five years, one or two local conventions were held by delegates from neighboring districts, but never before from all the States did delegates assemble, until in the great convention held in Philadelphia in 1787, which framed the present Constitution of the United States, and under which, after it had been adopted by the people, George Washington was inaugurated President (1789), and we began our national life.

XXII.

THE GENERAL ASSEMBLY ARRANGED FOR.

The movement in the Presbyterian Church began practically in 1785, when, as preliminary to constituting a representative judicature of last resort for the church throughout the whole land, a motion was made to divide the synod of New York and Philadelphia into three synods. The following year the motion was amended so as to read *three or more* synods; the latter provision covered the whole ground, as it left the number of synods to be extended according to circumstances, while over all it was in contemplation to constitute a General Assembly—the delegates to which, were to come as representatives from the presbyteries, not from the synods—the former being in more direct relations with the people or church members. There is not a self-perpetuating judicature in the church, since all its members derive their authority as such, ultimately from the church members themselves, with whom is lodged the power of choosing their representatives, as it is in our civil government.

Increase of the Church.—A brief notice of the American Presbyterian Church at this period may interest the reader. The synod of New York and Philadelphia had been in existence *thirty years,* and it was now to be divided into *four* synods. It had received 230 ministers as new members, and had grown from eight presbyteries to sixteen, under whose care were 420 churches; of these, 380 were south of New York State, while in the latter were forty. The great body of the ministers were native born and educated in the bosom of the church. The others came for the most part from the Presbyterian churches in Scotland and North Ireland. The synod had (1786) under its control churches on the Atlantic slope extending from the State of Connecticut to Florida, and also beyond the Alleghanies in Western Pennsylvania and in Middle Kentucky.

Four Synods Organized.—The synod of New York and Philadelphia, according to its own resolution, was divided and arranged into four synods, having the following names: New York and New Jersey, Philadelphia, Virginia, and the Carolinas. The first synod included the Presbyteries of Suffolk, Dutchess, New York, and New Brunswick; the second, those of Philadelphia, Lewes, New Castle, Baltimore, and Carlisle; the third, those of Hanover, Lexington, Redstone, and Transylvania; the fourth, those of Abingdon, Orange, and South Carolina. The third or Virginia synod covered by far the greatest extent of territory, as it alone extended beyond the mountains, including the Redstone Presbytery in Pennslyvania and the Transylvania in Kentucky.

It is easily seen that the ministers or pastors of these churches, scattered over so extensive a territory, found it exceedingly difficult to attend the annual meetings of the synod, as required by the rule, and that in consequence the important and beneficial influence of such frequent and fraternal intercourse was much diminished, but by having four synods such advantage could be in a measure retained, as the ministers would be more able to attend the meetings.

Alterations in the constitution being required in order to apply to the new condition of church affairs, a committee was appointed to prepare such constitution. The committee was instructed "to examine the Book of Discipline and Government, and digest such a system as they should think adapted to the state of the Presbyterian Church in America." It was also arranged that this draft or plan of the committee should be printed and sent down to the presbyteries, "who were required to report *in writing* their observations upon it at the next meeting of synod." The committee performed this duty and sent the plan to the presbyteries, and the latter presented their observations to the synod at its meeting in 1787. After thorough discussion and adoption of amendments, the plan of government and discipline agreed upon by the synod was then ordered to be printed and again sent to the presbyteries "for their consideration, and also for the consideration of the *churches* under their care," thus recognizing the propriety of consulting the church members. This plan of government was also to be reported and acted upon at the meeting of synod the following year, 1788. The plan having been discussed and approved by the presbyteries and churches was returned to the synod, which, in due form, ratified the former's action, and resolved: "That the true intent and meaning of the above ratification by the synod is that the Form of Government and Discipline and the Confession of Faith, as now ratified, are to continue to be our Constitution and Confession of Faith and practice unalterably, unless *two-thirds* of the presbyteries shall propose amendments, and these shall be agreed to and enacted by the General Assembly" (*Dr. Hodge, p. 414*).

The General Assembly Constituted.—On the adoption of the plan the synod ordered that the General Assembly about to be called into existence should consist of delegates from the several presbyteries in the ratio of *one minister and one elder* for every six members or ministers belonging to the presbytery. The synod divided itself into four, in accordance with the act of 1786, as already noted. Then it was ordered: "That the first meeting of the General Assembly to be constituted out of the above synods be held at 11 A. M. on the *third* Thursday of May, 1789, in the Second Presbyterian Church in the City of Philadelphia." Dr. Witherspoon was appointed "to open the assembly with a sermon, and to preside till a moderator was chosen." Its organization being completed, the presbyteries were enjoined, in accordance with the rules laid down, to elect and send delegates to the assembly which was to meet in 1789.

The Address to President Washington.—George Washington had been inaugurated President of the United States in New York City only a few weeks previous to this first meeting of the General Assembly in Philadelphia in May, 1789. In this connection we notice two coincidences. The leading men of the Presbyterian Church and the leading men of the States had been moving on parallel lines in the effort to secure a more comprehensive government both for the church and the nation. Both went into operation within a few weeks of each other, and both having remained virtually unchanged for more than a century, give evidence of the excellencies of the respective systems, which, as such, have been recognized by the people of the nation and by the members of the church.

It was under these circumstances that the assembly appointed a committee to prepare an address to the President of the United States. Its chairman was the celebrated Dr. Witherspoon, who was one of the signers of the Declaration of Independence, and had been a member of the Continental Congress during the troublous times of the Revolution, and was now president of Princeton College. Dr. John Rodgers was his alternate. The committee's report was quite lengthy, but being appropriate in terms and in tone, it was received and approved by the Assembly, who directed the presentation to be made. After referring to Washington's past career as a soldier, a patriot, and a statesman; to his voluntary retirement from public affairs to the longed-for rest and quiet of private life, and especially to his self-denial in the acceptance of the office of President, at the unanimous call of the people, they say: "A man more ambitious of fame, or less devoted to his country, would have refused an office in which his honors could not be augmented. * * * We are happy that God has inclined your heart to give yourself once more to the public. But we derive a presage even more flattering from the piety of your character. Public virtue is the most certain means of public felicity, and religion is the surest basis of virtue. We therefore esteem it a peculiar happiness to behold in our Chief Magistrate a steady, uniform, avowed friend of the Christian religion, and who on the most public and solemn occasions devoutly acknowledges the government of Divine Providence." They define also their own position, saying: "We shall consider ourselves as doing an acceptable service to God in our profession when we contribute to render men sober, honest, and industrious citizens, and the obedient subjects of a lawful government." They closed with the prayer that God would prolong his valuable life and continue him a blessing to his country. To this address Washington replied in appropriate terms, acknowledging his gratification at their good-will, and coinciding with them in declaring his "dependence upon Heaven as the source of all public and private blessings," and that "piety, philanthropy, honesty, industry, and economy seem, in the ordinary course of human affairs, particularly necessary for advancing and confirming the happiness of the country." He closed by thanking the assembly for their efforts "to render men sober, honest, and good citizens, and the obedient subjects of a lawful government," and for their prayers for the country and for himself.

Doctrinal Truth Guarded.—Doctrinal truth, as embodied in its standards, has been carefully guarded in the Presbyterian Church ever since 1729, when the adopting act (page 113) was agreed upon as a rule, by which examinations, thenceforth, were required as to doctrine of the ministers desiring admission to the church, as well as of their own licentiates. This rule had been virtually in force and carried out for fifty-nine years. Afterward, in 1788, when the synods of New York and Philadelphia, as we have just seen, took measures to organize a General Assembly for the entire church, they also, as a summary of Christian doctrine for the same, "ratified and adopted the Larger Catechism;" this summary has been in force in the church down to the present time. These two historical facts may account for one peculiarity that has always been present in the several divisions and reunions that have occurred in times past within the Presbyterian Church—*not* one of them has been on *distinctively* doctrinal grounds; other causes have intervened. It is true there have been within the last half century one or two instances in the church, in which individual ministers have been charged in regular form before their presbyteries with holding doctrines inconsistent with the Confession of Faith. But these exceptions did not impugn the doctrinal faith of the church itself. The charges appear to have grown out of misapprehension of the real views of these good and eminent men.

The salutary effect of this care in preserving in their purity the doctrinal standards of that church, is manifested in the uniformity with which the essential truths of the gospel are, and ever have been, preached by its ministers in good and regular standing. Though, as we have seen in relation to its own doctrines and polity, the Presbyterian Church is exceedingly strict, yet it is liberal toward other evangelical denominations, and deems as valid their rite of baptism in whatever form administered, and also recognizes the validity of their ordaining men to the sacred office, whether of one order or of three.

A Christianized Patriotism.—We will, therefore, speak only of those advantages that in the future may be the outgrowth of the free and untrammeled extension of the Presbyterian Church throughout the length and breadth of the Union, wherein, with the Divine blessing, it will have facilities for applying its principles in developing a *Christianized patriotism.* A patriotism that will have an eye not only to the material progress of the country, but to the promotion of a practical union of national feeling and sympathy between the people of every section; if they all practice the precepts of the golden rule. The type of patriotism includes an element unknown to the patriots of Greece and Rome. The latter looked no further than to promote the public safety and welfare, but only in a material point of view—for when did their leading men make an effort to elevate the people morally? Christianity adds the brotherhood of man, a principle that through the medium of the churches of every denomination can be applied specially to our own household—the American people.

Ex-officio Members.—In the meetings of the judicatures of the Presbyterian Church, there are, strictly, no *ex-officio* members. The only one that approaches that position is the moderator of a previous assembly, who, by the rule, "if present," preaches an opening sermon and presides till a new moderator is chosen. In truth, his presence depends on a contingency, because his presbytery may not send him as their delegate. History demonstrates that *ex-officio* or *hereditary* members of church judicatures or of parliaments—being less in direct sympathy with the church members or with the people at large—are the persistent opponents of changes and measures that are designed to result in reforms, and to which they seldom give their sanction unless compelled by popular pressure; much less do they lead in such movements.

Voting by Orders.—The system of voting by orders in church judicatures seems to be unfair, unless on the supposition that the members of the *higher order* have in the aggregate as much brains and intelligence as the aggregate of the same qualifications belonging to the members of the *lower*. The higher house or order has in number fewer members, but they are *ex-officio;* the lower has a greater number, but who are presumed to be equally educated. The result of such rule is, that a vote in the higher order, as the case may be, is worth from five to eight times as much as one in the lower—its value being in proportion to the number of members respectively present in each order. Nor is the unfairness of voting by orders obviated, when it depends upon the contingency of a limited minority of either order, demanding that the vote should be by orders. Such rule is very liable to be abused. It may be known, or supposed, that one order is in favor of a certain measure, while the other is not; the latter, by using the prerogative of a limited minority, can frustrate a full expression of opinion of both orders by preventing a joint vote.

The mode of constituting the General Assembly of the Presbyterian Church leaves the way open from year to year for a change in its membership, as it does not adjourn to meet the following year, but *dissolves,* while the choice and election of individual delegates to the next assembly depend upon the will of the presbyteries. The delegates, therefore, come fresh from the people or church members—a principle recognized in constituting the lower house of Congress and the House of Commons in England, hence the propriety of the rule that financial measures, in which the people are specially interested, must originate respectively in these two houses.

The Ecclesiastical Despotism.—All the Protestant denominations in the Union act in accordance with the spirit of the civil institutions of the land when they recognize the right of the laity to have a share in the management of their own church affairs. In this respect the government of the Roman Catholic Church is in marked contrast, inasmuch as the rule is entirely in the hands of the priests, the laity being rigorously excluded. By this system the intelligent and representative lay members of that communion have no opportunity, through being members of church judicatures, for cultivating fraternal and Christian intercourse with their fellow-members throughcut the Union. On the contrary, the government of that church is an ecclesiastical despotism; it ignores the rights of its own lay members, and is antagonistic to the spirit of our political institutions—State and National.

XXIII.

PRESBYTERIAN MOVEMENTS IN THE SOUTH.

We now resume the narrative. The Presbyterians in the southern end of the valley of Virginia continued to make inroads on the wilderness on either hand, numbers of them following the course of the Holston, formed settlements in its valley in Southwestern Virginia, and afterward in what is now East Tennessee. These immigrants increased so much that to supply their spiritual wants more effectively, the Presbytery of Abingdon was erected out of that of Hanover. To it was assigned the care of the churches in Southwestern Virginia, and in the adjacent parts of North Carolina, and those in the valley of the Holston in Tennessee. Within twelve years the Presbytery of Abingdon had under its care nearly forty congregations; of these nineteen were in Tennessee, seven in North Carolina and the remainder in Virginia, Numbers of these congregations, however, were without settled pastors, and were served by the neighboring ministers or by missionaries.

The Migration.—Down the Holston was the southwestern route of the pioneers of Presbyterianism, thence amid the Alleghanies into the valley of the Mississippi; it corresponded to the northern route, over the same mountains to the valleys of the head streams of the Ohio, already noted. Out of the Abingdon was carved in 1786 the Presbytery of Transylvania, which at first numbered only *five* ministers. One of these five, David Rice, was the first Presbyterian minister who went to Kentucky and who may be deemed the founder of that church in that region—he deserves a grateful recognition. After an uninterrupted labor of thirty-three years he was permitted to see his beloved church extended and exerting a benign influence throughout the entire State. A man of Christian temper and zeal and strengthened by decision of character, he commanded the respect of the outside world, and the love of church members, so that all joined in giving him the affectionate title of "Father Rice." He came from Virginia, where he had been a pastor beloved for a number of years, to the Territory of Kentucky in 1783—nine years before it became a State. A fine scholar, a graduate of Princeton; licensed by the Presbytery of Hanover and a well-read theologian. In his new home he took an advanced position in favor of education. He was a staunch friend of Transylvania University, and was for many years the president of its board of trustees. He battled successfully against errors in theology and the peculiar phase of *politico-infidelity* that was in vogue for a time in the State. The Master released him from his earthly duties in his eighty-third year (1816), but not until he was permitted to see the gospel triumphant where once infidelity alone seemed to reign.

The Presbytery of Transylvania had under its care the churches in Kentucky, and even across the Ohio, those in the immediate vicinity. An unbroken wilderness of two hundred miles intervened between these settlements in Kentucky and those in the beautiful valley of the Holston. The military grants of land given to settlers within the bounds of the Presbytery of Transylvania, induced an unusually large immigration of bold and hardy men, who had already been schooled in the peculiar trials and risks of a wilderness filled with skulking foes. Owing to this influx, the population within the bounds of Transylvania presbytery soon outstripped that of the Abingdon.

The Three Pioneer Ministers.—The first Presbyterian minister that came as pastor to the people on the Holston (1773) was the Rev. Charles Cummings, who was a member of Hanover Presbytery and had labored a number of years in Augusta County, Virginia. One hundred and thirty heads of families in two adjacent congregations signed the call for his services. The settlers were mostly from Maryland and Pennsylvania. The Revolutionary War was impending and the Indians were hostile. Mr. Cummings was often in danger of his life. He never went to his church without being armed, as well as the other male members of his congregation. On Sabbath morning he would "put on his shot-pouch, shoulder his rifle, mount his horse and ride to church." After placing his arms within reach, he would preach two sermons, with a short interval between. For more than thirty years this pioneer and devoted servant labored in Tennessee, till the Master withdrew him from the work. During this time, he, also, performed an immense amount of missionary labor among the scattered churches in the region.

Another strenuous laborer was added to this band of Presbyterian ministers when in 1785 Hezekiah Balch came as a missionary to the region now known as East Tennessee. He was a graduate of Princeton, and deeply imbued with the importance of education in a community. For more than twenty years he was indefatigable in the performance of his missionary and pastoral duties. (*See p. 135.*)

In 1788 Robert Henderson was licensed to preach the gospel by the Presbytery of Abingdon. He at once entered upon his duties as a missionary and a fitting colaborer of Mr. Balch. Henderson was unique in his character; a stranger to fear when duty commanded; no matter how hostile the audience, he would fearlessly preach the truth. A prevailing sin of the community at that time

REV. FRANCIS HERRON, D. D.
(271, 272.)

was the vulgar and senseless one of profanity. On one occasion Henderson determined to rebuke that form of vice in a sermon. Though he saw in his audience many men of influence, but who were notoriously profane swearers, instead of being over-awed, his courage never wavered, and he lashed them without mercy. He had "a matchles power of mimicry and a perfect command of voice and countenance and attitude of gesture—his flashes of wit or grotesquely humorous illustrations would break from him in spite of himself." Then, again, perhaps in the same sermon his bold, passionate and grand appeals would almost make his hearers tremble, or by his indescribable and earnest pathos allure them into sympathy with his own emotions. He influenced the people who were outside the pale of the church almost as much as those within it.

Retarding Influences.—The incident just related reveals a form of immorality that was common among the backwoodsmen of that region, and with which the ministers had to contend much more than their brethren in Western Pennsylvania. The settlers of the latter, before they moved across the Alleghanies into that section from New Jersey and Eastern Pennsylvania, had been better trained under gospel influences and were more prosperous in worldly affairs than those who migrated from Virginia and the Carolinas into the western wilderness. For a long time, the latter had been subjected to being burdened in the form of tithes paid to the established church, in addition to the support of their own churches and schools. In consequence of these and other drawbacks, such as the restrictions imposed by the colonial government in respect to the number and location of meetinghouses, the private members of the Presbyterian churches from which migrations went into Tennessee and Kentucky were not on so high a plane of general intelligence and of biblical knowledge as those who removed to Western Pennsylvania. The latter, having more advantages, were better trained in their youth by parents and ministers in the knowledge of Bible truths and in the Westminster Confession and the catechisms. The population on the head streams of the Ohio, had, therefore, in the main much more respect for religion and morals, than the settlers of East Tennessee and Kentucky.

The Sabbath Desecrated.—The immigrants to Western Pennsylvania, almost from the first, took with them their families, while it was many years before their southern brethren of Tennessee and Kentucky, because of hostile Indians, dared risk that privilege. Being thus deprived of the amenities of domestic life, these pioneers became quite rude in their manners—to reform which took many years. The main portion of these backwoodsmen seemed to have left their religion behind, when they crossed the mountains. They appeared as reckless of personal danger as they were fearless of the consequences of sin. Among them that efficient preserver of good morals—the Sabbath—was not merely disregarded, but was habitually desecrated; in contrast with its being religiously and even punctiliously observed among the Presbyterians on the upper Ohio. The custom of horse-racing, copied from the Cavaliers of Virginia, though then scarcely known in the north, was prevalent in the south. This amusement became the occasion of much betting and gambling and the kindred vices of drunkenness and profanity, and still worse, it was often patronized by men of standing in the community, thus giving the sport a certain phase of respectability. The Presbyterian ministers found it exceedingly difficult to counteract this evil influence. On the contrary, in the settlements in the valleys of the upper Ohio the vices of gambling, drunkenness and profane swearing were not much in vogue, as they were under the ban of the greater portion of the people, while horse-racing was unknown. In consequence of these characteristics of the population of this southern region, a different style of preaching was required from that in the northern, where the soil was better prepared for the reception of the seed of the gospel and the promotion of its growth.

The Surveyor and His News.—Tradition tells that certain of these Southern pioneers, who had advanced into the wilderness far beyond the old settlements, had agreed for their mutual benefit and to avoid future legal contests to have the boundaries of their respective clearings or farms definitely and legally fixed by the authorized surveyor, and their farms entered by land-warrants. An official surveyor was sent by the State authorities for the purpose, and in anticipation of his arrival, by mutual agreement the settlers from far and wide assembled at a central position in order to meet him. The place chosen was known as the *Fork;* that is, the junction of the rivers Holston and French Broad, which there form the Tennessee.

When the surveyor arrived he was questioned eagerly as to the news from the old settlements beyond the mountains. Amid the information of various kinds that he communicated, was incidentally mentioned that it was rumored a Presbyterian minister named Samuel Carrick was to be sent to them as a missionary. The whole assembly was startled, and still more eagerly they asked could it be true that a preacher was coming to them? The special work for which the surveyor had come was for the time thrust aside. Conscience was aroused, and these rough and stalwart men were overwhelmed with deep emotions. The prospect of a minister coming to them called to their remembrance the days of their childhood and youth when under the tender care of pious parents they had enjoyed the privileges of Christian homes and the services of the Lord's day. Amid the excitements and dangers of a frontier life, the hallowed influences that blest their youth had faded; for years they had been far away from Christian sanctuaries; the Sabbath with them had no longer been held sacred; they had become reckless of danger and fearless in sin. They at once resolved to invite the new minister to visit them and henceforth be their pastor. They manifested their sincerity by immediately taking measures to raise a fund sufficient for his support.

The Founding of a Church.—The surveyor carried back the invitation, and also told of the eagerness of these backwoodsmen to once more enjoy the religious privileges of their youth, and secure them for their own children. At length, Rev. Samuel Carrick came (about 1789), and a day was named on which he was to preach his first sermon. The place chosen for the meeting was an open space in the primitive forest, at the *Fork,* and near an Indian mound. On the same spot now stands the Lebanon Presbyterian Church. This first sermon was heard by a great crowd, some of whom came long distances, even from the adjacent counties, for the news of the preaching was sent far and wide. These settlers were all armed with their rifles as a guard against the hostile Cherokees, and they were clad in the coarse cloth of their domestic manufacture.

Carrick was most efficient, visiting from settlement to settlement and from house to house. Parents presented their children for baptism, and resumed their sacramental vows, while a blessed religious influence pervaded the region. Mr. Carrick finally settled as pastor of the Lebanon church in connection with one in Knoxville, across the river. After years of labor, Carrick was elected president of Blount College—since known as the University of Tennessee. On entering upon the duties of the office, he resigned the pastorate of the Lebanon church, but retained that of the one in Knoxville.

The Planters of the Church in Tennessee.—The ministers, Hezekiah Balch, Robert Henderson, Samuel Carrick, Gideon Blackburn and other worthies, were the men who led the way in planting the Presbyterian Church in East Tennessee. "They were men of varied gifts, untiring zeal and entire consecration to their work, and were eminently successful."

Gideon Blackburn deserves a passing notice. He was used to hardships, which taught him self-reliance and fitted him as no other training could for the sphere of usefulness he was destined to fill in that primitive community. Though dissimilar in his ministerial characteristics, he was a fitting co-laborer with Henderson. In preaching his words, his tone and manner were solemn and impressive, as though he was overwhelmed with the majesty of his subject. Thus he carried out his own rule of rhetoric, which he once gave his theological pupils: "Get your head, your heart, your soul full of your subject, then let nature have her own way, forgetting all rule." (*Sprague's Annals, IV., p. 43.*)

The foundations of the Presbyterian Church were thus laid in that new region, where afterward it was widely extended, as from time to time came other ministers to aid in the cause.

A Peculiar Type of Infidelity.—The ministers belonging to the Transylvania Presbytery in Kentucky were antagonized by a more complex immorality than their brethren in East Tennessee. This phase of evil was a type of infidelity originating among the French revolutionists and which had become popular with these settlers. In addition it had a political prestige emanating from the National capital, for "Jeffersonian influence was as strong west as east of the mountains." The French names given to the towns and counties in that region, are significant of the sentiment prevailing among people.

There was an unusual flow of immigrants from Eastern Virginia into that fertile region of which Lexington may be deemed a central point, and in consequence, the population within the bounds of the presbytery soon outstripped in numbers that of the original Abingdon, from which Transylvania had been taken (1786). The facilities for reaching these distant settlements may account for the rapid increase in their population. Instead of threading their way from East Tennessee, through a wilderness of two hundred miles or more, they passed over the Alleghanies on the Braddock road, commencing where Cumberland now stands, to Fort Redstone, now Brownsville, on the Monongahela, there embarking on capacious *flat boats*, built for the occasion, they floated down that river and the Ohio to their destination.

The Political Clubs.—A number of political clubs were formed at central points, such as Paris and Lexington. These clubs were branches of the one formed in 1793 in Philadelphia, and which prided itself on being modeled after the famous Jacobin Club of Paris. (*Four Hundred Years, etc., p. 583.*) "These clubs," says an authority, "were politically violent and dogmatic; morally they were corrupting, and in respect to religion, utterly infidel." This form of infidelity was vulgarly blatant in its opposition to Christianity in any form whatever; the legislature catching the spirit dispensed with the services of a chaplain. Through this influence "an apostate Baptist minister was elected governor of the State," and a sceptic placed at the head of Transylvania Seminary—afterward university. This institution was founded on the basis of Christian truth, and funds were contributed for that purpose. The effect of all this was an increase of vice and dissipation; it is stated that in this portion of Kentucky "a decided majority of the population were reputed to be infidel."

Some of the ministers of the gospel labored faithfully in resisting this tide of evil, but the outlook in respect to vital religion was gloomy in the extreme, when suddenly came the Great Revival—the most remarkable in the annals of the Presbyterian Church. It swept over a region that to human view "was proof against its influence. It effectually arrested the universal tide of scepticism and irreligion." This religious movement, though marred by some indiscretions that led to a few lamentable effects, exerted a power which put in motion influences that materially neutralized the evils of the *politico-French* infidelity already noted, and for more than a generation moulded to a great extent the moral condition of society (*See Chap. XXIV.*)

XXIV.

The Great Revival.

An efficient instrument of Divine Providence in promoting this revival was the Rev. James McGready. He was a native of Pennsylvania; a student of theology under Dr. John McMillan; was licensed by the Redstone Presbytery, and afterward removing to North Carolina commenced preaching in that State in 1788. His own spiritual life had been greatly quickened by his having recently participated in a revival among the students of Hampden-Sidney College. He was noted for his denouncing sin in every form, and in consequence he became exceedingly unpopular with those classes whose vices he rebuked. The spirit of practical religion that he had just witnessed in the revival was in great contrast with the conformity to the world and its allurements that he encountered in the community in which were the two churches to whom he had come as a pastor. Horse-racing, with its attendant gambling, profanity and intemperance prevailed to an alarming extent, and yet the nominal members of the churches were virtually indifferent as to the prevalence of these and other vices.

Mr. McGready labored here for about ten years, in what proved to him a *training school*. His pungent and continuous denunciation of the vices common in the community, at length, roused against himself *personally* an intense opposition on the part of those who remained unconverted. Every effort was used by these parties to counteract his influence, so that his preaching in respect to them became an instance of casting pearls before swine. He thought it better to seek a new field of labor, and he removed to Kentucky, at the invitation of a number of his church members, who had recently migrated to that region. McGready was then about thirty-three years of age and imbued with a spirit of fiery zeal.

Religious Conditions.—In that State he found a condition of society, morally speaking, more irreligious than even the one which he had just left, because, in addition to the prevalent vices in the latter community, was an under-current of scepticism, that neutralized almost every Christian effort. He took charge of three congregations (Jan. 1, 1796), that were located in most unpromising neighborhoods. Here he labored with varied success for four years. The religious and moral condition of that portion of Kentucky was exceptional, when compared with any other section of the Union; the lines were strictly drawn between a *politico-French* infidelity and Christianity, itself. Davidson, in his *History of the Presbyterian Church in Kentucky, pp. 102, 107,* says: "The French mania brought about a leaning to French infidelity of which Thomas Jefferson, who was idolized as a friend of the *West,* was a notorious advocate. * * * At the close of the century, a decided majority of the people were reported to be infidel, and as infidelity is the prolific parent of vice, it is not surprising to find that the whole country was remarkable for vice and dissipation."

This condition of affairs affected many of the members of the Presbyterian churches, and in consequence Christian duties were neglected almost everywhere. Still further, it was charged by a writer of the time—Crisman, historian of the Cumberland church—that some of "the ministry aimed at little else than to enlighten the understanding. * * * They spoke but little of individual accountability or spiritual regeneration, but of

the elect, the predestined, the preordained. * * *
Members were received into the churches, without professing a change of heart, or being aware of its necessity. * * * A stiff technical theology or a dry speculative orthodoxy thus left the heart and conscience unmoved."

At this crisis, when the few earnest Christian men and women were in despair came the outpouring of the Holy Spirit. It came with such power that the opposition for the time was appalled and swept away. We cannot go into detail of all the circumstances attending this marvelous religious movement, by means of which the moral character of the population of an extensive territory, not only in Kentucky but in portions of the neighboring States, was modified or changed, and gospel truth received an impulse, which from that day to this has blest the people of that entire region. (*Gillett II., pp. 158-200.*)

After the work commenced (July, 1799), its influence spread rapidly throughout the region, and a few other Presbyterian ministers, who were in earnest sympathy with the revival entered into the cause with great zeal. Prominent among these were Revs. John Rankin, William McGee, a Presbyterian, and his brother, a Methodist, and William Hodge. The latter and William McGee were converted under Mr. McGready's preaching when he was in North Carolina.

Characteristics of the Revival.—There were peculiar characteristics of this religious awakening that are well authenticated, and to explain which is as difficult to account for as the outpouring of the Holy Spirit on the day of Pentecost, if the inspired word had not made known the power that moved the souls of men on that occasion, while under the preaching of the Apostle Peter. Here in these modern days were bold and daring sinners, scoffers and blasphemers, some of whom had even come intending to interrupt these religious services, but instead were overcome and wept bitterly, bewailing their sins. The emotions of the soul were so intense that they affected the whole physical system. "Many were so struck with deep heart-piercing convictions that their bodily strength was quite overcome so that they fell to the ground and could not refrain from bitter groans and outcries for mercy." These manifestations were not confined to any special class, but all, old and young, black and white, were affected, some more, some less. Numbers of professed Christians, after a searching examination of their former hopes, were awakened to a new and heartfelt religious life, and thus the work went on with increasing power for a number of years.

Injurious Divisions.—Unfortunately divisions arose, doctrines were preached that were deemed unscriptural by many Presbyterian ministers and it became evident to the more judicious that such errors, if permitted to remain unimpeached, would retard the progress of the revival. Extravagancies, the legitimate outgrowth of these errors, had already produced evils in some of the churches. From the point of view of to-day the ministers who strove to avoid these extremes were right in their opposition, as the influence of such unscriptural and injudicious measures afterward proved. Although they did not sanction all the methods used, nor condemn them absolutely, yet they held that whatever permanent good that was done was through the Holy Spirit and the truth alone. They assumed that a genuine "work of God" would bear the test of His word. Prominent among these ministers were John Lyle, Thomas B. Craighead, Robert Stuart, J. P. Campbell and David Rice, who because of his age and disposition was characterized as "Father Rice." The advocates of the extreme measures most unjustly stigmatized these men as *Anti-Revivalists.*

Influence of the Revival Spread.—The news of these remarkable religious exercises spread far and wide, and great multitudes, impressed by an indefinable feeling on the subject, came from long distances to attend these services. Congregations one after another were brought under the same influence, till the whole region was reached, extending in every direction for at least a hundred miles. The indefatigable McGready visited and preached with tremendous power in places more than that distance from his home. In many instances these converts from classes of hardened sinners in expressing their thoughts astonished even the preachers themselves. Says Mr. McGready: "The good language, the good sense the clear ideas and the rational scriptural light in which they spoke amazed me. They spoke upon the subjects beyond what I could have done."

To instruct these multitudes the Presbyterian ministers labored incessantly. The meeting-houses were too small and during the summer the people thronged the groves in many thousands. There were often seen at the same time but at different places in the woods great congregations —in one instance seven—listening to sermons, but all impressed by a similar intense conviction of sin. Great numbers of the most careless and God-defying sinners experienced a change of heart and who manifested their sincerity afterward by living consistent Christian lives.

Camp Meetings.—The immense crowds that attended these services and the lack of buildings of sufficient size to contain them afterward led to holding in the summer months the larger assemblies in the groves. From the latter custom originated *camp meetings*. Regular encampments were formed at first by having canvas tents, but these in turn gave way to light structures made of wood, because more permanent, since the same encampment was oftentimes used from year to year. Some central position was chosen that furnished an abundance of pure water and a suitable forest. In time the custom of having such encampments was so extended throughout Kentucky and the neighboring States that a systematized form of evangelical work was inaugurated for preaching the gospel to the people at large during the summer months, when the groves could be thus utilized. This mode of holding large assemblies for evangelical work was suited to the conditions of the people, and therefore they became very popular and equally as useful as a means of preaching the word.

Uneducated Men Licensed to Preach.—These continuous and extensive revivals called for an unusual number of active ministerial workers. The Cumberland Presbytery of Kentucky endeavored to supply such by licensing men to preach who had not the usual qualifications required in the Presbyterian Church as to their classical and theological learning. This proceeding ran counter to the sentiment and traditions of its intelligent church members. About sixty years (1748) before the time of which we write an effort was made under almost similar conditions to lower the standard of the education of the ministry. That effort signally failed (*see p. 166*). In connection with other irregularities a number of uneducated but zealous men were thus licensed to preach. To this proceeding the Synod of Kentucky refused to give its sanction, and in the course of several years many attempts were made to reconcile the parties at variance, and also appeals were made to the General Assembly. The sum of the latter's final action was to sustain the course of the synod "as firm and temperate" in not licensing uneducated men to preach, but gave permission for the presbytery to "sanction catechists and exhorters." A number of these men were of exceptional ability, but over whom "the presbytery was to keep careful watch and supervision."

—*Cumberland Presbyterians.*—This decision failed to satisfy a number of the members of the presbytery, and the outcome was far-reaching in its influence, no less than the founding of the Cumberland branch of American Presbyterianism. There were other impediments, such as doctrinal differences that precluded a perfect adjustment of these controversies and the reconciliation of the parties at variance, since some of the doctrines preached contravened the Confession of Faith, while the licensing of uneducated men to preach was looked upon as inexpedient and fraught with future injury to the church.

Unavailing efforts were made during a number of years to reconcile these differences, but in 1814 the Cumberland Presbytery took in hand the Westminster Confession, which was "modeled, expunged and added to." In this proceeding they apparently "aimed to steer a middle course between Arminianism and the confession, rejecting the articles charged with teaching the doctrine of fatality." The progress of the denomination was rapid, its congregations increased in number to sixty; three presbyteries were formed and these constituted a synod. Under these conditions the General Assembly in 1825 defined its position as to the latter to be the same as that of "other denominations, not connected with our body." In a Christian spirit they each agreed to follow their own way in their respective spheres of usefulness.

The desire to promote education of a high order led in 1827 to the founding by the denomination of the Cumberland Presbyterian College at Princeton, Kentucky, and to which was also attached a theological department. If we may judge from the efforts made to-day to supply its churches with a thoroughly educated ministry, we would infer that the present members think that these good men on the point then at issue may possibly have made a mistake in respect to an educated ministry. The rule was again sustained by the General Assembly, as the secession of a portion of a single presbytery did not infringe the principle involved. The scholarship of the Presbyterian ministry has always kept pace with every branch of advanced secular and theological education, and to-day *the former study science much more than scientists study theology.*

Another Great Revival.—In this connection we give a brief account of a revival which commenced in the autumn of 1802, under the ministrations of Rev. Elisha Macurdy in Washington County, Pennsylvania. Macurdy was a farmer in Ligonier valley, Westmoreland County. In his twenty-eighth year he heard a sermon by Rev. James Hughes, who was on a missionary tour among the scattered Presbyterian churches in that region (1792). His attention was arrested by the doctrines expressed and warnings given by the preacher, who based them upon the word of God. Macurdy *bought* a Bible and began to examine its contents; the result was he professed himself a Christian, though afterward he experienced clearer views of his acceptance with the Saviour. He determined to devote his energies to preaching the gospel and, selling his farm to defray the expenses, he entered upon a course of study in the Canonsburg Academy. His study of theology was under the direction and instruction of Dr. McMillan.

He finished his course of study in 1798 and was licensed by the Presbytery of Ohio. Immediately he began work and as a missionary preached with great zeal and acceptance in the vacant churches and destitute settlements in that region, but ere long he became the pastor of two churches—known respectively as Cross Roads and Three Springs. Here he labored with remarkable success for thirty-five years.

The Counterpart.—This revival in certain characteristics was almost a counterpart of the one commencing in Kentucky two years before (1800) under the ministry of James McGready. The similarity consisted in the effects produced upon those who were convicted of sin, such as the physical system being overpowered by the emotions of the soul when under a pungent sense of guilt before God. But all were not thus affected, as the manifestations were varied in kind and in intensity; derangements of the nervous system being more frequent than the loss of physical strength. As for the length of time in which such conditions lasted, some were for only a few minutes, others for hours and even days. The mental powers of those thus exercised appeared to be intensely active in dwelling upon religious realities and things of eternity. Bold and hardened sinners were awakened and their mental agony was so great that often the body of the convicted became seemingly paralyzed and sank down helplessly. In one instance so great was the intensity of feeling that the greater part of the congregation did not disperse at the usual time in the evening, but remained in prayer and exhortation all night long and even till near noon the following day. There were scenes similar to those witnessed about the same time in the revivals in Kentucky, Tennessee and in both the Carolinas.

The Revival Spreads.—Meetings continued to be held at central points, as at Mr. Macurdy's churches and others in the vicinity. In all these were manifested, more or less, similar spiritual effects in the conviction of sin and in the powerful influence over the physical system. The revival spread to many other churches in the country round about, and finally its influence extended to the west into Ohio.

A calm but interested stranger—Rev. Joseph Badger— who happened on one occasion to be present, in writing of those who fell says: "They very nearly resembled persons who had just expired from a state of full strength.

For a considerable time pulsation could not be perceived. Their limbs were wholly unstrung, and respiration was scarcely perceptible; yet they retained their reason and knew what was said within their hearing." (*Gillett, I., p. 543.*) The preaching was "Calvinistic in sentiment, serious, earnest and pathetic. * * * The people were carefully instructed that there was no religion in the mere falling or in the bodily exercises, and against this idea they were repeatedly put on their guard."

The Contrast.—It may be said in contrast that when the revival burst forth in Kentucky it had to contend with the united force of a *politico-infidelity* and an almost universal scepticism, but in Western Pennsylvania, while there were many unconverted among the people, there was none of that blatant infidelity that prevailed in the former State, as Christianity had so far indirectly moulded the mass of the people that it was held in respect by the unconverted in the community.

It is interesting to note that James McGready, the leader in the revival in Kentucky, and also that Elisha Macurdy, who bore a similar relation to that in Western Pennsylvania, were both educated in the Canonsburg Academy, and in their theological training were under the direction and instruction of Dr. John McMillan.

In 1805 Mr. Marquis and Mr. Macurdy were commissioners from the Presbytery of Ohio to the General Assembly of that year, which met in Philadelphia. There they learned that certain incidents in this revival were severely criticised by "some of the ministers in the region of Philadelphia, especially those who retained the traditions and prejudices of the Old Side." The latter good men appeared to ignore that the Westminster Confession says the Holy Spirit "worketh when and where and how He pleaseth."

Revivals in New England.—It is proper to note incidentally that while these revivals were in progress in Kentucky and Western Pennsylvania there were also remarkable outpourings of the Holy Spirit in New England, especially in Connecticut and Massachusetts. These revivals commenced in Maine and continued for a number of years with more or less power to spread from congregation to congregation, and thus in one sense they were local, though they extended finally throughout that section of the Union, and far into the first quarter of the present century. In writing of these scenes the celebrated Edward D. Griffin, then a pastor in Hartford, Conn, says: "I could number fifty or sixty continuous congregations laid down in one field of divine wonders and as many more in different parts of New England." In 1802 a revival remarkable for its power occurred in Yale College.

XXV.

THE WAY PREPARED FOR THE PLAN OF UNION.

We have seen in the early colonial times in New England that the Congregationalists and the Presbyterians coöperated in their religious work, and while the form of church government was virtually reckoned a matter of expediency, uniformity in respect to Christian doctrine was deemed essential in order to the perfect harmony of the two denominations. We have already noted that even before, but especially soon after, the close of the Revolution large migrations composed mostly of Presbyterians crossed the Alleghanies into the fertile valleys of the headstreams of the Ohio, and also that a little later during the same period similar migrations crossed the same mountains further south into the rich and beautiful valleys of the head-streams of the Tennessee.

The middle and lower portions of the valleys of the Hudson and the Mohawk had been partially occupied by settlers nearly a century before the time of which we write and who for the most part belonged to the Church of Holland. Afterward came in Presbyterians, whose doctrinal creed harmonized with that of the latter church, while both recognized the parity of the ministry and a form of church government in which the church members were represented by laymen. A large emigration of Protestants—Lutherans—some five thousand, it is said, came from the Palatinate in Germany and settled in the valley of the Mohawk (1707). They were induced to come by grants of land given by the government of Queen Anne, and on the condition they would settle on the frontiers of the colony. Some time afterward came an immigration of Scotch Presbyterians, who took up lands and made their homes principally in the region north of Albany, and whose number was increased from time to time by others from their native land. In addition, in 1740 came to the same colony an entire congregation of Presbyterians under the direction and pastoral care of their minister, Rev. Samuel Dunlop. They migrated from Londonderry, New Hampshire, and settled in Cherry Valley; to the former place they had previously come from Scotland and the north of Ireland. Mr. Dunlop afterward (1763) became a member of the Presbytery of Dutchess County. Thus was prepared the way for the promotion of evangelical religion in that entire region.

Lines of Migration.—Owing to climatic reasons, people in the United States, when they migrate from one portion of their country to another, do so mostly on or near the same parallels of latitude on which they have been accustomed to live. Thus while the migrations across the mountains just mentioned were going on, others on the same principle were in progress further north, for New Englanders, chiefly from Connecticut and Massachusetts, were pouring into the valleys of the Hudson and the Mohawk and the lake region of Central New York. These streams of people were mostly Congregationalists, and they located as circumstances dictated side by side with the Dutch and the Presbyterians, and generally blended with the latter in their church relations and Christian fellowship, since both were agreed as to the essential doctrines of the gospel. Meanwhile to aid in supplying the religious wants of the people in these numerous settlements ministers as missionaries came from New England, who often preached to congregations composed of members of the three denominations mentioned.

Losses and Regains.—The churches of this entire region had unwonted trials and disasters during the French and Indian War (1753-1763), and afterward during the Revolutionary period. They were on or near the routes of the several invasions first by Indians from Canada and afterward by the British under Burgoyne. After the Revolution those who had been driven away returned to their desolated homes, and in time began to rebuild their churches. As soon as peace was assured the population in this fertile region began to increase rapidly and the churches also in a similar proportion, but even faster than pastors could be obtained to supply them. Such was the condition of the religious affairs of these settlements some years before and after the year 1800.

Interest in Missions.—It is remarkable that about this time special attention was directed almost simultaneously to missionary work amid the comparatively frontier settlements, and among the Indians who were yet living along the western borders of the States. This missionary spirit seemed to pervade the entire country, and the different denominations—Reformed Dutch, the Baptists, the Congregationalists, the Presbyterians and the Associate Reformed. The first to enter the field was the Missionary Society of New York, Nov. 1, 1796; soon after was formed the Northern Missionary Society, designed to operate specially in the northern and western portion of the State. The following year (1797) the General Association of Connecticut formed itself, as it were, into an *ex-officio* missionary society. Then in 1798 the Massachusetts society was formed; and soon after another, the Berkshire Columbian, was organized in the western part of the State. In Pittsburg (October, 1802) was organized the Western Missionary Society by the Synod of Pittsburg. Such were the comparatively feeble beginnings of domestic missions for those destitute of gospel privileges in our own land, the same influence expanded and ere long took in the foreign field. This liberal Christian spirit manifested itself in the increased intercourse between the different denominations and their uniting with one another for the greater efficiency in the work. The custom was introduced of interchanging ministerial services, as well as that of fraternal letters passing back and forth between their respective church judicatures. The General Assembly entered heartily into the "plan for correspondence and intercourse." At this time a vast field was opened to missionary work, one which extended from Middle New York across Pennsylvania and into Eastern Ohio, where multitudes of settlers were coming in from New England. They found homes for the most part on the territory known as the Western Reserve, which territory then belonged to Connecticut.

Plan of Union Suggested.—When Dr. John Blair Smith was president of Union College, a young Congregational minister—Eliphalet Nott—who had been sent by the Association of Connecticut as a missionary to the "settlements" in New York State, on his journey stopped at Schenectady and by invitation spent a night with the president (1795). They discoursed on the situation of the churches in the region round about, and also on the several points of doctrine that were held in common by the Congregationalists and the Presbyterians—the form of church government being held by both parties as nonessential. In the course of the conversation President Smith, after describing the religious condition of the several settlements, in thus having two distinct ecclesiastical organizations when both were orthodox in their views, asked: "Would it not be better for the entire church that these two divisions should make mutual concessions and thus effect a common organization on an accommodation plan, with a view to meet the conditions of communities so situated?" (*Gillett, I., p. 396.*) This young and eloquent minister was won over to the views of President Smith, and being also encouraged by a number of Congregationalists and Presbyterians he labored earnestly in the cause and the result was that numerous churches in that portion of the State were formed or strengthened in their work by their union with one another on this accommodation plan. Mr. Nott was induced by President Smith to accept the pastorate of the Presbyterian church in Albany (1798), to which he had been invited; six years later he became president of Union College—a position of great influence, and which he filled admirably.

Presbyterial Form Preferred.—It appears that at this time the sympathy of the Congregational churches of Connecticut was in favor of a virtual presbyterial form of church government (as they stood on "the semi-Presbyterian Saybrook platform"). The following statement in 1799 of the views and church polity of the Hartford Association shows that the constitution of its churches "is not Congregational, but contains the essentials of the government of the Church of Scotland or the Presbyterian Church in America." This is further illustrated by the statement that the "decisive power of ecclesiastical councils and consociation consisting of ministers and messengers or a lay representation from the churches, is possessed of substantially the same authority as presbytery." "As the eighteenth century drew toward a close, Connecticut's sympathies went out increasingly toward fellowship with the Presbyterian Church of the Middle States. Massachusetts, on the other hand, came to represent an increasingly independent type of Congregationalism." (*Church Hist. Series, Vol. III., p. 209—Walker.*) This polity of Connecticut is radically different from that put forth as the principles on which the original Congregational Church in Massachusetts was founded. (*See p. 71.*)

The Plan Proposed.—The General Association of Connecticut proposed to the General Assembly in 1801 "*A plan of union,*" which proposal was accepted by the latter body. In brief, the following regulations were agreed upon: A Presbyterian minister might be the pastor of a Congregational church and still continue his relations to his presbytery; and a Congregational minister might be the pastor of a Presbyterian church and still remain a member of his association. In case of trial the Presbyterian might appeal to his presbytery, or to a mutual council equally composed of Presbyterians and Congregationalists. In the case of the Congregationalist he might appeal to a mutual council or to presbytery; in the latter a delegate of the church had the right to sit and act as a ruling elder. In a Congregationalist church the male communicants constitute the *session;* in a Presbyterian the session or eldership is chosen by the church members as their representatives.

The preaching of the gospel in these peculiar circumstances was deemed paramount to technical or strictly ecclesiastical forms. Apparently the plan was designed to be temporary, since in respect to the church polity of each denomination it was a divergence and used only as an expedient. It will be noticed that the presbyteries were not overtured on this occasion by the assembly in accordance with the book and the usual custom; and that the Association of Connecticut in accordance with its constitution had no legislative authority in the premises.

Why the Churches Prospered.—The progress of the churches was much stimulated by the adoption of the Plan of Union, which enjoined "mutual forbearance and accommodation," as it enabled the ministry to be better utilized; when it required only one to supply the religious wants of the town or neighborhood, instead of two as heretofore, one was thus freed to preach elsewhere. This spirit of union pervaded the Christian community and the Middle Association—Congregational—was invited to become a constituent branch of the Synod of Albany, if the approval of the General Assembly could be obtained. This was secured with the understanding that the churches of the association could continue in their own mode of government, unless they would voluntarily adopt the Presbyterian form. The assembly (1808) gave its sanction to this arrangement. The jurisdiction of the association and that of the Presbytery of Geneva were virtually within the same limits. The three presbyteries of Albany, Columbia and Oneida were constituted by the Synod of Albany (1803), afterward the Presbytery of Oneida was divided, and from it the Presbytery of Geneva was set off, and from the latter was afterward formed the Presbytery of Onondaga.

Reasons for Material Prosperity.—The material progress of the entire State of New York, up the Hudson and the Mohawk and through the lake region to Lake Erie, was very rapid, owing in part to the immense migration from New England, especially from Connecticut and Massachusetts. These immigrants brought with them their love for the church and the school-house, and in that respect they had the full sympathy of those already in the field. Villages were increasing in number, while the fertile lands were rapidly brought under cultivation, and soon the wheat fields of the Genesee valley became famous. Further on the opening of the Erie canal (1825), connecting the lakes with the Atlantic through the Hudson, gave a new impulse to this migration from the East, while the increase in the native population was in an equal ratio.

Results of Christian Effort.—The several missionary societies were active in sending supplies of ministers to meet the the religious wants of the settlements of the whites, and also to the Indians yet remaining in the State.

As a result of these efforts as reported to the General Assembly of 1810, the number of ministers in the western portion of the State had in eleven years increased from two to nearly fifty. The local societies were active in the cause, but mainly through the distribution of religious tracts and books. These operations required funds and the whole church was more than usually stimulated to provide the means to support missionaries and other general expenses.

Effects of the Great Revival.—The influence of the great revival in Kentucky had extended north of the Ohio river and, as already noted, into Western Pennsylvania and thence to Western and Middle New York. Magazines were established for the purpose of diffusing religious information, while the assembly and the Connecticut Association went hand in hand in promoting the good work. At this period and for a number of years there was a general progress of religion in the form of revivals in almost every presbytery in some of the States, in North and also in South Carolina, in the Valley of Virginia, New Jersey and especially in Western Pennsylvania. The outpourings of the Holy Spirit were remarkable, and the influence of the gospel was often manifest in the change produced in the morals of society in general and in the new life that inspired the churches.

Standing Committees.—In 1802 the assembly appointed a "Standing Committee of Missions." It consisted of seven members, four ministers and three laymen; its duty was to take cognizance of the progress of missionary work during the year and report the same to the assembly. This committee was afterward increased to twelve; the five additional members were appointed from Philadelphia and vicinity in order for the convenience of a quorum being more easily convened. At that time the impression was abroad that as the Presbyterian Assembly had a charter as to its temporalities from the State of Pennsylvania, it could not legally meet and transact business in any other State.

The subject of ministerial education was not in the meantime overlooked, but greatly promoted by the contributions of the church members. Each synod was at liberty to designate a professor of theology, to whom students could resort for instruction; this measure was the harbinger of regularly constituted theological seminaries.

The Sad Interruption.—At this period the religious progress of the entire country was sadly interrupted. The Napoleon wars in Europe brought about misunderstandings that were followed by numerous aggressions in consequence of which the American people suffered greatly, especially in their trade upon the ocean and in the violation of the rights of their seamen, so that Congress thought itself justified in declaring war against Great Britain (June 18, 1812). (*Four Hundred Years, etc., pp. 623-628.*) The war itself lasted nearly three years, but including the public turmoil before and after it, the period was about five, during which a demoralizing moral influence permeated the whole land and very much retarded the legitimate work of all the churches.

During the period of religious disaster caused by the war and its concomitant evils the assembly appointed each successive year a day of fasting and prayer. Amid the general moral gloom that rested upon the churches, there were isolated cases of revivals in different portions of the land; some of these were quite extensive, and the assembly was cheered by reports of "scenes resembling those of Pentecost."

Efforts in Favor of Temperance.—The subject of intemperance, because of its evils, began about this time to attract almost universal attention, and it was proposed to arrest its widespread influence. The first effort was made from a medical point of view by the celebrated Dr. Benjamin Rush of Philadelphia in a pamphlet entitled: "An Inquiry into the Effects of Ardent Spirits on the Human Body and Mind." This pamphlet by order of the General Assembly was widely distributed.

In 1811 the General Associations of Massachusetts and of Connecticut and the assembly each appointed a committee to investigate the subject of intemperance and to coöperate in devising measures to restrain its progress. The Connecticut committee reported the following year, but was unable to devise any definite plan to remedy or remove these evils, which were increasing from year to year. In those days, strange to say, rum and whisky were both used as beverages even at ordinations and installations of ministers of the gospel. The baneful influence of the custom was not then fully realized by either the ministers or the members of the church, and much less by the people outside such relations.

Reports on Temperance.—Dr. Lyman Beecher was present when the report of the committee of the Association of Connecticut was made; he at once moved another committee to report on the subject as soon as possible to the association (1812). He was named its chairman and as such prepared the report, which by its cogent reasoning and illustrations startled the members who realized, as never before, the enormous evils of the custom of using spirituous liquors as a common beverage. The report glowed with the peculiar and vivid eloquence of its author; it was soon afterward followed by his sermons on the evils of intemperance; the latter were widely read and approved by the intelligent and well-disposed citizens of the land.

The assembly adopted the report of their committee and recommended their ministers "to preach as often as expedient on the sins and mischiefs of intemperate drink-

Rev. Charles Coffin, D.D.
(330, 331.)

ing and to warn their hearers, both in public and private, of those habits and indulgences which may have a tendency to produce it." It went further, and urged vigilance on the part of the sessions of the churches to use means by sermons and the circulation of tracts on the evil and to make efforts to limit the sale of intoxicating drinks.

XXVI.

Presbyterian Worthies.

It is fitting to recognize, though for lack of room very briefly, the worth of some of that galaxy of self-denying, learned and devoted Presbyterian ministers who during the latter portion of the last and the first half of the present century exerted a grand and consecrated influence. This they did as pastors directly upon the members of their own churches, but indirectly throughout the Union *in originating* the benevolent institutions that are to-day in their respective fields grand promoters of various forms of usefulness. These worthies, so prominent, were nobly aided and sustained by multitudes of their brother ministers of lesser note, whose names, perhaps, have been forgotten in this generation or found only in the stored-away records of their respective presbyteries.

Taggart, Dana, Morrison.—In the east was Rev. Samuel Taggart of the Presbytery of Londonery, New Hampshire. He combined consistently the statesman with the sacred office, being a member of Congress for several terms. A man of devoted piety and remarkable for his mental powers of memory and logical acumen. Dr. Daniel Dana of Newburyport, Massachusetts, and Dr. William Morrison, also of Londonderry, were men of far-reaching influence as pastors and of talents and learning that commanded the respect of the community in which they lived.

Blatchford, Nott, Porter.—In Northern New York was Dr. Samuel Blatchford of Lansingburg; a gift to the Presbyterian Church from the English Independents, a devoted friend of learning, philanthropy and missions; in the pulpit instructive and of wide influence. With him was associated Dr. Eliphalet Nott, president of Union College, who towered above his peers in sacred eloquence, and noted as a teacher and also as a moulder of the characters of the young men brought under his magic influence. Dr. David Porter of Catskill, a master in theology, and of keen sympathies, eccentric but of clear judgment. At Bridgehampton, Long Island, was Aaron Woolworth, a promoter of revivals in which he was greatly blessed, whose daily life "was a fragrance of goodness."

Rodgers, Perrine, Romeyn, Spring.—In the City of New York prominent among the Presbyterian clergymen were Dr. John Rodgers, Dr. Matthew L. Perrine, pastor of Spring Street Church; Dr. John Broadhead Romeyn of the Duane street, and Dr. Gardiner Spring of the historic Brick Church. One of the remarkable men of the period was Dr. John Rodgers, who was trained in the classical school of Dr. Samuel Blair, at Fagg's Manor. He was intimately connected as pastor with two Presbyterian churches in New York—the "Old" First and the "Historic" Brick, an offshoot of the First. During the Revolution he was compelled to flee the city, but meantime was chaplain of Gen. Heath's brigade which guarded the Hudson in the Highlands. The British evacuated New York on November 25, 1783; the following day Dr. Rodgers returned home to find both church buildings desecrated and almost ruined by the British, while the number of the church members was much diminished by death and removals. By his energetic labors these buildings were soon repaired, meanwhile the Presbyterians by invitation worshiped in the Episcopal churches St. George and St. Paul.

In every important movement in the church we always find Dr. John Rodgers prominent; he was the moderator of the first General Assembly (1789). He was a strong advocate for renewing the fraternal intercourse that had been suspended during the war between the Congregationalists of New England and the Presbyterians, "as brethren so nearly agreed in doctrine and forms of worship." He was blessed with mental ability of a high order, and a remarkable symmetry of Christian character; farseeing but not visionary; never acting till he saw clearly his way. He commanded the respect of the entire community and his influence was almost unbounded. He lived to a good old age and was succeeded in his pastorate of the Brick Church in 1810 by Dr. Gardiner Spring.

Dr. Matthew La Rue Perrine was installed pastor of the Spring Street Church in 1811. Here he spent nine years most usefully. Because of his gentle disposition and religious zeal he was characterized as "the beloved disciple," and because of his tact and prudence "as wise as a serpent and harmless as a dove." He was afterward chosen for a higher sphere of usefulness in teaching candidates for the ministry as professor of church history and polity in the Auburn Theological Seminary.

Dr. Romeyn came into the Presbyterian denomination from the Reformed Dutch Church. He was licensed when only twenty-one years of age; after filling acceptably as a minister one or two positions he was installed as pastor of the First Presbyterian Church in Albany (1804). This was a trying ordeal for the youthful pastor, as that city was the capital of the State, and to it was attracted "a large amount of cultivated intellect and professional eminence; and during the sessions of the legislature, particularly, the church was thronged with strangers—many of them persons of distinction, from various parts of the State."

Considerations in respect to his own health and that of his wife induced him to accept a call to the Cedar Street Church, New York, which afterward removed to Duane

(1808). He was its pastor for sixteen years. Never blessed with robust health, yet he labored on incessantly; his influence was felt and appreciated throughout the church, if we may judge from the important positions he was called upon to fill, one of which was in his thirty-third year to be moderator of the General Assembly. He was ever active in promoting the then infant benevolent institutions of the day and church. Especially were his labors blessed among the youth, and more young men became ministers from his congregation than from any other. He instituted catechetical classes, which were crowded by the young ladies regularly attending his Bible class, which was held especially for them; every one, it is said, became a professor of religion. Many of the most active members of the benevolent societies of the time were from the men trained under him. (*Sprague's Annals, IV., p. 216.*) The Duane Street Church under the pastorate of Dr. James W. Alexander moved to Fifth avenue and Nineteenth street (1854), and afterward under that of the late Dr. John Hall to Fifty-fifth in the same avenue (1875).

Dr. Gardiner Spring had intended to devote himself to the legal profession, but becoming deeply impressed in reflecting on religious subjects he changed his views and studied for the ministry. He succeeded Dr. John Rodgers of the Brick Church in New York in 1810, and for more than half a century he was an influential pastor and among the foremost of the Presbyterian clergymen of the day in promoting every work that aided the cause of Christ, as in the formation of the American Bible Society, in which he took an active part. He was at all times equally as zealous in advocating missionary societies—foreign and domestic—and other benevolent institutions.

Richards, Griffin.—In New Jersey's chief city were the

famous ministers, Dr. James Richards and Dr. Edward Dorr Griffin. The former by his practical wisdom and unfeigned piety was looked up to as a safe guide in all matters pertaining to ecclesiastical affairs. Dr. Griffin was remarkable for his imposing personal appearance, being of unusual stature and of symmetrical proportions, while his intellect was equally grand in its power and acquirements. Previous to his coming to Newark he had been pastor of Park Street Church, Boston, where he labored successfully in behalf of the essentials of Christianity in opposition to the most talented and learned advocates of Unitarianism, then in the height of its influence and which its devotees wielded with consummate skill. Dr. Griffin was an ardent promoter of all the benevolent institutions of the day and church till his death, November 8, 1837.

Green, the Alexanders, Miller, Finley.—Dr. Ashbel Green was inaugurated president of Princeton College in 1812. He exerted an almost boundless influence over the minds of the students, then collected from all portions of the Union. He was very decided in his views, which he persistently labored to carry out to their legitimate results. In manners of the old school, courteous but dignified and grave in his demeanor, standing by his convictions, which sometimes appeared to close observers to be near akin to theories. He took for many years a very active part in the ecclesiastical affairs of the Presbyterian Church. He has been styled "the connecting link between the old times and new."

Dr. Archibald Alexander was inaugurated August 12, 1812, the first professor of Didactic and Polemic Theology in Princeton Seminary. Here for more than thirty years he exerted an almost unbounded influence over many hundreds of theological students to the great advancement of the gospel and of the Presbyterian Church. He was a native of Virginia, where his example as an efficient pastor and preacher was highly appreciated by his brethren in the ministry and by the church at large, as were the same traits when afterward a pastor in Philadelphia. He married a daughter of the celebrated James Waddel, the "Blind Preacher," whom William Wirt so graphically describes. Dr. Alexander's sons, James Waddel and Addison, also (the one as a preacher and writer, the other as a professor) exerted in their respective spheres of usefulness a direct and blessed influence in the Presbyterian church. In the same seminary was Dr. Samuel Miller (1813), professor of Ecclesiastical History and Church Government. An urbane, scholarly gentleman, who in his special line of instruction was not inferior to that of his illustrious compeer, while the influence of his symmetrical Christian character was a power of itself.

Dr. Robert Finley, when quite a young man, because of his acquisitive mind and stability of character, gave an earnest of his future usefulness. At the age of sixteen he graduated at Princeton, and in that institution he served two years as tutor of the eight which he devoted to teaching. We find him in 1795 pastor of the church at Baskinridge, New Jersey, where he was remarkably successful in his ministrations. In order to give to his people more than usual biblical knowledge he established special classes for the purpose. Having thoroughly tested the method, and finding it the source of great edification to his own congregation, he laid the matter before the General Assembly (1815). After explanations and the account of the beneficial results, the assembly endorsed the plan and cordially recommended the practice to all its ministers and pastors. Here was the commencement of the system of Bible classes, which to-day are so numerous and so blessed in their influence.

In 1816 he devised the plan for planting a colony in

Africa, to which free colored men could emigrate and find homes for themselves and their families. He went to Washington City and in his intercourse with members of Congress and the officials of the government, secured the formation of the African Colonization Society, which ultimately founded the republic of Liberia. The first president of this society was Bushrod Washington.

Afterward Dr. Finley became president of Georgia University at Athens, in that State. But his intense labors and the debilitating effect of a climate to which he was not accustomed speedily ended his useful life, October, 1817.

Janeway, Wilson, Skinner, Ely, Patterson.—This catalogue of marked and efficient ministers found a counterpart in Pennsylvania, where lived and labored among other worthies Dr. Jacob J. Janeway, James Patriot Wilson, Thomas H. Skinner, Ezra Stiles Ely and James Patterson.

Dr. Jacob J. Janeway, long pastor of the Second Presbyterian Church, Philadelphia, exerted a beneficent influence, not limited to the city alone, but throughout the denomination. He was a native of New York City and a graduate of Columbia College (1794). He studied theology under the direction of Dr. Livingston of the Reformed Dutch Church. After remaining as colleague and pastor for twenty-seven years Dr. Janeway accepted a professorship in the Presbyterian Theological Seminary at Allegheny City, Pennsylvania, which he resigned after four years of service. His efforts were afterward specially directed to the promotion of a number of the benevolent enterprises of the church. The latter for the most part had been instituted within recent years and were gradually developing into fields of almost unbounded usefulness.

James Patriot Wilson—of Scotch-Irish descent—was pastor of the First Presbyterian Church of Philadelphia from 1806 to 1830. He was a graduate of the University of Pennsylvania (1788) and after studying law he entered upon its practice and obtained a reputation as a lawyer not exceeded by any one in his native State, Delaware. Sorrows crossed his path which had the effect, first of neutralizing his skeptical opinions and finally of leading him to become a Christian and to enter upon the gospel ministry. His talents commanded the respect of all, and being "the model of a Christian gentleman" he became one of the leading spirits of the Presbyterian Church and perhaps its foremost minister. An ardent student, with a disciplined mind, he was able to utilize his learning for the benefit of his fellow men. Of a logical mind, his sermons were well arranged and studied, though he never used a note in the pulpit. His aim was ever to elucidate the true meaning of the Scriptures and make the application to his hearers of the principles contained therein. He was one of the most learned men of the day.

Dr. Thomas H. Skinner was pastor of the Fifth Presbyterian Church of Philadelphia after having been some time co-pastor with Dr. Janeway in the Second Church. Within the latter difficulties arose. Some of the church members attributed to him "Hopkinsian tenets," when he "was decidedly Edwardian" in his preaching and in his theological views. The latter was misinterpreted, and in consequence charges of heresy were brought before the presbytery and by that body he was triumphantly vindicated. He remained pastor till his vindication was secured, when he resigned and a portion of the church members who sympathized with him also withdrew (November 5, 1815). Almost immediately he was invited to the Fifth Church, situated on Locust street, but in an undesirable location, the congregation being also in a very depressed condition. Here he labored faithfully for seven years, when he received a call to New Orleans (1822). In order to induce him to remain the place of the church building was changed to a more suitable locality, that of Arch street, where a commodious edifice was erected. Within a short time, when occupied, it was crowded with large assemblies, who were fascinated by the earnest and logical presentation of gospel truth. For a number of years Dr. Skinner remained a successful pastor of this church. Afterward he was a professor in Andover Theological Seminary, then pastor of the Mercer Street Church in New York and finally a professor in Union Theological Seminary in that city.

Ezra Stiles Ely, pastor of the Third Church and successor of Dr. Archibald Alexander, was a native of Connecticut, in which State he had been a pastor previous to his coming to Philadelphia. A man of great mental activity and zeal in behalf of the essential doctrines of the gospel, he entered into controversies with great zest, especially did he oppose "Hopkinsianism," a fruitful theme of discussion at that time among the leading minds of the Presbyterian Church. He was the author of several books on controversial subjects, while editor of the *Philadelphian*. For eleven years (1825-1836) he was stated clerk of the General Assembly, and in 1828 its moderator. In order to advance general and theological education he devised a plan to establish at Marion, Missouri, a college in connection with a theological seminary (1835). In this enterprise he labored a number of years, but the very extensive financial reverses of 1837 neutralized his efforts besides absorbing his fortune, and he returned to Philadelphia. Soon afterward he was invited to the pastorate of a Presbyterian church; here he labored with his usual zeal till a stroke of paralysis (1850) prevented his further preaching.

Rev. James Patterson became pastor of the First Presbyterian Church, Northern Liberties, in 1814. It had been a much-neglected field, and the population was composed mostly of the poorer classes. When he became pastor the entire number of the organization was only fifty-three, yet owing to his energy and apostolic zeal the house in a short time was crowded with interested listeners. The pastor visited the lanes and back alleys and found numbers of ignorant and vicious adults, while multitudes of neglected children swarmed in every direction. Having heard that a Christian lady of New Brunswick was in the habit of collecting in her own house on the Sabbath a number of poor and neglected children and there giving them religious instruction, he determined to make a similar effort, but on a much larger scale. The result was that in a short time more than a hundred children were brought together to receive Bible instruction. The work continued to prosper and "the Sabbath School Association of the Northern Liberties" was formed. Here was the germ of the Sunday school system in the city, as similar ones were organized in other churches and finally throughout the land.

Patterson also endeavored to interest his people in prayer meetings; the first one held had present besides the pastor only two apprentice boys. In the course of a few years this public beginning had increased to forty-four in number, held every week. His people "laid hold of the thing" and thus four thousand persons were brought under religious instruction. These prayer meeting services extended to the lanes and alleys of the city to a distance of four miles from the church.

Some of the measures he introduced would be deemed imprudent under ordinary circumstances, but his tact and whole-soul devotion were successful in making such measures available for the cause of Christ. He was in a peculiar position, amid a people who had been woefully neglected in their religious education, while on all sides vice in every form was rampant. During more than twenty years revival followed revival and "scores upon scores were received, successively, at single seasons of communion," and the original fifty-three became about twelve hundred communicants. (*Gillett, I., pp. 488-492*).

XXVII.

PRESBYTERIAN WORTHIES CONTINUED.

Hoge, Rice.—Among the representative Presbyterian ministers south of Pennsylvania, two held important positions of influence. These were Moses Hoge and John Holt Rice. They both were natives of Virginia.

Dr. Moses Hoge when quite a young man entered the Army of the Revolution, the classical school in which he was a pupil being broken up by the ravages of the war. We next find him in 1787 pastor of a church at Shepherdstown, in the Valley of Virginia. The religious condition of the church was at a low ebb, but twenty years of faithful and judiciously conducted services greatly increased the number of the congregation. His talents and acquirements attracted attention and he (1807) was elected president of Hampden-Sidney College, succeeding Dr. Archibald Alexander. His mind was one of unusual vigor and originality, well disciplined and well furnished with biblical knowledge. The Synod of Virginia resolved to establish a theological seminary within its own bounds and also in connection with the college, and to this professorship of theology it unanimously appointed Dr. Hoge (1812).

John Holt Rice, a man of ardent piety and more than usually blest with practical wisdom and charity, was pastor at Richmond (1812). At the time of his acceptance of that pastorate there were very few Presbyterians in the city, and they much scattered. This fact may account for the phraseology of the invitation sent him, as "a call from a number of persons in Richmond and its vicinity attached to the Presbyterian Church." After the pastorate here of about eleven years he was appointed by the Synod of Virginia to succeed Moses Hoge as professor of theology at Hampden-Sidney (1823). The seminary was in great need of funds and Dr. Rice took a journey to secure them. He visited many of the churches in New England and was successful in meeting a cordial reception for himself personally and substantial aid for the seminary.

His preaching, notwithstanding his peculiar manner, captivated his hearers by his noble thoughts and the loveliness of his Christian character. It is said by an authority that "among the ministers of the day he had not, perhaps, his superior in the mastery of sound, pure, vigorous English." He was devoted to the prosperity of the Presbyterian Church, which he believed could be obtained only through peace and unity, saying: "The church is not to be purified by controversy, but by holy love." His visit to the Northern States had an influence in drawing out the religious sympathies of the Congregationalists and Presbyterians toward one another, north and south. The times for such influence were propitious. The "era of good feeling" in the political atmosphere had the effect of alluring the people of the different sections into a broad patriotism, based upon Christian principles.

Dr. John McMillan.—We now pass beyond the Alleghanies into Western Pennsylvania and the adjacent territory. The inhabitants of this region were preëminently Presbyterian, since thither had migrated from east of the mountains numerous Covenanters and Seceders, besides the still greater number of the representatives of American Presbyterianism. In that portion of the church the most prominent theologian and instructor in theology during a period of a third of a century was Dr. John McMillan: "The father of Canonsburg Academy and of Jefferson College." His direct and most potent influence was over the minds of his pupils, not only of the many who studied for the ministry, but of those who entered other professions. He deemed himself not merely the instructor of his students but likewise their pastor, and that theory was carried into practice when afterward applied to Jefferson College, whose president was the *recognized pastor* of its students.

Porter, Power, Marquis, Dunlap, Ralston.—Among these worthy pioneers was Dr. Samuel Porter, who originally belonged to the Covenanters, his ancestors being of that branch of the Presbyterian family. Following the advice of Dr. McMillan and Dr. Joseph Smith he prepared himself for the ministry. He labored under the disadvantage of not having a full collegiate education. In respect to that requirement the presbytery in his case made an exception. Thirsting for knowledge and endowed with a vigorous mind, his attention was providentially drawn to reading and studying theological works. He as a layman became noted for his progress in that special field of knowledge.

He was licensed by the Presbytery of Redstone in 1789 and the following year was installed as pastor of the Congruity Church, in Westmoreland County; this, his only pastorate, lasted thirty-five years. He was a peculiarly gifted son of nature; remarkably eloquent, having the power to utilize his knowledge to the best advantage in presenting the truths of the gospel. He was characterized as the Patrick Henry of the Presbyterian pulpit. He was also a staunch patriot and stern lover of order; though not without personal danger, he boldly opposed in his sermons and addresses the unlawful actions of the famous whiskey insurrectionists in 1794. (*Four Hundred Years, etc., pp. 485-487.*) By his eloquent appeals he restrained their excited passions and modified their prejudices. He was quick at repartee, his imagery often startling, while his appeals were so overpowering that he held complete mastery of his audience and left the impression upon the intelligent hearer as that of a man of moral and intellectual greatness.

Rev. James Power, who has the honor of being the first settled pastor in Western Pennsylvania, was born in 1746 at Nottingham, Chester County, of that State. He graduated at Princeton, 1766, and in 1772 was licensed by the New Castle Presbytery. After preaching in Virginia for two years he crossed the mountains and entered upon missionary labors among the settlements of that region, within the territory of the now populous and rich counties of Fayette, Washington, Allegheny and Westmoreland. Afterward making a visit to the East for two years he returned with his family and continued in active duty as an itinerant missionary till in 1779 he became the regular pastor of two congregations, Sewickley and Mount Pleasant, in Westmoreland County. He was the first settled pastor in that region. His influence was of a uniform and strong character, the outgrowth of quiet and courteous manners and unremitting zeal as a pastor devoted to his special duties, while at the same time attractive to all as a graceful and instructive preacher.

Rev. Thomas Marquis was a native of Virginia, born in 1753, of Irish parentage. His father was a large landholder, but by his early death Thomas, the fourth son, and the other children were left destitute, since by the colonial law, following that of England, the landed estate went to the eldest son. When about the age of thirteen he commenced to learn the trade of a weaver. Tradition tells that in after life when working at his trade, to do which he was often compelled to eke out his support, he would fasten a book in a proper position in order that he might read and ply his loom at the same time, the only interruption being when replenishing the spool in the shuttle; and thus he became remarkably well read.

When twenty-three years of age and already married he migrated to Western Pennsylvania. After a course of private study in the classics under the tuition of Rev. Joseph Smith, and of theology under the direction of Dr. John McMillan, he was licensed by the Redstone Presbytery, April 19, 1793, in the fortieth year of his age. The following year he was installed as pastor of the Cross Creek Church in Washington County, and as such remained till 1826. It is interesting to note that he built his cabin in the woods near where the village of Cross Creek now stands, in order to be under the protection of Vance's fort, as hostile Indians were often prowling in the neighborhood. Here he became a Christian and was one of the original members of the church when it was organized (1779), and from the first one of its ruling elders till he was licensed to preach, and afterward its pastor for thirty-two years.

He was characterized as the "silver-tongued," "whose voice was music and whose art of persuasion was well-nigh perfect." Even in the last generation tradition continued to tell of his marvelous eloquence. How "he bore his audience with him on the tide of his own emotions, and sometimes their intenseness of feeling seemed to outvie his own." He was always deeply imbued with the importance of his divine subject, and of the responsibilities of the sacred office.

Ardent in his zeal for promoting missionary efforts in the numerous destitute settlements round about, he often seized the opportunity to go on tours himself, while encouraging the cause and judiciously directing the labors of others engaged in the work. Upon the whole there was no one of the worthies of the time thus laboring on the frontiers who *as a preacher* had so strong a hold upon the popular mind as Mr. Marquis. His eloquence was of a broad type, and adapted to other conditions than those on the frontiers; for illustration, when a commissioner to the General Assembly he preached to one of the most intelligent congregations in Philadelphia; his audience was deeply moved, while the pastor—the celebrated Dr. Ashbel Green—was equally as much affected by the matter and the manner of the discourse.

Other Honored Names.—Space forbids the pleasing task of enumerating, even briefly, all the names and labors of the many other worthies who filled their positions during this formative period of the Presbyterian Church in that distant region, designated "beyond the mountains." What a noble catalogue of devoted and public-spirited pastors we have in the names of such men as the Revs. Joseph Smith, John McPherrin, Robert Marshall, James Hughes, Dr. George Hill, Robert Johnston, James Guthrie, Elisha MaCurdy, the great revivalist; William Johnston, Ashbel Green Fairchild, and others; Dr. James Dunlap, a graduate of Princeton, a student of theology under James Finley, pastor of the Laurel Hill and Dunlap's Creek congregations, afterward president of Jefferson College. Dr. Samuel Ralston, born in Ireland in 1756, graduate of the University of Glasgow, 1794; imbued with the religious doctrines taught in the Bible and the Westminster Confession, migrated to Western Pennsylvania and in 1796 became pastor of the churches at Mingo Creek and Williamsport (now Monongahela City); here he labored for thirty-five years till the infirmities of age overcame his wonted energy. A man of great mental activity, of fine scholarship and withal of genuine piety, noted for his kindness of heart and gifted with the peculiar and graceful wit of his countrymen. An ardent friend of education, a trustee of Jefferson College, and for many years the president of the board. The pen, though reluctantly, must stop somewhere.

Let another—no one more competent—give a summary of the influence exerted by these worthies.

An Appreciative Estimate.—Rarely, if ever, in the history of the Presbyterian Church in this country has any of its missionary fields been occupied by a more able and devoted band of pioneer laborers than that which was covered by the Old Redstone Presbytery. In wise and sagacious forethought and provision for the prospective wants of the church, as well as in unwearied and faithful cultivation of their own fields, they have been rarely equalled and never surpassed. Their self-denial, their energy and their success alike entitle them to the highest honor. In spirit they were the successors to the Blairs, Finleys and Smiths of the revival period, who during the division adhered to the New Side and the cause of vital piety. (*Pp. 153-154.*) Many of them were rarely gifted, and would have done honor to the most exalted station, and the influence which they exerted upon the great western field then opening with inviting promise to eastern emigration cannot be estimated. (*Dr. E. H. Gillett, I., p. 267.*)

The Continued Influence.—In this catalogue comparatively only a few names have been mentioned of the noble, learned and devotedly Christian men, who during the period which includes a portion of the last quarter of the last century and the first half of this exerted a combined influence that permeated the whole Presbyterian Church. In this period, as an outgrowth of the Christian zeal of these men, originated the missionary and other benevolent institutions which to-day are a power in the land for doing good. All the pastors in their respective spheres, however humble, manifested their appreciation of the cause by impressing upon their congregations its vast importance. Here, though feeble at first, began a system of training individual church members to *realize their responsibility* to do their part by furnishing the funds requisite to carry the gospel to every portion of their own land and also to the world outside.

XXVIII.

PROGRESS OF THE CHURCH.

Formation of National Societies.—We have already noticed the formation of local societies for missionary purposes (*pp. 237-238*), but now the extension of the work demanded organizations on a larger scale to supply the religious wants of the people on the frontier, west of the older settlements. This was specially the case when the country settled down to peace and harmony after the close of the War of 1812. The Christian sentiment of sending the gospel to the destitute portions of our own country and to heathen lands was aroused and seemed to pervade almost everywhere the religious communities. This is evident from the great numbers of local missionary societies that sprung into existence and which did a grand local work. The time was, however, drawing near for the blending of these societies in the form of auxiliaries with others that were so comprehensive in their scope and operations as to be national in their character.

We will give a summary of the societies formed during the first third of this century, and to which in due time in order to promote their greater efficiency the existing local societies became auxiliary. In October, 1802, the Synod of Pittsburg, when in session in that city, organized the Western Missionary Society, its primary object being to meet the increasing and almost universal calls on the part of the people for more ministers of the gospel. This demand was the outgrowth of the great revival (*pp. 224-235*). There is a peculiar interest attached to this movement as it was the first instance in the Presbyterian body in which the theory of the church being *ex-officio* a missionany society took form in the announcement, "*The Synod of Pittsburg shall be styled the Western Missionary Society.*" This society had a far-reaching influence, as it was the germ of the present Presbyterian Board of Foreign Missions (1831). The American Board of Foreign Missions was formed in 1810, the American Bible Society in 1816, the Baptist Church entered fully upon the work of foreign missions in 1814, the Methodist Episcopal in 1819, the Reformed Dutch in 1832, Protestant Episcopal in 1838, and afterward others; in all fifteen societies were organized. It is seen by the formation of these societies that all the evangelical denominations throughout the land were manifesting unusual interest in promoting the cause of missions. (*Four Hundred Years' Hist., p. 636.*)

Reasons for Educational Societies.—In a line with these missionary movements was another, the supplying ministers in sufficient numbers to meet the increasing religious wants of the churches and of the people at large. To accomplish this object attention was directed to the expediency of aiding Christian and otherwise suitable young men, though of limited means, in obtaining the requisite education. The number is comparatively very, *very* small of Christian young men that happen to be sufficiently rich, and therefore able to bear the expenses of their own theological education, but who are also willing to devote themselves to the gospel ministry. On the other hand how slender are the hopes of success in a worldly point of view to induce students to devote sufficient time, labor and expense in preparing themselves for the ministry in either the Congregational or Presbyterian Church! The same may be said of the other denominations. The motive, therefore, for undergoing the expense and the labor in preparing for the ultimate object of the theological student must be in the desire to preach the gospel for its own sake. This may account for the fact that so many students of theology are willing to practice great self-denial in preparing themselves for the sacred office. From positive knowledge we know that as a class no students practice self-denial and labor so hard in their studies as do the theological.

The Union of Educational Societies.—There had been for a number of years local societies in New England and in some of the other States to aid theological students, but the call for ministers became so urgent and continuous that it was deemed expedient and even necessary to enlarge the field of the associations. The first to be inaugurated was the American Educational Society (1815), located at Boston. To this society in due time, to promote greater efficiency in the work, the local societies of that section for the most part became auxiliary. The Presbyterian Board of Education was established in 1819. This action of the General Assembly stimulated the movement and numbers of similar auxiliary societies were organized within the bounds of the church. Some of these, however, perhaps the majority, gave their contributions to the American society, evidently because of its better facilities of applying them practically.

A union of the American and Presbyterian Educational societies took place in 1827. The latter at this time had under its care about one hundred students, and its operations had been mostly within the bounds of the Middle States. The union of these two societies made one that was national in its influence. In truth the sentiment of nationality had greatly increased since the close of the War of 1812—sometimes characterized as the second war of independence—not merely in the political and industrial but in the religious world, and on this line of *religious policy* the missionary societies had gradually assumed a national character. In the year 1830 the American society removed its headquarters from Boston to New York City, it being a center of greater influence because of its geographical position.

Dueling.—The barbarous practice of dueling prevailed in portions of the land, though usually among those who prided themselves as being in the upper circles of society. In the minds of the Christian public, however, there was a strong undercurrent against the custom. In the vicinity where duels occasionally occurred, there was often roused an indignant feeling of disapproval, but which owing to the circumstances, was only local in its influence. Alexander Hamilton, recognized next to Washington, the statesman of the period, fell a victim of the custom at the hands of Aaron Burr. On this occasion, owing to Hamilton's position, was roused an intense and almost national sense of the atrocity of his virtual assassination. Dr. Lyman Beecher, then a young man, at the first meeting of the Synod of New York and New Jersey after the murder, introduced resolutions condemning in severe terms the custom of dueling. Although timidity adduced "strong political reasons" why they should not pass, the synod, nevertheless, in most emphatic terms, condemned the murderous practice. Dr. Beecher had already expressed his views on the subject in a sermon which startled his congregation, as he unveiled in vivid terms the criminality of the custom, which he characterized as a national sin, because of its prevalence within our borders, and he pointed out that those who honored the duelist were conniving at murder. Afterward, the sermon was published and, having a very large circulation, aided much in rousing an intense feeling against the practice.

Many other clergymen of the time did not hesitate to notice in appropriate terms the so-called "code of honor," such as Dr. John M. Mason of the Scotch Church, and notably among these sermons was one supremely eloquent, by Dr. Eliphalet Nott, then President of Union College. It was circulated in pamphlet form throughout the land, and had also a very great effect upon the public mind.

The following year the Presbytery of Baltimore instructed its commissioners to ask the General Assembly to recommend the ministers of the church not "to officiate at the funeral of any one who was known to have been concerned in a duel, or had given or accepted a challenge." The assembly (1805) took high ground, expressing its abhorrence of the practice, as "a remnant of Gothic barbarism * * * a presumptuous and highly criminal appeal to God as the Sovereign Judge." And in addition, also recommended that no persons thus engaged, unless they had given clear evidence of repentance, should be admitted to the distinguishing privileges of the church.

Opposition to Slavery.—In 1787 the United Synod of New York and Philadelphia expressed the views of the Presbyterian Church by resolving that they were in favor of "promoting the abolition of slavery"—a sentiment they had expressed again and again—and closed by "recommending the people under their care to use prudent measures consistent with the interest and state of civil society in the parts where they live, to procure, eventually, the *final abolition of slavery in America.*" This was the same year in which the Constitution of the United States was formed. The convention which framed it met on the 14th of May, in Philadelphia, and continued in session four months. The synod met also in the same city and at the same time, and its published utterance on the subject was not without influence.

The subject of slavery was also brought to the attention of the assembly soon after its organization on a national basis (1795). Twenty years later, in 1815, a number of elders, who had scruples in respect to the holding of slaves, petitioned the assembly to take action on the subject, and at the same time came an overture from the Presbytery of Ohio, asking for a deliverance in relation to the buying and selling of slaves. After expressing deep regret at the continuance of slavery, and also recognizing the difficulties in remedying the evil, the assembly urged the adoption of such measures as "to secure to the rising generation of slaves, within the bounds of the church, a religious education." It also emphatically condemned the "selling and buying of slaves by way of traffic, as inconsistent with the spirit of the gospel." It likewise condemned all undue severity in the management of the slaves, and in addition recommended the Presbyteries and sessions "to use all prudent measures to prevent such shameful and uprighteous conduct."

Deliverance on Slavery.—To preserve the connection, we give an account of the action of the assembly on the same subject, three years later (1818). It came up in a new phase; a member of the church had sold a slave, who was also a member of the church, and who was unwilling to be sold. The assembly made a somewhat lengthy deliverance on the general subject of slavery, concluding as follows: "It is manifestly the duty of all Christians who enjoy the light of the present day, to use their honest, earnest, and unwearied endeavors to correct the errors of former times, and as speedily as possible to efface this blot on our holy religion, and to obtain the complete abolition of slavery throughout Christendom, and if possible throughout the world." (*Minutes of that year.*) At the same time the assembly expressed its deep sympathy for those members of the church upon whom had been entailed the evils of human bondage, "wherein a great and most virtuous part of the community abhor slavery and wish its extermination as sincerely as any others." Every afterward, when the subject came up, the assembly was true to the principles thus announced.

Francis Herron.—Among the prominent ministers of this period was Francis Herron, a Pennsylvanian by birth, of Scotch-Irish descent, a graduate of Dickinson College (1794) under Dr. Charles Nisbet's presidency, and a licentiate of the Presbytery of Carlisle (1797). He entered at once upon his work, first as a missionary beyond the mountains; on his journey he spent a Sabbath at a settlement where Wilkinsburg now stands, and preached under the shade of a tree. He did not linger, but passed on through a little town called Pittsburg, toward the frontier, having a settler for a guide in the wilderness. On the way he spent a while among the Indians, who were encamped in the vicinity of Marietta. After spending some time as a missionary, he returned East, and on his way back he stopped at Pittsburg. The proprietor of the tavern at which he put up happened to be an acquaintance from his native place, Shippensburg. The latter asked him to preach, and Mr. Herron consented. Word was sent around, and a congregation numbering eighteen assembled to hear the sermon. The meeting was held in a rude log cabin, in which swallows having their nests flew out and in during the service. On the site of that log cabin afterward stood the First Presbyterian Church of Pittsburg, of which Dr. Herron was pastor nearly fifty years.

After a successful pastorate of ten years in the East, Dr. Herron was invited to Pittsburg (1810). He accepted the call. On entering upon his pastoral duties he was confronted with an unprecedented coldness on the part of the members of the church in respect to their Christian duties. An incident illustrates the prevailing religious sentiment. Dr. Herron proposed to hold prayer-meetings; but the proposition met with little favor. The first meeting was held in a school-room belonging to the Rev. Thomas Hunt, who was a teacher, but occasionally preached. At the first meeting were the two mininsters, one layman, and six women, and for a year and a half the number was not materially increased. At length the opposition took a more pronounced form, inasmuch as some men forbid the attendance of their wives and daughters, and finally Dr. Herron was told that such meeting must be discontinued. The reply was prompt and decisive: "Gentlemen, these meetings will not stop; you are at liberty to do as you please, and I also have liberty to worship God according to the dictates of my own conscience, none daring to molest or make me afraid." The prayer-meetings continued, and soon an unusual interest in religion became manifest, revivals followed, and numbers were converted from the world, some of whom were the leading members of the society of the city. During his long pastorate the church prospered and became a great power for good in the city, which, in the meantime, greatly advanced in population and proportionately in its material prosperity. Dr. Herron was an ever warm sympathizer in all measures for the promotion of education, of temperance, and the good morals of the community at large. "During his long pastorate he was a power in the city, beloved of his people, and influential in the church. * * * One such life is an infallible proof of the gospel, and puts infidelity to confusion." He was a prominent and influential advocate of the founding of the Western Theological Seminary, to sustain which he ever earnestly labored. Owing to the infirmities of age he resigned his pastorate at the age of seventy-six; the Master called him home in his eighty-sixth year. With the continued material progress of the city other Presbyterian churches were established. The *Second*—which had languished for a number of years—became a power for good under the pastorate of Dr. Elisha P. Swift (1819-1835), when he resigned to accept a professorship in the seminary

Other Presbyterians.—This region, of which Pittsburg may be deemed a center, from the earliest settlements within its bounds, was a favorite with Presbyterians of different orders. These all strictly held the same church policy, but differed on some points of opinion or doctrine which to the outside world appear to be non-essential. The city of Pittsburg in the early part of this century had a number of churches belonging to the Reformed Presbyterian and the Associate Reformed, etc. Here one of these bodies established a Theological Seminary. The leading pastors of these churches were Drs. Black and Bruce.

Revivals in the South.—In addition to the revivals in Kentucky and in Western Pennsylvania, which have been already noticed, were many instances of the special outpouring of the spirit in other portions of the country, almost contemporary with the former or in the immediately succeeding years. These later revivals were principally in the Carolinas and in Georgia and in the western portions of Virginia. They had to contend with a phase of infidelity, though not quite so political or pronounced and blatant as that which obstructed the work in Kentucky. It was a *deism* derived from the writings of Hume, Voltaire, and Paine. A similar influence that affected the physical system of the convicted in Kentucky was, to a limited extent, also experienced here. These abnormal exercises elicited much adverse criticism, and a number of Presbyterian clergymen came, some many miles, to witness these unusual scenes. Among whom was Dr. Moses Hoge of Virginia, who was one of the most judicious and conservative men of the time, and who made himself familiar with the experience of many of the converts. His prejudices vanished, and though he did not see the order and propriety that he wished, he deemed the work "very extraordinary," and expressed his conviction that it was "a work of God," and "was satisfied that he had before him the evidence of the operation of Divine truth and of the Spirit of God."

During the first twenty years of this century, owing to political disturbances, the advance of the Presbyterian Church in the number of its communicants, was not very rapid, yet the latter increased forty per cent, while the increase of the general population was only twenty per cent. During the same period there were, comparatively, isolated revivals in New Jersey and in Central and Western New York. Scarcely was there a Presbytery that did not report: "The triumphs of evangelical truth and the power of sovereign grace." The assemblies of the years 1802 and '03 took cognizance of these times of spiritual refreshings, and in gratitude to God made mention of "the very extraordinary success of the gospel" in many places. These, so to speak, isolated revivals continued for a number of years, and were thankfully recognized by the assemblies from time to time, but the War of 1812 sadly interfered with the general progress of vital piety in all the denominations, and of this deleterious influence the Presbyterian was by no means exempt.

Progress in Religion, How Promoted.—The progress of religion in both the Carolinas and in Georgia was greatly promoted by the labors of the noble corps of Presbyterian ministers resident in that section of the land; they were also greatly aided by a few finely educated ministers who migrated thither from the North. The oversight of the churches in these three States was, virtually, in the hands of the Synod of the Carolinas rather than in the control of the General Assembly, since the latter body could give but little aid, as it was overwhelmed with calls for ministers further west and southwest, which came most urgently especially from the Synod of Kentucky. The Synod of the Carolinas was, however, nobly sustained not only by the pastors but by the people — the church members themselves— in their zeal for the cause of religion and that of education. Thus they labored on and became more and more self-reliant and as a result the churches were imbued with Presbyterian sentiments. The latter phase was not in consequence of outside influence, since into that section comparatively few Presbyterian families and church members removed from the Eastern and Middle States; for obvious reasons the tide of migration of families from the latter was much larger toward the West beyond the mountains than toward the South on the Atlantic slope. The Congregationalists who happened to come fell in with the Presbyterians, and so, usually, did the Huguenots and their descendants. This may partially account for the uniformity in the Presbyterian influence in all that region. It is a matter of history that there has been less discrepancies in the interpretation of the Bible and of the Confession of Faith in the southern portion of the church than in the northern. There was less of critical Biblical scholarship in the South than in the North; and less material progress owing to the inefficiency of slave labor. The people moved along in the even tenor of their way, without being much affected by outside influences emanating from other portions of their own land, or from Europe, in the form of immigration, because of the existing slavery; neither were they to much extent affected by the stimulus of commerce, nor in the religious world by theological discussions.

The church members, however, did not cease to follow the traditions of their fathers in relation to an educated ministry, and that spirit pervaded the whole region, and numbers of the best educated pastors had each a few pupils whom they instructed in the classics, in Hebrew, in Greek, and in theology. In this manner these worthies labored incessantly to secure an educated ministry, and in due time theological seminaries were established.

The Migration of a Church.—A Congregational church and its pastor migrated from Dorchester, Mass., in 1695, to South Carolina, "with a desire to encourage the settlement of churches and the promotion of religion in the Southern plantations." They located on the Ashley river, eighteen miles above Charleston, and named the place after their former home. Fifty-seven years afterward, for sufficient reasons, the church members moved in a body, their pastor, John Osgood, a graduate of Harvard, accompanying them, and made a new settlement at a place named Midway, because of its position between the Ogechee and Altamaha rivers. Here upon lands granted them by the Georgia colonial authorities they began their new home in 1754, but in 1778 their house of worship and nearly all their rude private dwellings were burned by the British soldiers under the command of General Provost. The members of the church and society were scattered, but after the close of the war they returned and repaired their desolate homes. They erected a log church and true to their instincts they also founded an academy.

Afterward, in 1874, the Rev. Abiel Holmes, from Boston, was their pastor. He was the father of the late Oliver Wendell Holmes, and author of *American Annals*. Jedediah Morse succeeded Mr. Holmes in 1786. The latter was the author of the first complete American geography. This church united finally with the Presbyterian, and had a number of pastors under whose charge it did good service in furnishing a number of Presbyterian ministers for the churches in that region, among whom was Daniel Baker, the famed evangelist.

There was in this entire region during the period of twenty-five or thirty years commencing in 1790 a noble band of earnest and self-denying Presbyterian ministers, concerning whose labors we cannot go into detail, but whose memories are embalmed in the reminiscences of the direct descendants of those to whom they ministered, and in the dusty records of their respective presbyteries; such as the names of Thomas Cummings, Thomas Goulding, William Whirr, John Brown, famed as the President of the State University at Chapel Hill—a model teacher, loving and beloved by his pupils. To these may be added the brothers Caldwell, Joseph and Andrew, John McIntyre, Allen McDougal, and many others.

Prayer-meetings.—An outgrowth of the revivals just mentioned was the formation of a "praying society," an innovation upon the usual routine of indifference that prevailed among the churches. At first very few of the church members could be induced to take part in these social prayer-meetings or even attend them, but ere long a spirit of prayer manifested itself and the attendance began to increase greatly. In consequence, a series of meetings for prayer and preaching was commenced, to which came the people in crowds and in a spirit of devotion. The preaching was a practical presentation of gospel truth, and no undue effort was made to excite the emotions of the audiences. Decorum and good order prevailed, no sensational or unscriptural expressions were heard, yet in more than one instance numbers were stricken down in a manner similar to that which had occurred in Kentucky.

Union Meetings.—This spiritual interest prevailed to such an extent that Christians of other denominations were drawn more closely together, and what was unusual at that time, union meetings were held, at which thousands often attended. Several Methodist and Baptist clergymen took part in these exercises, though the greater number of preachers were Presbyterian. Here were converts in great numbers and of all ages, from children of ten years to persons of seventy. The influence of these meetings extended for numerous miles in every direction, since the converts, on returning to their homes, carried with them a spirit of prayer, and an aggressive religion that influenced their neighbors, and thus the work went on for a number of years. The infidelity and scepticism, once so prevalent, disappeared. Among those brought to Christ during these years were a number of young men who afterward devoted themselves to the ministry.

There was no portion of the Presbyterian Church during the period from 1790 to 1825 in which was manifested more genuine zeal for the gospel than in the Carolinas, Southwestern Virginia, Georgia, and East Tennessee. The people had very few facilities for the accumulation of wealth; as best they could they met from year to year the ever-recurring expenses of their families. They depended upon themselves alone for their household comforts of plain food and clothing of domestic maunfacture. Only in a few districts had they facilities by being within reach of the ocean for exchanging their lumber, tar, and turpentine for comforts, to them luxuries, obtained from the outside world. Yet, if we take into consideration these material disadvantages, the amounts they gave to sustain the institutions of the gospel were in proportion as great as in any other part of the Presbyterian Church.

Drs. James Hall and S. E. McCorkle.—We have scarcely room to merely notice two worthies, who labored in this Presbyterian field—Drs. James Hall and Samuel Eusebias McCorkle. The former was licensed by the Presbytery of Orange, and was afterward pastor for forty years at Bethany, North Carolina. His ministry is described as "a glowing scene of untiring activity and earnest zeal to win souls to Christ." At one communion he admitted eighty from the world and at another sixty. He was a native of Carlisle, Pennsylvania, and of Scotch-Irish descent. At an early age his parents removed to North Carolina, and he was brought within the bounds of the congregation which he afterward served as pastor for so many years. He graduated at Princeton in 1774, under the presidency of Dr. John Witherspoon. He refused the office of tutor, as he wished to devote himself entirely to preaching the gospel. He was accustomed to travel at certain seasons on missionary tours in the country round about, and revival after revival followed his labors, but none of which were more powerful than those within the bounds of his own congregation. He was not deaf to the calls of his country, and in consequence at one time he was an officer in the army of the Revolution. His eloquence inspired his men, many of whom were from his own congregation, to repel Cornwallis in one of his raids. Dr. Hall was offered the commission of Brigadier-General, but he declined the honor.

Dr. Samuel Eusebias McCorkle was a native of Pennsylvania, but his parents removed to North Carolina, when he was a child. He graduated at Princeton (1772) in the same class with Dr. John McMillan. Licensed by the Presbytery of New York, he was commissioned to labor in the South, under the direction of the Presbytery of Hanover and Orange. After preaching two years as missionary, he was settled over a church, Thyatira, N. C., within the bounds of the Presbytery of Concord. Here he labored for thirty-five years as a preacher, and also as the principal of a classical school named *Zion Parnassus*. His influence was greatly extended through his numerous students, not only in the church but in the world outside.

XXIX.

Progress of the Church Continued.

An increased interest in religious affairs became manifest in Maryland in 1799, especially in Baltimore and in the churches in that vicinity. Though these churches were nominally Presbyterian, there appears to have been no effort to organize them in accordance with the polity of that denomination. Means were taken in 1802 to remedy this defect by electing representative men as elders.

Drs. Inglis and Nevins.—About the commencement of the century Rev. James Inglis, of Scotch descent, a graduate of Columbia College, New York City, a student of law under the famed Alexander Hamilton, and afterward of theology under the direction of Dr. John Rodgers of the Brick Church, in the same city, was licensed by the Presbytery of New York. Soon afterward he was called to the pastorate of the First Presbyterian Church in Baltimore, where he remained eighteen years as a successful and laborious pastor. He was remarkable for his ease of manner in the pulpit, combined with a gracefulness of style and flow of finished oratory, but which did not betray the labor of its careful preparation.

The work laid down by Dr. Inglis in 1820 was taken up by Dr. William Nevins. The latter was a native of Norwich, Connecticut, and a graduate of Yale (1816) and of Princeton Seminary (1819). Within a few years his labors were crowned with success in an extensive revival whose influence was felt for many years afterward in his own church as well as in others within the city. This distinguished man was an original thinker, and had the aptness of clothing his vivid thoughts in graceful and appropriate language in the pulpit or out of it, and thus he became a recognized power in the religious literature of the time. In the midst of his usefulness he was taken away in his thirty-eighth year. He was universally lamented by the church and the community in which he labored, and also in the outside world.

Religious Interest in New Jersey.—In the State of New Jersey, commencing in 1802, and continuing for several years, occurred several revivals of religion. In their main feature they were more like those which had blessed Western Pennsylvania than the revivals in Kentucky or in the Carolinas. At the same time there were a number of finely educated and gifted Presbyterian ministers within the State, such as Drs. Robert Finley, M. L. Perrine, Asa Hillyer, James Richards, Edward D. Griffen—the latter two of Newark—Henry Kollock, and the venerable Dr. Alexander McWhorter, also of Newark, and many other worthy preachers.

On one occasion a meeting for religious services was held at Madison, where Dr. Robert Finley was pastor in connection with Baskingridge. An immense concourse of people assembled, and no less than twenty-three ministers from different portions of the State were present. The meeting was presided over by the venerable Dr. McWhorter. Because of the numbers it was found necessary to divide the multitude into two assemblies, the one meeting in the church and the other in the open-air.

The exercises were characterized by an unusual and deep solemnity and interest. The preachers' souls appeared to glow with devotion, to which responded the emotions of the Christians present with holy fear and trembling. There were, also, a large number of congregations in that region that were soon after visited by the outpouring of the Holy Spirit. Notably was this the case in Newark in the congregation under the pastorate of the celebrated Dr. Griffen. A day of fasting and prayer was held, which was followed by scenes described as truly Pentecostal. The number of conversions was about two hundred and fifty; they were of all ages, from nine years to three score and ten. Some of the latter had been resolute opposers to the Christian religion, and some were apostates and some abandoned characters.

Increase of the Church in New York.—The Presbyterian church increased more rapidly in the central and western portions of the State of New York than in the eastern. Within ten years (1800-1810) about fifty new churches were organized in the former region, and of this number nearly all became self-supporting and permanent, and within the next five years twenty additional churches were organized. In 1800 the General Assembly stationed the Rev. Jedediah Chapman of the Presbytery of New York at Geneva, and he became a sort of missionary bishop for that region. In succeeding years other ministers were sent to aid in the cause.

Dr. James Carnahan.—Among the Presbyterian pastors who labored in Central New York was James Carnahan, who deserves a passing notice. He was of Scotch-Irish descent, born in 1775 in Cumberland County, Pennsylvania, a son of a farmer, who left him an orphan at the age of twelve years. He at once entered upon a struggle to obtain an education, his early years being spent in farm labor. At the age of eighteen we find him beyond the mountains, entering upon a preparatory course of study at the Canonsburg Academy. When he was through his preparatory studies, Dr. John McMillan, appreciating the good qualities of the young man, loaned him the means to prosecute his studies at Princeton. Carnahan set out on

REV. JAMES CARNAHAN, D.D., LL.D.
(282, 283.)

foot across the mountains; his companion was Jacob Lindsley, who, after many years of service in the church as a preacher and pastor, was professor in Ohio University at Athens, in that State. Lindsley owned a horse and he generously shared the latter's service with his friend on the way. One would ride on ahead some miles, then tie the horse; the other would come up and, mounting, ride till he overtook his friend, thus reaching the end of their journey of about three hundred miles.

Carnahan on his graduation at Princeton (1800) received the highest honor of his class, and the following year was appointed tutor in the college, and four years later he was licensed to preach the gospel. His first pastorate was in Utica and Whitesborough, New York, but after a service of six years his health failed and in consequence he resigned and engaged in teaching at Princeton, and afterward in Georgetown, D. C. During these years, Dr. Carnahan, by his zeal and labor, kept himself in touch with the most advanced scholarship of the times, and yet he was as remarkable for his tact and accurate knowledge of the practical affairs of men. He was elected President of Princeton College in 1823, succeeding Dr. Ashbel Green. For more than thirty years he presided over that institution, and with unusual success; thus exerting in the Union a healthful influence in the promotion of education and morals, based on the truths of the Bible, as exemplified far and wide in the lives and examples of the numerous students that during nearly a third of a century had been under his care and direction.

Associations and Presbyteries in New York State.— The Connecticut Missionary Society during this period (1789-1815) continued to send preachers to visit the settlements in Central and Western New York. Among these missionaries occur the names James H. Hotchkin, Seth Williston, Jedadiah Bushnell, David Higgins, who was a native of Haddam, Connecticut, and a graduate of Yale, and many other worthies. In 1802, Higgins was installed by a council of Congregational and Presbyterian ministers as pastor of the church at Aurelius. Numerous revivals, the fruit of the labors of these devoted missionaries and pastors, prevailed throughout this region from 1797 for a number of years. These times of spiritual refreshing were followed by a succession of new churches that were in due time organized.

In 1803 the "Middle Association" was formed by the Congregationalists in what was termed the "Military Tract," in which lands were granted to settlers on liberal conditions. This area embraced the counties of Cayuga, Onondaga, Seneca, Cortland, and portions of three others. The territory thus named contained at this time an estimated population of 30,000. This association, after an existence of eight years, on its own motion, dissolved and its members individually united with the presbyteries of Cayuga and Onondaga. According to its constitution its "ministers and churches were held amenable both as respected doctrine and practice." In this rule the association partially adopted the Presbyterian policy.

The uniting in this manner with the Presbyterian denomination by the members of this association disclosed as a motive the fact that among the intelligent and thoughtful members of the Congregational churches there had originated a desire for a stricter order of government than obtained in their body. Rumors had reached them of the sad defection toward Unitarianism among their sister churches in Massachusetts. They recognized that under the Congregational system there was a lack of authority to enforce church discipline, even in a gentle manner. This feature was true, especially in respect to deviations from what was termed the orthodox or evangelical doctrines. In order to avoid an investigation and perhaps consequent censure, the accused minister or church had only to withdraw from the association. In accordance with the original system of independency as established in Massachusetts (*See p. 71*) the accused congregation was free from the censure of sister churches, except the *negative one,* implied in the non-recognition of Christian fellowship. The latter could withdraw from the association and assume the name, say, of the Second Congregational Church, and thus retain the prestige of that name while rejecting essential and characteristic doctrines of the Church of Christ. This sentiment among devout Congregationalists had permeated the entire region. It may be on this ground that when an effort was made—June, 1810 —to form a State (Congregational) association, the plan failed, because of the great diversity of opinion as to the expediency of the attempt, since some of the associations did not send delegates. The following year, as we have seen, the Middle Association dissolved itself. The outcome was a preference for a union in some manner with the Presbyterian mode of church polity, that ecclesiastical order might be maintained.

Religion West of the Genesee—Mr. Allen.—A partial idea of the condition of society at this time in the territory west of the Genesee river may be obtained from the notes of the Rev. Dr. William Allen, who was afterward the honored President of Bowdoin College. Beginning in 1804 as a missionary, he traversed this entire region on horseback, even to Niagara Falls, preaching as opportunity served, in the scattered settlements. He afterward published a brief but stirring "plea for the Genesee country." There were at that time only twelve Congregational and Presbyterian ministers in the region east of the Genesee, while "west of that river to Lake Erie, and from Lake Ontario to the Pennsylvania line there was no meeting-house, no settled minister nor missionary, except Mr.

Allen." The agent of the Holland Land Company—Joseph Ellicott—was, in his way, the most influential man in the section of the country west of the Genesee. He was a notorious infidel, after the then fashionable French type as represented by Voltaire, Volney, and Paine. A club whose members professed these sentiments, was formed and exerted its legitimate influence, and as a result the Sabbath was virtually ignored, and systematic efforts were made through the club to oppose Christianity and to such an extent that it passed into a proverb "that Sunday could not find its way west of the Genesee." A narrative of the state of religion in 1811, as found in the report of missionaries, ventures the opinion that the country bordering on Lake Erie was "among the most destitute in the United States." To this sad story may be added that of the Rev. R. Phelps: "In many of the settlements the state of society is truly deplorable. Scarcely is the form of godliness visible. The Sabbath is awfully profaned, and God's name is dishonored in various ways. Infidelity abounds to an alarming degree, and in various shapes."

Immigration Coöperation.—The tide of immigration continued, and with increasing volume, to pour into the central portion of the State; that is, up the valley of the Mohawk and in the lake region. Meanwhile the church organizations increased, but in a less proportion. The several missionary societies, as far as they were able, sent ministers and licentiates to supply the religious wants of the people. It was the custom of the settled pastors to devote a portion of their time in preaching tours among the more destitute churches and settlements.

The presbyteries frequently designated the portions of the country to be visited, and the preachers for that service. In this evangelist work the Congregationalists and Presbyterians labored in unison.

The General Assembly gave its unqualified sanction to

this coöperation in evangelical work, but it was found more advantageous for the promotion of the cause to depute its management largely to the synods and presbyteries, within whose bounds the missionary labor was to be done. As the entire church was interested, the assembly took measures to secure a certain amount of supervision by means of the annual reports of its standing committees. In accordance with this arrangement the portion of the country known as Northern Pennsylvania, Western and Central New York, came under the care of the Synods of Pittsburg, Geneva, and Albany.

In 1811 the Ontario Association, following the example of the Middle, dissolved itself, and its churches and ministers united with the Presbytery of Geneva. It is to be noted that the boundaries of these several presbyteries and associations overlapped one another, and as they were prosecuting the same work it was evident the latter could be more effectively accomplished under the control of one organization than of two or three. From this time forward for a number of years, there is no record of which we are aware of any Congregational association being formed in the State of New York.

XXX.

SETTLEMENTS AND CHURCHES IN THE WEST.

The Settlement of Marietta.—As early as 1785 the Continental Congress commissioned a Mr. Hutchins to survey the territory a portion of which afterward was included within the bounds of the present State of Ohio. The institutions of the church were introduced into that region when the settlement was made at Marietta on the Ohio river. This site was selected from others that were almost equally attractive. The visitors to that wilderness brought back glowing, but in the main fair, descriptions of the fertile soil which, when compared with that of New England, was apparently inexhaustible. They told of the great beauty of the scenery along the rivers; of the magnificent forests of stately sugar-trees, whose product was so necessary to the comfort of the household; the great oaks and the large black-walnut trees, and many other varieties of useful woods; the immense vines climbing the trees and loaded with clusters of grapes, while the open spaces, where the sunshine could reach the ground, bloomed with white-clover and other grasses, and all cheered by an abundance of brooks fed by perennial springs of crystal water, and in addition to these were found iron ore, coal, and salt. No wonder the younger portion of the people, especially, were eager to migrate to such a land.

Several bands from the East, mostly from New England, pressed on to inherit this land of promise. Between February and June, 1788—the year in which the Constitution of the United States was adopted—4,500 persons passed on their way by Fort Harmer, according to the report of the officer in command. One of these migrating companies set out from Danvers, Mass., in December, 1787, and in January, 1788, one from Hartford, Conn. They had the canvas coverings of their wagons labeled: "To Marietta on the Ohio." They passed through the intervening States and reached the east end of the famous Braddock military road at Wills Creek, now Cumberland, Maryland, and passed on it over the mountains. On the west side, for some unknown reason, instead of taking the nearer route down Redstone creek to the Monongahela, they went down the Youghiogheny to where the village of West Newton now stands. Thence in a crude flatboat which they built, they floated to the Monongahela and on to the Ohio, and then down to the mouth of the Muskingum, and landed on April 7, 1788, where Marietta now stands. The number of persons who arrived safely was only forty-seven instead of the one hundred who at first designed to be of the party, but numbers of the latter joined the colony in after years.

The plan for the migration was devised by Gen. Tupper, who had been an assistant of Surveyor Hutchins, and also an officer in the Revolution. He was greatly aided in the enterprise by Rev. Dr. Manassah Cutler of Massachusetts, and a number of other prominent gentlemen. Congress gave substantial aid in granting lands on liberal terms. George Washington commended the movement highly, saying: "I know many of the settlers personally; and there never were men better calculated to promote the welfare of such a community."

The progress of the first year of the settlement was very satisfactory, but soon after the settlers began to be annoyed in various ways by hostile Indians, such as stealing horses and capturing and plundering unprotected flatboats loaded with needed supplies. These depredations continued till August, 1794, when Gen. Wayne's overwhelming victory dispersed their savage enemies. (*Four Hundred Years, etc., p. 680.*)

Story, Lindsley, Hughes.—The first minister we have note of in this connection was Rev. Daniel Story, a native of Boston and graduate of Dartmouth College (1780), who nine years afterward began to preach in Marietta, and also in two other places in the vicinity—Waterford and Belpre. At Marietta, in the winter, the block-house was used as a place of worship, and in the summer services were held under the shade of immense forest trees. No church was organized at Marietta till 1796; about that time came missionaries who were sent by the Synod of Pittsburg. Rev. Stephen Lindsley, a licentiate of the Presbytery of Ohio, began his labors as pastor of a Presbyterian congregation in 1803; three years later the Rev. Samuel Prince Robbins from Connecticut, also entered upon his duties as pastor of the original church of Marietta—the presumption is it was Congregational.

It is stated that the Rev. Thomas E. Hughes was the first permanently settled pastor north of the Ohio. He was a graduate of Princeton (1797), and studied theology under the direction of Dr. John McMillan, and was licensed to preach by the Presbytery of Ohio.

Immigrants were rapidly flowing into these regions, and new settlements were forming from time to time, especially in the southwestern portion of the State, as that section was more easily reached by water than was the interior by land.

Cincinnati Founded.—The fertile soil of the territory between the two Miamis had attracted much attention, since Daniel Boone, when a captive (1778) among the Shawnees Indians, who lived in that region, made the fact known on his return home. The Hon. Cleves Symmes,

SETTLEMENTS AND CHURCHES IN THE WEST. 291

in order to verify the truths of these accounts of the richness and beauty of the territory, made a personal visit for investigation.

Symmes had been a member of Congress from a district in New Jersey. He now projected a settlement in that region. A company of thirty persons through his influence was induced to migrate thither (July, 1788). They went by land and were fully equipped to begin a settlement. They had four wagons, each drawn by four horses. They reached their destination in about six months, and laid the foundation for the city of Cincinnati (December 28, 1788), by forming a settlement on its site. Shortly after the colony had an accession of fourteen persons. They all went to work in the primitive forest, and built a few log cabins. and block-houses as a protection against hostile Indians. In a year's time the population was "eleven families and twenty-four bachelors." This was in addition to the United States garrison which had been sent to guard the infant settlement. Troublous times were caused by hostile Indians, and it was not till after Gen. Wayne's victory that the residents felt secure from their savage enemies.

Several settlements meantime were made in the surrounding country, but they were greatly hampered in their progress for a number of years by the continued fear of attacks from the Indians. For this reason immigration almost ceased till the power of the latter was broken; after which event the settlers had peace and continued prosperity.

The First Church Organized.—In laying out the town in 1789, the settlers, a majority of whom were from New Jersey, and presumably Presbyterians, designated certain lots for a church building and school-house. The following year "Father" Rice of Kentucky organized a church which afterward was known as the First Presbyterian

Church of Cincinnati. The congregation took formal possession of the premises thus set apart for religious purposes, but for a long time they were unable, for lack of means, to erect a suitable church building. They usually met for worship in a horse-mill, and in private houses, till they were able to build. The Rev. James Kemper, of the Synod of Kentucky, came in 1791 to minister to them, and so great was the joy in the prospect of having a settled pastor that a large number of the church members volunteered to escort him from Kentucky across the river to his new charge. A subscription was at once commenced to raise funds to build a church edifice. Meanwhile, the weather permitting, the people met for worship in the open air, on the designated lots, after having cleared a sufficient space from the native forest. They sat upon rude logs, hewn smooth on one side, each man having his trusty rifle by his side. The following year a church building was finished, and the four lots originally dedicated for religious purposes were enclosed; they were on the corner of Main and Fourth streets.

After Mr. Kemper left (1795) the church then had a membership of 226, in which were included the names of the baptized children, who were regarded as subjects of discipline. It had no settled minister till 1808, when Joshua L. Wilson became its pastor. He was a native of Virginia, but removed with the family to Kentucky. He was licensed to preach in 1802, and two years afterward we find him pastor of two Presbyterian churches, one at Bardstown and the other at Big Spring, Kentucky; from the latter he was called to Cincinnati to the pastorate of the First Presbyterian Church, which he faithfully served for thirty-eight years. About this time the town—in modern phrase having a boom—began to increase very rapidly in population and in general prosperity, while the churches grew in proportion.

SETTLEMENTS AND CHURCHES IN THE WEST. 293

It will be noted that the early settlements in the State of Ohio were on its southern border along the river of the same name, and afterward they extended gradually toward the north, the pioneers being attracted by the fertility of the valleys of the tributaries of that river, such as the Miami and the Scioto. Numerous isolated settlements were made; the more prominent at that time were those of which, respectively, the towns of Dayton, Chillicothe, and Columbus were the centers. These three were the first—namely, Revs. James Welch, Robert G. Wilson, and James Hoge—to have stated Presbyterian pastors of their churches. Meanwhile devoted missionaries were traveling and preaching in the smaller and scattered settlements throughout the entire region. It was estimated that in 1810 the population of all these amounted to 25,000

Settlements in the Reserve.—During this period a stream of immigrants was pouring into the northeastern portion of the State. These came principally from the States of Massachusetts and Connecticut, and they located on the Connecticut or Western Reserve. These settlers brought with them their love for the gospel and for a free and liberal education, and in consequence churches and school-houses were soon established wherever there was a population sufficient to sustain them. These churches, for the most part, were Presbyterian and Congregational, the latter predominating, though there was very often the blending of the two in Christian fellowship, when circumstances authorized such a union of the membership in the churches.

Ministers of the Ohio Presbytery.—The Synod of Pittsburg, from its position, had easier access to the churches and settlements in the Reserve than any other ecclesiastical body. One of its presbyteries, the Ohio, availed itself of this privilege, and sent numbers of missionaries to these destitute churches. The presbytery itself, as well as its individual members, manifested great ability and enterprise and true devotion to the cause of preaching the gospel in the settlements that were constantly forming by the multitudes of people who were coming from as far east as Massachusetts. Realizing its responsibility in the premises, the presbytery supplied, as far as possible, licentiates and ministers, who in turn, by their arduous labors and self-denial, exerted an influence that indirectly tells for good even to this day. The ministers thus sent by the presbytery were welcomed by the churches on the Reserve, and between them existed cordial relations. Though the Reserve belonged originally to Connecticut, the majority of the inhabitants, in 1813, were not from New England.

Prominent among the earlier preachers sent by the presbytery, was Rev. William Wick, a native of Long Island, but who removed to Western Pennsylvania with his father's family; received his education at the Academy at Canonsburg, studied under Dr. John McMillan, and was licensed to preach the gospel by the Presbytery of Ohio, August 28, 1799. Under its direction he entered upon his duties as a missionary to the people of the Reserve, where he became the first settled minister, when, in 1800, he was ordained and installed pastor of the Presbyterian churches of Youngstown and Hopewell. He made, however, yearly preaching tours among the neighboring destitute churches; in this he was sustained by the Connecticut Missionary Society. After three years his church at Youngstown was blessed with an extensive revival. One of its subjects was Thomas Barr, who afterward studied theology, was licensed to preach, and became one of the most laborious and successful preachers of the time in the Presbyterian Church.

Rev. Joseph Badger.—The name of Joseph Badger de-

serves remembrance perhaps more than any one of the
many devoted missionaries and pastors who blest these
regions by their labors. He was sent as their first minister
to the Reserve by the Connecticut Missionary Society.
He preached his first sermon in that region in the Presbyterian Church in Youngstown.

Badger was a native of Massachusetts, born at Wilbraham, in 1757; his parents were intimate friends of the
sainted David Brainerd, whose mantle seems to have fallen
on their son Joseph. Immediately after the battle of Lexington, though in his eighteenth year, he entered the army
of the patriots. He participated in the battle of Bunker
Hill, and went with Gen. Arnold in his expedition
against Quebec. After two years of service he was compelled by almost fatal ill-health to be discharged from the
army, though two months after his arrival at his home
he volunteered to aid in repelling the British under Gov.
Tryon, who had just burned Danbury, Conn. (1777).
His health having been restored, he again enlisted in the
army, but when his term of service expired he found himself penniless, as his pay in Continental money was nearly
worthless. Meanwhile, becoming a Christian, he determined to obtain an education. The progress in his preparation was slow, but his energy enabled him to surmount
every obstacle. To secure means he often labored at the
loom, and sometimes taught school. At length he presented himself to be examined for entrance into Yale, and
being accepted, he struggled through, often doing menial
service round the college. He graduated, and after studying theology was licensed to preach, and for a number
of years was pastor of a church in Blanford, Mass. Then
his sympathies were specially drawn toward the destitute
settlements of the West, and at his own request he was
dismissed to enter upon the duties of a missionary under
a commission from the Connecticut Society. The follow-

ing month he set out on horseback for his distant field of labor in the Reserve. During the winter and spring he traveled over the southern portion, preaching to destitute congregations. The badness of the roads, often only bridle-paths, did not deter him, neither did the swollen streams, which he taught his horse to swim. In the summer of the same year he visited the other portions of the region, finding his way to Cleveland.

The Presbytery of Ohio, about this time, requested Mr. Badger to accompany the Rev. Thomas Hughes in a missionary visit to the Indians in Detroit. He reported: "There was not one Christian to be found in all that region, except a black man, who appeared to be pious." The missions to the Indians by both the Congregationalists and the Presbyterians were, for the most part, unsuccessful, and for that reason they were, about this time, partially suspended. Under the influence of their medicine men, they refused to accept the good white man's religion; but preferred the bad white man's whisky and to imitate his evil habits.

Soon after Mr. Badger's return from this mission he set out for home, to report to the society under whose care he was. His health, meanwhile, was so broken by exposure and toil that he required assistance in mounting his horse, to which he could scarcely cling. Nevertheless, he resolutely pursued his journey, though weakened by disease, for which he daily took medicine, and by hunger, for on a portion of his five-days' travel in the wilderness, he was compelled to resort to chestnuts for food. At length he reached the town or settlement of Hudson, where from necessity he rested for a while. Meantime, he organized a church at Austinburg (October, 1801), consisting of fourteen members—eight men and six women. In course of time he reported to the society, and also announced his intention of removing to the Reserve with his family, which consisted of a wife and six children, and to devote the remainder of his life to preaching the gospel in that destitute region.

We find him a month or two later setting out on his long and laborious journey, with his worldly effects on board a four-horse wagon, which served the purpose of a carriage and also a tent for the family. In that inclement season, when his progress was retarded by a storm which covered the ground with snow two feet deep, he put his wagon-bed upon runners and hurried on, and after two months of such unprecedented toil, he arrived, in the early spring, at Austinburg. Within two weeks more his humble log-cabin was put up, in which was a floor of native earth, but neither chair nor table, nor even a door, while the chinks between the logs were unfilled. It was now time to plant a garden; that essential work he left for his wife and family to do, while he himself, as in duty bound, set out on a preaching tour from which he did not return till the middle of the following June (1802).

In order to have more fully the sympathy of brother ministers, about this time he connected himself with the Presbytery of Erie, which had been recently set off (1801) from those of Ohio and Redstone. When asked why he, a Congregationalist, wished to change his church relations, he answered: "I believe you are ministers of the gospel. I am alone; I need your watch and counsel." He ever after acted in evangelical work in connection with the Presbyterians. We have not room to go further into detail concerning his trials, privations, and incessant labors.

Woman's Self-denying Labors.—In closing this sad story of labor and toil under numerous distressing circumstances there is presented a phase of the subject that deserves the attention and ought to enlist the earnest sympathy of all Christians. It is a sad fact, in the histories of the Presbyterian Church in the United States, that the self-denying labors of the women who have been the wives of devoted ministers of the gospel are virtually ignored; their names and noble deeds left to be recorded in a book that will be open for inspection in the Judgment Day alone. They shared toils with their husbands; cheered them in hours of gloom that so often overshadow the homes, especially of missionaries on our frontiers. The wife of the home missionary to-day may not have to endue trials similar to those of Mrs. Badger, in her long and toilsome winter journey, which was devoid of comfort and replete with deprivations, that the wives of ministers of to-day cannot realize when they travel. But there are other discomforts equally as pungent in giving pain to the educated, refined, and sensitive wife, who has left her home, delightful in its associations, to share with her husband in the new settlements the trials and deprivations incident to frontier life. The labors of the wives of ministers are not limited alone to those of missionary life. Self-denying wives are found in cultured and refined associations, where they are truly helpmeets for their husbands, to relieve them of many domestic and annoying cares that interfere with the proper preparation for the pulpit or other pastoral duties. Tradition tells that the great Jonathan Edwards once asked his wife if the grass in the meadow ought not to be cut. The answer was "My dear, the hay has been in the barn three weeks." No doubt there may be exceptions, but, on the other hand, are multitudes and multitudes of the type of Mrs. Edwards. It is a sad reflection; but throughout the history of the Presbyterian church, whenever we read of the lack of material support for its ministers and missionaries, it always implies sufferings entailed upon their wives and children.

Population and Preachers.—Immigrants continued to pour into the Reserve, and the Connecticut Society, though it could furnish the means to support them, had not the men to supply the religious wants of these people, and at the end of a struggle lasting six years, it had only one missionary in the field. The great distance and the numerous obstacles in the way of travel had, no doubt, much to do in preventing ministers and their families migrating thither, while the pressing religious wants of the churches nearer home, as fields of prospective usefulness, were equally urgent in demanding their services.

The Synod of Pittsburg came to the rescue, as it was nearer the scene of operations and had, also, more young men about to enter the ministry. The Canonsburg Academy had developed into Jefferson College (1802); in past years the students of the former in an unusual proportion had devoted themselves to the sacred office, and the same ratio was kept up in the college. Numbers of these students had become Christians during the great revival in that region, already noted (*p. 231*). The labors of these men were not without success, since in 1808 it was estimated that nearly twenty churches had been organized, while in addition were many preaching stations, with the prospect of their becoming established congregations. The region of the Reserve was blessed repeatedly by revivals; the missionary tours of Revs. Joseph Badger and Thomas Robbins, and preachers from the Synod of Pittsburg, were often greatly blessed. The General Assembly, also, aided the cause by sending quite a number of missionaries who traversed the new settlements that were constantly forming in the desirable and fertile districts outside the Reserve.

Among these immigrants were great numbers who had been church members in their Eastern homes, and they appreciated at their full value the services of these preachers. In addition, they were all in favor of promoting education for their children. In some places where they had no preaching, these Christians established *prayer-meetings* and conducted them as best they could. The leaven of former instruction received in their youth was working among them and preparing the way for a fuller reception of the gospel when presented in after years by a more settled ministry. This is virtually a summary of the reports made by the traveling ministers and missionaries, who went from place to place in preaching to the feeble churches that had only a few members, and were dependent upon the Synod of Pittsburg and the General Assembly for their supply of preachers.

The war between England and the United States (1812-1815) had a most deleterious effect upon the spirituality of the churches throughout the Nation. In no section of the Union was this disastrous influence more vividly felt than in the Reserve, as some of the exciting scenes of the war occurred on Lake Erie and around its shores. (*Four Hundred, etc., pp. 630-640.*) Everywhere in these scattered settlements, when in their normal condition, the traveling missionary was heartily welcomed by the people.

XXXI.

INCREASE OF THE CHURCH.

The growth of the Presbyterian Church from 1816 to 1826 is shown from statistics. At the former date the number of presbyteries was forty-three and at the latter eighty-six. Meanwhile the five hundred and forty ministers had increased to more than eleven hundred and forty, and the nine hundred and forty churches had become more than two thousand. The number of church members in 1816 was less than 40,000, but in 1825 was more than 122,000—an increase of three-fold in less than ten years. It will be remembered that 1816 was the first year after the close of the War of 1812, and the latter's evil influence lingered long among the churches and the people outside of them. As a general rule, during this period of ten years there was an unusual prevalence of harmony in the promotion of church work, one phase of which was an increased interest in favor of ministerial education. Collateral with the latter was an effort to promote the cause of missions, domestic and foreign.

Accessions from Other Bodies to the Church.—During these years Congregational families migrating from New England, who came into the vicinity of Presbyterian churches, usually united with them, while there were, also, accessions in many instances from the Associated Reformed Church. More striking than these were revivals, some of which were quite extensive, that prevailed in a number of localities. The greater increase in church members was in the North and West. This was especially the case in Central and Western New York, Ohio, Indiana, and the neighboring States. The plan of union in the first of these States had the effect of promoting Presbyterianism, for the reason mainly that its home was on the ground, while the center of influence of Congregationalism was comparatively distant; either form of church government was utilized as a matter of expediency according to circumstances. There appeared to be no rivalry and jealousy involved, and church members fell in with that which seemed the best adapted to the existing conditions.

Reports on Revivals.—During this period the reports to successive General Assemblies made mention in almost every one of the outpouring of the Spirit within the bounds of the different presbyteries, so that there was scarcely a locality which at one time or another had not been visited. The assemblies of 1819 and 1820 were specially cheered by the reports concerning revivals, extending from Northern New York down toward the south as far as East Tennessee. In the latter year about eighty churches were blessed with such seasons of spiritual refreshing. The report of 1821 showed an aggregate of conversions from the world within the bounds of the church to have been between nine and ten thousand. It was estimated that during this period of ten years not less than 50,000 were added to the church from the world as the outcome of revivals.

Board of Missions.—In 1816 the assembly increased the membership and the power of its Committee on Missions, and changed its name to the "Board of Missions." The members of which board were to be elected annually by the assembly, and it was empowered to appoint missionaries at its discretion, and also provide for their support and designate the amount of salary to be paid. On this occasion the idea was suggested for the first time that the Presbyterian Church should be *ex officio*, a missionary society, as the command was to the *collective* body of the disciples to preach the gospel to all nations. The time, however, had not yet come to carry into effect that theory, since there were other denominations in connection with that church engaged in missionary enterprises, and in addition there were indications that a society on missions might be formed that would unite in the effort with the Presbyterians, the Reformed Dutch, and the Associate Reformed. A constitution was drawn up by a committee appointed for the purpose, and which was approved by the committees of the three bodies above mentioned. Finally, on July 28, 1817, the society was duly organized under the name: "The United Foreign Missionary Society." (*Gillett, II., p. 217.*)

The assembly of that year in its pastoral letter gave its sanction to such missionary associations, to Bible societies, and plans for the distribution of religious tracts, and also exhorted its church members to support them "vigorously" with their contributions. Within a short time, to the care of this society were transferred the stations and likewise the funds of the New York and the Northern missionary societies, and other similar organizations in the State, as the work could be carried on more efficiently, their efforts being thus concentrated. The receipts of funds for the society show that the church members became more and more interested in the subject, and in proportion recognized their responsibility. For illustration, in the first year they contributed $2578; in the second, about $3400, and in the third, more than $15,000

Efforts for an Educated Ministry.—The Congregationalists of New England were zealous to have an educated ministry, and local educational societies were organized in those States, and also within the bounds of the Presbyterian Church in other States. The Board of Education was established in 1819, in view of the demands for ministers. In a worldly point of view the inducements are very small for young men to enter upon the expense, the laborious study and trials in preparing for the sacred office. Under these conditions the obligation of the church to furnish ministers of the gospel for her service is similar to that of the United States to provide educated officers for its army and navy at West Point and Annapolis. The cadets of the Nation are not only lodged, clothed, and fed at the public expense, but they have the assurance, when they graduate, of employment at a liberal salary. The West Point cadet has only *four* years to serve as a student, while the Presbyterian theologian has in his whole course of study usually *nine* years, and under expense the whole time. Meanwhile, the Educational Society is careful to furnish only a small moiety of that expense. He, it is true, is taught self-reliance in the school of self-support, or nearly so, and when he graduates and is licensed to preach he turns to the church for employment as a missionary or a pastor, on a mere pittance of a salary, and that sometimes uncertain. The student who under such conditions seeks the sacred office must be actuated by a higher motive than pecuniary gain.

The great number of feeble congregations in the various presbyteries was startling, and the General Assembly of 1825 called upon the churches "to consider very seriously the case of the destitute parts of our country, especially of the many thousands of families in the new States in the West and in the South, which are growing up almost destitute of the preaching of the gospel and of all religious instruction." (*G., II., p. 228.*) The problem of the future of the Nation, in relation to its Christian character, was earnestly urged in support of domestic missions, not only by means of preaching the word, but

Rev. Gardiner Spring, D. D.
(248, 249, 472.)

in giving encouragement to the cause by sustaining those institutions that promote the education and general welfare of the people at large.

Revivals in Colleges—Theological Seminaries.—During the period under review several colleges were blest with revivals, and, in consequence, the number of professing Christians among the students had much increased. In three such institutions—Union and Hamilton, New York, and Princeton, New Jersey—the number who professed themselves Christians was one hundred and ten; of these, seventy were in Union. Dr. Eliphalet Nott was then President of Union. To supply the wants of the churches the question of having more theological seminaries was now earnestly agitated. The presbyteries of Northern and Central New York succeeded in having one established in 1820 at Auburn in that State. A similar question was most earnestly discussed for a year or two among the churches in Western Pennsylvania, Ohio, and Kentucky. The outcome was the Western Theological Seminary, which was located in 1826 at Allegheny, Pennsylvania. In the South, about the same time, Union Seminary, in connection with Hampden-Sidney College in Virginia, received a new impulse from the same cause. It had been retarded in its progress by an insufficient endowment, and at the request of the trustees, it was taken under the care of the General Assembly in 1826.

Churches in Need of Pastors.—The continued increase of the churches was faster than they could be supplied with pastors, though in the ten years, 1816 to 1826, the number of missionaries sent out annually by the board had increased from fifty to more than eighty. To meet these numerous demands the efforts of the board became more systematized, and more attention was given to aid feeble churches then in existence to become self-supporting, and thus permanent centers of Christian influence, rather than to organize new ones, to linger along for a few years and then, perhaps, die for want of proper care and sustenance. The tendency of the times was toward concentrated efforts, that might be more effective than those that were so much diffused by the action of local societies, which were doing their duty as best they could, but by their desultory measures much power and influence were lost. In view of these obvious reasons, in 1822 a movement was inaugurated that finally united several local missionary societies in the State of New York, into one, *"The United Domestic Missionary Society."* The latter organization was the outcome of a convention of delegates from the local societies, numbering altogether eleven, whose names we need not enumerate, and all of whom were engaged in the same evangelical work. One prominent evil was neutralized by this consolidation. A number of these local societies were so situated that their *assumed* boundaries sometimes overlapped one another, and this circumstance, though inadvertently, led to rivalries which greatly interfered with the progress of the work.

The officers of the new society issued to the public a summary of the reasons for uniting all of these organizations under one control, which reasons appear to have been satisfactory if we may judge from the increased contributions to the cause. Under the former desultory mode "some destitute regions had been regularly visited by missionaries of these different societies, while others equally in need had been passed by." The new society entered upon its duties with twenty-nine missionaries in the field under its control, while it hoped "to excite a fresh and deeper interest in the cause of home missions." As an indication of its work: "Its first report showed that within twelve months of its formation it had in its employ sixty missionaries, mainly within the bounds of the State. This report took decided ground in favor of aiding, specially, the feeble churches to become self-supporting, and making that feature prominent, hereafter, in organizing new churches. The auxiliary societies, six in number, were "entitled to designate the stations where the funds which they contributed were to be employed in supporting missionaries." The appointments of the latter, were however, in the hands of the main society, in order to secure uniformity. Sometimes the application of such funds was left to the discretion of the General Society. (*Gillett, II., pp. 227-229.*)

The General Assembly of 1819 commenced a mutual correspondence with the synod of the Associate Reformed and Dutch Reformed churches; this had been asked for some twenty years before, but for some reason declined. The Associate Reformed entered into the arrangement and the Dutch Reformed three years later.

Action of the Charleston Association.—The Charleston (South Carolina) Association appointed a committee to investigate the principles of the Presbyterian Church as to its mode of government and other distinctive features. In consequence of the favorable report of the committee, the association voted (1822) to dissolve itself and unite with the Presbyterian Assembly, which resolution was carried into effect the following year. To meet the case, the assembly constituted the Charleston Union Presbytery so as to include the ministers of the association with a portion of those belonging to the Harmony Presbytery.

Action on Psalmody—Intemperance—Sabbath Desecration.—The assembly of 1819 directed its attention to providing a suitable book of Psalmody, to be used in church services. The outcome of the measure was not published till 1830, when the book was adopted by order of the assembly.

Successive assemblies during this period endeavored to direct public attention to a number of questions that had arisen among its members and congregations, in respect to certain evils and their moral bearing on society at large. Among these evils were prominent those of intemperance and Sabbath desecration. Petitions were prepared and signed by great numbers of Presbyterian church members, as well as by a multitude of church members of other denominations, and of citizens outside the church who recognized the moral obligations to observe the day of sacred rest. Similar petitions were presented to Congress, from time to time, praying for the repeal of the law demanding the mails to be carried on the Sabbath day.

Increased Interest in Missions.—The subject of missions at home and abroad had become an absorbing topic in religious circles, and a monthly concert of prayer for missions was agreed upon in order to elicit an interest in the cause. This movement often received the approbation of the assembly, and in the session of 1830 it specially directed the attention of its own churches, and likewise those of other evangelical denominations, to the importance of this union or monthly concert of prayer. At these concerts it was the custom, in addition to the service of prayer, to give the recent information obtained from the respective mission fields. The latter phase of the monthly concert has been virtually superseded by the numerous periodicals published exclusively on the missions and kindred subjects by the several evangelical denominations. Owing to these circumstances the monthly concert has been more or less discontinued.

The great good to be received by the training of children in Sunday-schools during this period was recognized by the assembly at its full importance, and the cause was recommended to all the churches. Numerous examples of the blessed influence of instructing children in

INCREASE OF THE CHURCH. 309

this manner in Bible truths, were afforded, especially in the cities, wherein were greater facilities for prosecuting the work among the children of the foreign population and of others outside the evangelical churches.

A Deliverance on Slavery.—The assembly of 1818 was noted for a deliverance, as it is termed, on the subject of slavery, and which condemned the system as unchristian, and expressed the desire for its total extinction, but at the same time deprecating any measures that might endanger the tranquillity of the country. It exhorted the members of the church, who were so unfortunate as to be in contact with the system, to do their utmost to give religious instruction to the slaves. It expressed its sympathy for those portions of the church upon which the evils of slavery had been entailed, saying: "When a great and the most virtuous part of the community abhor slavery, and wish its extermination as sincerely as any others."

XXXII.

INCREASE OF THE CHURCH CONTINUED.

The progress of the church from 1825 to 1835 was unusually rapid. The number of synods increased from fourteen to twenty-three, and the presbyteries from eighty-one to about one hundred and twenty-five. The number of ministers in 1825 was one thousand and eighty, but ten years later it was about two thousand eight hundred, and during the same period the churches numbered seventeen hundred and seventy, while the church membership had more than doubled, amounting in round numbers in 1835 to more than two hundred and fifty thousand. This unusual increase was the outcome of numerous and extensive revivals, which, during the period, extended almost over the entire Union. These revivals induced renewed action in favor of union measures for evangelical labors throughout the land. In promotion of this work, plans for the first time were devised by the evangelical denominations to place the *Bible in every family* in the Nation, and special efforts were made by Presbyterians to organize Sabbath-schools in the valley of the Mississippi. The American Tract Society, then recently brought into existence, greatly aided the cause by the liberal distribution of religious tracts and books. The temperance reform continued to be discussed in the churches. This reform went hand in hand with the revivals of the period. On the same line special attention was given to the monthly concert of prayer for missions, both foreign and domestic.

Increased Missionary Effort.—During this time an ardent religious sentiment seemed more than usual to permeate the inner life of the church members of all the denominations. As they realized more correctly the greatness of the religious destitution of the land. In consequence, the churches began to press forward with unwonted zeal to remedy these evils by sending missionaries to supply, as far as possible, the existing religious wants; and in addition they took measures to support these laborers in their Christian work. On this line of evangelical effort were organized a number of local missionary societies which in time became auxiliary to the national society. By this means the attention of church members in such localities and in their immediate vicinity was more fully directed to the importance of the cause of domestic or home missions.

Of these local associations, the Western Missionary Society of Utica, New York, formed in 1826, was perhaps the most effective, as it sent out ministers whose sphere of labor was extended to about fifty towns and villages in the State;—it is said that in eight of these villages no church had yet been organized. Among other local societies was one in connection with the First Presbyterian Church in Philadelphia, and likewise one in Monroe County, New York; both of these did effective work. To promote unity of action and more efficient work, these local societies in the various portions of the Union, when the necessities of the time demanded the change, became auxiliary to the Home Missionary Society.

A convention of the friends of home missions met in the City of New York in 1826, during the May anniversaries and proposed a comprehensive plan, in order to concentrate the efforts of all the local organizations. The outcome of the convention was the formation of the American Home Missionary Society, with which, in due time, the local organizations became affiliated as auxiliaries. The United Domestic Society, formed in 1822, was the first to fall into line. The new society, in the extent of its plan, became national in character, and accordingly assumed the responsibilities, financial and otherwise, of the various locals that became its auxiliaries, the latter passing over to it the missionaries under their care.

The list of the first officers of the society, about twenty in number, comprised the names of great influence in their respective denominations—the Congregational, the Dutch Reformed, and the Presbyterian. The organization of this society, so national in its character and purpose, gave great satisfaction to these three denominations. It was hailed with joy throughout the country, if we may judge from the letters of congratulation that its management received, especially from the South and West, the regions wherein its ministrations were so greatly needed.

Influence of the First Address.—The first address issued by the committee to the churches, which were to aid the cause by their contributions, confirmed with great earnestness the purely national character of the society in its object and in its plan of operation. It announced that its aim was not to interfere "with the benevolent exertions of those who might deem it their duty to act apart from its advice." It was preeminently a voluntary association to send the gospel in its purity to the destitute portions of the Union, while the upright, practical, and christian character of its officers was a guarantee that its operations would be judiciously managed and the disbursements of its funds carefully made. Its missionaries went forth in the name of Christ, to be cheered by receiving a cordial welcome wherever they came. This was specially the case in the South and West.

Eastern Christians soon became largely interested in the subject, because the agents of the society and its publications made known more clearly and definitely the religious wants in the various destitute regions of the Union. It was discovered very soon by investigation that to supply properly these demands of the people of the Western States alone, would require at once five hundred ministers, in addition to the three hundred already in the field, while equally urgent requests for preachers were coming in from the South and Southwest. Even in the older States were numerous weak churches that were languishing for spiritual food. Under these circumstances the inauguration of a missionary society, so comprehensive in the outlines of its intended operations, was hailed with joy and enthusiasm, especially in the Presbyterian and Congregational churches.

As has been indicated, the spirit of missions was abroad, and while a number of local societies had done a local work, there were large sections in the Union that were beyond the influence of Associations so limited, both in men and funds, and the numerous facilities that naturally increase in proportion to the number of men and the amount of pecuniary means. At that time, no one of the three denominations specially interested was sufficiently strong, either in the number of its church members or in the available funds at its command, to sustain a missionary society that was truly national in its character. It was in the future when their numbers and financial circumstances would authorize any one of these denominations, singly and alone, to sustain a society that could station its missionaries in every portion of the Union.

Destitution in New York, Pennsylvania, and the Great Valley.—In Western New York in 1828 there were about fifty Presbyterian churches vacant or but partially served, while were coming urgent calls from fifty more in districts that were almost destitute of any Christian ministrations. Similar statements were made in relation to the religious condition of the northern portion of Pennsylvania. In Ohio, within the bounds of the Synod of the Western Reserve, were eighty-seven churches, and within the same limit only forty-two Presbyterian ministers, while the churches were, for the most part, not having many members each. It ought to be taken into consideration that where now are rich farming regions and villages, there were then only scattered settlements, while the greater portion of the territory was unoccupied. The larger tide of immigrants for some time had been going through and past Ohio into the States of Indiana and Illinois.

In 1827 it was estimated that Indiana had nearly 300,000 inhabitants; the region bordering on the Wabash river was fast filling up because of its exceptionally fertile soil. Within the limits of the State, however, were only twelve resident Presbyterian ministers, and about the same number who were missionaries, traveling from place to place, and about sixty churches, some of whom with scarcely more than a name. In the State of Illinois were only six or seven settled Presbyterian pastors, while in the State of Missouri were five or six missionaries of the same church. The Presbytery of Detroit, Michigan, had only seven ministers in 1830, when the territory had a population of 30,000. Further south, in Kentucky, with a population of quite 600,000, were only *forty* settled Presbyterian pastors. The number of ministers of the same denomination in East Tennessee was small, indeed, compared with that of the population and its religious wants, while the western portion of the State was even less supplied with Presbyterian ministers. To meet the demand for such preachers the Synod of Tennessee resolved in 1827 to found a theological seminary in connection with Cumberland College, which had recently been placed under another name —Nashville University—and better auspices, when Dr.

Philip Lindsley assumed its presidency in 1824. For some reason the seminary was not established.

The Church in New Orleans and Mobile.—From the extreme South the cry for ministers came equally as urgent. In New Orleans, with a resident population of nearly 50,000, which in the business season swelled to 70,000, was only one Presbyterian church. The latter had been gathered by Dr. Elias Cornelius and the eloquent Rev. Sylvester Larned; of this church Rev. Theodore Clapp was pastor (1827). Outside of that city were only two Presbyterian ministers in the State of Louisiana, while west of the Lower Mississippi was not one. The Presbytery of Mississippi then included that State and Louisiana, and with a total population of nearly three hundred thousand there were altogether twelve Presbyterian ministers and only nine of these were engaged in active and stated work.

The Presbytery of Alabama was earnestly calling for ministers to supply the vacant churches within its bounds. The church in Mobile was organized in 1827, with one hundred and twelve members, but they could only obtain preaching once a month by Rev. Lucas Kennedy, who was commissioned (1819) as missionary by the General Assembly. The people had gone to work earnestly and erected a building to serve as a church, an academy, and a Sunday-school room. Urgent calls continued to come to the presbytery from Pensacola and from Tuscaloosa and the vicinity.

The Church in Huntsville.—The Young Men's Evangelical Missionary Society of New York sent to Huntsville, Rev. Isaac W. Platt (1819). In this prosperous village was no organized Presbyterian church or stated ministry, yet Mr. Platt testifies that: "Its inhabitants will suffer nothing by a comparison with those of most other towns in our country, as respects intelligence, refinement, and wealth." The town, because, perhaps, of its beauty of situation, became a favorite summer resort of the wealthy planters in the South. In consequence, in after years Huntsville held an enviable position in the educational world by means of fine schools, especially for young women. Through Mr. Platt's exertions and influence a handsome church building was erected. About this time Presbyterian churches were established in Tuscaloosa, Tuscumbia, Selma, and other places in the State. The whole number of Presbyterian ministers, including settled pastors and missionaries, in the State in 1825 was seventeen.

The Church in Georgia, Carolinas, and Florida.—Other churches continued to be organized in this tier of Southern States. Georgia had a great number of vacant churches, while there were only seventeen ordained Presbyterian ministers in the State. Meanwhile the number of churches was increasing *five-fold* faster than that of the ministers to supply them. A similar reign of destitution prevailed in the Carolinas and Florida. In the eastern portion of the latter was a population of 6000, mostly in the vicinity of St. Augustine, in which village vice was represented as bold and rampant, gambling houses were licensed by law, and intemperance prevailed unblushingly. In St. Augustine was organized in 1824 the first Presbyterian church, through the exertions of Rev. William McWhirr. He ordained elders and administered the ordinances of the church, then went to work to raise money in order to build a suitable dwelling for the new church and persevered till he had accomplished that most desirable object.

South and North Carolina Churches.—The Presbytery of South Carolina was composed of twelve members, but within its bounds were thirty-five churches (1827), which, in the main, were not self-supporting, and some were even

REV. PHILIP LINDSLEY, D.D.
(315, 497-499.)

on the border of extinction. The ministers, in order to meet the wants of the people as best they could, supplied more than one church, even three and four, and they often a number of miles apart.

The Presbyterian churches of North Carolina were at this time equally destitute of the stated supply of the ministry, and in like manner was the portion of Virginia west of the Blue Ridge, while in the eastern part were numerous vacant churches, and others, having been so long without stated preaching, were almost on the verge of dissolution. Reports from missionaries and others revealed the religious wants of Maryland and Virginia east of the Blue Ridge. Even the church building at Drummondstown, in which Makemie had preached, was a ruin, and the one on the banks of the Nanticoke, where Presbyterians once worshiped, had totally disappeared. Within the boundaries of the Presbytery of Lewes, in Delaware, were about eight churches, but it numbered only four ordained ministers.

The Church beyond the Mountains.—The reports from the field of ministerial labor beyond the mountains, north and south—that is, in the valley of the Mississippi—made known as the great destitution of the churches, and unceasingly urged their fellow Christians of the East to come to their assistance by sending them the gospel. Many of these looked for help to the assembly's board, but more, after its organization, to the concentrated facilities found in the Home Missionary Society.

XXXIII.

Theological Seminaries.

Founding of Theological Seminaries.—The increasing demand for preachers of the gospel led to an earnest effort to educate a ministry for the purpose, and it was evident more seminaries were required. The Synod of Geneva, at a meeting held in Rochester in 1818, urged the propriety of establishing one somewhere in Western or Middle New York. The following May the proposition was laid before the General Assembly. The latter body, though not prepared to assume the responsibility of establishing and sustaining such an institution, yet it did not oppose the plan. After much discussion, a partial endowment being provided, the outcome was the founding in 1820 of a theological seminary, located at the village of Auburn. A board of commissioners to supervise the institution was selected from the presbyteries interested in the cause. In October, 1821, the professors having been chosen, it commenced operations. Dr. James Richards was elected Professor of Theology, but did not enter upon his duties till 1823, his place being supplied by Dr. M. L. B. Perrine of New York, who was Professor of Ecclesiastical History and Church Polity. In after years the institution continued to be manned by equally able and learned men.

The same reasons led to a theological department being connected with the college at Hudson, in the Reserve. This seminary labored under great difficulties for a number of years. Its students at one time numbered about forty, but there seemed to be impediments in the way of complete success—at least for a time (1828).

The Presbyterians of Indiana took measures (1828) to promote a higher education, and at first they established a classical academy, under the care of Dr. John F. Crowe, and which afterward grew into South Hanover College. It is worthy of note that in its earlier days a large majority of its students were professing Christians. To this college was added in 1830 a theological department, in which Dr. John Matthews was unanimously chosen Professor of Theology by the Synod of Indiana, and Dr. Crowe by the same authority was appointed second Professor.

Western Seminary, Allegheny.—The lack of ministers still continuing, the Presbyterians, especially of Kentucky, desired to have a theological seminary modeled after that of Princeton, and if possible located within their own State. The matter was brought to the attention of the General Assembly in 1825. It was deemed essential by all the parties concerned that the prospective seminary should be located in the Great Valley, but it was difficult to decide where should be that location. After much discussion in the presbyteries and in the newspapers—religious and secular—Allegheny, in Western Pennsylvania, was chosen by the assembly as the site for the institution (1827); more funds could be secured for that location. That position was on the eastern edge of the valley, and therefore it did not meet satisfactorily the wishes of the more western presbyteries, and measures were taken to have a theological seminary located further west, under the plea that its location should be nearer the *center of the population* of the Union and also of the valley. This center of population, according to the *first* census, in 1790, was east of Chesapeake bay, near the thirty-ninth parallel of latitude. It has moved west from census to census, and at the time of the location of this seminary (1827), was almost directly south of the city of Allegheny, and near the same parallel. It is remarkable that this center has thus far crossed and recrossed the thirty-ninth parallel *four times*. The census of 1890 places it in the State of Indiana, at a point about fifty miles west by north from Cincinnati, and not far from the same line. The center of the territory of the United States—excluding Alaska —is near Abilene, Kansas, and also near the thirty-ninth parallel. (*Four Hundred Years, etc., p. 1092.*)

The result of this agitation was the founding of Lane Seminary at Walnut Hills, near Cincinnati. The name was given in gratitude.

Lane Seminary.—Two brothers, whose name was Lane, residents of Boston, gentlemen of intelligence, liberal and patriotic, and of far-reaching views, on visiting the Great Valley, learned of the religious wants of its people. Impressed by the situation, they deemed the most feasible means to supply these wants would be a theological seminary, where young men seeking the ministry could study theology among the people for whom they expected to labor. The Messrs. Lane were Baptists, and they first offered the funds they proposed to give to their own denomination; the latter, however, was not prepared to accept the proposition. The object was so important in their view, that they paid the Presbyteries the compliment of offering the funds to them.

This institution, as originally designed, was to have two departments—a literary and theological. The former was the first to go into operation, but it was afterward transferred to Miami University, over which Dr. Robert H. Bishop then presided. The theological department languished for lack of funds. At length Mr. Arthur Tappan of New York City proposed to endow a professorship of theology if Dr. Lyman Beecher should be appointed to the chair. The proposition was accepted, and Dr. Beecher, then in the height of his influence, was installed, September, 1832.

Religious Condition of the Great Valley.—Previous to this time, the attention of American Christians, especially in the Northern and Eastern States, had been drawn to the religious conditions of the Great Valley. Multitudes were migrating thither from the States east of the Alleghanies, while perhaps as many were pouring in from Europe. About twenty years previous the center of the population of the Union had come within the valley, and from census to census, was steadily advancing westward—along the thirty-ninth parallel, which it crossed back and forth four times—apparently, the time was not far distant when here would be also the center of the political influence of the Nation. Far-seeing minds, both in Church and State, began to forecast the ultimate outcome of the movements of these energetic and ever-progressive people. Thousands upon thousands of church members, sad to say, who came from other States, appeared to have grown careless in respect to their religious vows. To the Christians of the East came, however, the cry from their brethren in the valley, who were still faithful, for more preachers of the gospel, in order to counteract the undue influence of infidelity and irreligion. In addition, was a great influx of immigrants of European birth, industrious and frugal, and good citizens, but the majority were imbued with the indifference so characteristic of German rationalism, in respect to the essential principles of Christianity. This statement applies more justly to Cincinnati and vicinity than to any other locality of the valley.

Such was the state of religious affairs when Dr. Beecher entered upon his duties as professor in Lane Seminary. He was fresh from his conflicts in Boston with Unitarianism, and with the multiform evils of intemperance, and who, by his boldness of speech and his impressive personality, was, perhaps, the only man of the time that could effectually withstand the pressure of the evils then prevalent in the West. He might impress his strong individuality upon his students and send them forth imbued with his own zeal, if not with his pungent eloquence. These were the hopes cherished by the intelligent Christians, who were thus able to appreciate the religious and political conditions of the Great Valley. Nor were they disappointed in Dr. Beecher himself; but untoward circumstances, to be noted further on, unfortunately, for a time, retarded the onward flow of his legitimate influence.

Seminary at Marysville.—The Southern and Western theological seminary is known as Maryville College, and is located at that place, in Blount County, East Tennessee. It was under the control of the synod, and was doing a good work. It stood isolated from any similar institution by a distance of 400 miles (*see Log Colleges, pp. 127-137*), and yet it was in a central position, amid an estimated population of two millions. Here was adopted the manual labor system, by means of which the individual expenses of the students were somewhat reduced by their earnings. The success of the institution was not then as great as its merits seemed to justly demand; it has since grown in its usefulness, and at this writing (1899) its students of all classes number 450.

The demand for more ministers pervaded the church in the Southwest, and the Presbytery of Mississippi, though comparatively weak in financial resources, resolved to establish a theological seminary within its bounds. The outcome of the movement was not as intended, but resulted in founding Oakland College, in Claiborne County (1830), which did good service in the cause. The Rev. Jeremiah Chamberlain was its first president.

Union Seminary, Virginia.—In Southern Virginia, Union Theological Seminary, though much crippled for funds, for a number of years had been strenuously engaged in its appropriate work. At length, by request of the Board of Trustees, it was taken under the care of the General Assembly in 1826. The celebrated Dr. John Holt Rice was appointed a professor. He entered upon his duties with his usual energy, and soon afterward visited the cities of Philadelphia and New York in order to obtain funds to place the institution on a firm basis. The churches of the former city gave ten thousand and those of the latter thirty thousand dollars. Within the Synods of Virginia and North Carolina an additional twenty thousand was obtained.

The reader will observe that this unusual interest in establishing and aiding theological seminaries was during a period of about ten years. It is gratifying, also, to note that the general interest in this subject has never flagged since. The church members having been true to their traditions, as best they could, have gone hand in hand with the presbyteries in furnishing funds for providing and sustaining both colleges and theological seminaries. Collateral with these movements during this time were special efforts made to aid young men who desired to preach the gospel in securing an appropriate collegiate and theological education.

In intimate connection with the theological seminaries should be recognized the healthful influence exerted by the management of the colleges founded within the Great Valley. We have already noticed (*p. 132*) two academies or schools, the precursors of two colleges—Washington and Jefferson—that were and continue to be prominent in that respect. They had the advantage of being early in the field, commencing their career as soon as they were needed to supply the educational and religious wants of the settlers in that fertile region of which Pittsburg may be deemed the center. It is stated on good authority that the number of graduates from Dr. McMillan's school and afterward from Jefferson College, who became ministers of the gospel, was much greater in proportion than any other college in the Union.

Dr. Matthew Brown.—Entered upon the presidency of Jefferson College in 1822, which office, because of declining health, he resigned in 1845. He was a graduate of Dickinson College in 1795, when it was under the presidency of the celebrated Dr. Charles Nisbet. Presbyterians owe him a debt of gratitude for what he did during these twenty-two years in the promotion of education and of religion within the college itself and outside that, indirectly, for the advancement of their own church through the labors of the students whom he had trained.

What was the secret of this benign influence? In his sphere of usefulness as president of the college, Dr. Brown did all that was possible under the circumstances for the promotion of genuine scholarship, while in his relation as *pastor* of the students he was peculiarly successful. He was accustomed to visit them in their rooms and pray with them; within a few weeks after the commencement of the college session he would visit every new student and learn of his antecedents, of which he took note. He often urged the older students to meet the new ones in a kindly manner, and, as he expressed it, make them feel at home. In consequence, the barbarous and vulgar custom of hazing was never known at Jefferson.

His innate fondness for young persons attracted to him all the worthy students; he won their respect by the scholarship that he manifested in his department, and secured their love by his kindly care, so blended with sympathy; decided in character, his influence was an ever-present stimulant for the best students to labor in their respective duties. During his administration of twenty-two years there were *eleven* revivals of religion in the college. The services connected therewith were held at hours so as not to interfere with the regular duties of the college—the latter he never would relax. His theory was that regular duties faithfully performed were not a hindrance, but rather a stimulant, to religion. At one time during his presidency, with only one exception, every student in the college was a professing Christian. Let results testify. During Dr. Brown's presidency seven hundred and seventy students were graduated; of these, nearly *one-half* chose the gospel ministry as their profession. That this spirit thus received an impulse which still prevails, we infer from the fact that since the union of the two colleges, Jefferson and Washington, in 1865, more than *forty* per cent. of the graduates have devoted themselves to the sacred office. (*Sprague's Annals, IV., p 258. President Moffat's Historical Sketch, p. 27.*)

XXXIV.

Louisiana Bought.

The acquisition of Louisiana by purchase in 1803 had, in a business way, increased the interest already felt by the American people in the lower portion of the valley of the Mississippi. This might be said specially of those who lived west of the Alleghanies, and in the valley of the Ohio, who now, by way of the great river, had free outlet for their products to the outside world and to the markets on the Atlantic slope. These products were carried in huge flatboats down to New Orleans, and there transferred to ships, and thus taken to their destination.

This lower region was easy of access by means of the many tributaries to the main river, and in consequence, even before its purchase, quite a large migration had gone thither. Natchez and vicinity being an attractive locality, numbers had settled there, and the church soon began to follow these settlers with a preached gospel. The religious wants of the people of these distant settlements had, through the missionaries to the Indians, become known to the Synods of the Carolinas and Virginia, since to them, because of their location, naturally fell the supervision of these missions. The Synod of the Carolinas, therefore, directed the Presbytery of Orange, North Carolina, to ordain James Smylie (1804) as a missionary to be stationed at Natchez, at which place he had previously labored. The Rev. James Hall of North Carolina, a veteran in the cause of Presbyterianism in the South, had also, under a commission of the General Assembly (1800) labored in Natchez and vicinity. He was assisted by two other brethren, who were commissioned by the Synod of the Carolinas. Here were established the first Protestant missions in the lower Mississippi valley—that is, below Vicksburg.

Indian Mission in the Southwest.—Rev. Joseph Bullen was sent in 1799 by the New York Missionary Society to labor among the Indians of the Southwest in what is now the State of Mississippi. It would seem that the Indians in that portion of the country had been hitherto overlooked. Bullen, on his journey, visited Rev. Dr. Gideon Blackburn, who was then a pastor at Maryville, East Tennessee. The latter had been planning to send the gospel to the Cherokees, and now, by his intercourse with Bullen, he was induced to put forth more efforts in the enterprise. He laid the matter before the Union Presbytery, of which he was a member, but the poverty of the people was an almost insuperable obstacle in the way of the project.

Blackburn was a commissioner to the General Assembly in 1803. He had already devised the outline of a plan to carry the gospel to the Cherokee Indians. He appeared before the committee to which his paper was referred, and explained to it the importance of such missionary effort being made, and also demonstrated the feasibility of the plan. In the end he secured from the assembly an appropriation of two hundred dollars to aid in support of the mission. The recommendation of the assembly enabled him to obtain about four hundred dollars additional among his friends in East Tennessee, after his return from the meeting of the assembly in Philadelphia.

Dr. Blackburn had already enlisted in its favor the Indian agent of the government, Col. Return Jonathan Meigs, while the President, John Adams, also sympathized with the movement and directed Col. Meigs to aid the cause. A council of about two thousand Indians—Cherokees and Creeks—was held and the proposed plan of giving them instruction, such as is given to the children of white men, was explained to them. The Indians, after some delay in consulting among themselves, approved the measure, and the mission was commenced in 1804. Dr. Blackburn labored incessantly in the cause, practising great self-denial in his individual exertions and contributing much from his own limited means toward defraying the necessary expenses. He went on a tour through a portion of the South in order to obtain funds, and succeeded to the amount of fifteen hundred dollars. The following year (1805) he visited the North, and returned with more than four thousand dollars, all of which he used judiciously. This missionary enterprise was entirely in individual hands, and was thus sustained. It had, however, the commendation of the General Assembly, and was effective in its work until the evil influences exerted by the War of 1812 wrought its ruin.

Indian Missions in Georgia.—Some years later (1817) the missions to the Cherokees and Creek Indians came under the care of the American Board. The latter commissioned the Rev. Cyrus Kingsbury to labor among them as missionary and teacher, and soon after the Choctaws were brought within the influence of the mission. The chiefs of these tribes were anxious to have schools like the white men. The location chosen for the mission-station was at Brainerd, thus named in honor of the devoted Indian missionary. The mission at this place largely increased in the number of pupils and also in competent teachers, some of whom were laymen with their families, to give instruction in civilized domestic life. For some reason in 1822 the mission was divided and the members distributed among the tribes. The number of converts in the course of years led to the organization of four churches, which were in connection with Union Presbytery, East Tennessee.

Removal of the Indians.—For twenty years the good work of Christianizing these sons and daughters of the forest had gone on prosperously, and as a result great numbers, especially of the younger portion of their several communities had adopted civilized modes of living. A dark cloud of misfortune was overhanging this prosperity. It first presented itself in the agitation of the question as to the removal of these Indians to a territory beyond the Mississippi. This cruel and unjust measure was carried out to the letter in 1833-1835. The State of Georgia obtained possession of their lands, their private dwellings and their cultivated farms and improvements, at a price which avarice dictated—their school-houses and church-buildings went to ruin. Their missionaries, Dr. Elisar Butler and Rev. S. A. Worcester accompanied them to their distant and wilderness homes, and continued to labor for their good. In this cruel, illegal and arbitrary act the President—Andrew Jackson—disregarded the solemn treaties of the government with these Indians and the recent decision of the Supreme Court of the United States in their favor. (*Four Hundred Years, etc., p. 706.*)

Individual Influence.—It is worthy of notice, that in evangelical work in the South that individual men exerted more personal influence than individual men did in the North. The reason for this statement may be found in the general intelligence of the people at large, being much less in the South than in corresponding classes in the North. This difference in the diffusion of useful knowledge among the Northern people was owing to the prevalence of public schools, wherein *all* the youth were made readers, while in the South the public school system, as it was in the free-labor States, was then unknown, and none but the well-to-do slaveholders could educate their children. Meantime, the great mass of the youth in that respect were woefully neglected. In a state of society thus constituted, it was reasonable that the educated man would loom higher in public estimation than in a community wherein much greater intelligence prevailed.

Dr. Charles Coffin.—Among the most devoted and prominent ministers who labored in East Tennessee was Charles Coffin. He was a native of Newburyport, Mass.; graduate of Harvard, studied theology under the direction of Dr. Daniel Dana of Ipswich, and of Dr. Samuel Spring of his native town. When a boy he was remarkable for his precocious intellect, and for his ardent zeal for knowledge, and withal for his uprightness of character. He graduated with a high reputation for his proficiency in the studies prosecuted in the college course. He was licensed to preach the gospel in 1799 by the Essex Middle Association. Not being of robust constitution and his usual health having been impaired, it was thought best for him to undertake a preaching tour in the South. He, in consequence, ministered for a season to a small Presbyterian congregation in Norfolk, Virginia, which met in the town-hall. Afterward, he traveled on horseback southwest through Virginia and North Carolina, finally reaching Greenville, Greene County, East Tennessee. For a season he preached in that region, meantime becoming much interested in the college located at that place, and in its prospective usefulness. Remaining sufficiently long to make himself familiar with the situation, in relation to the educational and religious wants of the people, he returned to the East in order to enlist the benevolent in procuring funds for the college as a promising field of great usefulness.

Obtaining what funds he could as an endowment of the college, he came back to Greenville, and identified himself with it as vice-president (1805). The Rev. Hezekiah

Balch being president, at whose death Dr. Coffin was elected his successor (1810). Here as president he labored for seventeen years, performing the duties of his office with great efficiency, when he was called to the presidency of East Tennessee College—now University of Tennessee—at Knoxville. After six years of successful labor his health failed and he was compelled to resign.

During all these years he was remarkably blessed in his preaching and building up churches; still greater, was his benign and lasting influence over his students. His fine scholarship, and clear judgment and decision of character commanded this respect, while his amiable, generous, and courteous manners won their love. "Even to old age his intellectual energies were fresh and his activity scarcely abated. Long will his memory live in the region in which he was known and loved, and in which he scattered seed for harvests that succeeding centuries will reap." (*G. II., p. 206.*) The Master withdrew him from his work at the age of seventy-eight.

Isaac Anderson.—The Rev. Dr. Isaac Anderson is another minister who deserves to be remembered with gratitude by the entire Presbyterian Church, as well as his contemporary fellow-citizens and their descendants, for whom he labored during his long life. Of Scotch-Irish descent, and imbued with the influence of the traditions of the principles for which his ancestors fought at the siege of Derry, he was by heredity a genuine Protestant of the Presbyterian type. His father, a farmer of Rockbridge County, Virginia, where the son was born, migrated in 1799 to Grassy valley, Knox County, East Tennessee. The son was then nineteen years of age, but the year previous he had consecrated himself to Christ.

He had studied for several years at Liberty Hall Academy, under the care of Rev. Dr. William Graham, celebrated in that day as a classical teacher. He made great proficiency in his studies, and until he became a Christian his intention was to enter the legal profession, but the cause of the Redeemer loomed so high that the anticipations of future distinction in that line vanished in comparison with the importance of preaching the simple gospel. In preparing for the ministry, Rev. Samuel Carrick was his first theological instructor, but the talented pupil soon outstripped the teacher, and began to ventilate speculations which at that time Carrick deemed unorthodox, and in after years the same view was held by Anderson himself.

Carrick was by no means able to cope with the metaphysical dogmas of Hopkinsianism—a fruitful theme of controversy in that day—as presented by his precocious pupil, and he handed him over to Dr. Gideon Blackburn, then at Maryville, Tennessee, in charge of a church and of the college. Almost at their first interview the instructor and the pupil entered upon a discussion of the then controversial questions of theology. This friendly and candid discussion lasted long into the night, and ended in the conviction of the young student that his theories were not sound according to the scheme of the gospel as revealed in the Word of God. Afterward, Anderson expressed his sentiments by saying he found his "head as empty as a barrel," and "his whole system of theology completely set aside and utterly demolished." In due time, after much study and prayer, he came to look upon the views of Blackburn as "sound, scriptural, and true."

Anderson was licensed to preach by Union Presbytery in April, 1802, and soon after was installed pastor of Washington Church. Here he remained nine years. He happened to own a farm, perhaps by inheritance, and he cultivated it to eke out the pittance of a salary from the church. His active mind was ever engrossed on sacred themes, and he preached the gospel without intermission, not only in his own congregation, but arranged for making extensive preaching tours throughout that region. Never did his energy flag nor his self-denial diminish.

President of Maryville College.—Nine years after his licensure (1811) he succeeded Dr. Blackburn, who was called to another field, and finally to be president of Centre College, Kentucky. In his new position at Maryville, Dr. Anderson found a second sphere of aiding the cause of the church. It was suggested by the spiritual desolation that prevailed all over that region, and the impression seized his mind that the only remedy was in providing more ministers. With his wonted energy and Christian zeal he took in hand to supply them. He had no material means, but he had an inexhaustible fund in his trust in God. First he wrote to one or two missionary societies in the North; but they were unable to send him preachers; at last, driven to this extremity, he determined, putting his trust in Providence, to do what he could himself. He established a school of theology, commencing with a class of five (1819). This was the beginning of the Southern and Western Theological Seminary, now known under its chartered name, Maryville College. The motive of the founder may be stated in his own words: "Let the directors and managers of this sacred institution propose, as their sole object, the glory of God and the advancement of that Kingdom purchased by the blood of his only son."

Dr. Anderson started a boarding-house for the students, and appointed a suitable person to take charge of it, meantime becoming himself responsible for the supplies. Students absolutely unable to pay received their board gratis. Oftentimes he did not know how he could provide for his score or more of students, but at the critical moment the aid would come. Often a plain Christian farmer would drive up to the door with his wagon loaded with provisions as a gift to the institution; sometimes the merchant of his merchandise sent appropriate articles; others, again, at the proper moment sent money. Thus the work went on; but we cannot go into detail. Let it suffice that Dr. Anderson by these his exertions, in the course of forty-two years, sent forth about one hundred ministers of the gospel, nearly all of whom were Presbyterians. At this writing (1899) this institution has about 450 students—male and female.

The personal appearance of Dr. Anderson is represented as being very imposing; the evidence of intellect was stamped upon his brow, a kindly expression of countenance accompanied a piercing eye; he was conciliatory in his manner, and impressed his hearers from the pulpit and his students in the class-room with his Christian sincerity of purpose—as such he was venerated and loved. He was released from his earthly labors at the age of seventy-seven (1857).

James White Stephenson.—The Rev. James White Stephenson was of Scotch-Irish parentage and a native of Virginia, born in 1756, but his childhood was spent in the northern portion of South Carolina, his parents having removed thither. It is not known definitely where he received his education, but that he had a classical school near the North Carolina line, and tradition tells that Andrew Jackson was one of his pupils. Stephenson took an active part in the War of the Revolution, and afterward prepared himself for the ministry, and was licensed in his thirty-third year by the Presbytery of South Carolina in 1789. He at once entered most earnestly upon his active duties, and his ministry was remarkably blessed. He was specially diligent and prayerful as a pastor, and soon his congregation became imbued with a similar spirit.

Migration of a Congregation.—We now notice a movement similar to some in earlier colonial times, as, for instance, when Minister Thomas Hooker, in 1636, led his congregation from near Boston through an unbroken wilderness to the fertile valley of the Connecticut. (*Four Hundred Years, etc., p. 115.*) Stephenson became much interested in the great field for missionary work in the fertile region now known as Middle Tennessee. Numbers of his congregation caught his spirit, and the result was that under his lead, in 1808, a caravan consisting of twenty families of his congregation set out from South Carolina, and after much toil in crossing intervening mountains and making their way through the wilderness and partially settled regions, reached their destination in what is now Maury County, Tennessee. The distance was five hundred and seventy miles—more than four times as far as Hooker led his congregation. They settled on a large tract of land which had been given by the government to General Nathaniel Greene, in recognition of his services during the Revolution; from his heirs they purchased their homes.

The congregation of Dr. Stephenson, being in full sympathy with him, entered heartily into his plans of making known the gospel to the region in their vicinity. His church—Zion congregation—was in connection with the Presbytery of West Tennessee, and the latter with the Synod of Kentucky. The members of the congregation took much interest, as individuals, in giving private religious instruction to the colored people in their respective neighborhoods.

They also, under their pastor's leadership, engaged in practical missionary labors among the Indian tribes within reach. This became preeminently a Christian colony under the fostering care of the pastor, who for twenty-four years labored and exerted a remarkable and benign influence upon the community at large, till in his seventy-sixth year death ended his earthly service (1832).

Characteristic Zeal.—It was characteristic in that early day of the Presbyterian ministers of Eastern Tennessee and Kentucky, to be self-reliant and full of zeal. Gideon Blackburn, after leaving Maryville (1810), we find him the following year at Franklin, Middle Tennessee, where he remained about five years, preaching with great success, meanwhile having charge of Harpeth Academy and a number of theological students. He then removed to St. Louis (1816), where his preaching attracted great attention, even that of the Catholic French population. It is related that a prominent French lady was much affected, and attended his services regularly. Her priest chided her because she wept under his preaching. "You never weep when I preach," said he. The answer was: "If you will preach like Mr. Blackburn, I will cry all the time."

Dr. William W. McLane, in his sketch of Blackburn, says: "It was as a preacher, however, that he was specially gifted. His commanding presence, his benignant countenance, his sweet and silvery voice, his graceful gestures, and his fine power of description gave him the attention of his audience and control over them." He was called to the pastorate of the First Presbyterian Church in Louisville in 1825; then, in 1827, to the presidency of Centre College, at Danville, Kentucky, which he resigned in 1830, being succeeded by Dr. John C. Young.

An incident in Dr. Blackburn's early ministry illustrates one phase of his character. A slave, John Gloucester, was converted under his preaching, who, by his mental gifts and ardent piety, attracted the attention of Blackburn. The latter, thinking he might be of great use to his race, bought him and had him prepare for the ministry. Gloucester did so, and was licensed and ordained by the Union Presbytery, from which he was dismissed in 1810 to that of Philadelphia. In that city he was the devoted pastor of the African church till his death in 1822. That church was organized through the special influence of Dr. Archibald Alexander.

Gloucester commenced as a missionary to his own people in the city. He had musical talent of a high order and a strong and sympathetic voice. For a time he preached in private houses and in a school-house. In fair weather it was his custom to take his place at the corner of Shippen and South streets, and commence singing a hymn. A miscellaneous crowd would soon collect, and then he would preach. He won by his prudence and fervent piety the confidence of his brethren of the presbytery, and of the entire community. The means were subscribed and a church building was erected on the corner of the streets where he used to preach. In addition, money was supplied by friends in England and at home to purchase the freedom of his family—he, himself, having been freed by Blackburn long before.

XXXV

New Orleans—The Towns along the River.

The People of New Orleans.—New Orleans was at that time one of the most interesting and most difficult fields in the Union for missionary cultivation. The original population was peculiarly heterogeneous, and as it had quite recently come under the jurisdiction of the United States, the mass of the people were unacquainted with American institutions. The French portion were nominally Roman Catholic, but not deeply imbued with the true spirit of Christianity; some, the more devout, went to mass in the forenoon of the Sabbath, in the afternoon desecrated the sacred day in amusements of doubtful morality. Another class—the boatmen—free from the restraints of Christian influence of their surroundings up the river, were easily tempted to indulge in gambling and sensual vices. To these were added the many sailors on shore from ships that represented almost every port in the world. The population was also very unstable in its numbers; at one portion of the year, the busy season, it was about twice that of the dull season. The stated population was in 1804 about eight thousand, and in 1820 it was more than twenty-seven thousand. So many of the people being only temporary residents was of itself a great impediment to the successful preaching of the gospel and founding Christian institutions. In addition, the moral evils incident to the War of 1812 apparently exerted more influence in New Orleans than in any other place in the Union.

Elias Cornelius.—The Connecticut Missionary Society 1816 sent Rev. Elias Cornelius to make a missionary tour in the Southwestern States, but specially enjoined him to visit New Orleans. His instructions were to inquire into the moral conditions of the city, while preaching as opportunity served. He found only one Protestant church in the place—an Episcopal. He invited the Congregationalists and the Presbyterians that happened to be in the city temporarily, or who were permanent residents, to join him in religious services, and to aid in establishing a church. Cornelius was indefatigable in his labors, in carrying out his instructions and in preaching every Sabbath. He secured a cabin of a ship and there preached to a congregation of sea captains and sailors, and often during the week conversed with the latter personally. He visited the hospitals in which were many seamen; he noticed the neglected condition of these inmates and suggested remedies for the evils present, many of which, in consequence, were removed. He also preached to and taught a congregation of colored people, numbering about two hundred.

Sylvester Larned.—On January 22, 1818, Cornelius was joined by Rev. Sylvester Larned, a student of Princeton, who had been appointed to assist him in the mission. The two labored together diligently for three months, and succeeded in establishing the first Presbyterian church in the city. Cornelius then left for another sphere of usefulness.

The brilliant young preacher captivated all hearts, and the people came forward promptly and, under the circumstances, contributed liberally for the purpose of erecting a suitable building, whose corner-stone was laid a few days less than a year after the arrival of Larned. The latter, in his eloquent manner, manifested the greatest zeal in the cause, while all his movements were guided with discretion, so that he seemed to be specially fitted for the position, but, sad to say, his usefulness was cut short by a premature death.

Religious Condition of Towns along the River.—The moral condition of the inhabitants of the towns along the river from Vicksburg down was in many respects similar to that of New Orleans. There was a large population of temporary residents at certain seasons, when the flatboats from the upper country floated down with their cargoes of produce. The crews of the latter were for the most part indifferent to the claims of the gospel while here, but which they recognized more when at their homes. The permanent residents had been so much neglected by the denominations in the East and the North that they, too, were in a sad condition. There were good Christian men among these residents who meant well when they essayed to preach on their own responsibility, but they were so illiterate as to fail in attracting the attention of the more intelligent permanent residents, while they repelled the temporaries who had been accustomed to hear an educated minister at their native homes. The settlements up the Red river in Louisiana were in a similar moral condition, if we accept the account of a writer who says: "The population of Natchitoches was a conglomerate of various tongues and creeds—Americans, French, Spaniards, Indians, and negroes; Roman Catholics, Protestants of different kinds, deists, infidels, and heathen."

Samuel Royce.—To such communities the Connecticut Missionary Society sent the Rev. Samuel Royce (1817). He made his journey thither on a missionary tour, and as opportunity served he preached to congregations that were destitute. He was then only a licentiate, and as such connected himself with the Presbytery of Mississippi. He commenced his labors on the west side of the river, opposite Baton Rouge, on ground "never trodden before by a

Rev. Charles Hodge, D. D.
(165, 499.)

Protestant minister;" that is, one who was properly educated for the office.

Mr. Royce was ere long invited to Alexandria, on the Red river, and there he settled. Here he was almost entirely isolated from ministerial friends, as there was scarcely a brother minister within a hundred miles. He labored incessantly, after making missionary tours through the adjoining region. Great numbers of his hearers had never before heard a Protestant sermon. Infidelity abounded, the French type of which seemed a sort of epidemic, extended by means of immigrants, many from Kentucky. Now and then he was cheered when he happened to be cordially received by Christian men and women, who had migrated thither from homes that were within reach of gospel privileges. He said: "Their countenances and tears, more than words, revealed emotions easier to imagine than to express." Here, as far as we know, Mr. Royce spent his ministerial life.

Educational Society.—Dr. Elias Cornelius was appointed in 1826 secretary of the American Educational Society, which was located at Boston. The following year the American and the Auxiliary Educational Society, which was Presbyterian and in New York, were united under the name American, and three years later (1830) the offices of the general society were transferred to the latter city, since its location was more central in respect to the country at large.

The labors of Cornelius were remarkably successful, especially in New York City, where his presence seemed to inspire those with whom he came in contact with his own consecrated enthusiasm. The influence spread beyond individuals, and some churches came forward and proposed at their own expense to educate a number of young men for the ministry. Interest in the cause gradually penetrated other and distant portions of the church, the effect of which was to greatly increase auxiliary societies and their contributions; the latter, in due time, were doubled and also in proportion the number of the candidates, which, within two years, reached more than two hundred. The society, because of its new location and of its many auxiliaries, secured the prestige of being national in its character, as we have seen was the case of the other benevolent societies. The hearts of all Christians who appreciated the significance of the situation rejoiced.

The assembly's Board of Education had not been nearly so successful, as many of the contributions of its own churches were drawn off to the society, which had recently become *national* in its character, and, in consequence, its facilities for usefulness were thought to be greater, and, moreover, both were evangelical in doctrines and designs. The time had not yet come when in numbers, wealth, and influence, any one denomination could become national in its character; that is, extend its benevolent efforts to all portions of the Nation.

The American Board.—On the same line the American Board of Foreign Missions had acted, and also had been so admirably managed in every respect as to secure the confidence of the Presbyterians as well as that of the Congregationalists, and in consequence to it the former gave, for the most part, their contributions. The Board had recently introduced, in addition to the monthly concert of prayer, the custom of preparing papers containing accounts of the current progress of the cause of missions in foreign lands, and which were published in the *Missionary Herald*. This information, so new and fresh, by its diffusion, roused an unusual interest in the subject among intelligent Christians, especially in the Presbyterian Church.

The organization known as the New York Missionary

Society blended with the United Foreign Missionary Society, and under the latter name a plan of union was proposed with the American Board. The General Assembly of 1826 favored such union, though a respectable minority did not heartily sanction the movement. The tide of influence at that time in the Presbyterian Church seemed in a measure to run in favor of voluntary missionary associations rather than in denominational. The United Foreign Missionary Society was a voluntary association, and, of course, was not in direct connection with the Presbyterian Church, though the members of the latter, by their contributions, largely sustained its operations. At that time, the necessities of the foreign field seemed to require the union of the efforts of the two denominations most interested in the cause—the Congregational and the Presbyterian. This increased interest in missions to the heathen was, evidently, the outgrowth of revivals that prevailed in the sections of the country in which these societies had more specially their home, and the tendency was to utilize, as much as possible, the concentrated facilities of the American Board for carrying on the work, which had already been well organized.

The American Board took proper measures to enlighten the church members on the subject of its work in the foreign field by means of the *Missionary Herald*. As the churches thus learned of the trials and the success of these missions, they were induced, in view of their *own responsibility*, to aid the cause by their contributions. As outgrowths of this interest, many local missionary societies became auxiliary to the American Board; one or two of these were as far South as South Carolina and Georgia.

The Action Ex Officio.—Meanwhile, there was an undercurrent of thought in the minds of many influential men in the Presbyterian Church that the denominations, as such, should be *ex officio* missionary societies. In after years this theory began to be recognized in contradistinction to the voluntary system, though for the present the latter appeared to be the more expedient. In due time, the denominations having, respectively, increased greatly in the numbers of their church members and also proportionately in wealth, took up the missionary cause, virtually, *ex officio,* and the results have been grand. Their church members and ministers, under these new conditions, began to realize as individual denominations, *their responsibility* in the cause more vividly than was possible for them to do in connection with mixed or voluntary associations. The several denominations thus entering independently into the missionary field, has no doubt, as facts prove, advanced the cause throughout the world much more than if they had continued to act as auxiliaries to a vast voluntary association, though it conducted its work in the best manner that intelligent Christian and self-denying men could devise. This result can be accounted for on the principle that, on entering upon separate mission work, these denominations assumed a certain responsibility, the influence of which became so diffused as to reach the individual church members, and thus the whole body—the rank and file and leaders—became imbued with the same spirit and desire to sustain the cause.

XXXVI.

Numerous Revivals.

For several years, commencing in 1827, there were many revivals in Presbyterian churches throughout the Union. These awakenings were more local than universal, yet there was an awakened interest in nearly all the churches, some more decisive than others, during this period, and great numbers on professing their faith united with the church. Within the bounds of several presbyteries in the State of New York occurred a number of revivals; this was specially the case in those whose bounds included the City of New York and up the Hudson to and beyond Troy. Many of the churches in the city were blessed with powerful revivals. More than a thousand persons were added to the churches, and mostly on the profession of their faith (1829). The blessed influence extended to the western portion of the State and pervaded the churches to an unprecedented extent. The interest felt was so great that the secular press for the *first* time often noticed the meetings and the progress of such spiritual awakenings. This marked work of grace continued among the churches of that region for several years. The religious services were conducted with great zeal, and sometimes measures were introduced that afterward appeared to have been of doubtful utility, but the good results far overbalanced the evil of the injudicious measures.

During this period other sections of the country were visited by the blessed influence of the Holy Spirit, as in

Eastern New Jersey and in Pennsylvania. Such was strikingly the case in Philadelphia, where a number of churches enjoyed scenes of spiritual refreshing, and many hundreds within a year or two were added to the churches on examination. These revivals extended toward the West, and within the bounds of the Synod of Pittsburg many of the churches had seasons of the outpouring of the Holy Spirit. In these seasons there seemed to be a deep pervading religious influence that impressed itself not merely upon the Christians but threw a shade of solemnity over the non-professors who came in contact with the churches.

Revivals in Ohio, Indiana, and Illinois.—The State of Ohio was also visited, and many churches were specially awakened in different portions of the State, but more especially in the City of Cincinnati and vicinity. The revivals in the city itself were greatly promoted by the labors of two evangelists, Revs. James Gallaher and Frederick Ross, who came from amid revival scenes in Kentucky in order to aid the several pastors of the city at the request of Dr. Joshua L. Wilson, pastor of the First Church. These evangelists also made preaching tours throughout the State, and were greatly blessed in their labors. They were characterized as most admirably qualified for their special work. Within the year 1828 there were added to the First Church, alone, on profession of their faith, three hundred and sixty-four. During the same time revivals were progressing in ten neighboring churches, in which great numbers were converted and connected themselves with these churches. The same influence extended to the interior of the State, and nearly thirty towns and villages are mentioned in the reports to the presbyteries, where revivals prevailed during this period, and altogether thousands professed to be converted and joined the churches. To accommodate the multitudes who were interested in these religious services, the Presbyterians held camp-meetings. The first one being under the direction of the Presbytery of Cincinnati, was held in the vicinity of that city. Others were held at different times and places, and were attended by thousands, and the preachers were very successful in presenting the gospel to multitudes who perhaps seldom, if ever, went to the ordinary church. The meetings were conducted with proper decorum, though it was charged that questionable methods were sometimes introduced. Great numbers professed to have experienced a change of heart and on examination were admitted to church membership. Leading Presbyterian clergymen in the city and State took an active part in conducting these services. These revivals, so general in their characteristics, extended into the States of Indiana and Illinois, and great numbers of Presbyterian churches scattered over these States were visited by seasons of spiritual blessings, though the churches therein, for the most part, were comparatively feeble in point of the number of their members respectively.

Revivals in Kentucky, the Carolinas, and Georgia.—The revivals were not limited to the States north of the Ohio, but passed to the south, and Kentucky was greatly blessed. The benign influence was specially felt in the towns of Paris, Lexington, Danville, and other places of note. Conversions in the State were numbered by thousands. "The whole aspect of society [in some localities] was changed; vices before prevalent and unblushing almost entirely disappeared." For more than two years this interest in religious subjects continued in the State. Protracted meetings were held in numerous places throughout the country, in order to accommodate the attending thousands. The individual churches shared in these blessings and great numbers in the aggregate were converted. The Synod of West Tennessee, in their narrative of religion in 1827, said: "Never before has there been in the same length of time, so much attention given to the means of grace, or so many additions to the church as during the last year."

The same spiritual influence spread still further throughout that southern portion of the Union, it also crossed the mountains toward the East, and reached the States on the South Atlantic slope, the Carolinas and Georgia. In the latter a striking instance occurred in the college, now the University of Georgia, at Athens. Previously there was not known to be a single professing Christian among the students, when in 1822 seven of them undertook the Christian work of establishing a Sunday-school and to hold prayer-meetings. Five years later in the institution commenced a revival of religion among the students, and which pervaded the entire vicinity. Presbyterian camp-meetings were held in different places in the State, which were attended by immense numbers, and hundreds were added to the various churches. Says a writer (1828) who was conversant with these scenes: "I hear daily of hundreds being added to the churches, and of thousands inquiring for the bread of life." As an outcome, a large number of new churches were organized within the State, and the missionary spirit received a new and strong impulse, and in consequence a domestic missionary society was formed.

South Carolina also participated in the blessings of these revivals, and in that State great numbers of the churches enjoyed seasons of spiritual refreshings. Presbyterian camp-meetings were also held to which flocked thousands from the neighboring regions, numerous conversions were confessed, while multitudes were apparently deeply impressed. The meetings of the presbyteries were largely attended, and in consequence the precious influence extended far and wide. North Carolina for a time seemed to be passed by, when in 1828 the outpouring of the Spirit came in answer to the prayers of the faithful. The synod of that year reported the admission of about four hundred to church membership within its bounds, and likewise an increase in the numbers of the ministers of the gospel.

Revivals in Virginia.—The blessed influence also reached Virginia, and revivals commenced in many of the churches connected with the several presbyteries. Such was the case in the churches in the tidewater region, as in Norfolk, Williamsburg, and others in that vicinity. Quite a number of the churches more in the interior, as those connected with the famed Presbytery of Hanover, were also blessed by the presence of the Holy Spirit. The evangelist, Rev. Asahel Nettleton, whose labors had been so much blessed in the State of New York, at the special request of Dr. John Holt Rice, visited Virginia. In connection with his labors a number of revivals commenced, principally in Prince Edward County, while the influence reached the neighboring congregations, and in the end extended far and wide throughout the State.

The Sabbath—Sunday Mails.—For a number of years the desecration of the Sabbath had increased to such an extent as to arrest the attention, especially of the religious portion of the Nation, including *all* denominations. The moral aspects of the subject were discussed extensively in the newspapers and in meetings of the people called for the purpose. In order to remedy the evil the national government in Jackson's first administration was urged by numerous petitions to use its influence in the cause of good morals, by refraining to carry the mails on the Sabbath. There were, also, counter petitions presented by those who had no sympathy for preserving the sacredness of the day. In the lower house of Congress these petitions were referred to a committee of which Richard M. Johnson of Kentucky was appointed chairman. This committee made a report in 1830. It is not our intention to point out in detail the fallacies of this report, nor the sneering innuendoes against the petitioners.

The Famous Report.—The report had unequivocal internal evidence that Johnson did not write it. Dick—as his intimates called him—never on any other occasion gave evidence that he had been a Sunday-school scholar or a learner in a Bible class, but his report bristled with Biblical and theological criticisms on the Sabbath laws of the Israelites, and so on down through the Christian ages to the finishing sentence of the document. For a long time the Hon. Amos Kendall had the popular credit of writing this report, but in his autobiography he denies the charge and says the writer was a Baptist minister at whose house Johnson was boarding at the time.

The animus of that report may be inferred from the following sentence: "So far from stopping the mails on Sunday, the *committee* would recommend the use of all reasonable means to give it greater expedition and a greater extension." The *italics* in this sentence are the committee's. The report was received and adopted by the House and the committee discharged.

The report made the assertion that if the government on moral grounds refrained from carrying the mails on Sunday, as the petitioners had asked it to do, "that Congress in so doing would be legislating upon a religious subject, and therefore the act would be *unconstitutional,*" as it would be to all intents and purposes a union of Church and State!

When this report was published, a righteous indignation, such as was never known before, burst forth from the entire Christian portion of the American people. This protest and condemnation were, however, treated with contempt. The composition of the majority of the members of that House of Representatives, and of many successive ones, was such as to discourage for a generation efforts to secure a better observance of the sacred day by the national government.

Ratio of Representation.—The General Assembly in 1826 modified the ratio of its members. By the rule adopted, that each presbytery consisting of less than twelve ministers was entitled to send one minister and one elder as delegates or commissioners; if a presbytery had more than twelve ministers, it could send to the assembly two ministers and two elders.

The General Assembly has always been accustomed from year to year to keep abreast with the movements of the age, and to give its influence in favor of benevolent societies and of those designed to promote good morals. In 1826 it commended to its churches the interests of the Colonization Society; in 1827 it encouraged the temperance reformation, and approvingly noticed the American society for the promotion of that cause; in 1828 lotteries were unequivocally condemned; and since they were in some States sanctioning by law, they were characterized as "legalized gambling."

Statistics of the Church.—The increase of the church during four years—1827-1830, inclusive—may be inferred from the number of presbyteries organized to meet the wants of the churches, and for the convenience and advantage of having frequent intercourse between the ministers and the representatives of the church members—the eldership. The number of presbyteries thus erected was twenty-two. As the boundaries of not one of these remain the same to-day as they were originally, it is scarcely necessary to record their names. During the years mentioned above, and for similar reasons, were formed five synods; these were West Tennessee, Indiana,

Utica, Mississippi, and Cincinnati. The membership of the churches increased, meanwhile, from "about one hundred and thirty thousand in 1826 to about one hundred and eighty-five thousand at the close of 1830." The reader will perceive that this increase was on an average of nearly fourteen thousand a year. It is proper to remark that as a general rule these numbers do not represent a perfectly accurate account, as churches sometimes failed to report the number of their respective numbers to the presbyteries.

XXXVII.

Societies—Church—Colleges.

Home Missions.—As has been already noted, the missionary societies, foreign and domestic, or home, including the assembly's board and the Connecticut Society, and also the educational, were formed previous to 1820, and had become virtually *national* in the scope of their operations. From that time forward home missionary work was conducted in connection with these societies and without special friction till near the division of the Presbyterian Church in 1838. Much attention during this period was given to the field designated in missionary work as the Northwest and West, thus including the States of Ohio, Indiana, Illinois, and Missouri. The territory of the latter was then the most populous west of the Mississippi, St. Louis being a center for trade and its most important town.

Numbers of preachers of the gospel were sent by these societies, who supplied as best they could the churches throughout that region, then but sparsely settled, except at certain locations. In some of the latter churches had become self-supporting, while the others were so scattered and feeble in the number of their church members that they were unable to sustain settled pastors. Meanwhile the character of the population was continually changing, because of the influx of immigrants, some of whom came from the Eastern States and others from foreign lands. The southern portion of these States bordering on the north shore of the Ohio had large accessions from beyond that river. Most of the latter did not wish to bring up their families amid the demoralizing influences of slavery, especially upon the inner life of the people. Unfortunately, as a general rule, the latter immigrants were not as intelligent as those who founded settlements in the middle and northern portions of these States. The people of the slave-labor States never had the advantages of public schools, while they were only partially trained to support the ordinances of the church and gospel. On the other hand, west of the Mississippi, even before Missouri became a State (1821) but much more afterward, because she held slaves and had a very fertile soil and fine climate, an immense migration moved thither from the slave labor States, not from Kentucky alone, but especially from Eastern Virginia and the Carolinas; they could take with them their slaves, and to better their condition they bid farewell to their exhausted fields.

Organizing Churches.—In giving the gospel to these destitute Territories and States the missionaries found only a few centers of influence in which to concentrate their efforts, but they had to pass from settlement to settlement, and preach to the people thus scattered abroad. They often met those who in the homes of their youth had enjoyed religious privileges; these settlers always welcomed the preachers of the gospel. The latter, often taking these professing Christians as a nucleus, and when the conditions warranted the movement, organized a church. Churches being thus established, the missionaries visited them in turn. Some of these churches soon became self-supporting, as when under favorable circumstances two or three would combine and sustain a pastor. The detail in giving an account of the founding of individual churches would, alone, require a volume, and therefore we give only the salient points, and indeed the reader woud find such recollections rather monotonous, as they are very similar in almost every respect.

The first Presbyterian church in Indiana was organized at Vincennes in 1806, ten years before the Territory became a State. The first resident minister was Rev. Samuel Thornton Scott, who came from Kentucky and preached in that church. In the years immediately succeeding a number of licentiates and ordained ministers were sent to that region by the General Assembly to fill missionary appointments of different lengths of time, and were assigned to special districts in order to reach as many as possible of the people. These ministers traveled on horseback throughout the Territory, and afterward the State, visiting and preaching in the numerous isolated settlements of that time.

Father Dickey.—Rev. John M. Dickey, of Irish descent, a native of South Carolina, found his way into Kentucky and was licensed to preach by the Muhlenberg Presbytery. He visited Indiana in 1814 as a missionary; after remaining one year and exploring the region as a field for Christian effort, he made arrangements to bring his family and settle therein permanently. When we read of his trials and those of his family, we get a glimpse of similar ones endured by other ministers laboring in the same region. He settled over a church at the forks of White river, near where now is the town of Washington. The cost of the ferriage over the river for his family and furniture was fifty cents more than the money in his possession. His salary was fifty dollars a year for half his time; the other half he devoted to *volunteer* missionary work in destitute places or churches; for this labor he scarcely received enough to defray his traveling expenses. In order to eke out a support for his wife and children he often had recourse to manual labor, and sometimes he gave instruction in vocal music. His district or "Presbyterian diocese" was in area about six-

teen miles by ten. He thus labored on with unflagging
zeal; once he changed his location to a more destitute district near Lexington, Scott County, and finally became
pastor of two churches located further south and nearer
the Ohio river. During the twenty-five or thirty years
of ministerial labor, he was instrumental in gathering a
large number of churches which in due time were organized. He was the sixth minister to enter that field of
settlements so heterogeneous in character, and which were
then almost entirely destitute of gospel privileges. He
was ever diligent in the work, and in the end it prospered
to such an extent that within the State he saw presbyteries and synods organized to meet the wants of the
church. His indefatigable labors were crowned with success, and thus encouraged, he labored on till the infirmities
of age forbid. It was no wonder that the people affectionately called him "Father Dickey," as he had a claim
more than any other man to be recognized as the father
of the Presbyterian Church in Indiana. (*G., II., p. 396.*)

The Immigration of Farmers—Mr. Derrow.—In 1816
Rev. Nathan B. Derrow, who under a commission from
the Connecticut Society had been laboring for seven years
in the Western Reserve, left that field under a missionary
appointment of the same society to preach in Indiana and
Illinois, then Territories but soon to become States. He
found the field inviting because it was quite destitute and
the people willing to hear the gospel. Great numbers of
immigrants were pouring in; these were principally farmers who desired to secure homes for their families. An
unusual number of these settlers were illiterate, especially
in the southern portion, and scarcely a book was to be
found in their cabins. "In a large number of instances
extreme indigence was connected with extreme ignorance.
When tracts were presented by the missionary, he was
asked to read them by those who declared they could not

read themselves." There also prevailed, to a certain extent, a roving and restless disposition on the part of some, who, instead of clearing the virgin soil and living permanently on their own cultivated farms, preferred to be on the move toward the frontier, as if neighbors were an annoyance. As the country became more densely settled, greater portions of the land were brought under cultivation, and this roving class either settled down or disappeared. Mr. Derrow accomplished an immense amount of ministerial work by traveling throughout the country and preaching. He organized a number of churches and was cheered in his labors by an increasing attention on the part of the people to hear the gospel.

The Time of Commission Limited.—The missionaries usually had an appointment for half a year, and also to each one a district was assigned by the committee of the association by which they were commissioned. The Rev. Orin Fowler was sent in 1818 by the Connecticut Society to labor for six months in Indiana. He was directed to visit some ten counties in the middle and eastern portion of the State. In relation to this region which he had explored, he reported that: "The people were anxious to hear the Word preached," and that urgent requests were pressed upon him almost daily to visit and preach to assemblies or congregations, that would hear him gladly. The interest manifested was so great that the news of his approach was spread far and wide, as is evidenced by the people coming ten miles or more to hear a sermon. During the period of his appointment, Mr. Fowler felt warranted in organizing *only* two churches, a number, however, had been previously thus established in these counties by other missionaries, but in the entire State, at that time, not one appears to have been able, alone, to support a settled pastor.

The main portion of the population of this new State

was in its eastern section, and in the southern part, bordering on the Ohio, and in the fertile valleys of its tributaries, that of the Wabash securing the larger share. A limited number of immigrants had come into this southern region from Ohio, but comparatively few from the Northern States. The latter, for climatic reasons, were more inclined to migrate due west. On the parallels of latitude to which they were accustomed in their native homes.

There had been a number of missionaries sent into the State, some of whom were commissioned by the General Assembly, and others by the Connecticut Missionary Society, but only for a limited time, scarcely ever longer than six months; the lack of funds had much to do with these short-time appointments. In 1820 there were only seven Presbyterian ministers in the State, and only two of these were settled pastors. Soon ofter this time the population commenced to increase very rapidly. An immense immigration of settlers came in and with the intention of being permanent residents. These were mostly from the Northern and Eastern States.

The Church at the Capital.—Indianapolis, then a small village, had become the capital of the State, and in consequence the number of its inhabitants began to increase. Here, in the summer of 1821, was preached the first sermon by a Presbyterian minister, and that to a very small congregation. The following year, commencing in May, the Rev. David C. Proctor, a missionary sent by the Connecticut Society, preached a few sermons and then left, but returned the following autumn and began his labors for a year. In July, 1823, he organized a church of *fifteen* members; after three-fourths of a year's service—the other fourth being given to a church at Bloomington about seventy miles distant—Mr. Proctor was called to another field, and the following year the Rev. George Bush commenced to supply the church, which he did for several years. Afterward Mr. Bush became professor in the University of the City of New York.

Rev. Isaac Reed, a native of Granville, New York State, a graduate of Middleburg College, commenced in 1818 his work as stated supply for a year at New Albany. The church numbered thirteen members, but within a year the number increased to thirty-five, and a Sabbath-school —the first in the State—was organized and soon had sixty scholars in attendance. The population was nearly eight hundred. A great moral change was brought about through the influence of the gospel. The Sabbath was previously desecrated, being a sort of half holiday, the stores for the most part were kept open, but now they were closed. Mr. Reed appears to have been commissioned by the Connecticut Society, but for some reason it did not give pecuniary aid to the church in New Albany, and the latter, not being able to support a pastor, Mr. Reed, for that reason, removed to Kentucky. Three years afterward he returned and had partial charge of the Presbyterian church at Indianapolis, and later (1824) became pastor of Bethany Church in Owen County. The latter was a new enterprise, and Mr. Reed with his own hands prepared the logs for his parsonage; he states that winter was coming on, and his neighbors were too busy with their own preparations to aid him except in raising or putting the logs in place, which he was unable to do with his own strength. Thus was put up the rude logcabin, one story high, and the openings between the logs above the joint-plates where the roof rested were unfilled with clay or plastering when the family moved in to enjoy Christmas in their new home. This rude hut the devoted missionary in his letters styled "the Cottage of peace." Mr. Reed has done the church a service by giving a graphic account of the trials of these missionaries, their wives, and their families, and also a general sketch of the country and the churches, in a book, entitled "The Christian Traveler."

Notwithstanding his self-denying labors Mr. Reed was forced within a few years to give up the "Cottage of peace," and seek another settlement because of a lack of support, as he had not received one dollar in money for two years. We cannot adequately realize what must have been the trials, even the sufferings of the self-denying wives and families, of those devoted servants of the cause of Christ.

Number of Churches and Ministers.—The population of the State of Indiana was estimated in 1825 at 200,000. The number of Presbyterian and Congregational churches was only forty-three, while the number of their ministers was ten; one-half of whom were settled pastors, the other were missionaries under appointment from the societies. One of the hindrances to the spread of the gospel was the baleful influence of New Lights and Dunkards, which prevailed in neighborhoods wherein the people were grossly ignorant. When the gospel and education came hand in hand these errorists began to disappear and are now virtually extinct, though in the days of which we speak they were a power for evil.

The destitution continued very great, and yet under the circumstances much progress had been made, as was manifested in the better moral tone in general society. Immigrants were still crowding in, many of whom were careless in respect to religion. Sabbath-breaking prevailed to a certain extent, while profanity seemed to be everywhere, and intemperance, the handmaid of many vices, was almost unblushing, and gambling was common.

From 1825 onward to 1837 there is nothing special to note, but the cheering fact that the churches grew in number and prospered. Missionaries continued to fill

SOCIETIES—CHURCH—COLLEGES. 361

their appointments in many settlements, and individual churches were organized and became self-supporting and local centers of influence. Thus was laid wide and deep the foundation of the Presbyterian Church in the State of Indiana, as we now see it, in its educational and religious institutions.

The Presbyterian Church in Indiana had in 1837 sixty-nine ministers and one hundred and twenty-two churches, while the church membership was nearly five thousand. It must be confessed that numbers of individual churches were feeble and were not self-supporting. Many of the sixty-nine ministers were missionaries and traveled in their allotted districts, and served, as they were able, the churches as stated supplies, while others became pastors in the growing towns and the more densely populated portions of the agricultural districts.

Missionaries in Illinois.—The first recognition of Illinois as a separate field for missionary labor was, in 1816, two years before the Territory became a State. Hitherto the Societies had connected it in their operations with Indiana, which took the lead at first in population. With Presbyterians and Congregationalists, education in all its bearings went hand in hand with home missions. Thus the Rev. J. M. Ellis, a Presbyterian missionary, realized the importance of founding a college in the new State of Illinois to meet the wants of the rising generation, whose parents were coming in and forming settlements. When he had been a missionary for two years he began to enlist the sympathy of his fellow members of the Presbytery Center of Illinois, to aid him in the undertaking. The latter body deputed Mr. Ellis in 1828 to visit the East and lay his plan before the benevolent. The design was to move cautiously, and first to establish an academy, which might eventually become a college. Mr. Ellis visited New Haven and also the City of New

York; in the latter, the Presbyterians and the Dutch Reformed sympathized with the object and responded quite liberally. With the funds thus obtained, buildings were erected and the following year the institution, in that respect, was ready for pupils.

Illinois College.—How remarkable are the providential ways in which benevolent purposes are carried out! At this very time seven young men—Yale theological students—had been impressed with the idea that it would be a sphere of great future usefulness to go as missionaries to Illinois, and in time found in that growing State a college that should become a center of good influence. Rumor was continually telling of its beautiful prairies and exceedingly fertile soil, all ready for the plow of the husbandman and for prosperous settlements. To avail themselves of these natural treasures, as well as a fine climate, an immense migration of desirable people was crowding in to become citizens of this garden of the West.

The names of these young men were Mason Grosvenor, John F. Brooks, Elisha Jenney, William Kirby, Asa Turner, J. M. Sturtevant, and Theron Baldwin. They pledged themselves to God and to one another, and in accordance with that pledge they all, on the completion of their theological course, migrated to the State—except Grosvenor, whose poor health forbid his going—and became missionaries and settled in different places, but within reach of one another. They had inquired by letter, and thus became familiar with the plans of Mr. Ellis, and exerted their influence in favor of the college. Three other ministers were on the ground, and with them, six of these young men were named trustees in the charter, which established Illinois College at Jacksonville, in that State.

In this connection it is proper to note the founding

of another institution of learning in the State. Dr. Gideon Blackburn, after his resignation of the presidency of Center College in Kentucky, removed in 1833 to Illinois, on the invitation of some gentlemen interested in the cause of education. He here directed his energies to establish a theological seminary. The outcome was the founding of Blackburn University at Carlinsville, Illinois. By its charter it offers a regular college course of instruction, and also one in theology. After five years of labor in the enterprise, death in 1838 ended the useful and active life of Gideon Blackburn, in his sixty-sixth year. He left as a legacy to the church two sons—successful ministers.

XXXVIII.

The Relation of Churches to Certain Presbyteries.

The reason has already been given (*See p. 222*) why the settlements in Northern Kentucky, bordering on the Ohio river, were formed so rapidly. Meanwhile, because of the easy accessibility by the same river settlements were as rapidly established on its north shore and up the valleys of its tributaries. Thus the southern portions of the now States of Ohio, Indiana, and Illinois were first occupied by enterprising immigrants who floated in flat-boats down the river from Western Pennsylvania and Eastern Ohio. These pioneers occupied in time prominent points from Marietta down to and beyond Cincinnati. The Presbyterian ministers, who were among the first to visit these settlements, came across the river from Kentucky. And when churches were organized and needed the care of a presbytery, it was more convenient because more accessible, for these churches to be connected with the Presbyteries and the Synod of Kentucky, than with those in Western Pennsylvania or Northern Ohio. We find that this rule prevailed until the number of churches and the increase of population warranted the formation of presbyteries and synods on the north side of the river.

In those early days of Christian work there was much inconvenience incident to the proper supervision of the churches by the presbyteries. For illustration, the Presbytery of Center Illinois was in connection with the Synod of Kentucky, and the Presbytery of Missouri, which had a number of churches under its care in Illinois, was itself connected with the Synod of Tennessee. The bounds of the Presbytery of Washington, which was erected in 1799, out of that of Transylvania, Kentucky, was divided by the Ohio river, and on its north side included the churches of the territory, taking the town of Cincinnati as a center. The Synod of Kentucky was formed in 1802; the churches in that region had been, hitherto, under the care of the Synod of Virginia. Of the churches of Illinois, some were connected with the Presbyteries of Transylvania and Muhlenburg, in Kentucky, while others were under supervision of the Presbytery of Missouri. These various arrangements had no influence upon the missionary societies: the Presbyterian Board, the Connecticut Society, the Home Missionary and Young Men's Missionary Society of New York, and minor associations. These all sent their missionaries to fill appointments for Christian work in these new settlements, wherever needed; to preach and establish churches, and, if opportunity served, to become settled pastors, stated supplies, resident missionaries, or evangelists. The missionaries themselves acted in harmony with the societies and with one another; sometimes they were permitted to exercise their own judgment, and if one found a field occupied he would go to a more destitute district. They utilized every facility to carry the gospel to all the settlements, and thus the work went on, meanwhile the population was increasing by immigration, and the people were becoming more stable in their habits, cultivated farms increased rapidly, and towns were fast coming into existence.

The Presbytery of Salem, in the State of Indiana, was erected in 1823. It consisted of nine members, and had under its care most of the churches of the State. The number of the latter continued to increase, but they were so much scattered that in 1825, in order to secure for them closer supervision, the Presbytery of Salem was divided, and from the original two presbyteries were set off—Wabash and Madison—and on the same line, the following year the Synod of Indiana was organized. Afterward with the latter synod was connected the Presbytery of Center Illinois (1828). The boundaries of these presbyteries and synods were arranged as a matter of convenience, and not in respect to the State or territorial lines. The Presbytery of Missouri, which was erected in 1818, had, seven years later, nearly one-half the churches under its care across the Mississippi in the State of Illinois, while it was itself connected with the Synod of Tennessee. Five years later the churches in Illinois belonging to the Presbytery of Missouri were set off to another within the State. These changes were continually going on in consequence of the increase of population and the corresponding increase of churches.

Why the Interest in Missouri?—The new State of Missouri elicited an unusual interest in missionary operations. This was owing to its location, it being then the most important territory west of the Mississippi occupied by American citizens. St. Louis had been for years the starting point and the fitting-out place of the companies of French and other fur traders, who went across the plains to the Rocky Mountains and to the Northwest, now known as the States of Oregon and Washington. An effort was made by Rev. Dr. E. S. Ely (noted elsewhere, *see p. 254*) to found a college in 1834 in the village of Marion, the intention being to meet the expected wants of the youth of the American immigrants who were so rapidly occupying this much-lauded region. After the labors of years by a number of eminent men, and, as it seems, injudicious expenditure of large funds, the enterprise was abandoned. The settlers were mostly from the slave-labor States, and brought with them their slaves. For obvious reasons these people took very little interest in an advanced education, which they were really unable to appreciate, and in addition the financial troubles of 1837 gave the finishing touch to the ruin. The fertile soil and fine climate, and the advantage of being adjacent to navigable rivers and in a central position, was unable to cope with the negative influence of the lack of general intelligence at that time prevailing among the early inhabitants of Missouri.

Religious Character of St. Louis.—The town of St. Louis, originally settled by the French, was the largest in the territory and a center of traffic, but a very difficult missionary field to cultivate. Here were great numbers of French people, who were Catholics and hostile to the Protestants, or indifferent to any religion, whatever. In addition, the boatmen up and down the rivers, when on shore, often spent their time in gambling and drinking, while the streets were in a continual turmoil of traders to the Indians, who were absorbed in disposing of their furs or fitting themselves out for new expeditions. The Sabbath day was almost unknown, and yet in St. Louis were a few Christians who had come from the older States, and longed for the gospel privileges of their native homes. Protestant ministers were rarely seen and seldom heard preach; an itinerant Methodist minister had preached in the town perhaps once a month—this was in 1816. As far as reported by Mr. Giddings and other missionaries, there were at that time only three Presbyterians in the town. The general morals of the territory may be inferred from the fact that the Sabbath was desecrated everywhere, and given up to idleness and pleasure, one form of the latter was horse-racing, a custom imported from Virginia and Kentucky. One illustration may suffice: The Rev. Mr. Flint on one occasion was announced to preach on a certain Sunday at the town of St. Charles. When he arrived at the building in which he was to officiate he noticed that a great crowd was collected. A horse-race was to come off, and as he was about to commence the services, he heard the signal given for the horses to start.

Samuel J. Mills's Tour.—The Rev. Samuel J. Mills and the Rev. John F. Schmerhorn, graduates of Williams College, were commissioned by the Massachusetts Missionary Society, and others, to make an exploring tour on the frontiers through the West and Southeast, in order to acquire accurate knowledge in respect to the moral and religious wants of the people of that entire region. They set out on their journey in the autumn of 1812, and spent about a year in traveling from point to point, preaching by the way, and when it seemed expedient, tarrying long enough to make proper investigations. In this manner they passed through a portion of the State of Ohio; visited many settlements in the Territories of Indiana and Illinois, and the towns along down the Mississippi to New Orleans, where they spent some time, and on their way back they visited the Territory of Missouri at its principal town, St. Louis. (*G. II., p. 423.*)

They made an elaborate report on the religious and moral condition of the people, and also on the destitution that prevailed in the entire region in respect to preachers of the gospel. This report was published and widely circulated, and it aroused an unusual interest in the Eastern churches, which was manifested in an increased number of missionaries that the societies representing these churches sent out. The authors of the report having been on the ground, and after thorough investigation were able to suggest judicious measures to meet the religious wants of the people. They urged the policy, adopted by the Presbyterians, of occupying important points, and there establishing churches and sustaining them till they become self-supporting and centers of local influence. This plan was in contrast with the injudicious custom, that sometimes prevailed, of organizing churches with a mere handful of members, and afterward, because of the lack of men and means, leaving them to dwindle away and perhaps pass out of existence.

This report commanded the confidence of the religious community. Previous to this time, by his persevering efforts in urging privately upon prominent clergymen and others his views of the churches having a practical missionary spirit, Mr. Mills, more than any other man, had promoted the formation of the American Board of Foreign Missions, in 1810. (*Four Hundred Years, etc., page 636.*)

Rev. Salmon Giddings.—To no one does Missouri owe more as a missionary than to Rev. Salmon Giddings. He was an intimate friend of Samuel J. Mills, and after the latter's return from his tour of observation he learned from him of the peculiarities of the country and of the religious wants of its people. Giddings was then a tutor in Williams College, and had recently been licensed to preach. Being deeply impressed with the importance of the subject he determined to make the West his future home and field of missionary work and St. Louis the scene of his labors. The Connecticut Society, having learned of his purpose, sent him a commission to labor in the "Western country." In December, 1815, he commenced his long journey on horseback, advancing slowly across the State of Ohio and the Territories of Indiana and Illinois. On the way, he preached on the Sabbath and often, when opportunity served, on week days. It was not till April 6, 1816, that he reached St. Louis. During the three previous years the country had been much agitated by the War of 1812, which interfered very sadly with home missionary work, as well as with the general piety of the people. But now the war being ended, an unusual impulse was given to business, especially in the line of migrations to the West, and therein on its rivers.

St. Louis, as already noted (*p. 367*), had all the elements of a hard place for an evangelist to begin his labors. Giddings was peculiarly adapted for his work, being blessed with a Christian and kindly disposition, scholarship, and common sense, and withal self-reliance; he was able to adapt himself to surrounding circumstances. He was under the necessity of walking through the town from house to house to obtain a lodging-place and board. He happened to pick up a little St. Louis newspaper, in which was an article headed *"Caution;"* the people were warned against himself. They were told that a missionary society in New England was about to send out preachers to the West, but that it was done for a political purpose, and, moreover, the project had its origin in the Hartford Convention! The latter was a favorite bugbear at the time, and used on almost every occasion on the stump or in the newspapers by a certain class of demagogues. The motive of the latter was, no doubt, to prejudice the Southern people against those of New England.

Mr. Giddings spent the first year in visiting a number of settlements and preaching in the Territory. He sought out the Presbyterians and organized a church in the Belleview settlement some eighty miles southwest of St. Louis (August 16, 1816). This was said to be the first Presbyterian church organized in the Territory. There is a special interest attached to this church, inasmuch as in 1807 there migrated to Missouri from the same church in North Carolina four Presbyterian elders

REV. LYMAN BEECHER, D.D.
(244, 268, 321, 395, 408–413, 415.)

and their families, who found homes at this place. Though they had no preaching, they were careful to keep up a weekly prayer-meeting and to meet together on the Sabbath and read sermons. After some time the settlement was visited by a Methodist circuit rider, and they worshiped with them until Mr. Giddings came, when he organized a church consisting of thirty members.

Rev. Timothy Flint.—The same year (1816) came the Rev. Timothy Flint, commissioned by the Connecticut Society. He traveled much as an itinerant, directing his attention to the settlements up the Missouri river. He wrote a graphic description of the country as to its fertile soil and salubrious climate, and also described the Territory as a most important field for missionary labor. Immigrants in great numbers were coming in and settling on farms or moving on further West. For a time, the crowd was so great that, as Flint states, as many as one hundred immigrants passed daily through St. Charles. He reported that not one family in fifty had a Bible.

Reasons for the Migration.—In order to understand the reasons for this movement the reader will notice as one of them, the material condition of the country at that period. The War of 1812 had recently closed. It had had a most depressing effect upon religion as well as on the business prosperity of the older portion of the Union. In the seaboard States, ocean commerce, especially the carrying trade was destroyed; mechanical industries were ruined by the influx of foreign—especially English— manufactured articles, purposely put in even at cost; workmen were thrown out of employment, and in consequence thousands upon thousands who happened to have the means, sought to better the condition of themselves and families by migrating to the fertile valleys and prairies of the West. This movement continued for a number of years, since it took a long time for business in its various forms to recover in the older States from the unwonted depression into which it had been plunged by the embargo and similar measures. The result was, these new and fertile regions were occupied by energetic settlers who were not afraid to labor, and that influence passed over into succeeding generations, so that proverbially, the people of the West became and continued to be industrious and competent in business matters, and in due time promptly did their full share in sustaining the Union in its time of trial, as well as the ordinances of the church and the cause of education.

The Presbyterians of Missouri, as well as its early settlers, owe a debt of gratitude to the energetic and self-denying missionary labors of Giddings and Flint. They journeyed far and wide, and preached by the way, encouraging numbers who in their old homes had been professing Christians, but in their new ones had become indifferent to form themselves into congregations, and afterward, when circumstances permitted, into organized churches and then to sustain them by their own personal efforts. Meantime every effort was made to secure for these churches ministers either as stated supplies or evangelists.

Mr. Giddings, to eke out his very limited salary, established a school in St. Louis, but continued to preach, and managed for a portion of the year to make preaching tours throughout that region and sometimes across the river in Illinois. When teaching he gave special attention to a feeble congregation, which he finally organized as a church (November 23, 1817). Such were the beginnings of the First Presbyterian Church in St. Louis. It had only *nine* members, and it was eight years before they were able to build for themselves a suitable home. Mr. Giddings became its pastor and served it faithfully for eleven years, till his death. In that relation he was succeeded by Rev. (Dr.) William S. Potts (1829), who did a grand work as its pastor. During the years of his pastorate Mr. Giddings was ever diligent in the labor, when the occasion required, of itinerating, and devoting his energies as much as possible to every work that would have good influence upon the public welfare. He was specially interested in the French Catholic population, distributing among them Bibles and Testaments in that language, and in addition, manifesting toward them his good will by many acts of kindness.

Mr. Flint, who had previously been a missionary in Indiana, was during this period very active in his labors, the scene of which was up on the Missouri river at St. Charles and vicinity. He visited and often preached in the neighboring towns, traveling much during the year, and as he could not afford a horse oftentimes on foot. He also, sometimes, visited the more distant new settlements on both sides of the river, and on one of his missionary excursions, lasting seven weeks, he crossed the Missouri sixteen times. Mr. Flint, in his journal, when speaking of the scenes and people, says: "Many of them live and die without any thought of eternity. So engaged are they in making new settlements in the woods that they seem to regard nothing besides." Yet he was often cheered by being most cordially received by those with whom he had previously conversed and given Bibles, and who listened joyously to his sermons. Mr. Flint, after remaining ten years in the West as a Missionary, returned to the East, and wrote with great success on the characteristics of the scenery of the Great valley and of its then inhabitants.

A Number of Missionaries—John Matthews—From time to time other missionaries were coming into the Territory, who were usually commissioned for six months, some of whom remained and settled permanently over churches. Rev. Thomas Donnell, from North Carolina, was one who was eminent as a Christian and for his usefulness. Rev. Charles S. Robinson, from Mississippi, was sent by the New York Young Men's Evangelical Society (1816). Rev. William McFarland was sent in 1817 by the General Assembly to St. Louis for six months, and to visit destitute places in the Territory. The General Assembly commissioned Rev. Jeremiah Chamberlain in 1819 for six months to the Territory of Missouri. Rev. Francis McFarland was commissioned in 1820 to visit the region up the Missouri river.

The Connecticut Society commissioned Rev. John Matthews to itinerate six months in Missouri in 1819. Matthews was a native of Beaver County, Pennsylvania; of Scotch-Irish descent, a graduate of Jefferson College, and studied theology under Dr. John McMillan. After being a pastor for several years within the bounds of Erie Presbytery he felt it his duty to become a missionary to the destitute portions of the Western territories. After receiving his appointment from the Connecticut Society he went down the Ohio on a flatboat, landing at Louisville. Then traveling on horseback and preaching by the way, he passed through Indinna and Illinois, and finally joined Mr. Giddings in St. Louis, and immediately entered upon his work. Passing up the Missouri to the vicinity of St. Charles, he took charge of a church in Pike County; here he remained seven years, a portion of which time he engaged in teaching to aid in his support. Afterward he took charge of a church in Southeastern Missouri, and two or three years later we find him a pastor of a church in Kaskaskia, Illinois. Matthews, though indefatigable in his ministerial labors, managed to become a well-read student, and found time in the course of years to write out a system of theology.

These ministers continued to visit the various settlements and gave special attention to the churches recently organized. The destitute portions of the Territory made urgent calls for more preachers, while those in the field were incessant in their efforts to answer these calls.

Missions in Michigan.—The territory now known as Michigan was previously visited by the French, who in 1610 established a trading-post on the strait—Detroit. After the Treaty of Paris, 1763, it passed into the hands of England, and all the French forts on the lakes were occupied by English garrisons. After the American Revolution, when a boundary was arranged between Canada and the United States, the line was drawn through the middle of the Lakes and their connecting streams, and thus the Territory of Michigan became the property of the latter.

The first settlers at Detroit and in the vicinity were French, who in 1749 were sent out at the expense of that government to form a settlement. At the close of the Revolution "The French at Detroit were numerous; they tilled their farms as well as engaged in the traffic of furs." This trade was carried on from Detroit as a center along the shores of the upper lakes.

In 1805 the United States Government organized the Territory of Michigan, but four years previous missionaries had visited Detroit, though more especially to the Indians (*p. 296*). The town had the reputation of being "a most abandoned place;" it was stated that only one person in it—a colored man—appeared to be pious. Two other missionaries, a Methodist and a Congregationalist, made similar efforts, but both were unsuccessful. About this time (1804) a destructive fire burned ever house in the place except one.

The Trials of the Early Settlers of Michigan.—Detroit being on the line between Canada and the United States, was, if possible, still more demoralized than ever by the War of 1812, and not till after its close was special effort made by the General Assembly to send missionaries thither. The population consisted largely of the resident garrison; in addition were white traders and Indians of different tribes, and the descendants of the original French; the latter were Catholics. The character of the people in 1816 is thus summed up: "The profaneness of the soldiers exceeds anything I ever imagined"—by the way, the garrison had no chaplain; . . . "there is no Sabbath in this country." Such are the words of Rev. John Monteith, who in 1817 was sent to Detroit and vicinity, by the assembly's board, for one year, but his commission was renewed from year to year. Though ignorance and wickedness prevailed to a frightful extent, there were a few who welcomed him most cordially; he labored on faithfully, and commanded the respect of all classes by his self-denying zeal in the cause of pure religion. He said he was lonely, as the nearest Presbyterian brother was two hundred miles distant. He took one month in the year as a vacation, when he went on missionary tours to the surrounding region. Thus he occasionally visited the settlements on the river Raisin, and as far on the lake shore as Sandusky and Cleveland. The Methodists had also preaching from itinerant ministers, and they manifested in the community their usual Christian zeal.

Labors of Rev. Monteith.—Mr. Monteith made a report of his preaching tours, and the assembly in 1818 commissioned a missionary for six months to the settlements on the Raisin, and this was for a year or two following.

Mackinaw, on the straits of the same name, from its position, was an important center for missionary work, since through these straits there was every prospect that in time an immense coasting trade would pass. This trading-post was in 1820 visited by Rev. Jedediah Morse, who preached to the people for a season. The moral character of the town may be inferred from the statement that "the Christian Sabbath had not got so far." Two years later the Rev. W. M. Ferry came under a commission of the United Foreign Missionary Society. Though at first he could not find much encouragement, he labored on for ten years, and had his reward in seeing the moral character of the place quite changed for the better.

Mission at St. Mary's Straits.—The Western Missionary Society of the Synod of Pittsburg established a mission at the straits of St. Mary. At this location were a number of English-speaking families, as well as French, the latter nominally Catholic, besides numbers of Indians of different tribes, who still resorted to these waters in order to obtain supplies of fish. This was an important missionary station, as the trade of the upper lakes, which evidently would have a great future, must pass through these straits, and it was hoped it would become a center of Christian influence and effort. The United States Government had established here a military post, and here at that time resided its Indian agent, Mr. Henry R. Schoolcraft.

The special missionary, Rev. Robert M. Laird, was earnest in the performance of his duties, and he was blessed in his labors among the soldiers and residents, numbers of whom attended his special services for those inquiring on the subject of religion, as he reported to the General Assembly in 1824. He made it a point to distribute Bibles and religious books to the scholars in the Sunday-schools, and also to adults.

The General Assembly continued from year to year to make appointments for the entire region around the shores of the lakes, and the adjoining settlements in the interior of the Territory of Michigan, till it became a State in 1837. An immense population kept pouring in from the Eastern States for a number of years, and the calls for preachers of the gospel were incessant. The Presbytery of Detroit was formed in 1827, and put in connection with Western Reserve Synod. Meanwhile the number of people and churches continued to increase, so that it became necessary, as a matter of convenience, to divide the Presbytery of Detroit, and two others were set off from it, that of St. Joseph's and Monroe. These three presbyteries numbered thirty-two ministers, and the churches fifty-nine, and in 1835 the Synod of Michigan was organized.

The Reports—Views of Missionaries.—It is unfortunate for the historian and for the reader that so few of these pioneer ministers—not more than three or four, it seems—took notes or wrote specially of the varied conditions of the people living in these new communities. To be sure, they sent regularly their reports to the respective societies under whose commissions they labored. These reports were condensed as ordinary business documents. These devoted men had an instinctive delicacy which prevented their making complaints to the committee of the society. It is only now and then we get hints derived from their private letters, of their trials, and those of their devoted wives, who underwent with them the dangers and the hardships incident to such frontier life. When the timid statement is made of the lack of support, it always means deprivation for the family of the necessaries of life—of luxuries they had none. The great services of these wives and mothers have been almost literally ignored; if we only had a record of them we could obtain a clearer view of the inner life of the people among whom they and their husbands labored. How often would the journal of the wife of a missionary throw light upon the characteristics of these frontier communities? In every instance when the missionary presented himself, the women of the frontier settlements were always the first to give him a hearty welcome, with tears of joy and a burst of gratitude for bringing them the gospel which they loved to hear in their native homes, and now, for obvious reasons, more lovingly cherished than ever. May we not hope that a better day is dawning, when the fruitful labors of the wives of home missionaries will be more appreciated and become a subject of record, and thus stimulate their sisters to greater exertions in the cause?

XXXIX.

The Change of Policy.

We are now approaching an important era in the history of the Presbyterian Church—no less than its division. This act led to a complete change of its policy in missionary operations; namely, from the union with other denominations in voluntary societies, to a separate and individual action on the part of the church. This was in accordance with the theory, which had been suggested some time before, that the Presbyterian Church, as a denomination, should be *ex officio* a missionary association. The reader will note that the several denominations in the Union at this time—1900—conduct their missionary operations, foreign and home, in their individual or organic capacity. The only voluntary benevolent associations at this day are the American Bible Society, Sunday-School Union, and American Tract Society. Within the last half-century all the evangelical denominations have each advanced so much in the number of adherents and in material prosperity that they can in a separate capacity do more effective work in extending the influence of the gospel than by coöperating with voluntary associations. This separate action brings home more vividly to their respective church members each one's *individual responsibility* in the matter than under the voluntary or combination system. The American Board was originally a voluntary association, and because of its having been admirably conducted financially, as well as judiciously in its general management, it commanded the confidence of the entire religious public. It has now, however, become virtually denominational, since it is the agent of the Congregational Church alone. What a grand career it has had for nearly ninety years! The voluntary system is better adapted to the Congregational Church polity than to any other denomination. Since its polity enjoins "the equality of all believers, including the officers of the church; the equality of the several churches, free from the jurisdiction of ecclesiastical court or bishop, free from the jurisdiction of one church over another, free from the collective authority of them all." (*Bancroft's U. S. Hist., pp. 238, 239. Last revision.*)

The Progress of the Church.—In the progress of the Presbyterian Church from 1830 to 1837, the average annual number of persons admitted to it on examination in the first four years of that period was 23,340, and of the last three the average was only 14,463. During these latter three years there was much agitation in the church, because of ecclesiastical trials of clergymen and other controversies, which resulted finally in 1838 in its division; this may account, in part, for the falling off of conversions from the world. In 1837 the number of synods was twenty-three; presbyteries, one hundred and thirty-five; ministers, two thousand one hundred and forty; churches, two thousand eight hundred and sixty-five, and of church members, two hundred and twenty thousand, five hundred and fifty-seven.

The Awakened Interest.—The sentiment had been increasing in the minds of men of comprehensive views that the church in its organized capacity should be virtually a missionary society. It was agreed that such a stand taken on the subject would develop a greater missionary spirit among the church members. The discussion and diffusion of knowledge on the subject awakened an interest never before known. The great difficulty in the way of realizing these expectations was that the American Board was doing a grand work; and why not let well alone, rather than break off and try experiments on a separate line? On the same ground the Home Missionary Society was a voluntary association, but was doing a good work. In consequence of this success Presbyterians, for the greater part, gave their contributions to these voluntary societies, and that habit crippled those belonging to the church proper. It is probable that a much longer time would have elapsed before the majority of the Presbyterian ministry and intelligent laymen could have become willing to withdraw from that system and adopt the denominational, had not other causes intervened.

The Changes in Thirty Years.—The plan of union had been the means of accomplishing a grand work since it was first established. The two denominations, the Presbyterian and Congregational, in their missionary labor, often overlapped one another in occupying the same ground, and thus they came in friendly competition. The plan of union was therefore adopted in order to utilize more effectively the power of both parties. (*See pp. 238-240.*) But in the course of more than a third of a century the conditions had very much changed. Both denominations had increased in the number of their church members; while the field for their missionary operations had increased in a still greater proportion. The Congregationalists had extended on parallel lines of latitude across Northern and Western New York, and, passing over Pennsylvania into Ohio, occupied mainly the region known as the Western Reserve. The Presbyterians continued to hold their own in the South, along the Atlantic slope. In early days they crossed the Alleghanies and took possession of Western Pennsylvania, then extended their lines into the Territories, afterward the States lying between the Ohio and Mississippi rivers; meanwhile their missionaries from the South Atlantic slope, on similar lines of latitude, were penetrating the Territories, afterward States, bordering on the north shore of the gulf, and also on the north of the latter were occupying Kentucky and Tennessee. The Presbyterians of Western Pennsylvania and Eastern Ohio were at the same time passing down the rivers Ohio and Mississippi, taking in only the towns on the north shore of the former but on both shores of the latter to New Orleans. On the west side missionaries were sent to the Territories of Arkansas and Missouri. From these fields of early ministerial labor the Presbyterian Church never receded, but continued to advance toward greater efficiency in proclaiming the gospel.

Missionary Territorial Areas Compared.—With the exception of a limited number of isolated churches in different localities, and those in the Western Reserve, there were scarcely any organized Congregational churches west of the Alleghanies. The home of the great influence of that body of Christians was in New England; but how nobly they labored to promote the cause of Christ within the Union, especially in the great West! The immense territory just described was, in an ecclesiastical sense, occupied for the most part by the Presbyterians. To aid in evangelizing the people therein, they invited and cordially welcomed great numbers of ministers, who were sent and supported by the missionary societies of Massachusetts and Connecticut. The ministers and missionaries, Congregational and Presbyterian, agreed in the essential doctrines of the gospel, and on this basis they fraternized. As to the form of church government, though each party had its predilections, it was deemed by both non-essential or a matter of expediency, and in consequence changes were often made by ministers from one denomination to the other. The result was that in the West the missionaries from New England fell in with the Presbyterial polity and connected themselves, when occasion required, with their presbyteries and synods.

The area of these new territories occupied by the Presbyterians was comparatively so much greater than that of New England that it required a proportionally greater number of ministers to meet the religious wants of the population, which, in addition to the rapid and natural increase, was augmented by thousands and thousands migrating thither from the old States. Still more, in after years, hosts of immigrants were almost daily coming in from Germany and Ireland. Some of those from the former were evangelical Lutherans, while others, indeed the much more numerous class, were indifferent to religious subjects, especially those who were rationalistic in their views. The latter had scarcely any respect for the Sabbath as a day of sacred rest, they being accustomed to the "Continental Sabbath." Those from Ireland were, for the most part, unfortunately, grossly illiterate and priest-ridden Catholics.

What Presbyterians Had at Stake.—The Presbyterians had a great deal at stake, since they, as a denomination, had adopted a system or Confession of Faith, and catechism, church polity, and discipline, that had stood the test for two hundred years, and proved itself, as they believed, to be in substance in accordance with the teachings of Holy Scripture. On the contrary, the Congregationalists had no such complete system of Christian doctrine around which a great denomination could rally, as each congregation usually had its own confession framed by the congregation itself. No two of these creeds were alike, word for word, and occasionally individual churches changed the terms of their summary of doctrine. The

Presbyterians did not relish this desultory element having a foothold within their well organized system of theology and church discipline. It was often said that the Congregationalists took the Bible as their Confession of Faith, but they did not do that one *whit more* than the Presbyterians.

Church Discipline.—There was another phase of the subject, that in relation to church discipline, which was in contrast with the polity of the Presbyterian Church. In the latter, if a minister was charged with preaching doctrines that contravened those of the Bible and of the Confession of Faith, he could be summoned before the presbytery for trial; if the result of the latter was not satisfactory, the accused could appeal to a higher court, even the highest, the General Assembly. If he refused to obey the regular summons his name, under the charge of "contumacy," was dropped from the roll of the presbytery, that he might no longer preach as a recognized Presbyterian. In the Congregational system, if a clergyman preached not in accordance with the received doctrines of Christianity or of the Bible, he could be summoned before the association to answer the charge. He was not accused of contravening a confession of faith, which perhaps he himself had framed for the individual church of which he was the pastor. If he did not wish a trial by his peers, he could avail himself and his church of the principle of being "free from the jurisdiction of [an] ecclesiastical court," and withdraw from the association, and preach any doctrines he pleased, and also claim to be pastor of a Congregational church.

After some years of observation, a number of leading Presbyterians became alarmed, when they noticed that under the conditions of the plan of union ministers who had been trained in accordance with the Congregational method of church discipline, and who apparently sanctioned the same, were received without examination into presbyteries in certain localities. Complaints had also been made that "committee men," not ordained, as were elders, came from churches that were organized in accordance with the plan of union and took part, as voting members in the higher judicatures of the church. The question naturally presented itself, would not such influence, in the end, impair the efficiency of the Presbyterian mode of church government? The discrepancies on these points did not alienate the cordiality of the two denominations as represented by their respective missionaries in the great West; they blended together in a beautiful Christian harmony in preaching the gospel to the people. In this manner that grand work went on and prospered for a third of a century.

Irresponsibility of Societies.—Other elements of discord were in existence. One of these was the dissatisfaction in the Presbyterian Church because of its coöperation with the voluntary societies that were *irresponsible*, as far as that church was concerned, though it contributed liberally to their funds. This feeling was quietly increasing from year to year, when it suddenly manifested itself in the General Assembly of 1829, when a resolution was introduced to continue its coöperation with the Home Missionary Society. The discussion made manifest the undercurrent of a desire that was becoming stronger and stronger to have the Presbyterian Church in its organic capacity and in its right and duty, to put forth more strenuous efforts to sustain the missions that were distinctly its own. This was the beginning of the end of the plan of union, or coöperation, with voluntary missionary societies. The resolution was, however, not passed. The General Assembly of the following year (1830) was remarkable for the harmony and good feeling that prevailed among its members.

The Assembly's Board and Education.—Two organizations appealed very strongly to the Presbyterian church members for support; these were the assembly's Board of Missions and its Board of Education. In order to enlighten them on the subject, a periodical, *The Missionary Reporter and Education Register,* was established, and by extraordinary efforts its subscription list became large and its circulation extensive. As a result of the interest thereby elicited, auxiliaries to these two societies were formed in great numbers—nearly two hundred. Throughout the church the members entered into the enterprise with an enthusiasm hitherto unknown, and that practically, as was evidenced by their contributions to the funds of the societies. At the end of 1829 the former had commissioned more than one hundred missionaries and the funds amounted to $7665. In 1830 it employed one hundred and ninety-eight, and in the course of the year more than three hundred feeble churches had received assistance, and the funds in the meanwhile had nearly doubled; the following year the funds had increased to about $19,000, and the missionaries of the society to more than two hundred and fifty.

These results had a decided effect in strengthening the theory of the church becoming *ex officio* a missionary society, as well as acting in that capacity in all its benevolent operations. It was also seen that in order to induce the members of the churches to realize their *individual responsibility* in sustaining by their contributions the cause of missions, foreign and home, and as collateral with them that of educating a ministry, was only to give them proper information on these subjects.

Elements That Caused Friction.—Notwithstanding the union which existed between the Presbyterian and the orthodox Congregational churches in coöperating in missionary work, there was gradually introduced an element that caused no little friction. In the General Assembly appeared delegates who were not ordained as elders, but "committee men" from the churches that had been organized under the plan of union, and who sat in the assembly and voted on questions pertaining to the Presbyterian Church *alone,* and in which a Congregationalist could have no special interest, and for him to vote upon such questions was deemed out of place. This was a contingency never contemplated by the good men who projected and formed the plan of union. This question first arose in the Assembly in 1820, and some objected to the innovation as contrary to the order and discipline of the church; this element of irritation continued for some years. In this first case the committee to whom the question was referred reported in favor of the principle "that the rights of a committeeman were the same in regard to delegation as those of a ruling elder." Six years afterward a similar case came up and was decided in the same manner as the former; but in opposition to the latter was entered a strong protest signed by forty-two members; a similar one came up in 1831, and was decided as the two former; against this was a still more vigorous protest, signed by sixty-eight members. Afterward, the assembly decided to leave to each presbytery to judge of its own members, and either party had the right to appeal to the synod as a *final* authority, but not to the assembly. This decision was evidently owing to the fact that only in a comparatively small portion of the church could this innovation occur. This element of discord was thus eliminated from the assembly by a compromise.

An Important Movement.—In the midst of this clashing of opinions in respect to the policy of coöperating with voluntary societies, a movement was in progress that had a decided effect in settling the question within the Presbyterian Church. This movement culminated when the Synod of Pittsburg, as such, in 1831, constituted itself: "The Western Foreign Missionary Society of the United States," thus taking that position as the representative of its ministers, its church sessions, and its church members. This action was in accordance with the synod's own well-grounded theological opinions and also of its theological surroundings.

Scotch Presbyterians.—Pittsburg itself and the fertile region around it for more than one hundred miles were settled extensively by Scotch and Scotch-Irish, though there were, perhaps, equal numbers of English descent. These settlers were nearly all stanch Presbyterians; loyal to the Bible, to the Sabbath day, to the Westminster Confession and its catechisms. They taught the latter faithfully to their children from generation to generation, and not one of those thus instructed, when grown to manhood and womanhood, ever regretted the religious teaching they had thus received. The majority of these Presbyterians were, however, of the American type, as modeled after the English, and were more liberal in their characteristics than those of the pure, unadulterated Scotch type—Seceders, Covenanters, Associate, and perhaps a name or two more. A portion of the ancestors of the latter came to America from Scotland about the middle of the eighteenth century and in 1754 organized "the Associate Presbytery of Pennsylvania subordinate to the Synod of Edinburgh (*G., II., p., 233*). They did not sympathize with the liberality of American Presbyterianism that had taken form in the *Adopting Act of 1729.* (*See p. 113, 114.*) In the ranks of these Scotch Presbyterians were found numbers of celebrated men, as the Drs. James Proudfit, John Mason, John M. Mason, his son; Matthew Henderson, and others. Great numbers of the descendants of these pure Scotch Presbyterians, under different designations, migrated to the Pittsburg region, and by their sympathy sustained those in connection with the General Assembly who were opposed to the lax methods and the supposed "heretical and metaphysical theology of New England."

We cannot go into detail in respect to the ecclesiastical divisions that obtained among the Scotch Presbyterians in America, even back in colonial times nor after we became a nation. An outgrowth of these differences was "The Associate Reformed," which was constituted in 1804. This latter was decidedly far in advance of the others in liberal sentiments toward American Presbyterianism. In consequence, perhaps, of this well-known fact, overtures were made inviting that body to unite in organic union with the General Assembly. This union was made in 1822, when the Associated Reformed Synod, but it would seem in an irregular way, voted to unite with the assembly. The comparatively liberal settlements within the synod, just mentioned, were greatly promoted by the influence of the celebrated Dr. John M. Mason, one of its ministers, though that influence appears on his part to have been exerted unconsciously, but in a most effective manner. Dr. Mason was one of the most remarkable men of that period; as a preacher he had no peer, a fine scholar and theologian, of generous sympathies, and of commanding and consecrated talents, and withal of liberal and charitable views in relation to Christian fellowship; he did not hesitate to commune in the ordinance of the Lord's Supper with Presbyterians outside of the Scotch church; his refined taste and perhaps other reasons preferred the hymns of Dr. Watts to the metrical version of the Psalms by Rouse. He was in full sympathy with the General Assembly in its work, then in its infancy, on

REV. GIDEON BLACKBURN, D. D.
(221, 327, 328, 330, 363.)

the lines of missions—domestic and foreign. He was thus for years in spirit with the progress and labors of American Presbyterianism.

The Ground Taken.—The Western Foreign Missionary Society boldly took the ground that it was national in its character, and it carried out that principle to its legitimate result, by inviting the coöperation of all Presbyterian churches, presbyteries and synods, and by implication that of the General Assembly itself. The synod had taken an irrevocable step toward the solution of the problem: should not the church and its representatives be *ex officio* a missionary society, and not be a mere auxiliary to a composite or voluntary association, though it may have been, hitherto, admirably managed, yet irresponsible to any organized body or denomination?

XL.

Unsubstantial Rumors.

A number of rumors were at this time afloat in intelligent church and theological circles, concerning certain defections from the orthodox and essential doctrines held by the great majority of the Congregational ministry and of the fairly read members of that church. These rumors were not traced to their origin and thus verified or disproved, as they should have been, but were permitted for some time to pass virtually uncontradicted, and in consequence they became greatly exaggerated and many believed them to be founded on facts. There appeared, at most, only one center whence the evil was emanating, yet in certain quarters in the Presbyterian Church almost the entire Congregational ministry were treated in a suspicious manner, as if they all were in sympathy with these reputed errors. Hundreds of devout men, pastors of Congregational churches, were as much opposed to the doctrines deemed erroneous that were promulgated from that center, as were the ministers trained as Presbyterians. It was reasonable that the observant and leading minds in the Presbyterian Church should take alarm at these defections, thus reported, since numbers of young ministers were coming from New England into the service of their church. These young men often located in different portions of New York State and in the Western Reserve, but perhaps the half, if not more, cast their lot with the Presbyterians of the Great West.

An animated discussion of the subject was carried on between prominent clergymen in New England, New York State, and New Jersey. Professor Leonard Woods, of Andover Seminary, expressed the general sentiment when he said: "I believe that there is an alarming looseness among young preachers, and that there is a fixed determination to maintain a party holding loose opinions." The "young preachers" alluded to were understood to have been educated in the New Haven school or seminary. Other clergymen wrote of the "loose speculations which have come from that school;" and the fear was expressed that these "notions would undermine the fair fabric of our evangelical churches and spread a system, unscriptural and pernicious." The Presbyterians of Middle New York and of the Western Reserve, as a general rule, came more specially in contact with these discordant elements, because of their intermingling in churches organized in accordance with the plan of union.

Conflict of Theological Opinions.—During the year 1831 what proved to be a prominent cause of disquiet in the churches was suddenly brought into public notice in New England. It was in relation to a conflict of theological opinions. Professor Nathaniel W. Taylor of the Divinity School of Yale College, was credited with holding views in respect to the atonement that contravened the doctrines on that subject as held not only in the Congregational but in the Presbyterian Church. It was charged that he "virtually and substantially rejected" the orthodox view of the atonement. These views of Dr. Taylor were strongly contested by Professor Leonard Woods of Andover Seminary and Professor Bennet Tyler. Presbyterian papers also joined in the discussion, notably the *Christian Advocate* of Philadelphia, edited by Dr. Ashbel Green, former President of Princeton College. This controversy elicited the attention of the leading minds in religious circles, especially among those who were known as Calvinistic.

The reason why the Presbyterians took so much interest in these conflicts of theological opinions was that numbers of young ministers trained under such influences were coming into the Presbyterian Church. The question suggested itself to some minds: can a minister holding the views attributed to Dr. Taylor, really and truly preach Christ crucified? Dr. Taylor's forms of expression were of a metaphysical character, and therefore susceptible of being differently interpreted, and often in accordance with the predilections of the reader or hearer. Said the venerable Dr. John Holt Rice, when writing of these theological discussions: "The evangelical men are disputing, some for *old* orthodoxy and some for *new* metaphysics." And again: "I do not know what our brother Taylor is driving at. I find it hard to understand him. Is the fault in me or in him?" Dr. Rice thus expressed the sentiments of hundreds of educated men on the theological opinions of Dr. Taylor. These metaphysical theories became a fruitful source of theological speculations; even if the latter were harmless to their authors, they did more or less injury to the church at large.

New Measures.—In connection, in time, with these discussions revivals in certain portions of the church were in progress. These were conducted, for the most part, by the aid of evangelists for whose employment arrangements were made. They preached as to length of time according to the interest manifested by the audiences in attendance; sometimes the meetings continued for weeks and even months. Some of these evangelists introduced what were termed "new measures," that were extreme in their character and, to say the least, were often injudicious, but despite these hindrances, great good was done. They left, somewhat, the beaten track of routine preaching and strenuously made their assaults upon sin and worldliness in an aggressive manner that attracted the attention of the unconverted, more than hitherto. Their labors were wonderfully blessed, and thousands of souls were brought to Christ from the outside world.

In Western New York were prominent scenes of these revivals, and in connection with them Rev. Charles S. Finney adopted measures that were disapproved by such eminent ministers as Dr. Asahel Nettleton—a graduate of Yale College and Seminary, and himself a remarkably successful revivalist—and Dr. Lyman Beecher. But as usual under similar conditions, Mr. Finney had many imitators, who carried these novelties still further than he did himself. "There were extravagances and questionable measures, indiscretions of men who hastily assumed the office of evangelists, and which only worked mischief; but the results, sad as they were in some respects, were by no means such as permanently to affect the integrity of the churches as a body." (*G., II., p. 457.*)

Unjust Suspicions.—Accounts of these scenes were published and distributed far and wide, and unfortunately were often exaggerated. For the greater part, these scenes were enacted in connection with Presbyterian churches, which, more or less, were the outgrowth of the plan of union, and in consequence, right or wrong, these objectionable measures were associated with the views of theology emanating from New Haven, with which all New England was unreasonably credited. This assumption, made without proper discrimination, did great injustice to some of the best Congregational clergymen in the latter section, as well as to some of the most liberal-minded and successful pastors among Presbyterians, especially in the cities of New York and Philadelphia. The latter were thoroughly evangelical, and were equally aggressive as the evangelists mentioned above, in their assaults upon sin in every form, and yet without resorting to measures of doubtful propriety. The Head of the church blessed their labors abundantly, yet in certain quarters of the church these men were deemed not orthodox, but the advocates of errors that would eliminate the vital principles of the standards of the Church. These suspicions, it was said, were put forth by those who were so extremely conservative as to preach their congregations into a semi-comatose condition. The measures and forms of expression used by many workers in the Salvation Army of to-day grate upon the critical taste of the refined and educated, but they reach a class that the cultured and equally spiritually minded preachers have never fully reached and, perhaps, never will.

We will not go into detail by citing examples. It is a sad reflection that devout ministers and whom the Master greatly blessed in their work, and whose names tradition has cherished in the memories and affections of the descendants of those to whom they ministered, should have been the victims of such unwarranted suspicions. It was natural that Presbyterians living beyond the immediate bounds of these scenes became alarmed because of their influence, especially when it was rumored that some of the presbyteries, apparently in accordance with the general principles of the plan of union as now interpreted, received ministers from Congregational associations without requiring their assent fully to the standards of the Presbyterian Church.

An Important Rule Adopted.—The assembly of 1830 adopted a rule by which "ordained ministers [when about to enter the Presbyterian Church] were required to give their assent to the questions proposed to the licentiates of the Presbyterian Church when about to be ordained." This rule had not been complied with in some instances. In the assembly of 1832 the Western Reserve Synod was charged with being delinquent in that respect. In its reply to the charge the following year the synod declared to the assembly there was no ground for the complaint since the promulgation of the rule in 1830. That synod had more churches organized on the basis of the plan of union than, perhaps, any other and it admitted that previous to the time when the rule was made some of its presbyteries had received ministers "without the formal profession of adopting the Confession of Faith of the Presbyterian Church." In this reply, however, cropped out unpresbyterial opinions in respect to the eldership when it said that "the intermingling of Congregationalists and Presbyterians in many churches was a sufficient reason for the non-existence of the eldership, according to the conditions of the plan of union." The assembly accepted the report, but repudiated the views of the synod in relation to the eldership.

Ministers Ordained Injudiciously.—Other causes of irritation and complaint were in existence. When young men were licensed to preach it had not been the custom to ordain them immediately, but for them to exercise their qualifications for some time, virtually as probationers; unless the circumstances were urgent, as, for illustration, when the candidate was going on a foreign mission. It was quite different when the candidate was expected to labor at home, and within the bounds of another presbytery; in that case the rule, the outgrowth of propriety and of Christian courtesy, dictated that the ordination should be performed by the presbytery within whose bounds he was laboring. A memorial to the General Assembly of 1834 complained of this custom. It stated that recently eighteen young men had been licensed and at once ordained by two presbyteries—that of Newburyport, Mass., and the Third, of New York City. These ministers, for the greater part, were commissioned to preach within the bounds of other presbyteries, but in the service of the Home Missionary Society. Their fields of labor were designated mostly in the West, and from that region came the "Cincinnati Memorial" to the assembly, protesting against the custom. The memorial was signed by eighteen ministers and ninety-nine elders. It was also said that other young men were thus occasionally licensed and ordained by Congregational bodies, and who, also, were destined to labor within the bounds of presbyteries and in the service of the same society. The plan of union was credited with opening the way to these irregularities, since by its provisions men were admitted to the presbyteries who had no sympathy with the presbyterial polities, and this was deemed an "evil operating in the Presbyterian Church toward the general change of its form of government and the character of its creed." (*G., II., p. 483.*)

XLI.

THE TRIAL OF ALBERT BARNES.

In 1830, amid the clashing of theological opinions in the Congregational Church, and whose influence produced a similar agitation in the Presbyterian, Albert Barnes became colleague to Dr. James P. Wilson (*see p. 252*) in the pastorate of the First Presbyterian Church of Philadelphia. Mr. Barnes was a native of New York State, born in 1798; a graduate of Hamilton College and of Princeton Seminary; was licensed to preach in 1823, and is described as a "thoughtful, spiritual preacher." When invited to this new field of labor he had been for about six years a successful pastor at Morristown, New Jersey. We may, in passing, note that he never accepted a college title or degree.

The Sermon.—Previously to his removal to Philadelphia Mr. Barnes had published a sermon, entitled "The Way of Salvation." In it were some "unguarded expressions," as was admitted freely, and to these exception was taken, attention being drawn to them, perhaps, partly in consequence of the theological controversies going on at the time. When the church in the usual form asked leave of the presbytery to prosecute the call to Mr. Barnes, and a motion to that effect was made, Dr. Ashbel Green opposed it, basing his objections on the expressions in the sermon, to which allusion has been made. Dr. Green contended that fundamental errors were contained in the sermon.

A spirited discussion ensued, lasting for four days,

and in which many members of the presbytery took part. The ministerial character of the accused was referred to as that of a devoted pastor, even by some who differed from him in the views expressed in the sermon. Others deemed the opposition out of order, unfair, and unkind, since Mr. Barnes was not a member of the presbytery; they argued, let the call be presented in the usual form, and when he becomes a member, it will be in order to put him on trial. The presbytery voted, twenty-one to twelve, to grant the request of the church. Within a month's time Mr. Barnes presented his certificate of dismissal from the Presbytery of Elizabethtown, with the usual recommendation to that of Philadelphia. His reception was vehemently objected to by his opponents, but the presbytery, by a vote of thirty to sixteen, received him as a member. When the presbytery afterward met to install him as pastor, the minority, in order to prevent that action, presented charges against him, but in very general terms—"for unsoundness in the Faith." The moderator ruled the presentation of the charges out of order, "as the present meeting was called for a special purpose."

The Appeal to the Synod.—The minority (October 27, 1830) then appealed to the synod, which sustained the appeal and enjoined the presbytery to hear and decide in relation to the orthodoxy of the sermon. Within a month the presbytery met to act in compliance with the injunction of the synod. Charges were now presented against the doctrines said to be contained in the sermon, and at great length by Dr. Green. This document contained many charges as to the orthodoxy of Mr. Barnes and also implied censures. He urged the presbytery to adopt his paper as its own, but by a decisive vote that proposition was declined. On the other hand, the friends of Mr. Barnes contended that the mode of procedure was unconstitutional, and they entered their protest against such action as "charges being presented without responsible accusers," which mode was contrary to the discipline of the church or book. Mr. Barnes requested the presbytery to put him on trial, "either on the ground of common fame or by responsible accusers," but the request was refused; he then gave notice that he should appeal to the General Assembly. Strange to say, the presbytery declared he had no right to such appeal, "on the ground that he had not submitted to a trial." Charity, at this distance, would say that these good men must have had in mind his refusal to be tried in the mode which they themselves had proposed—that is to say, the accusers being also judges.

The Matter Submitted.—Finally, by both parties conjointly, the whole matter was submitted, without argument, to the assembly of 1831. That body referred the case to a select committee. The latter, after investigating the whole subject, made their report, in which, after complimenting the presbytery for its zeal in striving to preserve the purity of the church, and noting "some unguarded and objectionable passages" in the sermon, recommended that the presbytery suspend further proceedings in the case. The report, which virtually acquitted Mr. Barnes, was adopted by the assembly.

Elective Affinity.—The assembly, at the same time, recommended that the presbytery should divide itself in such manner as to promote peace within its bounds. This was merely a compromise to be brought about by applying the principle of *"elective affinity,"* by which the parties in the controversy could form a new presbytery out of the old, not limited by geographical lines, but based on the similarity of views—that is, the conservatives in one presbytery and the liberals in another. This was only an expedient for the time being, and a fallacious one at that; the theory of elective affinity in constituting presbyteries or synods, because of its pernicious influence, was ere long repudiated by both parties (1835).

We shall not impose upon the patience of the reader a detailed account of the various forms of conflict that ensued during several years between successive assemblies and the synods of Philadelphia and Delaware, and their respective presbyteries. The agitation lasted about six years, to 1836, and thus infringed upon the Christian harmony that ought to have prevailed, as the outgrowth of mutual concessions based on the recognition of the purity of motive of both the parties, while acknowledging that neither was infallible.

Biblical Notes.—During these years of turmoil, Albert Barnes, the laborious student and faithful pastor, was preparing a series of notes on the gospels. These were designed to supply a great want in religious communities for a more simple and concise commentary than the ponderous ones of Henry, Scott, and others. It was soon recognized by lay teachers that the notes were well adapted to aid them in giving instruction in Sunday-schools and the Bible classes. In 1832 the notes on Matthew were issued, and three years later appeared those on the Epistle to the Romans.

The Second Trial.—Rev. Dr. George Junkin—who had come into the Presbyterian Church from the Associate Reformed—a member of another presbytery and of a different synod, took exception to certain views presented in the notes on Romans, which he thought contravened the standards of the church. He presented charges against Mr. Barnes before his presbytery, Philadelphia Second, which then belonged to the Synod of Delaware. The indictment contained *ten* specifications. The presbytery patiently reviewed all of them, and in its decision acquitted Mr. Barnes, as it deemed the charges had not been sustained, as they were based on *"inferences* drawn from the language of Mr. Barnes." The presbytery illustrated, saying that mere "inferences" were not a legitimate basis on which "to convict of heresy or dangerous error, affecting a sinner's hope or the Christian's to eternal life." And that he had not taught in his "Notes on Romans," "any dangerous errors or heresies contrary to the word of God and our standards." The presbytery cited as a precedent for their not admitting charges *based on inferences,* the decision on that point in 1824, of the General Assembly, in the famous trial of Rev. Thomas B. Craighead.

Since this case has been referred to as a precedent in subsequent trials, the intelligent Presbyterian reader will appreciate the following extract from the minutes of the assembly of 1824: "A man cannot be fairly convicted of heresy for using expressions which may be so interpreted as to involve heretical doctrines, if they also admit of a more favorable construction . . . he has a right to explain himself; and in such cases, candor requires that a court should favor the accused, by putting on his words the more favorable, rather than the less favorable construction. No man can rightly be convicted of heresy by inference or implication; that is, we must not charge an accused person with holding those consequences which may legitimately flow from his assertions . . . it is not right to charge any man with an opinion which he disavows. (*See Minutes of that General Assembly.*)

Dr. Junkin appealed from the decision of the presbytery to the Synod of Philadelphia (1835). Under the rule the records of a presbytery are subject to the revision of its synod, but the presbytery refused to give up the records of the case, because at the time of the trial it was subject to the Synod of Delaware, which in the meantime had been dissolved. The synod censured the presbytery for its refusal to comply with the former's request. Mr. Barnes, under these circumstances, presented a paper giving his reasons for his action, and then withdrew. The synod, however, went on and heard Dr. Junkin in his plea, and at its close, in mere form, the name of Albert Barnes was called, but of course he did not appear. The synod at once, on the *ex-parte* plea of Dr. Junkin, "suspended Mr. Barnes from the exercise of all the functions proper to the gospel ministry."

The Appeal to the General Assembly.—Mr. Barnes then, in due form, gave notice of his intended appeal to the General Assembly. The latter met in Pittsburg in May, 1836, and numbered two hundred and fifty members. It spent one week in carefully hearing the case, and the result was that the appeal of Mr. Barnes was sustained by a vote of one hundred and thirty-four to ninety-six. In addition, by a vote of one hundred and forty-five to seventy eight, was reversed the decree of the synod suspending him from the gospel ministry. As soon as the vote was announced, the minority introduced a resolution, prefacing it in substance that, as he had published in his "Notes on Romans" opinions contravening the Confession of Faith, that he be enjoined to "again revise the work and modify still further the statements which had grieved his brethren."

The Synod of Philadelphia being a party in the case, was, by the rule, excluded from voting on this resolution. The latter was rejected by a vote of one hundred and twenty-two to one hundred and nine. This vote elicited a protest from the minority, and in answering that protest an opportunity was given the majority to express their sentiments more fully. They asked "Whether a man who held views at the time of his

REV. MATTHEW BROWN, D.D., LL.D.
(134, 324, 325.)

licensure and ordination, who had held and preached them for ten years, and who held them in common with no small part of two thousand ministers in the same connection, was to be allowed peaceably to hold them still, and to labor under the influence of these views in endeavoring to save souls; or whether he was to be pronounced heretical and unsound, his character to be ruined, so far as a decision of his brethren could ruin it, himself to be harassed in his feelings, embarrassed in his preaching, and the large number of ministers, elders, and communicants in the churches, who held the same views, declared unworthy an office, a name, and a place in the church of God?"

Though the resolution mentioned above did not pass in the Assembly, yet Mr. Barnes, in order to avoid the appearance of disrespect toward his brethren who opposed him, did afterward, voluntarily, revise the "Notes on Romans," and without changing his views, used forms of expression that were not obnoxious to those who differed from him more in words than in doctrine. He at once resumed his pastoral duties, and was cheered by being welcomed back by an affectionate people. During almost six years he had undergone these harassing trials, and yet he was never heard to utter a harsh word nor manifest defiance of ecclesiastical authority, but in a self-respecting manner and Christian spirit abided the time when his integrity would be vindicated. For nearly thirty-five years after this trial, Albert Barnes remained in charge of the same church, laboring as a writer and pastor, with almost unexampled industry, as long as his health permitted, till in his seventy-second year he was called home by the Master. With a Christian's cheerful vision he wrote these, almost his last written words: "I shall close my eyes in death with bright and glorious hopes in regard to my native land, to the church, and to the world at large."

Bible Study Promoted.—It is only just in this connection to notice a remarkable movement and its corresponding influence that originated with Albert Barnes. God in His providence used him to promote in a marked degree the study of the Bible, especially among American youth. Seeing the want of a more concise and clearly defined commentary on the word of God, and one better adapted for giving instruction in Sunday-school and Bible classes than the ponderous volumes of Henry, Scott, and others, he issued in 1832 "Notes on the Gospel of Matthew." The good effects of the work were soon seen in the spirit in which it inspired the Bible teachers themselves and in the reflex influence upon their classes, by creating in their members a corresponding interest in the study of the Scriptures and their history. The earnestness in thus studying on the part of both teachers and pupils was the legitimate outgrowth of being familiar with the spirit of piety, and of the judicious, concise, and suggestive manner in which the "Notes" were written. Here was the beginning of what has since been done on that line of instructing the youth of the land—from the infant class upward—in Bible knowledge and in leading multitudes of them to the Saviour.

The notes were popular because they were useful for instructing Bible classes, and the work went on with increased zeal among the youth of all the Protestant denominations. Meantime, as experience dictated, were prepared and published simpler froms of instruction for the younger scholars. In order to increase the efficiency of the work, the religious sentiment of the teachers and people being propitious, the "International Sunday-school Lessons" were introduced. That system has had an increasing influence in directing the attention of Christian parents and teachers and youth throughout the Union to the practical study of the word of God—a stimulus to which was that of the same lesson on the same day throughout the land. During the last twenty-five years these lessons have been an instrument in leading millions of American young people to become Christian and among them has originated that most important movement, the Christian Endeavor Society, and other kindred associations. The beneficial influence of these is recognized to-day in all the Protestant churches of the land. This influence will tell still more in the next generation, when these young people will have become heads of families, and will train their children in the same Christian principles.

The Example Followed.—Following the example of Mr. Barnes were others who wrote notes or brief commentaries on separate books of the New Testament. In the Presbyterian Church, Professor Charles Hodge of Princeton wrote on the Epistle to the Romans, and Professor Melanthon W. Jacobus of Allegheny Seminary, on the Gospels and on Genesis. Since then numbers of brief commentaries on single books of the Bible have been published by writers of different denominations.

Terms of Distinction.—About this time came into use the terms Old and New School, to designate the parties that had come into existence within the Presbyterian Church. They correspond very nearly to the terms Old and New Side, used for a similar purpose in the church, about one hundred years previous. (*See pages 152, 153.*)

XLII.

THE TRIAL OF DR. LYMAN BEECHER.

The period in which occurred the trial of Mr. Barnes was fruitful of similar ecclesiastical trials elsewhere in the Presbyterian Church. Rev. (Dr.) George Duffield, pastor of a church in Carlisle, Pennsylvania, published a sermon on Regeneration, to which exception was taken. His trial was attempted, but in an irregular and unconstitutional way, and in consequence it came to no definite results. Meantime, Dr. Duffield accepted a call to a church in Philadelphia, and thither he removed and became a member of another presbytery and the prosecution was dropped (1835).

A Feeling of Unrest.—In portions of the Presbyterian Church prevailed a feeling of unrest, in respect to certain opinions on theology, which were deemed inconsistent with its accepted standards, and rumor reported that these objectionable opinions were held by some of its ministers. During a few years previous to the time of which we write, much interest was elicited among intelligent Christian citizens, both East and West, in relation to the religious condition and future moral prospects of the Great valley. (*See p. 340.*) Dr. Lyman Beecher, who as we have already noted (*p. 320*), was elected by the directors to the chair of theology in the newly founded Lane Seminary at Walnut Hills near Cincinnati (1832). Dr. Beecher, though a native of New England, was a Presbyterian in his views of theology and also of church polity. On examination he was ordained by the Presbytery of Long Island, and he signed "the confession as a systematic view of the truths contained in the word of God." His first pastorate was at East Hampton, on that island, and when there was sent as a commissioner to the General Assembly. He remained for about ten years at Hampton, and then removed to Litchfield, Connecticut. While there he preached and published his sermons on intemperance, famous because they gave the first effective impulse to the cause of temperance in the Union. In 1826 he went to Boston and became the pastor of the Hanover Street Congregational Church.

There is no doubt that an unwarranted prejudice against the orthodox ministers of New England, even though they opposed the New Haven school, did pervade the minds of certain Presbyterian clergymen in the Middle States and in the West. This circumstance may partially account for the prosecution of Dr. Beecher before the Presbytery of Cincinnati, by Dr. Joshua L. Wilson, pastor of the First Presbyterian Church of that city.

The Recommendations.—The appointment of Dr. Beecher to the theological chair in Lane Seminary was hailed as an immense gain to the religious force in the Great valley, by many eminent clergymen and by the intelligent religious public generally. He had also the commendation of the professors at Princeton, who had been consulted, and of Dr. Ashbel Green, afterward one of the prosecutors of Albert Barnes, but who a year or two previous urged Dr. Beecher to accept a call to a church in Philadelphia. And even Dr. Joshua L. Wilson was the first to sign a letter sent by a committee of the trustees, to the members of the Hanover Church, urging them to sanction Dr. Beecher's removal to Lane Seminary, giving as a reason the benefits that would accrue to that institution, saying: "We feel that the church will be deprived of his most important service and influence unless he is permitted to impress the important lineaments of his character upon the rising ministers of the West;" and much more in the same strain. (*The Trial, pp. 26, 27.*)

Disproved Suspicions.—Soon after Dr. Beecher entered upon his professorship unfounded suspicions, as it was afterward proved, became rife as to his orthodoxy; that is, from the standpoint of Dr. Wilson and a few others. It was used to the disadvantage of Dr. Beecher that he had brought a certificate and recommendation from the Congregational Church in Boston to the Third Presbytery of New York City, and from that body to the Presbytery in Cincinnati. In New York City at that time were three presbyteries: New York proper, the Second, and the Third—the latter does not appear on the minutes of the General Assembly until 1831. Why a prejudice was entertained in respect to the orthodoxy of Dr. Beecher, in the minds of a few Presbyterian leaders in the West, seems difficult to explain. One reason has been given, that, although his orthodoxy was unimpeached, yet he had brought a certificate and recommendation from the Third Presbytery of New York. Even in that case the suspicion could not have been based on the comparative lack of Christian work and success in the cause of Christ, on the part of the Third Presbytery, since in the four years, 1831-1834 inclusive, its churches had admitted to membership on examination 2843 persons, while the churches of the other two presbyteries combined, during the same time, admitted only 1352—less than half as many as the third alone. (*Minutes of Ass. for these years.*)

The Third Presbytery was constituted on the principle of *elective affinity*, and was reckoned on the New School side of the questions then at issue in the church. This circumstance was assumed by the same parties to afford evidence that Dr. Beecher in his theology was not in sympathy with the standards of the church;—an assumed offence, with which they also charged the presbytery itself. No one of the disaffected was willing, however, to take the responsibility of presenting charges against him to the presbytery—that is, in the regular and constitutional form. In consequence, an effort was made to attain the same end by inducing that body to appoint a committee to examine Dr. Beecher's sermons, "and report if they found doctrines at variance with the standards of the church." The presbytery refused to send a committee to rummage his writings for any such purpose. Then the complaining parties appealed to the synod, but that body threw out the appeal, and justified the Presbytery in not violating the rule in trying a member when there was no responsible prosecutor; then an appeal was made to the General Assembly of 1834, and it was referred to the Judiciary Committee, and the latter also recommended to throw out the appeal, in which action the assembly acquiesced. Thus the entire proceedings from the first were deemed illegal and contrary to the rule in such cases, at the respective sessions of these three judicatures of the church.

At length, after so long fighting shy of the responsibility, Dr. Wilson, the prime mover of the affair, presented charges against Dr. Beecher in the regular form before the Presbytery of Cincinnati. These charges were grouped under seven heads, including those of "slander" and of "hypocrisy or dissimilation." Of this trial we will give a concise account, going into detail sufficient only for that purpose, but refer the reader to the history of the trial itself.

Dr. Beecher and Dr. Wilson.—On June 9, 1835, the trial was commenced, and in its proceedings was manifested an unprecedented interest on the part of the whole church, and also in a large and intelligent portion of the outside community. The chief parties in the trial were both remarkable men: Dr. Lyman Beecher was one of the most successful preachers, competent and influential men of the period. He was a graduate of Yale College, and studied theology in the divinity school under Dr. Timothy Dwight; had had much influence in promoting the cause of temperance, and success in religious controversy. When a pastor in Boston he came in conflict with the most learned and cultivated minds among the Unitarians.

Dr. Joshua Lacy Wilson was born in Virginia, but in early childhood moved with his parents to Kentucky. The son of a farmer of limited means, he labored as a blacksmith, and at the age of twenty-two "he had no education beyond what his mother taught him." He about this time became a Christian, and selling his farm began to prepare for the ministry in a neighboring academy. He had no college education of which to speak, nor systematic instruction in theology, but he was mentally *unusually* gifted. He was licensed to preach in 1802, and after laboring in different places in Kentucky as a minister, was called in 1808 to the First Pesbyterian Church in Cincinnati, where as a pastor he spent thirty-eight years. (*Davidson's Hist. Pres. Church in Ky.*, pp. 364, 365.)

The Charges Not Sustained.—The trial continued for several days and was conducted with great skill by both parties; but the presbytery, by a vote of nearly two to one, decided that the charges were not sustained. Dr. Wilson appealed to the synod, which, within a few months, met at Dayton, Ohio, and before that body the whole case was again gone over carefully. The synod decided almost unanimously—about ten to one—as the presbytery had done—that the charges had not been sustained. The synod adopted a minute on the occasion. After first declaring that the charges "of slander" and "of hypocrisy and dissimulation were not proved," but by way of explanation the minute gives "the opinion that Dr. Beecher had indulged a disposition to philosophise, instead of exhibiting in simplicity and plainness these doctrines as taught in the Scriptures; and has employed terms and phrases and modes of illustration calculated to convey ideas inconsistent with the word of God and our Confession of Faith, and that he ought to be, and he is hereby admonished to be more guarded in the future." Dr. Beecher acquiesced promptly in the decree of the synod, which also requested him to publish a concise statement of his views on the points of theology involved in the charges, among which was specified "Natural and Moral Ability." (*Biography of Dr. B., II., p. 359.*)

After some hesitation, Dr. Wilson announced that he should appeal to the General Assembly, which was to meet in Pittsburg the following May, 1836.

Dr. Wilson Withdraws His Appeal.—When the assembly of 1836 met the case of Mr. Barnes, already noted, came before it on appeal, and as it involved, virtually, the same principles as those in the case of Dr. Beecher, Dr. Wilson said his "friends besought him earnestly to withdraw his appeal"—which he did. They brought forward several reasons, among which it was very probable the assembly would sustain the action of both the presbytery and the synod. Is it uncharitable to suppose from the mental characteristics of a man—a minister whose judgment and plea had been overruled by his peers in his presbytery and also in his synod, and that by overwhelming majorities, and who still acted as though he could not make a mistake, and had the pluck to be on hand with the avowed purpose of prosecuting the case before the assembly, must have had, in addition, a more potent reason than the remonstrances of a few friends? May not that urgent reason be found in the fact that on board the steamboat on his way from Cincinnati to Pittsburg, his overcoat was stolen, while in the pocket of which were the papers he intended to use in the presentation of his appeal. (*Gillett, II., p. 465.*) The apologists for Dr. Wilson urge he was sincere; that, no doubt, was true; but sincerity proves only itself; nothing more; a person can be sincere in error, as well as in truth; the crank can be as sincere as the man of the most profound judgment. If Dr. Wilson had had a thorough collegiate and well-read theological education the presumption is, he never would have become the prosecutor of Dr. Beecher. Such an education would have broadened his theological views, and he would have held nonessentials in Christian doctrine at their true value, and never permitted minor differences of opinion to usurp the domain of Christian charity.

Suggestive Considerations.—There are many considerations to be recognized before charges of heresy should be brought against a fellow minister of the gospel, and thus disturb the peace of the church. As long as men are differently constituted mentally they will have different shades of views on the application of Christian truths to the wants of the human soul. In that process there can be so many metaphysical phases, and because of their idiosyncrasies men may have on certain points their peculiar views, yet on the essential doctrines of the gospel they may agree perfectly. When they thus agree, shall a minister who has a *theory* about "Natural and Moral Ability," which another has not, charge the latter with heresy?

Abstract Phases of Thought.—In these two famous ecclesiastical trials the charges in both cases were based on abstract phases of thought or opinion, that did not interfere with the respective holders thereof, receiving the gospel in its fulness and purity, nor, on their line of thought and interpretation of Scripture, in directing the sinner to the Saviour.

Where are the men of that generation whom the Master honored more in His service; on the one hand by giving an impulse to the study of the Bible, whose influence still remains (*see pp. 406, 244*); and on the other, in inaugurating a temperance movement that permeates the Nation; in vindicating the doctrine of the Trinity against Unitarianism, and, finally, giving instruction to theological students, and inspiring them with his own vivid zeal in the cause of the Redeemer, than Albert Barnes and Dr. Lyman Beecher? The question arises in the mind of intelligent Presbyterians, why were men of such recognized mental abilities, learning, and consecration to the cause of Christ, and so blessed by the Master, arraigned for heresy in the courts of the church?

There is, however, no doubt, although Dr. Beecher came out triumphant and labored successfully for years as professor in Lane Seminary, that there lingered in the minds of certain sincere Presbyterians an indefinable suspicion, which lessened his influence, simply because of the *stigma* attached to the fact that he had been charged with heresy before the judicatures of his church. This was an evil that might and ought to have been avoided.

XLIII.

MEASURES LEADING TO THE DIVISION.

That the reader may have a connected narrative of the measures that led directly to the division of the church, we will endeavor to give of them a concise account.

The results of the trials of Mr. Barnes and Dr. Beecher did not allay the agitation that existed, especially in that portion of the Presbyterian Church which had come only indirectly in contact with the operations of the plan of union. We are not aware that a single church was ever organized on that plan in Western Pennsylvania; nor were there any such in the eastern portion of that State, taking Philadelphia as a center, nor south of that on the Atlantic slope; the same may be predicated of Southern Ohio, having Cincinnati as a center. There were, however, numerous churches thus constituted in the Western Reserve section of Northern Ohio, and these were in connection with the presbyteries and synods of that portion of the country. The latter judicatures bordered on those of Western Pennsylvania; to these churches must be added those formed on the plan of union in Western New York State. In regard to church polity, the tendency was more for Congregationalists to fall in with that of the Presbyterians, than for the latter to combine with the former. Says Dr. Lyman Beecher: "Three-fourths of the churches formed under the plan of union become Presbyterian. . . . It was in this way that the New School element increased in the Presbyterian Church, wholly, wholly." (*Autobiography, II., p. 340.*)

REV. ALBERT BARNES.
(399, 401-407, 415.)

The New and the Old School.—How are we to define the New Schoolism of the time of which we write? Wherein did it differ from Old Schoolism? We might characterize the latter as *conservative,* and the former as *liberal;* yet that distinction does not give a clear conception of the difference. Many of those who were termed New School were Calvinist in doctrine; were fervent in spirit when preaching the gospel, and the Master blessed their labors. Some of the most successful revivalists of the period were Calvinists, while some, strictly speaking, were not; of the latter class was reckoned Charles S. Finney, and of the former, Asahel Nettleton. They both appeared to preach with an earnestness similar to that of Saint Paul, the original Calvinist. Thus an ardent preacher or revivalist was usually characterized as a New Schoolman, while those who were not so ardent were deemed Old School. In the minds of the church members only these surface distinctions were recognized, but the theologians went farther back to certain metaphysical and doctrinal distinctions, of which the ordinary lay members knew scarcely anything. Statistics show that the number brought into the church from the outside world by the New School preachers was much greater than that brought in by the Old School.

We do not intend to enter upon a discussion of the theological questions of the time; the study of such is more appropriate to the theological class-room than in a history designed, more especially, for the intelligent private members of the church. This view, however, does not militate against the importance of every candidate for the ministry in the Presbyterian Church, making himself familiar with all the phases of thought that have been brought out in the theological investigations and discussions of the past. It is, also, essential that he be fully equipped in his scholarship, to answer objections that may be presented in his own day against the Christian system, and be able, likewise, to detect and refute *theories* that in their application would, virtually, sap the foundation of the truths presented in the word of God, and to recognize the legitimate effect of opinions which may influence the proper presentation of the gospel. This scholarship is required in the Presbyterian Church of to-day, more than ever before, inasmuch as its private members stand on a correspondingly higher plane of intelligence in respect to the doctrines of the church as contained in its standards. Genuine theological scholarship will never put forth as original opinions and theories which have been advanced and refuted, perhaps, again and again in the discussions of former times.

Conditions on Which Ministers Were Received.—The internal affairs of the Presbyterian Church were approaching a crisis—that of its division. The movement toward which, though unintentional, began in 1826, when the Synod of Pittsburg made known its apprehensions to the General Assembly in relation to the admission of ordained ministers coming from other denominations into the church, without being required to accept and assent to its standards. In this case nothing more was required of such ordained ministers than was of the church's own candidates for licensure or ordination, and therefore there ought to have been *no complaint* on the part of outsiders. Three years later an attempt was made to secure uniformity in the instruction given in the seminaries, and finally in 1830 the assembly made a rule, already noted (*p. 396*), which enjoined that licentiates or ordained ministers, when about to enter the church, were to be received on their accepting the conditions on which their own licentiates were admitted to ordination.

During these years of ecclesiastical turmoil many charges were made that at this distance of time seem to have been sometimes based on insufficient grounds. The American Home Missionary Society was charged with having ambitious plans—whatever that charge means;— that its influence was subversive of the polity of the Presbyterian Church; that its agents and missionaries, when opportunity served, as in the General Assembly, nearly always voted to sustain the innovations of which complaint was made. It is not strange that Presbyterians, who thoroughly believed in the governmental polity of their own church, should deprecate the introduction within it of the lax methods that obtained in the Congregational polity of licensing and ordaining ministers, or in having "committeemen" instead of ordained elders.

The Memorial Charges.—A memorial presented to the assembly of 1834 (*p. 398*) charged that the latter, on the occasion of the first trial of Mr. Barnes (1831), had in its decision evaded the doctrinal merits of the questions at issue; that by its compromise had "smothered the claims of truth;" and it was also asserted that the highest judicature of the church by its procedure had neutralized the principles of the constitution of that church, and had brought its government "to spiritual anarchy." The memorial also presented a series of errors said to be contained in the writings of several prominent ministers, whose names were given and who were designated as New School men. Finally, in view of the lax manner in which subscription to the standards of the church were made, these evils had grown out of the connection with the plan of union, and the memorial asked the assembly to annul its relations with that system.

The assembly of 1834, after due consideration, refused to recognize as proper the censures of previous assemblies, expressed or implied in the memorial. It thought it inexpedient to disturb its relations with the plan of union. It disapproved of publishing to the world the names of ministers in good and regular standing in the church, as holding views that were subversive of the gospel, while the same had not been brought to trial in the way provided by the constitution. Moreover, the charges were based on *inferences* drawn from isolated passages taken from the publications of the ministers named. The assembly also urged most earnestly the presbyteries and synods to exercise charity and forbearance, and, as far as possible, to settle among themselves these difficulties and not publish them to the world by bringing them for adjustment before that body. This reasonable request was evidently based on the fact, geographically speaking, that the influence of the plan of union in organizing individual churches was within quite a limited area, when compared with the vast territory wherein such influence was unknown, and over which the bounds of the church extended.

The Protest Not Received.—The above decisions were arrived at by the assembly after a long and animated discussion of the various charges contained in the memorial. A protest against the latter's general action was drawn up and signed by thirty members of the minority and presented to that body. This paper was couched in such terms the self-respect of the assembly demanded it should not be received. It censured that body for refusing "to discharge a solemn duty enjoined by the Confession of Faith, and loudly and imperiously called for by the circumstances of the church." The refusal to entertain the charges contained in the memorial greatly disappointed and even irritated those who had presented them. The minority were earnest in their efforts in some way to relieve the church of the evils which, from their standpoint, were impending over its good order, both in its polity and in the doctrines contained in its standards.

The Act and Testimony.—In order to influence more

effectively the next assembly, that of 1835, the minority afterward drew up a paper known as "The Act and Testimony. This document was to be signed during the intervening ecclesiastical year by ministers and elders throughout the church, and which, when presented, was designed to impress upon the assembly the views of the signers. The paper was also intended to direct the attention of the private members of the church to certain innovations that had been creeping into it, in respect to its doctrines and governmental polity. It was charged that the evils came in through the operations of the plan of union and the voluntary missionary societies, and to such an extent that pure Presbyterianism was in eminent danger of being subverted.

The act and testimony, in its charges of swerving from the standards of the church, followed the line of arraignment laid down in the recent rejected memorial. It was even more aggressive than the latter in its indictment of previous assemblies, especially the last one (1834). It was not altogether lacking in the accuracy of some of its statements; for illustration, its charge was true that there were some ministers who had avowed their adherence to the confession, but who, nevertheless, held doctrines at variance with those of that confession. The number of the latter was small, indeed, and not of so much importance as to warrant the charge of disloyalty to the church, brought against hundreds of godly ministers, who could not see the propriety of signing an *unauthorized document*, as was the Act and Testimony, and thereby give their sanction to suspicions concerning many of their brethren, whom they knew to be as true as steel to the church in every respect. In truth, the movement was inaugurated by irresponsible persons—ecclesiastically speaking—though they were highly respected because of their standing in the church, and for their sincere and ardent zeal in behalf of its standards.

Signers and Objectors to the Act.—The assembly of 1834 did not sanction the extreme measures which the memorialists proposed, and no doubt if occasion required, would do the same in regard to the similar ones put forth by the signers of the act and testimony. The latter document urged the members of the church not to encourage preachers and teachers who held the heretical opinions that had been pointed out in the paper, and also to subject such to the discipline of the church judicatures, and called upon all ministers and individual elders, as church sessions, to sign the act. The original act was signed by thirty-seven ministers and twenty-seven elders. The most prominent names of ministers were Drs. Robert J. Breckinridge, James Latta, Joshua L. Wilson, Ashbel Green, and George Junkin—the three last had been or were prosecutors of Dr. Beecher and Mr. Barnes.

The action of the authors of this movement did not meet cordial favor from all the conservatives of the church. The Princeton *Review*, the recognized organ of that class, condemned the measure most decidedly, as setting up a new standard of orthodoxy within the church. It pointed out the "gross injustice that was done to multitudes of our soundest and best men." It also called in question the facts that were assumed in the paper; and it deprecated the movement because it led to the division of the church, and finally, that the entire act was "an unauthorized assumption, and fraught with injustice, discord, and diversion." Saying in addition: "We have not the least idea that one-tenth of the ministers of the Presbyterian Church would deliberately countenance and sustain the errors specified." This sentiment was echoed in many instances in different portions of the church.

A Convention Called.—The signers issued an invitation for a convention of those who sympathized with the views contained in the act and testimony, to be held in Pittsburg just previous to the meeting of the assembly in May, 1835. The convention was to take measures for preserving the standards of the church in their original purity. Numbers of the private members of the church and of the eldership did not relish the position about to be assumed by the convention. It seemed as if the design was *to coerce* the assembly by outside pressure, and moreover, they were loth to believe that so many men, who had long been held in esteem in the church as ministers and as such blessed by the Master, were so derelict of duty as was implied in the charges and innuendoes of the paper.

The Effects of the Agitation.—At no previous time was there so much discussion within the Church as from the adjournment of the assembly of 1834 to the meeting of that of 1835. The agitation penetrated individual churches, dividing the eldership, and even threw a shadow over friendships among the private members themselves. The religious papers engaged in all the absorbing controversy, while some of the secular press took a hand in the fray, and, as usual, often showed a lack of true knowledge of the questions at issue.

This unusual agitation alarmed the private church members and through its influence was sent a majority of Old Schoolmen to the assembly of 1835. The convention summoned as we have seen, met in Pittsburg a few days before the meeting of the assembly. In it were representatives from forty-one presbyteries and also from the minorities of thirteen others. Many of the members of the convention were likewise commissioners to the assembly.

Grievances—Elective Affinity.—A list of grievances of which the convention complained was presented to the

Assembly. This list embodied, for the most part, though in modified terms the same complaints that had been in the memorial. Though a majority of the assembly sympathized with the convention, yet it was unwilling to adopt the extreme measures that the original authors of the act and testimony, desired. For illustration, it would not censure presbyteries for receiving ministers of good standing who came from sister ones on their presenting a certificate from the latter and a letter of recommendation. It recognized the principle of any judicature condemning publications of a minister of the same body, which were regarded as injurious in their tendency, though the author may not have been called to an account in a legal way. It repudiated the principle of *elective affinity* in constituting presbyteries and synods, and it made the repudiation practical by dissolving the Synod of Delaware. It deprecated the continuance of the connection with the plan of union, and gave its sanction to the theories of the act and testimony in respect to the doctrinal errors that had recently been creeping into the church. It refused, however, to break off the usual fraternal correspondence with the Congregational churches of New England, nor did it condemn in absolute terms the labors of the Home Missionary and Educational societies, though in many instances their operations were within the bounds of some of the presbyteries, but being voluntary organizations they were not under the control of the assembly.

Changes in Opinion.—Within a few years an important change in opinion had been in progress in the leading minds of the church in relation to missions conducted on the voluntary plan. The trend of that opinion was in favor of the Presbyterian Church being *ex-officio* a missionary organization—covering both the foreign and domestic fields. The time was rapidly approaching, if not already at hand, when the church would be able, because of the increased number of its private members, and of its wealth and general influence to conduct missions at home and abroad independently of sister denominations. That it could and ought to assume the responsibility of not only bearing the expense of such action, but also of furnishing from its own members the needed missionaries. The indications of the impending change of policy cropped out distinctly in certain resolutions adopted in the assembly of 1835, which foreshadowed the movement of entering upon the work as a separate denomination. These expressions were as follows: "That it is the first and binding duty of the Presbyterian Church to sustain her own boards." This was said in allusion to the Western Foreign Missionary and Domestic societies. Again: "We have done so little—comparatively nothing—*in our distinctive character* as a Church of Christ to send the gospel to the heathen. . . . As a nucleus of foreign missionary effort and operation, the Western Foreign Missionary Society should receive the countenance of those who cherish an attachment to the doctrines and order of the church to which we belong (*Minutes of the Assembly of 1835*). The members of the Presbyterian churches had been in the habit of contributing generously to benevolent and voluntary associations, some of which were admirably managed, and on whose boards were many Presbyterians as directors. No fault, to much extent, was found with these, except there was some friction in respect to the mode of conducting the Home Missionary Society, but which, at this distance of time, seems to have been rather the outgrowth of misunderstandings than otherwise.

A Committee of Conference.—In accordance with the sentiments expressed above, at one of its early sessions the assembly appointed a special committee to confer with a similar one of the Synod of Pittsburg, in relation to the transfer of the latter's Foreign Missionary Society to the care and supervision of the General Assembly. This committee was directed to report to the next assembly, that of 1836. It was, meanwhile, to ascertain the terms on which the transfer could be made, and also devise a plan for conducting the proposed missions about to come under the direction of the assembly.

The majority of the assembly of 1835 was strongly conservative or Old School. The alarming statements in regard to the number of alleged defections from the standards of the church as represented by the memorial and afterward supplemented by the Act and Testimony had much to do in creating that majority. In this connection it is interesting to note that within twenty days after the adjournment of this assembly was initiated the trial of Dr. Beecher, and in the following autumn the Synod of Philadelphia, in an unusual manner, suspended Albert Barnes from the ministry. (*See pp. 399, 408.*)

Misleading Statements.—During the following ecclesiastical year the private members of the church who kept up with the times, and great numbers of the eldership and of the ministry, appeared to have had forced upon them the impression that the statements mentioned above, concerning the defections from the confession, were greatly exaggerated. These same members began to inquire among themselves where are these derelicts? In some localities of the church none such were found; in others, there were some ministers who, from the standpoint of the conservatives, were under suspicion—but justly or unjustly was a question. It dawned upon the leading minds of these church members that the half dozen prominent leaders in this movement might possibly have gone too far in their indiscriminate charges against the orthodoxy of so many efficient pastors and preachers in the church. This view was strengthened by some of the religious newspapers declaring that they knew no minister in their locality holding the unorthodox doctrines attributed to them in the memorial and in the act and testimony. Charity forbids impugning the motives of these leaders, saying "their efforts were the outgrowth of honest but inflamed zeal"—but none the less unjust. The agitation in the church continued unabated, the reactionary result of which was the majority in the assembly of 1836 was in sentiment the reverse of that of 1835.

Instructions Transcended.—The assembly of 1836 also met in Pittsburg, and in the regular course of proceedings the committee appointed by that of 1835 to consider the transfer to the assembly of the Western Foreign Missionary Society, reported. The committee in conference had agreed upon terms of the transfer, and had devised a plan and framed a constitution under which the proposed Board of Foreign Missions should be conducted. The committee transcended its instructions; it was only to report progress, but it had, *virtually*, consummated the transfer. And still further, in view of contingencies that might arise, further assemblies were by a stipulation in the agreement, in legal phrase, put under bonds "never hereafter to alienate or transfer to any other judicature or board, whatever, the direct supervision and management" of the missions thus transferred. In thus binding future assemblies to carry out the above stipulation the committee again went beyond its instructions. In addition, the transfer was made contrary to the rule, as the presbyteries ought to have acted upon the question of accepting or rejecting the transfer. In consequence the ratification of the terms proposed was refused. As already noted (*pp. 404, 413*) this assembly took action on the cases of Albert Barnes and Dr.

Beecher, and acquitted them both of the charges brought against them.

Union Theological Seminary.—While these ecclesiastical controversies were in progress, some of the leading minds, ministers and laymen in the Presbyterian Church in New York were discussing the problem of founding a theological school in that city. The outcome of the movement was that in January, 1836, Union Theological Seminary went into operation. The following statement gives the reasons therefor: "It is the design of the founders to provide a theological seminary in the midst of the greatest and most growing community in America, around which all men of moderate views and feelings, who desire to live free from party strife, and to stand aloof from all extremes of doctrinal speculation, practical radicalism, and ecclesiastical domination, may cordially and affectionately rally."

In its organization it was thoroughly Presbyterian. A rule was adopted by which the professors on entering their office were required to sign a declaration of their acceptance of the Westminster Confession of Faith, and thereafter, once in three years, to renew their signatures to the same; none but members of the Presbyterian Church could be members of the Board of Directors. The seminary appealed for support in the form of endowments to the sympathy and patronage of the Presbyterian churches in the city—and nobly has that appeal been sustained. Many reasons may be given in favor of the location of such an institution in a large city; and especially in the American metropolis; among others, the facilities for becoming familiar with one form of pastoral work in the numerous Sabbath-schools—church and mission. These bear a similar relation to a theological seminary that a hospital does to a medical college. In view of this line of usefulness, in 1873, to the duties of the Professor of Pastoral Theology and Church Polity was added that of mission work. This is the first instance, as far as known, in which the last mentioned phase of ministerial preparation was introduced in "the regular curriculum of theological study in this country." Again, in respect to individual support, in a large city, opportunities are often afforded students for teaching by the hour as private tutors or in classical schools, and in the form of salaries for labor performed in missions, as teachers and as visitors in families whose children are pupils in such schools. No small item of advantage is afforded the students for hearing different styles of preaching, and also unusual facilities of becoming acquainted with the great moral movements in progress in the world.

XLIV.

The Division of the Church.

The decision of the General Assembly in the cases of Mr. Barnes and Dr. Beecher removed for the time theological questions out of the way, and now the undivided attention of the Old Schoolmen was directed to remedy the evils that in their judgment had grown up within the Presbyterian Church in consequence of its connection with the plan of union. During the twenty years immediately preceding this time the material progress of the country had been remarkable, but there was now approaching a crisis of unprecedented financial disaster. Meanwhile the advancement of the two denominations specially interested —the Congregational and Presbyterian—had also been equally great in the increase of numbers and wealth. The recognition had come to both, more vividly than ever, of their responsibility to send the gospel to the destitute regions of their own country, and abroad to the heathen. The plan of union had been in existence thirty-six years, and had been a source of blessing to both the Congregationalists and the Presbyterians, but now conditions had changed so much that the question arose, could not each denomination working separately in its own sphere and mode, accomplish more for the cause of Christ than in the present system of combined effort? Then, again, the turmoil of the last few years, occasioned by clashing theories and discordant opinions, had hindered the usefulness of the church as evidenced in the decrease of conversions from the world, and also forced upon many leading minds the conviction that a separation from the plan of union was essential to the peace of both parties, and it was hoped to the promotion of the general progress of the gospel in the land.

Plans Laid for Future Action.—Just before the final adjournment of the assembly of 1836 the leaders of the minority, or Old Schoolmen, met in private consultation and took measures to secure a majority of the next assembly (1837) which was to meet in Philadelphia. A committee was appointed to write in confidence to those ministers and elders, who, they had reason to believe, were in sympathy with the movement to abrogate the plan of union. The persons addressed were urged to exert their influence in securing a majority of the commissioners to the next assembly, who would act in union with the authors of the memorial and of the act and testimony.

The committee issued a circular which was distributed far and wide within the church. As is usually the case, an account of this secret movement soon appeared in the public prints. Certain questions were propounded in the circular, to which *confidential* answers were requested. Charges were made against the voluntary societies, the Home Missionary and Educational, and by implication the American Board. A decisive step, it was intimated, must be taken; a pamphlet was circulated which declared: "In some way or other these *men must* separate from us . . . we cannot continue in the same body." Meanwhile the New Schoolmen were not idle in their undiguised efforts to secure a majority in the same assembly; and the whole church was sadly agitated during the intervening year.

The Philadelphia Convention—Its Recommendations.
—A convention, similar in character to the one at Pitts-

burg the previous year, met in Philadelphia a few days before the meeting of the assembly of 1837. It consisted of more than one hundred members, nearly all of whom were also commissioners to the assembly. Warm and earnest discussions took place in the convention as to how they should manage the affair; all was uncertain until the assembly should be organized, since it was a mooted question which party would have the majority. In view of this uncertainty it was asked, how should they act if in a minority? Should they secede and constitute themselves the assembly, or a new assembly? If in the majority, should they cite the synods, against whom rumor made charges of irregularities to appear at the bar of the next General Assembly? That idea, however, was soon dropped as too dilatory; decisive action must be taken, and that speedily.

The convention resolved to present to the assembly another memorial, which contained a summary and recitation of the errors in doctrine said to be prevalent in the church and against which the assembly was called upon to testify in the most emphatic terms. It stated that church order had been violated by the principle of "elective affinity"—but that principle had been repudiated by the assembly of 1835. It was charged that presbyteries had refused to examine ministerial applicants who came to them with regular certificates of dismission from sister ones, thus violating the rule which the assembly of 1830 had adopted. But the Western Reserve Synod, against whom that rule was specially directed, had stated in 1833, that since the rule had been enacted, its presbyteries had obeyed it (*p. 397*). Again the memorial charged that presbyteries licensed men to preach who had professed to adopt the confession only for "substance of doctrine." One hundred and eight years before (1729) the synod of the Presbyterian Church in

"Guarding the Faith," required its ministers and licentiates to accept the Confession of Faith and the Catechisms, as being in all essential and necessary articles, good forms of sound words and systems of Christian doctrine (*p. 114*). The formula "substance of doctrine" was designed to express the same general idea in a more concise form.

The convention in its memorial condemned "the needless ordaining of evangelists," such having caused "spurious excitements" in the church, and sometimes brought the office of the pastor into contempt. It also condemned the formulation of special creeds for individual churches; this custom was the outgrowth of Congregationalism, and which was adopted in some Presbyterian churches organized on the principle of the plan of union. It censured in harsh terms the decisions of former assemblies; and deprecated the irresponsible character of voluntary societies and their influence upon certain presbyteries. It must be recognized that there was reason for genuine Presbyterians being greatly dissatisfied with the anomalous condition of the order and discipline of their church, when in connection with Congregationalism as developed through the influence of the plan of union. Under these conditions it was forced upon intelligent and conservative minds, even, of the private members of the church, that it would be better for its spiritual progress to be severed from a connection that seemed fraught with so much contention.

The convention was radical in its recommendations. It urged the abrogation of the plan of union on the plea that it had outlived its usefulness; and also that the original arrangement was unconstitutional inasmuch as it had not, according to the rule, been submitted to the presbyteries for their approval; and as to the Association of Connecticut, it had only advisory influence, but no legislative authority to make a compact and, therefore, in the abrogation, that body could be ignored (*pp. 238-241*). It recommended not to countenance nor aid the operations of the plan within the bounds of the presbyteries, and to dissolve or exclude individual churches that were thus organized, though nominally connected with a presbytery.

A Special Grievance.—It is proper to note that the Old School were much grieved, especially at the action of the assembly of 1836, in refusing to sanction the committee's transfer of the Western Missionary Society to the care and supervision of the General Assembly. This action was interpreted to mean that the voluntary system of conducting missions would henceforth be imposed upon the Presbyterian Church, and thus deprive it of being as a collective body a missionary society. If the church was *ex-officio* a missionary organization it ought to have a supreme judicature to which its missionaries and the officers of its societies were responsible, and should report, in contradistinction to the, virtually, irresponsible voluntary system.

The Assembly of 1837.—The General Assembly of 1837 met on May 18th of that year, in the Central Church of Philadelphia. The lines had been drawn more definitely than ever before between the parties in the church, usually designated the Old and the New School; each one on this occasion had marshaled for the contest its most talented and influential men. The vote for moderator indicated the relative strength of each party; the nominee of the Old School, Dr. David Elliott, received one hundred and thirty-seven votes and his opponent, Dr. Baxter Dickinson, one hundred and six; thus the former had an apparent working majority.

To the most important committee—that of Bills and Overtures—were referred a number of overtures from presbyteries, and in addition, the memorial of the convention. The latter contained a list of *fifteen errors,* which were declared to be more or less prevalent in the church. Some members of the assembly thought the schedule too long; others wished four more to be added, while others declared there were errors mentioned in the list of which they never before heard. Numbers of the errors cited were of a class involving metaphysical distinctive and subtile definitions, in which the great majority of even intelligent church members, from the nature of the case, could take little or no interest—such questions being appropriate only for the class-room in a theological seminary. A resolution was, however, passed to postpone for the present the consideration of the errors named, and instead take up the report on the plan of union.

Expression of Good Will—Reasons for Action.—A preliminary expression was made by the assembly before entering upon the consideration of the plan of union, urging that between the original parties to that arrangement there should continue mutual respect and sympathy, saying: "It is expedient to continue the plan of friendly intercourse between this church and the Congregational churches of New England, as it now exists." Then were indicated three reasons for the future action of the Assembly: First, that the plan of union was adopted specially to meet the wants of new settlements, and by implication, it was not adapted to the changed conditions of the present time; second, that the act was unconstitutional, inasmuch as the presbyteries had not been consulted and their sanction given to the measure; and third, that the General Association of Connecticut, according to its constitution, had no authority to legislate on the subject. These after-thought objections were adduced when the plan of union had been mutually acted upon for thirty-six years.

The report of the committee in respect to the plan of union was then taken up, and after a protracted discussion the following resolution was adopted, that "the Act of the Assembly of 1801, entitled, a Plan of Union, be and is hereby abrogated" (May 23). The vote stood 143 to 110. The principle involved in this action, that is, on the ground of being organized in connection with the plan of union, would cut off all individual churches, and also synods and presbyteries thus constituted.

Against this action was presented an earnest protest signed by one hundred and three members of the assembly. The protest argued that the repeal was a breach of faith with the Association of Connecticut. It was also an objectionable feature in adopting the measure, that it was dictated by the convention, an outside party, unknown in a legal sense to the assembly; and that a majority of the committee recommending the repeal had been members of that convention.

An Ominous Vote—Amicable Division Proposed.— The report on doctrinal errors was again in order, but was again postponed. And instead, a committee, on motion of Dr. Wm. S. Plumer, was appointed to devise suitable plans by which "such inferior judicatures that are charged by common fame with irregularities" could be cited to the bar of the next assembly. The resolution elicited a warm discussion, lasting through the better portion of two days, and which revealed insuperable objections to the measure, though it was finally adopted by a vote of one hundred and twenty-eight to one hundred and twenty-two (May 26). This vote was ominous; the majority was so small that another measure was proposed in order, it would seem, to obviate the danger of a minority becoming a majority, if the measures proposed were too radical.

Dr. Robert J. Breckinridge, it is said, in accordance

Rev. Robert J. Breckinridge, D.D., LL.D.
(422, 436, 439, 502.)

with a suggestion of Dr. Absalom Peters, now introduced a resolution to appoint a committee of ten—five from each party—to devise a plan for an amicable division of the church. This committee, composed of prominent men in whom all had confidence, met several times and discussed the subject in hand, but were unable to come to a satisfactory and definite conclusion. Manifold difficulties presented themselves, such as the dividing lines that must run through the presbyteries and the individual churches, thus interfering with their private members, causing alienation of Christian fraternal feelings, and to these were added the financial interests involved; the supervision of the theological seminaries and the care of missions, domestic and foreign. Under these circumstances the committee, as it desired, was discharged, and the whole matter was indefinitely postponed (May 30), the vote being one hundred and thirty-eight to one hundred and four. It now became evident that other methods must be adopted to secure a solution of the problem, since a voluntary and mutual division of the church seemed impossible.

Excision of Synods.—On the discharge of the above-mentioned committee, the time, in view of the majority, had come for more decisive action. Says the Princeton *Review* (July, 1837): "The real object which the majority desired to attain was to put an end to the contentions which had so long disturbed the church, and to secure a faithful adherence to our doctrines and discipline." Immediately after the discharge of the committee Dr. William S. Plumer offered a resolution to the effect "that by the operation of the abrogation of the plan of union of 1801 the Synod of the Western Reserve is, and is hereby declared to be no longer a part of the Presbyterian Church of the United States of America." It was charged that many irregularities existed in the synod, and that "an overwhelming majority of the churches within it were not Presbyterian." The latter statement was denied by the members of the synod on the floor of the assembly. It was argued that the effect of the exscinding act would be "to dissolve churches and unclothe ministers blessed of God;" and that remedies more in accordance with justice and prudence could surely be devised. The reply was that churches would not be dissolved nor ministers interfered with, and "if there were true Presbyterian churches in the region, they would come out and unite with the Presbyterian Church on the true principle, while others would follow their predilections." Finally the vote was taken, and one hundred and thirty-two were in the affirmative and one hundred and five in the negative (June 1).

The majority appeared to think there was no other mode but "excision" to remove the troubles in which the church was involved, therefore on the same line a resolution was adopted (June 1) recommending "that the so-called American Home Missionary Society and American Education Society . . . cease to operate within any of our churches." Upon this the vote stood one hundred and twenty-four to eighty-six. Charges were made that these societies "were exceedingly injurious to the peace and purity of the Presbyterian Church." These charges were unequivocally denied by the minority.

Then followed the exscinding of the Synods of Utica, Geneva, and Genesee, for the same reason as in the case of the Western Reserve (June 5). It was on this occasion announced that "the assembly has no intention to affect in any way the ministerial standing of any members of either of said synods." Within these three synods were churches of mixed character, they having been organized on the basis of the plan of union, and also others that were strictly Presbyterian. To this action was appended an invitation "directing churches and ministers, Presbyterian in doctrine and order, to apply for admission to the presbyteries most conveniently located." The vote stood one hundred and fifteen to eighty-eight.

It was adduced as an explanation of the action of the assembly of 1837 that the plan of union was abrogated as a compact, null and void, because of its having been made in an unconstitutional manner, and it therefore followed that all compacts made in accordance with that plan were also null and void. In the latter category were classed individual churches thus organized. The General Assembly has authority to organize synods, and it has impliedly equal authority to dissolve them. In this instance, however, instead of dissolving these synods the assembly left their organization intact, and thus opened the way by which churches and ministers, who were strictly Presbyterian, could remain or connect themselves with a presbytery, and thus with a synod, and by such process become separated from certain incompatible elements. The exscinding of these synods was also claimed to be *extra*-constitutional. Five other synods— New Jersey, Albany, Cincinnati, Illinois, and Michigan— were admonished to take order on the doctrinal errors within their bounds, and to report in writing to the next assembly.

Dealings with Presbyteries.—The majority, or Old School, determining to make a complete end of the matter, took in hand the presbyteries, two of which, on motion of Dr. Breckinridge, were singled out to be dissolved—that of Wilmington and the Third of Philadelphia, but afterward the former was permitted to remain undisturbed (June 7). The Third of Philadelphia was apparently very obnoxious, especially to the leaders of the convention of 1837. Of this presbytery Albert Barnes was a member, and it had been organized on the elective affinity principle. It may be interesting to note in this connection that within the last four years in the Presbyterian churches in the rest of Philadelphia "there had been a marked decrease" of conversions from the world, and meantime "the Third Presbytery had gained nearly one thousand members." As in the case of the exscinded synods, the ministers and churches of the dissolved "Third of Philadelphia" were directed to apply for admission to other presbyteries.

Board of Missions—The Protests.—The assembly, having as far as possible devised measures to prevent in the future a recurrence of the evils of which complaint had been made within recent years, proceeded to enter upon a course of policy peculiarly its own, in conducting missions and other forms of Christian work. It adopted the Western Foreign Missionary Society, and on that basis established a Board of Foreign Missions (June 8). The Princeton *Review*, in referring to these proceedings of the assembly, says the question is "whether this division has been effected in the way which will commend itself to the approbation of good men? We think not." In respect to these enacted measures the members of the minority were by no means silent, but ably opposed them in debate and then by earnest protests. The latter were graphic in their arraignment of such legislation. They showed how contrary to right, to rule, and to precedent, members of the church and its ministers in good and regular standing, and who from their childhood and earliest Christian life had been consistent Christians, and of their substance had contributed liberally to the funds of the church, were excluded from that church without trial, and their pastors, without the impeachment of their doctrinal views. The inquiry was natural, could not this end have been attained in a manner less harsh? Could not a specified time have been named—say three years, as was proposed—in which the members of those churches known as mixed could have separated in a friendly and Christian manner, and thus become strictly Presbyterian or Congregational?

Errors Acted Upon.—The consideration of the "errors in doctrine," as enumerated in the list of the convention, having been postponed from time to time, was now acted upon. In the vote taken the errors, one and all, were emphatically condemned, and by an almost unanimous vote of the majority and the minority. It was said that if one or two of the statements had been somewhat modified the vote would have been unanimous. This vote was very significant and worthy of the reader's notice. It showed, conclusively, that the charges which had been *so persistently* proclaimed for the previous six years, to the effect that "doctrinal errors" were prevalent in the Presbyterian Church, were grossly exaggerated, having comparatively little foundation. There was, however, no doubt that a very limited number of ministers were in the church who held doctrinal views which were not strictly in accordance with its standards. The Princeton *Review* declared "there *were not one in ten*" of the Presbyterian ministers who held the doctrinal errors thus charged.

The Connecticut Missionary Society.—The assembly of 1837, deeming it essential for the peace and prosperity of the church, abrogated the plan of union and exscinded four synods. How pleasant it would be if we could find in its minutes a recognition of what the Connecticut Missionary Society did, indirectly, for the advancement of the Presbyterian Church. In the year 1797 the General Association of Connecticut formed itself—*ex-officio*—into a missionary Society. Among its first gifts to the Presbyterian Church was Eliphalet Nott, first as pastor of a Presbyterian church in Albany and afterward for fifty years President of Union College, wherein his influence was a continuous blessing to the church of his adoption. Numbers of that society's licentiates, and who were supported by it, labored in Western New York, and mostly in connection with the Presbyterian Church, while in the course of twenty-five years it sent to and sustained numerous missionaries in the valley of the Mississippi, who with scarcely an exception, heartily coöperated with the assembly's board. It sent that self-denying and indefatigable missionary, Joseph Badger, to the Western Reserve, but who died a member of the Presbytery of Erie (*pp. 295, 297*). Elias Cornelius was one of its missionaries, and who organized the First Presbyterian Church of New Orleans, and in the same service it supported the eloquent Sylvester Larned—a graduate of Princeton Seminary (*p. 339*). That society commissioned Salmon Giddings, the apostle to Missouri, and who organized the First Presbyterian Church in St. Louis, and also Timothy Flint (*p. 372*) who labored in the same State, and they together founded several such churches. This society sent may others, among whom was Samuel Royce (*p. 287*), the first educated Protestant minister to preach west of the lower Mississippi. He connected himself with the presbytery of that name, and spent his life at Alexandria, Louisiana, and for a long time had scarcely a ministerial brother within a hundred miles; the region round about was his parish. When it was unable to send men it appropriated money to support other missionaries in the Great valley; of these there were more than twenty, all connected with the Presbyterian Church.

Sad Statistics.—In connection with these continuous controversies within the church it will not be out of place to refer to statistics as to the number of its communicants. In the report of 1833 the number of church members was 233,580, while in 1830 it was about 173,000, and in 1837, 220,557. From 1830 to 1833 the average annual *increase* from the world was about 20,000, and from 1833 to 1837, the annual average *decrease* was 3256. This decrease was largely in the Northern presbyteries, which fact may be partially accounted for because an unusual number of the churches in that region had been organized in accordance with the plan of union, and the agitation that was going on affected them more than the churches elsewhere; and in consequence great numbers of these mixed churches withdrew from the Presbyterian Church. The main cause of this decrease, however, was that the proper work of the church was interfered with and religion languished; it was not, as in previous years, when the church was united and pressing on in its appropriate duties. There were also during this period disturbing elements in the commercial and industrial world, which finally resulted in the terrible financial crash of 1837, that affected the whole Nation.

Difficulties Attending Assemblies.—During these years of controversy there existed much dissatisfaction among the Old School Presbyterians west of the Alleghanies in the Great valley because of the many difficulties in the way of their commissioners attending the meetings of the assembly when held so far East as Philadelphia. This grievance was first put forth by the Synod of Pittsburg in 1831; the circumstances being such there was quite a reason for the complaint. At that time there were no railroads, as now, but instead only two stage routes across the Alleghanies; one, the famous national road, from Cumberland, Maryland, to the Ohio and beyond, and the other up the Susquehanna and the Juniata rivers, and thence across. The modes of travel were by private carriage, on horseback or by canal and stage-coach combined, and in the Great valley on the rivers by steamboats. The time spent at the assembly and on the journeys to and from, and the expenses, often deterred, especially, the elders commissioned by the Western presbyteries from attending. The same could be said of the lay commissioners from the presbyteries of the Atlantic slope, south of the Potomac, and of the Southwest. The church of that day was ill able to systematically defray the expenses of its commissioners to the assembly. It was complained that owing to these conditions the churches in the West were not as fully represented in the assembly, as those east of the mountains; that some thirty or forty commissioners came every year from the portion of the church wherein the system of voluntary societies was specially popular, while the western portion was only a little more than half represented. For illustration, an investigation revealed the fact that in the year 1828 the portion of the church east of the Alleghanies and north of the southern line of the Synod of Philadelphia, having forty presbyteries, sent to the assembly thirty-four elders, and the other portion, having fifty presbyteries, sent only four. Again, in 1831, the former portion, having forty-four presbyteries, sent fifty-one elders, and the latter, having sixty, sent fifteen. It appears from the minutes of the assembly that a similar ratio prevailed in previous years.

The Action on Slavery.—For a number of years previous to 1837 the subject of slavery had been agitated in the South, the tendency of which was to secure the gradual emancipation of its victims. Societies having this end in view were first formed amid the evil. "In 1826," says an authority, "of the one hundred and one anti-slavery societies in the country, less than one-fourth were in the free-labor States." North Carolina had forty-one of these, Tennessee had twenty-three, Virginia had many, and Kentucky six. In the latter State the Presbyterian Church took a more active part than it did in any of the others. The synod of that State, in considering overtures on the subject, declared the system to be a moral evil, and contrary to the word of God. It went so far in 1834 that by an almost unanimous vote it appointed a committee "to prepare a plan for the instruction and future emancipation of the slaves." It reported the next year, and depicted the domestic evils of the system in a graphic manner and took decided ground in favor of emancipation. The synod accepted the report, but did not adopt it, deeming the sentiment of the people at large not fully prepared for so radical a measure. A change, meanwhile, was taking place in the minds of the Southern people, and which was occasioned by the agitation on the subject then going on in the North, that manifested itself by sending South through the mail publications that were deemed incendiary. It was charged that such papers often came in packages of goods in order that they might more certainly reach the eyes of the slaves themselves. The reaction became excessive, and led to enactments by some of the States of very stringent laws in respect to the slaves; even their religious meetings were forbidden and their Sabbath-schools discontinued.

The Presbyterian Church in the free-labor States had nothing to do with sending these objectionable publications. The subject had been brought to the attention of the assembly of 1836 in the form of a report of a committee appointed the previous year. The matter was discussed at length, but finally, on the ground that the assembly "had no authority to assume or exercise jurisdiction in regard to the existence of slavery." The whole subject was postponed by a vote of one hundred and fifty-six to eighty-seven. A protest was presented that was signed by twenty-eight members.

The Presbyterians in the South began to attribute what

there was of anti-slavery sentiment among their Northern brethren to only the portion of the church that was denominated the New School. In this opinion or assumption they were clearly mistaken, for the great majority of the ministry and of the private members of the church who intelligently kept up with the times did recognize the evils of slavery, but they were unable to see how they could be remedied. In accordance with their views, it was not strange that Southern presbyteries saw in a division of the church the only means of freeing it from the anti-slavery agitation. Several of their presbyteries and of their synods, two or three, expressed themselves in favor of a division, and with this sentiment coincided some of their religious papers.

In 1837 the number of ministers in the Presbyterian Church was 2140; churches, 2865; communicants, 220,557; funds for missions, $163,363; for education, $90,833; theological seminaries, $20,431.

The Pastoral and Circular.—The assembly of 1837, as usual, issued a pastoral letter to the churches. The plan of union was spoken of as having been "projected and brought into operation by some of the wisest and best men the Presbyterian Church has ever known." Then follow some of the objections to its practical workings, because the original conditions were so much changed. "By that act committeemen belonging to the Congregational Church, and under its government, were introduced into our presbyteries, our synods, and General Assembly. . . . The act in question goes to the subversion of the Presbyterian Church." The pastoral concludes: "That on whatever side the principal fault of our present disturbances may be the whole church has abundant cause of deep humiliation and repentance before Almighty God" (June 8).

The Assembly also issued a special circular letter ad-

THE DIVISION OF THE CHURCH. 447

dressed to the churches, the design of which was to present to them an explanation or vindication of the various acts of the assembly. The spirit of the circular was in marked contrast with that so clearly manifested in the pastoral letter. The subject of slavery, which came up at the assembly, was laid upon the table by a vote of ninety-three to twenty-eight. (*Minutes of the Assembly of 1837.*)

XLV.

THE TWO ASSEMBLIES.

The members of the assembly of 1837, who represented the presbyteries and churches within the four exscinded synods, before leaving for their homes, held a council. After consultation it was understood that the subject of their complaint would be fully considered at a convention soon to be called and to which delegates were to be sent by the aggrieved churches. These four synods had under their care nearly thirty presbyteries, while the number of their church members was about equal that of the whole church at the beginning of the century.

Complaint and Acts of the Convention.—The convention, accordingly, was called and met in Auburn, New York, on August 17, 1837. The number of delegates in attendance, ministers and lay, was about one hundred and seventy. Many of its members were prominent in the church as preachers and theological professors, such as Drs. James Richards, N. S. S. Beman, Lyman Beecher, Thomas McAuley, Samuel Hanson Cox, and many others. The members of the convention deemed themselves the victims of a gross injustice, inasmuch as they had been cut off, or virtually expelled, from the church of their fathers, not for reasons concerning doctrinal errors affecting their Christian character as ministers of the gospel or lay officers, but on grounds that were unconstitutional. The convention recommended the synods and their presbyteries to preserve their organizations intact, and send to the next assembly their usual number of commissioners.

The recommendation was complied with for the most part, as only a few churches severed their connection with their presbyteries. There was a tacit understanding to test the case on the floor of the General Assembly of 1838. In order to place the motives and the reasons for its action before the churches, the convention appointed a number of committees to prepare papers for publication and distribution throughout the church: first, to give reasons for the action of the convention; second, to define the rights of membership in the Presbyterian Church, and how they are guaranteed or forfeited; third, to direct the attention of judicatures and ministers to its present lamentable condition; fourth, to prepare a summary of doctrines as held and maintained by the portion of the church thus exscinded, as charges of defections in doctrines had been presented in memorials to former assemblies, and also a committee of correspondence, in order to confer as to the best method of securing the objects aimed at by the convention.

The Assembly of 1838.—The General Assembly of 1838 met on the 17th day of May of that year in the Seventh Presbyterian Church of Philadelphia. A number of questions had to be discussed and, if possible, settled before the regular organization could be completed. There were on hand commissioners from the exscinded synods, who deemed the excision acts unconstitutional, and therefore null and void, and they were present to claim their seats. The question was still an open one, since no competent authority had decided as to the legality of the exscinded acts, while as to the different opinions of the parties interested they were equally without authority. Another important question arose, how was the roll of the assembly of 1838 to be completed?

The ordinary exercises in opening a new assembly were conducted in the usual manner. At the close of these preliminaries the moderator, Dr. Elliott, called upon the permanent clerk to report the roll. At this time Dr. William Patton of the Third Presbytery of New York rose and asked permission to offer a resolution, but the moderator declared him out of order until the roll was completed. Dr. Patton appealed from the decision, but it was not sustained. The permanent clerk, in preparing the roll, had left off the names of the commissioners from the four exscinded synods, and this roll he reported. At the close of its reading the moderator, according to rule, asked if there were commissioners from presbyteries belonging to the Presbyterian Church in the United States of America, whose names were omitted from the roll; if so, it was in order to present their commissions. Upon this announcement Dr. Erskine Mason of the Third Presbytery of New York moved that the names of certain commissioners whose commissions the clerk had refused to receive, be added to the roll. The moderator inquired to what presbyteries they belonged; the answer was, to the synods of the Western Reserve, Utica, Geneva, and Genesee. The moderator stated that the motion was out of order. Dr. Mason, in a courteous manner, appealed from the moderator's decision, but the latter refused to put the appeal to the house, and immediately asked for the names of commissioners from presbyteries in connection with the assembly.

The Crisis Had Come.—The Rev. Miles P. Squier—the only one from an exscinded synod to take part—rose and stated that he had a commission to the assembly from the Presbytery of Geneva, which the clerk had refused to receive, and he now presented the same to the assembly, and claimed by right his seat. The moderator inquired if his presbytery belonged to the Synod of Geneva; being answered in the affirmative, the moderator declared the application out of order, curtly saying: "We do not know you, sir." Dr. John P. Cleaveland of the Presbytery of Detroit, rose and amid interruptions began to read a paper, the purport of which was that as the moderator had failed to do his duty in putting the appeal, it was therefore incumbent that the assembly be at once organized, and he moved that Dr. N. S. S. Beman— a moderator of a previous assembly—take the chair until a moderator be chosen. The motion was carried, and Dr Beman took a position in an aisle of the church. Clerks were immediately chosen—Dr. Erskine Mason and Dr. E. W. Gilbert. Then some one nominated Dr. Samuel Fisher of Newark Presbytery for moderator; he was chosen. These various motions were passed, there being very few negative votes. The other portion of the house sat quietly, taking no part. A motion was made and passed that the assembly, as thus organized, adjourn to the First Presbyterian Church, which was accomplished in order. The division of the Presbyterian Church was now complete. It is worthy of note that if the commissioners from the four exscinded synods be added to those who retired, a careful estimate makes the number one hundred and thirty-six, while those who remained in the Seventh Church number one hundred and forty. Here was an anomaly in church history—two denominations having the same name, adhering faithfully to the same standards of doctrine, and occupying side by side the same territory. Thus they continued for thirty-two years, and then reunited on the acceptance of the doctrines of the church as contained in the Confession of Faith.

In order to avoid confusion we will designate the assemblies as Old and New School—these terms being, at the time, well understood—instead of by the church in which they *happened* to meet.

The Old-School Assembly Organizes.—After a portion of the members had adjourned, as noted above, to meet elsewhere, those who remained proceeded to organize the assembly as if nothing unusual had occurred. In the minutes the withdrawal is briefly stated, without comment. Dr. William S. Plumer was elected moderator, and the Old-School Assembly entered upon routine business, such as the appointments of the usual committees, the election of trustees and of directors in the Seminary Board. In these were now an unusual number of vacancies owing to the withdrawal of so many members. Numbers of overtures were referred to appropriate committees and were considered in order; action was also taken on the missions of the church, foreign and domestic.

A resolution was passed to the effect "that the names of those who had left the assembly and were in attendance on an assembly in the First Church be transmitted to their respective presbyteries." Another measure was passed, saying: "In the present condition it is inexpedient to repeal the resolution which makes it imperative on presbyteries to examine ministers applying for admission."

The Question of Slavery.—The leading minds in the Old School tacitly decided in relation to the question of slavery "to let the Southern brethren manage their own concerns in their own way." And accordingly, when that question was brought before the assembly, it was laid upon the table. Both branches of the church, in their respective assemblies, had this question presented for their consideration from year to year, and they both condemned the system as wrong, yet from the nature of the case they were unable to do anything more efficient than to proclaim its condemnation. That form of agitation continued for twenty-three years, till the firing on Sumter occasioned a more effective mode of argument. We will not, therefore, impose upon the patience of the reader the monotonous details of these annual discussions and resolutions.

which were unsatisfactory to both assemblies, and are now of much less interest.

The assembly had already accepted the Western Foreign Missionary Society from the Synod of Pittsburg, and on the basis of which had constituted its Board of Foreign Missions. This transferred society was free from debt and had an increasing income from year to year, that was "larger than was then given to foreign missions by all the other churches of the denomination."

The New-School Assembly Organizes.—The New School Assembly of 1838 entered upon routine business in the usual mode. As a mere form, but for a legal purpose, the moderator called for the reports of the usual committees appointed by the assembly of 1837, and directors were elected for the Seminary at Princeton. The assembly repealed certain measures of the previous one, such as the latter's resolution in respect to the Home Missionary and Educational societies, and it went further in commending them to the good will and patronage of the church. It was emphatic in declaring the act of exscinding the four synods as contrary to the constitution of the church, and therefore null and void. It made no new arrangements of presbyteries or synods, except in one instance, when it constituted a new synod, known as that of Pennsylvania. It was to embrace the ministers and congregations of the presbyteries of Philadelphia Second, Philadelphia Third, Lewes, Wilmington, Carlisle, Huntingdon, and Northumberland. It also appointed a committee of twelve to supervise its legal rights and its pecuniary interests, as such questions might arise in the future.

Effort to Effect a Compromise.—It passed unanimously the following resolution: "That this body is willing to agree to any reasonable measures tending to an amicable adjustment of the difficulties existing in the Presbyterian

Church, and will receive and respectfully consider any propositions which may be made for that purpose." In accordance with the sentiment thus expressed propositions were made to the Old-School Assembly indicating a desire for a compromise or reunion, but an answer was received which implied that the latter still adhered to its exscinding acts. In view of this answer there was only one alternative, to test in the civil courts which one of the assemblies was the legitimate *chief judicature* of the whole Presbyterian Church. Though not stated, it was a fact that the private members of the churches cut off by the exscinding acts had previously been in proportion as liberal in their contributions in aid of the colleges and seminaries of the church as those who were not thus excluded. This consideration involved the rights of property, also, and the first question to be decided was which one of these assemblies—the New or the Old School—was the legitimate successor of the General Assembly of the church before the division. The New School elected members of the Board of Trustees of the Assembly under the charter of 1789. The method adopted to reach the case was to test the right of these newly elected members to a seat in the board. The New-School Assembly was the plaintiff and the Old School the defendant.

The Two Civil Court Trials.—The suit was brought —March 4, 1839—in the Supreme Court for the Eastern District of Pennsylvania, and before a special jury and a *single* judge—Rodgers—and after a trial lasting three weeks, was decided in favor of the plaintiff, on the ground that the exscinding acts which deprived the latter of their rights were *"unconstitutional."* This decision made the New School "The General Assembly of the Presbyterian Church in the United States of America."

The defendant now appealed to the Court in Bank, in which all the judges participate. In that trial the question as to the correctness of the decision of the previous court was ignored, and a different issue introduced, which had respect to whether the majority of the assembly of 1838 was in accord with the Old School. On this issue the Court in Bank decided in favor of the latter. It is a singular fact that in view of the premises in each case, both these decisions were correct. The New School were satisfied with the decision of the first court and jury, namely, that the exscinding acts were unconstitutional, and therefore null and void, and in consequence *no stigma* could be attached to the victims of said acts. On this ground the New-School Assembly assumed the title "Constitutional," which after some years appears to have been quietly dropped. Both parties were wearied of the turmoil and willing to let the contest cease for the sake of peace. Each one retained its property and tacitly agreed to let bygones be bygones, and go on in their appropriate duties as churches and separate denominations. So great was the desire to have peace that numbers of both parties remained with their respective individual churches when their sympathies were with the other party. After all, they both adhered to the same confession; meanwhile, the attrition of charity and good feeling and mutual forbearance in the course of years wore away the harshness incident to the different doctrinal views which did not interfere with individual piety nor with Christian work.

XLVI.

The Two Assemblies Continued.

The Old-School Assembly met May 16, 1839, in Philadelphia. Dr. Joshua L. Wilson of Cincinnati was chosen moderator. It very properly on May 21st celebrated with appropriate ceremonies the semi-centennial anniversary of the organization of the first General Assembly, which occurred on May 21, 1789 (*pp. 207*). The Assembly devoted itself to the usual routine business connected with the cares of the churches, which at this time were numerous and various, and required special prudence. Its trustees were authorized and instructed to oversee the affairs of the church, financially, which were then involved in civil suits. The report on domestic missions told of their continuous prosperity, but complained that probably "not more than two-thirds of our pastors and churches do at present render any assistance to the cause." By resolution it was declared "that the Presbyterian Church is by nature and constitution a missionary society . . . that the distinction between foreign and domestic missions is made only to secure a division of labor." The Board of Education was earnestly recommended to the churches for their sympathy and support. On the same line the Board of Publication was recognized and its duties defined as to the character of the books it was authorized to issue.

Synods Dissolved.—This assembly, owing to the peculiar conditions of the time, dissolved a number of synods but so arranging them that the private members and presbyteries could make their choice of either school. According to the minutes, the number of communicants in the church was 128,043; the ministers, 1243; churches, 1823. Funds contributed for domestic missions were $33,989, and for foreign, $51,307.

Abbreviated Creeds.—The New-School Assembly met in Philadelphia on the third Thursday of May, 1839. Dr. Baxter Dickinson was chosen moderator. Among the reports of the committees was one on "Abbreviated Creeds." This report was accepted and adopted. It spoke in general terms of approbation of these various creeds in respect to doctrines, alluding only to very few exceptions. The necessity for this investigation by a committee of the assembly had arisen from the custom of individual Congregational churches formulating creeds for themselves, and that some of these were in connection with presbyteries. The committee say: "We have found the creeds adopted by these presbyteries [their number was twenty-five] and recommended to their churches, with few exceptions, full and sound to a gratifying extent." Some were used "merely as a form of public consecration by adopting which candidates are received to the communion of the church." In view of this report, the assembly requested all presbyteries "to examine this subject, and if forms are used by any of their churches, to look at their character."

The assembly proposed a plan of division to the Old-School Assembly, but the proposition was declined. It recommended to students the following theological seminaries: Auburn, Lane, that of Western Reserve, and Union in New York City. The minutes showed the member of communicants, 100,850; ministry, 1181; churches, 1286; funds for missions, $45,686; for education, $12,718.

The Old-School Assembly of 1840 met in Philadelphia on May 21st of that year.

The session was characterized for its unanimity and for being careful in its routine business in relation to the wants of the churches.

The minutes of 1840 show the number of communicants to have been 126,585; ministers, 1615; churches, 1673; funds for domestic missions $35,113, and for foreign, $48,523. Here it will be noticed that the whole amount contributed in 1840 fell short of that of 1839 only $1645, while the decrease of ministers was 208, with perhaps a corresponding diminution in the number of the churches. This change, no doubt, was brought about in consequence of the assembly of 1839 having dissolved so many synods, thus giving an opportunity for changes on the part of those who wished to withdraw, whether ministers or churches.

The New-School Assembly met in Philadelphia on the third Tuesday of May, 1840. Dr. William Wisner was chosen moderator. The minutes for that year stated there were 102,060 communicants, 1260 ministers; churches, 1375; and also that 7421 were added to the church on their examination, and 4180 on certificate.

Characteristics of Each School.—The close of the two assemblies of 1840 marked their division complete, in the sense that between them there were to be no more legal contests. Each one was equipped to proceed in the line of its respective duties, independent of the other. The Old-School Assembly with its adherents was a harmonious and compact organization, homogeneous in its character; that is, agreeing in doctrine and church polity. The New School, on the other hand, was not homogeneous in all respects. There were quite a number of its members who had been reared as Congregationalists, and with whose church polity they sympathized, though they had united with the Presbyterians, more, perhaps, because of their surroundings than from choice. While those originally Presbyterians accepted the Confession of Faith, the appointment of a committee to look after the abbreviated creeds and its report thereon was evidence of a lack of harmony within that body in respect to doctrinal views.

Committee ad Interim.—The New-School Assembly instead of meeting annually, resolved to meet triennially, and in consequence it deemed it expedient to appoint a *committee ad interim,* or consulting committee of five ministers and five ruling elders, in connection with its *three* clerks, who were to be *ex-officio* members. This committee had power to act as the agent of the assembly in certain respects, and was enjoined to report to the next assembly, which was to meet in Philadelphia three years hence, on the third Thursday of May, 1843.

The Two Plans for Mission Work.—Which plan was the better—the voluntary or the denominational—in conducting missionary and educational work, was now to be more fully tested. The former had been in practice for more than a quarter of a century and had produced good results, for which reason the New-School brethren were not willing to make a change for the latter, which partook of the nature of a theory that had been only partially developed. One argument urged that by uniting in evangelical work a Christian fraternal feeling would be promoted among the private members of the various churches and denominations thus engaged. On the other hand, it was contended that the *ex-officio* or denominational plan would enlist the sympathies of the private members of the denomination more, when it engaged in the work of missions alone, than in connection with others. It would certainly induce a more vivid sense of *responsibility,* individual in character, among its intelligent private members, and in consequence lead them in their respective duties and contributions to make unusual personal sacrifices to aid the cause. The history of American missions at home and abroad, for the last half century, has given striking evidence of the utility of the denominational plan, and that recognition has led to its adoption by the respective denominations. The American Board of Missions—originally voluntary—is to-day virtually the agent of the Congregational Church alone; a similar relation to a denomination may be predicated of every other missionary society—foreign or home—in the Union. This change has been brought about by the influence of conditions being constantly modified during the last fifty years; such as the gradual rising of church members to a higher plane of general intelligence, the prominence that has been given to the study of the Bible by the youth of the Protestant churches, while consistent with this progress is also a clearer sense of *individual responsibility* resting upon the ministry and the church people or members. To these conditions may be added the increase of population and of wealth, and the greater facilities of intercourse between the different sections of our own country and with the outside world. Even the disturbing events of a civil war have been overruled by Divine providence to develop, more than hitherto, an interest in missions to every class of the destitute in our own land.

An Indirect Influence.—The intelligent American Christian who understands the condition—spiritual and temporal—of the church in countries where it is so united with the government as to be dependent upon it for support, may well be thankful that the principle of the separation of church and state is embodied in the constitution of his own country. Though this separation may in one sense be true, yet there is an important and intimate connection between the two. The State can in certain respects have an indirect and powerful influence upon the support of the church in sustaining its appropriate work. For illustration, in efforts to maintain itself and meet the expenses incident to extending the gospel and a Christian civilization throughout the Union, the church depends entirely upon the voluntary contributions of its friends, whose ability so to do may also depend, more or less, upon the financial and economical measures that are introduced, especially by the general government. All financial measures must, of necessity, affect, either beneficially or adversely, the industrial and commercial interests of the Nation, and thereby on a similar line, but indirectly, the support of the churches and their work. All such measures affect the church beneficially when they encourage legitimate industries, thus giving employment to the workpeople; and adversely when their influence depresses wages and incomes, and thereby diminishes the ability of Christian people to sustain by their contributions the ordinances of the gospel. For that reason and many others it is clearly the patriotic duty of members of the church to become sufficiently intelligent to exercise properly, and that in a conscientious manner, their *rights as citizens,* and thus aid in preventing such evils, by judiciously choosing their representatives to the legislative bodies—State and National. If they do not perform this patriotic and likewise Christian duty, they are so far responsible for the consequences. The financial affairs of the church should be conducted on correct business principles.

Financial Disturbances.—At this period (1833-1843) there were unprecedented disturbances in the financial affairs of the Nation, but more especially in those of the people themselves, for it is a remarkable fact that they were virtually bankrupt while the government itself was *rich.* The industrial and commercial interests of the former were at length prostrated by the tremendous crash of 1837. (*Four Hundred Years, etc., pp. 731-734.*) The evils thus induced lasted for five or six years longer, and amid these discouragements the entire Presbyterian Church, in both divisions, exercised much self-denial and went forward nobly in the efforts to sustain its work.

In order that the reader may have a true conception of the *inner history* of the church, we deem it necessary to thus notice the contemporary public measures, that often have financially so much to do, though indirectly, in retarding or in promoting its prosperity. The intelligent reader can remember and easily divine the reason why the General Assembly of 1895 adjourned with all its boards burdened with an unusually heavy debt.

XLVII.

THE TWO ASSEMBLIES CONTINUED.

Protests and Criticisms.—We will notice briefly some of the consequences of the division. The work of adjusting the affairs of the church began and went on until completed in both divisions. The process affected synods and presbyteries, invaded individual churches, and often alienated friendships of long standing among the members. There were large numbers of intelligent private church members who had been close observers of the proceedings by which the division had been secured, and who adhered to the Old School, but were not in sympathy with the mode in which that result had been attained. There were also numbers of ministers, some prominent in the church, such as Dr. Gardiner Spring, pastor of the historical Brick Church of New York, and Dr. Ichabod Spencer of Brooklyn, who protested most earnestly against the exscinding acts. There were also outside well-wishers toward the Presbyterian Church, who were made sad. The venerable Professor Leonard Woods of Andover Seminary, wrote: "When I heard of them [the exscisions] I was grieved and astonished, and constrained to ask whether there is anything in the Bible or in the constitution of the Presbyterian Church which can warrant such proceedings." Others of the outside world could understand the practical workings of the exscinding measures if they could not comprehend the importance of the doctrinal differences and policies that had been under discussion in the church judicatures from year to year, and they also made adverse criticisms. Ardent Congregationalists, especially, seized the occasion to fulminate charges against the Presbyterian polity, which could authorize such arbitrary measures. These good friends, in their zeal, did not recognize the fact that the prime movers in this affair knew better, and never claimed that the exscinding acts were in accordance with the constitutional polity of the church, but deemed them *extra*-constitutional. They were constrained to apologize for their action by pleading the extreme emergency of the case. Under the circumstances they were compelled to accept what appeared the less of two evils: either to continue in a connection that produced incessant turmoil, which was crushing out the spiritual life of the church and would eventually impair its polity, or by a stringent measure cause an excision of the synods, but in such manner as to leave the way open for their discordant elements to separate, and then, in accordance with their respective wishes, unite with one or the other division.

It is worthy of note that numbers of ministers and intelligent church members, who kept themselves in touch with the ecclesiastical trials and other movements; who were beyond the bounds of the direct influence of the plan of union, and who, in their doctrinal views, were in full accord with the Confession of Faith, yet in their church relations allied themselves with the New School, as was the case, partially in the Southern presbyteries. There were also numbers in other portions of the church who had been reared amid Congregational influences and whose sympathies were in the same direction, but allied themselves with the other school.

The Adjustments.—At the close of more than half a century after the times of which we write, it does not seem expedient nor profitable to tax the reader with a monotonous detail of the numerous adjustments in synods, in presbyteries and churches, that grew out of the division. These adjustments, though each one was of a local character, continued for a length of time. Numbers of them were sad in their results, as when a church self-supporting and doing a good work, was divided into two, each half not self-supporting and the good work paralyzed. Yet there were some instances in which such separation was graciously overruled for the general good.

The church in Kentucky was greatly disturbed; more, indeed, than in any other State, and the evil effects of the unusually long turmoil had a deleterious influence upon its progress. (See Davidson's "Kentucky.") In other portions of the valley of the Mississippi the results, so unfortunate, were plainly visible, especially because of the marked falling off of the home missionary work, to renew which to its former efficiency took some years. We can have only a partial conception of the confusion that must have prevailed within the church during these years of readjustments. More than twenty synods and their respective presbyteries were agitated on the questions involved, and yet the evil consequence that affected these judicatures in themselves, was as nothing when compared with that which interfered with the peace and piety of the church members.

The Work of Both Assemblies.—The two branches finally in an earnest manner took up their appropriate work. The New School continued to contribute to the funds of the voluntary associations, the American Board, and the Home Missionary and American Educational societies, and still maintained their liberal views and policy. The Old School, as soon as possible, entered independently upon a similar line of Christian work, and its churches came forward and nobly aided the cause by liberal contributions. The promptness in the latter respect was credited by some outsiders, to mere denominational zeal, but when we analyze the motives of these donors, it seems rather the result of a recognition of the *responsibility* that pervaded the minds of intelligent church members, since they clearly realized that the Presbyterian Church in its distinct organization was a missionary society, and that its *individual* private members ought to do their share by furnishing the funds necessary to carry on the work. Certain leaders might have been partially actuated by denominational zeal, but among church members such motives were scarcely known, but to perform a Christian duty in promoting the gospel was an ever-present stimulus.

Both the assemblies at their respective sessions in 1843 celebrated with appropriate ceremonies and addresses the two hundredth anniversary of the meeting of the Westminster Assembly.

At the New-School Assembly of 1843 the committee *ad interim* reported and their report was adopted. The assembly "commended the zeal and fidelity of the committee in the novel circumstances in which in the province of God they had been placed." That assembly was dissolved, and its successor was to meet in 1846.

Aloof from Slavery Agitation—Conversions.—The Old-School Assembly kept aloof, as far as possible, from the anti-slavery agitation, referring as occasion required to its deliverance on that subject in 1818. In consequence of this policy the portion of the church that was in the slave-labor States, though only partially satisfied, continued in connection with that body till the firing on Fort Sumter brought matters to a crisis. This assembly had the advantage of being quite homogeneous, inasmuch as those who were not perfectly in sympathy with all its modes of action, did not withdraw, but remained in the connection and aided the cause with their means and influence. It resigned all interest and claims in the other missions to which it had contributed funds, and instead, entered upon its own foreign and domestic mission work; looked after the education of young men for the ministry, and made provision in its Church Extension Committee to aid feeble churches and in providing houses of worship. Its pathway was comparatively smooth, but the political agitation immediately preceding the Mexican War and during its continuance, had the effect of causing a decrease in the number of conversions from the world. In 1844 these conversions were twelve thousand and sixty-eight, which number gradually diminished till in 1847 it was only seven thousand six hundred and two, after which year the number began again to increase till in 1853 there were reported eleven thousand eight hundred and forty-six. The Old School in 1844 had one hundred and sixty-six thousand four hundred and eighty-seven communicants, and in 1853, two hundred and nineteen thousand two hundred and sixty-three. The New School in 1843 had one hundred and twenty thousand six hundred and forty-six communicants, and in 1853, one hundred and forty thousand four hundred and fifty-two.

Difficulties in Coöperation.—After the completed division in 1838 the New School and the Congregationalists coöperated for some years harmoniously in their appropriate work. The former gave their contributions nearly all to the common fund of the voluntary societies. In relation to foreign missions there appears to have been no difficulty in their being carried on conjointly, but in conducting home missions there happened to be more or less friction, which hampered the work. The New-School branch, as a denomination, was retarded in its progress because of its not being truly homogeneous nor in perfect harmony with itself. Its members, those who were originally Congregationalists, seeing the effects that resulted from the excision acts, became more and more inclined to act in their missions independently as a denomination, and in consequence began virtually to withdraw from coöperating in the Home Mission and Educational societies. This action seems to have arisen from the fact that some of these churches thus aided were Congregational, some Presbyterian, and others that were mixed or composed of both parties. There appears to have grown up, as incidental to such conditions, a sort of rivalry, perhaps unconscious, between these congregations. The Presbyterians complained that their mission churches did not receive the amount of aid to which they were entitled; that is, in proportion to what they contributed. The answer to the complaint was that the rules of the society, in a measure, restricted donations to Presbyterian churches, and when an appeal was made to the Eastern Congregational churches the request was denied. Then the Presbyterians, in order to aid their own churches, took up special collections in addition to what they had contributed to the general fund; the Home Missionary Society complained of these collections, contending that they, too, should go into the general fund. In 1860 this question came up in the General Assembly, and its minutes say: "We deeply regret that our relations to the Home Missionary Society seem to grow more and more complicated and embarrassing. . . . The leading Congregational associations in their action seem to forbode a speedy dissolution of the copartnership in that society." Then in allusion to the fault-finding with Presbyterians making special collections to aid strictly Presbyterian churches, the assembly says: "We have never expressly nor by remote implication bound ourselves to make that society the exclusive agent of our church in the home missionary work." The assembly in order to provide against future deficiencies had seven years before, in 1853, determined to raise a fund of one hundred thousand dollars, by its own exertions, to be used specially in aiding such churches. The effort was at length successful, and this fact stimulated the members of the church to greater exertions in aiding the cause.

The Secession of Synods.—There were other elements of discord, and in 1858 in consequence of the slavery agitation, six Southern Synods withdrew from their connection with the New-School Assembly. They were the Synods of Missouri, Virginia, Kentucky, Tennessee, West Tennessee, and Mississippi; in all, twenty-one presbyteries and more than fifteen thousand church members. They constituted themselves "The United Synod of the Presbyterian Church." That body stood aloof until 1864, when the two Southern branches united under the present title, "The Presbyterian Church in the United States."

The American Missionary Association.—This organization was distinctly Congregational in its management and denominational in its operations. It would, however, aid churches that were constituted on a mixed basis. This arrangement appears to have had the effect of drawing off to the Congregationalists numbers of churches thus organized, which were nominally Presbyterian, and as such were counted in the statistics. In consequence of these two depletions the New-School branch was weakened to a large extent.

The Revival of 1857.—A revival in which the Presbyterian as well as other evangelical denominations participated, commenced in the City of New York in the autumn of 1857. It was remarkable inasmuch as it came upon men as "a still small voice;" there were no special leaders nor concerted action. It came at the end of a period of about ten years of unusual anxiety in the nation—the Mexican War, the discovery of gold in California, and the excitements and enterprises that were its outgrowth. The American people seemed weary and needed rest; which came in a manner that was undesirable, though it was overruled by a beneficent providence to result in untold blessings. The rest came in the stagnation of nearly all the mechanical industries of the land—the political and economical causes of which we need not here trace. Multitudes were thrown out of employment; a great depression in business became universal. In the midst of these material disasters, men engaged in their ordinary affairs seemed to be moved by an all-pervading, indefinable influence, that turned their attention to sacred subjects. Impressed by this unusual fact, a Christian man, Jeremiah Lamphier, sexton of the Collegiate Church in Fulton street, opened one of its rooms for a midday hour of prayer. Only a few attended at first, but soon came crowds, mostly business men, and other rooms were required for their accommodation. The influence spread, and within less than a year about twenty such daily meetings for prayer were held in different parts of the city; a prominent theater in one of its busiest portions was crowded by earnest men, who were instructed by eminent ministers in the gospel truths pertaining to personal religion. The same spirit spread far and wide, and ere long other cities and towns were reached until there was scarcely one in the whole land that did not have a number of similar prayer-meetings. They were union in spirit and conducted in a Christian and brotherly manner; ministers of the evangelical denominations led in turn and often well-known Christian laymen. "This revival was the introduction to a new era of the nation's spiritual life. It was a training-school for a force of lay evangelists for future work,

THE TWO ASSEMBLIES CONTINUED. 471

eminent among whom is the name of Dwight L. Moody." (*Am. Christianity, p. 344.*)

It is estimated that through the influence of these prayer-meetings 1,000,000 persons were brought into the church from the outside world. The public interest was so great that the leading newspapers noticed these meetings from day to day, and from that day on the secular press has been accustomed to notice more or less fully the religious movements of the times. The Fulton street "noonday prayer-meeting" still continues.

XLVIII.

THE TWO ASSEMBLIES CONTINUED.

A Decided Stand Taken.—The affairs of the Nation were now rapidly approaching a crisis, unprecedented in its history—the commencement of a civil war that resulted in consequences second only in importance to those of the Revolution.

About one month after the firing on Fort Sumter both the New and the Old-School assemblies met in Philadelphia, May, 1861. They both took high and patriotic ground in respect to the war thus wantonly inaugurated. The New School, in condemnation, traced its cause to the deliberate purpose of those who had thus insulted the flag of their country, to sustain and make perpetual the then existing system of slavery. During the sad conflict its members maintained the same high standard of patriotism and made great sacrifices to preserve the Union.

The Old School enunciated the sentiments of the church, when on motion of Dr. Gardiner Spring it resolved: "That the members of this General Assembly, in the spirit of that Christian patriotism which the Scriptures enjoin, and which has always characterized this church, do hereby acknowledge and declare their obligation, so far as in them lies, to maintain the Constitution of these United States in the full exercise of all its legitimate powers, to preserve our beloved Union unimpaired, and to restore its inestimable blessings to every portion of the land." The vote stood one hundred and fifty-six in the affirmative to sixty-six in the negative. In justice to the limited number of the members from the free-labor States who voted in the negative, it should be stated that they were not disloyal to the Union, but they believed the church, as such, should act only on spiritual affairs, and not even by implication take part in those that were secular. The Southern members, then and afterward, almost universally held the extreme view of the church keeping itself aloof from acting on secular affairs. This may be inferred from the fact that in the minutes of their assemblies held during the Civil War allusion is scarcely ever made to that subject, though to all it must have been of absorbing interest.

The above resolution, with others of similar import, deeply offended the portion of the Old School branch within the slave-labor States. These members, accordingly, withdrew and formed "The Presbyterian Church in the Confederate States of America."

We have already seen (*p. 469*) the New-School Assembly, to a certain extent, freed by the secession of synods, from the continuous and bitter discussions of the question of slavery, and now the Old School experienced a similar relief. These discussions had been very disturbing in their influence, as they often produced harsh feelings because of misunderstandings arising from extreme views of both parties coming in collision and ignoring a middle course, that might not have compromised the church with the evil and yet could have consistently labored for its removal. It is better, if possible, to look at the question from the standpoint of the good and earnest men, who in that day confronted the evil face to face, than from the point of view taken after an experiment of thirty odd years.

A Change in the Mode of Conducting Missions.—Owing to the continual dissatisfaction in conducting missions on the voluntary or coöperative plan, the New School began to verge toward the *ex-officio* system. The Congregationalists, as we have seen (*p. 468*), had already given indications of their moving in the same direction. Their General Assembly of 1861, as an earnest of this change of policy, resolved "to assume the responsibility of conducting the work of home missions within its bounds;" which theory of action was declared to be in accordance "with the constitution of the church." In consequence, a permanent committee was appointed, "The Presbyterian Committee on Home Missions." The report of this committee to the next assembly made known the encouraging fact that the churches had promptly and liberally responded with their contributions to thus carry on the work. Notwithstanding the increasing dissatisfaction with the voluntary plan, the New School churches in great numbers still continued to contribute to the funds of the Home Missionary Society, which the same year (1862), "receipted for nearly forty thousand dollars from persons known to be Presbyterians or from churches connected with presbyteries, or places where there was known to be a Presbyterian church alone." (*Gillett, II., p. 562.*) From this fund, "or any considerable portion of it," because of certain rules—which could have been easily changed—"Presbyterian churches could derive no aid." The committee on ministerial education, it appears, had not been specially successful in its work owing to the coöperative plan, and in that case, too, it became necessary "to harmonize the plans and concentrate the energies of the church." Another distinct denominational effort was previously made in establishing in 1852 a board known as "The Presbyterian Publication Committee," which two years later was directed "to publish such works of an evangelical character as may be profitable to the church at large." The latter work languished so much as to attract attention, and in 1863 an appeal was made to the churches to furnish a fund of fifty thousand dollars, and they responding liberally, contributed the amount.

The Old School Unhindered.—While the New-School brethren were thus unfortunately trammeled, the Old School, free from such hindrances were vigorously prosecuting their work. The latter had the essential appliances for so doing, especially in their missions, foreign and domestic; they had also boards of ministerial education and of publication and church extension. The church in its individual capacity being harmonious in its management and not hindered by uncongenial combinations, went on in a quiet manner and in a moderate degree increased its membership by additions from the world. From 1858 to 1869 was a time of unparalleled turmoil in the Nation itself, including the special agitation preceding the Civil War, that itself, and the Reconstruction period. The influence of these for each special time, had a depressing effect upon the progress of spirituality in both churches and in the whole land. For several reasons the Old School held its own in the slave-labor States up to 1861 and was successful in its duties, while it was equally energetic in the different fields in the West and among the churches in the Northern States. From the division up to the time of firing on Sumter it had had peace within its borders, and was thus free to promote its appropriate work.

Emancipation—The Freedmen.—The Proclamation that freed the slaves, January 1, 1863, prepared the way for opening a vast field for domestic missions in aid of the freedmen. The latter would now be permitted, and even urged to learn to read and write, and have the gospel presented to them untrammeled by laws antagonistic to the principles of Christianity, as embodied in the Golden

Rule. Their future, even when their freedom was proclaimed, was under a cloud. The Presbyterian Church in both its branches, began as soon as the way was opened, to do its share in lifting that cloud, by means of self-denying missionaries and teachers, while the liberal contributions of its private members sustained the work. Here was a race emerging from a servitude lasting more than two hundred years, in which the cruelty of the bondage was enhanced by laws designed to keep the victims in a state of mental imbecility, by forbidding under severe penalties their being taught to read—a wanton outrage, unknown even to the slaveholders of ancient heathen Rome. When the conditions under which they have labored are considered, the progress of the freedmen since that time is simply marvelous, in almost every respect. Nor must we overlook the leaven of the gospel that in spite of such laws had been placed in the minds of these people by the limited means of oral instruction in the truths of Christianity, and which led them to believe that their deliverance would come from the *outside*, similar to that of the Israelites of old—in this respect their trust in Providence was marvelous. They themselves were passive; they were waiting for a Moses to lead them out. (*Four Hundred Years, etc., p. 966.*) To fully understand the difficulties in the way of the church, it must be recognized that this question had another side, one that involved economical principles which led to political action on the part of the National government and also within the several States. These measures in the minds of the Christian portion of the people gave tone to the moral aspects of the case, though that feature was apparently overlooked by a certain class of public men, who sneered at Christian statesmen as being of the "Sunday-school order."

Innovations Attempted.—We have seen that as soon as

the division was completed a desire for a change from the perfect presbyterial order began to manifest itself in the New-School branch. The innovation was first made in respect to the annual meetings of the General Assembly, which were hereafter to be *triennial*. The presbytery and the synod were left intact as to their legislative and disciplinary powers. The change to the triennial assemblies impaired the utility and the symmetry of the system of presbyterial oversight of the churches. Other changes were, also made. "Unfortunate in their leaders . . . they [the Presbyterian portion] allowed the project of modifying the Constitution of the Church to pass without opposition, only a few years later to repudiate their inconsiderate mistake by a prompt restoration of the 'Book' to its original integrity." (*G., II., p. 554.*) These respective changes can be traced directly to the influence of Congregationalism, that had been for a number of years creeping into the Presbyterian Church and for the most part produced the New-School phase of that body. It is consistent for an advocate of a polity that makes every church organization independent of all others, singly or combined, to oppose church judicatures that have legislative power, and on the other hand, to sanction a council that has only the *negative* authority of being advisory in its character.

From this independency of individual churches rose the voluntary missionary associations, but about 1852 and onward the theory that the church in its denominational capacity ought to carry on missionary work, began to prevail among Congregationalists, many of whom were members of churches in connection with the New-School Assembly, and who seemed to be preparing to follow the Connecticut Association, which in 1797 declared itself in almost so many words to be *ex-officio*, a missionary society. This sentiment culminated in 1852 at Albany, when the Congregational Convention repudiated the plan of union of which in 1837 they were such strenuous advocates. The result of this decision was the abandonment of the Presbyterian Churches that had hitherto contributed to the Home Missionary Society and in proportion depended upon it for the needed aid. These Presbyterian churches thus thrown upon their own resources withheld their contributions from that society and applied them to sustain their own churches.

Triennial Assemblies—Protests.—The experiment of triennial assemblies was continued up to the meeting in 1846 wherein the almost interminable discussion on the slavery question was protracted at intervals for three weeks, and in consequence an immense amount of routine and important business was left unfinished. Meantime, protests were coming in against the present system of triennial meetings and the anomalous *committee ad interim.* The protests came principally from the Western churches. They complained: "That in the absence of an annual assembly, our churches had been left for a longer time than formerly without the visible bond of unity and without the frequent supervision and control of the highest judicature of the church." The assembly of 1846, therefore, found it necessary, in consequence of the wants made known by these protests, to meet the following year, and designated Cincinnati as the place. This was the first instance of a General Assembly meeting outside the State of Pennsylvania. Once more it was thought best to meet triennially and that assembly resolved to meet in Detroit, Michigan, in 1850. The comparative utility and necessity for annual meetings made it plainly expedient to return to them, and thus the original custom was resumed after 1850 and continued to the reunion in 1870.

The Singular Results.—Owing to the secession of the

THE TWO ASSEMBLIES CONTINUED. 479

seven Southern synods in 1858 the minutes of 1860 of the New-School Assembly revealed a falling off of sixty-seven ministers and one hundred and forty-five churches, and about fifteen thousand communicants. From 1860 to 1869 its ministers increased in number three hundred and twenty-five, while its churches during the same time increased only one hundred and forty-nine. The minutes of the latter year show eighteen hundred and forty-eight ministers and sixteen hundred and thirty-one churches—*that is, two hundred and seventeen more ministers than churches*. In consequence of the secession of the "Presbyterian Church South" in 1861, it was shown by the minutes of 1863 that the Old School had lost six hundred and fifty-four ministers and eleven hundred and forty churches. In referring to the minutes we find that in 1863 to 1869 it increased in its ministers one hundred and seventy-six, and in its churches one hundred and ninety-four. The statistics of 1869 for that year show the total number of ministers to have been two thousand three hundred and eighty-one, and of churches two thousand seven hundred and forty—*that is, three hundred and fifty-two more churches than ministers*.

XLIX.

The Reunion.

Within a few years after the division took place great numbers of private members in both branches of the church began to look upon the separation as a misfortune to the cause and the progress of religion itself. These Presbyterians were willing and even desirous to let the harsh measures and bitter sayings of the past be forgotten and to mutually condone the mistakes that had been made by both parties. Such was, undoubtedly, the undercurrent of the sentiment of reconciliation that began to pervade the thoughts of that class of church members, who took note of the developments and the influences at work in both divisions of the church. The wish for a reunion thus had its origin, but that wish became a longing desire, so earnest and effective as, at length, to accomplish the hoped for end. The influence of fervent prayer and kindly sentiment reached both assemblies, and fraternal letters were interchanged, and when opportunity served they celebrated together the Lord's Supper.

Preparing for Reunion.—For several years previous to the outbreak of the Civil War certain causes and their influence were evidently preparing the way for a reunion. Perhaps the more striking of these were the contrasts in conducting missions—foreign and home. The Old School stood upon an independent basis, having all the appliances for the work, and these had been utilized to advantage ever since the division. The New School, on the other hand, was not so happy in effective work; it had no mission fields of its own, and was unable to act independently, since it was hampered by being in connection with the voluntary societies. The association with the American Board was comparatively pleasant, but even in that was more or less friction. The troubles with the Home Missionary Society had given those Presbyterians an earnest of the difficulties of conducting that particular phase of missions on the voluntary plan. These hindrances had taken a more decided form ever since the Albany Congregational Convention had in 1852 repudiated the plan of union, thereby manifesting a desire to discontinue the custom of conducting home missions in connection with the New-School body. This convention "brought Congregationalists East and West into a friendly acquaintance and sympathy, which had been lacking before." It resolved to discontinue the plan of union, giving as one reason for so doing, that "it had resulted in Presbyterianizing hundreds of churches, out of New England, which might otherwise have been—and which in right should have been—Congregational." (*Congregationalism, by Dexter, p. 516.*) Among others, a similar reason—only the very *reverse* in substance—was given when the General Assembly of 1837 abrogated the same plan (*p. 436*)—namely, that Presbyterian churches were often Congregationalized by means of the plan of union. This and similar measures induced the true Presbyterians—those who accepted the theology of their standards and their church polity—and who were thus situated, to cherish their desire of union with the other branch. Technical theological questions of former days were held in abeyance or deemed settled, while the differences that once loomed as very important, had now become non-essential in the minds of those who once were their most strenuous advocates.

The Civil War.—While these Presbyterians were in

this state of agitation came the Civil War. The exciting events connected with it drew aside the attention of the church members from the situation of the two branches, but toward its close we find the interest in reunion received a new impulse. This interest was indicated in the numerous letters that passed back and forth among the intelligent Presbyterians of both parties, who were in touch with the movements of the times—secular and religious. The matter was often a subject of prayer in church meetings, and was often alluded to in the religious papers, and sometimes discussed at length. These incidents prepared the minds of the church members of both branches to hail with joy the movements toward a reunion, for which so many were praying.

The unanimity with which the private members, with the elders and ministers of both branches, supported the National government in its efforts to maintain the Union intact, drew the parties together in sympathetic patriotism and from that standpoint the transition was easy for them to be drawn to still closer unity in church bonds, under one name and constitution.

Renewed Difficulties.—For a year or two after the close of the war the New-School brethren had difficulties similar to those which they had immediately preceding that event. In addition, that body was weakened by the withdrawal of some of its members, who took sides in theory at least with the Confederates, but in proportion this number was far inferior to that which withdrew for the same reason from the Old School. The New School, notwithstanding the excellent standing of its preachers and pastors and high scholarship of its professors, was relegated more than ever to a subordinate position in the management of the voluntary societies. The Congregationalists in exercising their inherent right were meanwhile becoming more decidedly denominational in their proceedings, especially in relation to the control of the Home Missionary Society, which had virtually become their recognized organ, rather than that of the combination of the New-School Presbyterians and themselves.

The Cry for Help.—As soon as the Rebellion collapsed the Presbyterian Church, now untrammeled, took note of the spiritual desolations of the country caused by the demoralizing influence of that dismal war. In addition to the wants of the feeble churches on the frontiers came the freedmen crying for help, and thus presenting a new field for domestic missionary enterprise, and to that sphere of usefulness the Northern Presbyterians were instinctively drawn. These peculiar and new circumstances suggested numerous reasons for the union of the branches of the church, that thus united they might pursue their appropriate work with redoubled energy, stimulated by a sense of Christian duty and the cheering hope of success.

The Committees on Reunion—The Basis.—The movement for reunion took a preliminary form in 1864 when a correspondence on the subject commenced and fraternal letters were exchanged; in 1866 both parties conjointly appointed a committee, which reported progress in 1867. The movement continued until 1868, when both the assemblies united in appointing a Committee of Conference on the reunion of the two branches, which was to report to the assemblies of the next year. This action was only the exponent of the desire for reunion that had grown up in the hearts of the great mass of the church members of both branches. The question had penetrated their inner life, as was evidenced by the prayers that they offered to the Master to bring about the reunion.

The two assemblies, the Old and the New School, met in New York City in May, 1869; the former in the Brick Church and the latter in the Church of the Covenant. The Committee of Conference appointed the previous year reported as follows: that it "shall be reunited as one Church under the name and style of the Presbyterian Church in the United States of America." . . . "The reunion shall be effected on the doctrinal and ecclesiastical basis of our common standards; the Scriptures of the Old and the New Testaments shall be acknowledged to be the inspired word of God and the only infallible rule of faith and practice; the Confession of Faith shall continue to be sincerely received and adopted as containing the system of doctrine taught in the Holy Scriptures; and the government and discipline of the Presbyterian Church in the United States shall be approved as containing the principles and rules of our polity."

The assemblies were to submit to their respective presbyteries the *Basis of Reunion;* the latter were required to meet on or before Oct. 15, 1869, to express their approval or disapproval, etc. Each presbytery was to transmit to the stated clerk of its assembly the result by the first day of November, 1869.

Statistics.—According to the minutes of 1869 the Old School had one hundred and forty-three presbyteries, two thousand three hundred and eighty-one ministers, two thousand seven hundred and forty-nine churches, and two hundred and fifty-eight thousand nine hundred and three communicants; the New School had one hundred and eight presbyteries, sixteen hundred and ninety-four ministers, fourteen hundred and seventy-nine churches, and one hundred and forty-three thousand six hundred and forty-five communicants.

The above numbers give in the aggregate the whole membership, at that time, of the united church, but as the synods and presbyteries of the two branches occupied the same territory and often overlapped one another, committees were appointed by the assembly of 1870 to adjust that difficulty. The several adjustments thus made, of necessity, diminished the number of the synods and also that of the presbyteries by blending them together. The report of these arrangements was made to the General Assembly of 1871. According to the minutes of that year we find that the number of synods was thirty-five and of presbyteries one hundred and sixty-seven; ministers, four thousand three hundred and forty-six; churches, four thousand six hundred and sixteen; communicants, four hundred and forty-five thousand three hundred and seventy-eight; admitted on examination, twenty-seven thousand seven hundred and seventy. The union was thus completed.

Woman's Work.—The assemblies of 1872 and 1873 were marked by no special measures; the machinery of the church being in perfect order its work prospered. The admissions to the church on examination during these two years were 55,456. The assembly of 1874 highly commended the "Woman's Missionary Associations," which had been formed within recent years, for their raising funds and promoting the cause, closing as follows: "There will be no watchword rallying a mightier force in all the land than that of *"woman's work for woman through the whole world."* This is, if we mistake not, the first notice given by the assembly of the movement thus auspiciously begun by Presbyterian women, and which thus inaugurated that very important phase of missionary effort. In this connection it is worthy of mention that the "Narrative" of the assembly of 1877 also uses the following language in allusion to "women's work." "The daughters, wives, and mothers of happy Christian homes are combining, all over the church, to give Christ and his love to all within their reach, and especially to the daughters of sorrow and of heathenism. . . . We rejoice in their good works and bid them God speed."

Proffered Fraternity—Sabbath Respected.—The General Assembly of 1875 received the report of a committee appointed the previous year to confer with a similar one from the "Assembly South." The design was "to secure closer fraternal relations between the two bodies." The committees met and discussed the subject very carefully. The report, after giving a summary of the discussions thus held, concludes in the following terms: "Your committee regrets that they were disappointed in their own personal desire as well as that of the whole church, which they represent, to establish fraternal relations with the Assembly South on terms of mutual confidence and respect, Christian honor and love." The report was accepted and the action of the commitee approved.

The General Assembly of 1876, that being the year of the Centennial Exposition, expressed its sentiments on the subject of the latter being closed on the Sabbath, saying in a resolution: "Recognizing the constant and bountiful goodness of God to the people of the United States during the first century of the National Independence, record with satisfaction the fact that the commissioners having the exhibition in charge have decided by an emphatic vote to close its gates on the Lord's day."

Synods Consolidated—The Discipline Revised.—The synods had so much increased that in numbers they ranged from six down to two in a single State. This increase was a matter of convenience in order to obviate the difficulties arising from the distance to be traveled by the delegates, since all the ministers and commissioned elders within their respective bounds were to meet in the synod in the same ratio as in the presbyteries. In response to overtures the General Assembly of 1881 took action on the subject, and passed an enabling act, directing the several synods in their respective States to be consolidated into one and bounded by the State lines. The synod was also made a representative body. The presbyteries took action promptly, as was enjoined by the assembly; the result appeared in the minutes of 1882, in which the number of synods reported was twenty-three, instead of thirty-eight in those of the previous year.

The subject of revision of the Book had been before two or three assemblies, and the report as to the action of the presbyteries upon the same having been adopted, the moderator of the assembly of 1884 formally announced that "The Revised Book of Discipline with the Revision of Chapter X. of the Form of Government, had been adopted, and were now a part of the Constitution of the Church."

Statistics of Spiritual Progress.—We may obtain a partial glimpse of the spiritual progress of the church for the time being by comparing four items in its history, say, for a period of ten years, namely, the increase of the number of communicants, and that of the admissions on examination; the attendance of Sunday-school scholars, and the amount of contributions. For illustration, the number of communicants, according to the minutes of the assembly of 1876, was 535,210, and in the same of 1886 it was 661,809.

The minutes of 1876 also show that during the previous year were admitted on examination 48,240, which number in the latter year began to diminish gradually till it became only 20,196 in 1878, as recorded in the minutes of 1879, in which year the number commenced to increase, and thus continued till it reached 51,177 in 1886. It is proper to note that during this period were held the Centennial Exposition, and also two Presidential elections. The interest taken in these two subjects, no doubt, interfered with the spiritual progress of the church members, and also allured the attention of the non-Christians from religious impressions. Again, a restful change came over the minds of the American people, when the long-continued anxiety and discussions in respect to financial affairs virtually came to an end on the resumption of specie payments on the first day of 1879—was not this disturbed state of mind to a certain extent a hindrance to the reception of religious impressions? Be that as it may, the fact remains that the admissions to the church from the world on examination during the following ecclesiastical year exceeded those of the previous one by nearly 7000.

On a similar line of illustration it is worthy of notice that during these ten years the increase in the attendance of Sunday-school scholars seemed to be *unaffected*, but was very uniform. In 1876 the attendance was 555,347, and in 1886 it was 743,518. In about the same ratio are the total contributions of the church in sustaining its various operations. In 1876 they were $9,810,223, in 1886 $10,502,331. These sums include all the benevolences of the church and congregational expenses. The progress of domestic and foreign missions and the number of missionaries employed increased in about the same ratio. It is not expedient in this connection to go into detail, and the reader is referred to the usual reports on the latter subjects.

Thus in the absence of more definite data we obtain a partial conception of the *inner Christian life* of the church members. This life is often modified adversely by certain conditions, such as financial and industrial troubles and political agitation, and it behooves all, especially Christians, for more is expected of them, to labor in such manner as to remedy that class of evils, which under our government can be done by honest and intelligent voting. In this respect the Christian must not shirk his duty as a citizen, for in proportion to his influence in his own immediate community he is as responsible for the performance of such duty as the highest official in the land.

THE REUNION.

The Presbyterian Centennial.—The General Assembly of 1886 at Minneapolis appointed a committee of arrangements for the centennial celebration of the organization of the first General Assembly, that of 1788. By resolution the churches, the presbyteries, and the synods were enjoined to collect facts of their respective histories, which were to be ready by the autumn meetings of the presbyteries and synods. They were to forward these historical publications "two copies to the stated clerk of the General Assembly, and to the Presbyterian Historical Society, respectively." Each of the boards of the church were directed to prepare a brief account of their "History and Outlook," and also during the years 1887-8, special contributions were to be made for the work of the church, as specified.

In addition, a fraternal letter was written to the General Assembly of the Southern Presbyterian Church, then in session in Augusta, Georgia, most cordially inviting their branch to unite with the Northern, in Philadelphia, in 1888, celebrating the centennial anniversary "of the organization of the General Assembly at Philadelphia in 1788 (*see p. 207*). A committee was also appointed to arrange the method and plan of such coöperation." Favorable replies having been received from the Southern Church, the assembly of 1887 took measures to have a programme of the celebration prepared, in which the subjects of the orations and the speakers of the same were mutually agreed upon and equally divided.

According to the programme laid down by the conference committees addresses appropriate to the occasion were made on May 24th by delegates from the Southern and the Northern branches of the church. These addresses were comprehensive in their scope, taking in the numerous phases of the great subject in hand. We have not room for even the headings of the topics discussed by the many speakers. The spirit of piety and a patriotism molded by Christian principles, that pervaded these addresses, cheered the hearts of those who heard them, and when published, their beneficent influence was recognized throughout the church. The display of genuine learning in treating these various subjects was grand, and may be taken as an indication of the scholarship and the training of the speakers, ministers as well as laymen. The Presbyterian polity stimulates intelligent Christian laymen to take an interest, and even diligently study the workings of the system, inasmuch as they are often called upon as representatives of the church members, to have a share in the discussions and actions of all the boards and the judicatures of the church.

Church Periodical—Seminaries.—The assembly of 1888, adopting the suggestions of the committee who had the matter in charge, established the magazine *The Church at Home and Abroad,* which was intended to supersede the other church periodicals, and of itself represent all the boards of the assembly.

This assembly, also, through its standing committee expressed itself as "glad to see that our seminaries, as especially shown by the reports of Princeton and Union, employ their students in active work in Sunday-schools and among the poor and neglected. Such practical engagement of time and effort must contribute largely toward a preparation for successful labor and properly balance the retirement of the class-room and cloister," or private study.

As an evidence of progress it was reported to the assembly of 1889 that the gifts of the church members for the support and spread of the gospel during a period of ten years, advanced from an average of $14.37 per member in 1879 to $17.75 in 1889—a gain of $3.38 per member or 23.5 per cent. Meantime "the purely benevolent contributions to our boards and like agencies of evangelism," have advanced from $3.39 per member in 1879 to $5.56 in 1889, a gain of $2.17 per member or 64 per cent."

Revision Desired.—The committee on methods of effecting revisions in the Confession of Faith and the Constitution of the Church, that was appointed by the assembly of 1887, and continued by the assemblies of 1888 and 1889, was now enlarged in 1890 and continued. The assembly of 1889 had sent down to the presbyteries an overture in the words: *First:* "Do you desire a revision of the Confession of Faith?" The answer was *yes* by 134 presbyteries out of 213. *Second:* "If so, in what respects, and to what extent?" The answer to the latter question opened up a wide range for discussion. In consequence of the differences of opinion on the subject expressed by the presbyteries, the assembly deemed it expedient to appoint a committee on revision of the Confession of Faith. This committee consisted of *fifteen* ministers and *ten* elders. It was enjoined to consider the answers to questions number *two*, and "formulate and report to the assembly of 1891, such alterations to the Confession of Faith as in their judgment may be deemed desirable." This committee was unable to make a full report to the assembly of 1891, which met in Detroit, and it, also, was continued.

The assembly of 1892 met in May of that year at Portland, Oregon. It adopted an official seal, and for a device "an open Bible upon a circular field."

This assembly took note of the disposition of the amounts of money paid by Congress to Roman Catholic schools for Indians. The latter, alone, having obtained in round numbers 400,000 dollars of the 600,000 appropriated for all the denominations combined (*Minutes, p. 45*). It also condemned the principle of the general government appropriating money to sectarian schools. It manifested much interest in the home missions pertaining to the mountaineers in Kentucky, Tennessee, and North Carolina, and the two Virginias. The committee on the Confession of Faith reported progress.

REV. EDWARD ROBINSON, D. D., LL. D.
(493-497.)

L.

PRESBYTERIAN WORTHIES.

Professor Edward Robinson, D.D., LL.D., son of Rev. William Robinson, was born in Southington, Connecticut, April 10, 1794, of Puritan ancestry, which in church affairs is traced back to 1636. His mother, Elizabeth Norton, a lady of fine education, was a sister of Professor Seth Norton of Hamilton College. On her dying bed she sent to her son Edward, who was absent, a characteristic message, urging him "to do as much good as he could in the world." His father was under the necessity of cultivating a farm, and during his boyhood Edward thus worked, and also for a while in a country store. In school he ranked high as a scholar, a devourer of books and of untiring industry in search of knowledge, manifesting in his boyhood characteristics for which he was afterward noted, sound moral principles, kindly disposition, cautiousness in his decisions and accuracy in his studies. We give an incident. When a boy away from home at school, great excitement arose because of the appearance of smallpox in the neighborhood; Edward obtained some of the virus of cow-pox, took it home, and successfully vaccinated the whole family.

We find him at the age of eighteen in the Freshman class in Hamilton College, where he soon took position at the head of his class in every branch of study. Graduating in four years, he commenced the study of law in 1817, but soon gave that up to accept a more congenial work of tutor in mathematics and Greek in Hamilton

College. Three years later, in 1821, he went to Andover, Mass., to superintend the publication of his first book, an edition of eleven books of the "Iliad." Here under the influence of Professor Moses Stuart he commenced the study of Hebrew in which his progress was so rapid that in less than a year and a half he was appointed instructor in Hebrew in the seminary, which position he filled for three years with great acceptance. During this period he studied theology and was licensed to preach, but afterward preferred to devote himself to sacred scholarship. Resigning his position in the seminary he sailed for Europe in order to perfect himself in his chosen studies. He spent nearly three years at Halle and Berlin in assiduous study. He had the privilege of numbering among his intimate friends eminent professors in these universities, such as Gesenius, Tholuck, and Roediger in Halle, and Ritter and Neander in Berlin. In 1828 he married Miss Therese Albertine Louise von Jacob, daughter of Professor von Jacob of the University of Halle. This lady already held a high position in the literary world of Germany because of her original writings and translations, especially of "Servian Popular Songs." In 1829 Dr. Robinson returned to the United States, and soon after was appointed Professor Extraordinary of Sacred Literature at Andover.

We will anticipate, somewhat, in the order of time. Dr. Robinson published a number of books in his line of study, whose titles we need not give. Of these the most important in their influence were the translation of the "Hebrew, Latin Lexicon" of Gesenius, and his own Greek "Lexicon of the New Testament." The former in a number of revised editions, the last in 1854, and the latter in 1850. The one was a boon to the students of Hebrew, and gave an increased impulse to that study in the theological seminaries of different Protestant denominations in the Union; while the other was equally influential in promoting the study of New Testament Greek. Meanwhile he published a "Greek Harmony of the Gospels," and also established the "Biblical Repository" in 1831, and afterward, in 1843, the "Bibliotheca Sacra." He himself, at first, writing a majority of the articles.

Dr. Robinson's theory was that, in order to obtain vividly the precise meaning of the Holy Scriptures, they must be studied in the tongues in which they were originally written. To do this properly required the knowledge and appreciation of the surroundings, natural and historical, amid which their authors wrote. His strong desire, therefore, was to raise the standard of Biblical learning to as high a grade as possible. As a teacher he was strenuous in having the lessons prepared carefully; to shirk such preparation was in his eyes not a venial offense. When a boy he chided a younger brother, who was idling at his study, with the remark: "That the loss of a minute is just so much loss of life." In recitations, he never took his class in regular order, but skipped here and there, and if any one asked to be excused for not being prepared he was sure to be called upon next day, and if he then made it evident that he had neglected his duty, he was quietly called upon at the the next recitation, and so on till he gave evidence that he had prepared himself properly.

After declining professorships elsewhere, Dr. Robinson accepted in 1837 that of Biblical Literature in Union Theological Seminary in New York City, then recently founded. This acceptance was with the understanding that after delivering a preliminary course of lectures he should have leave of absence to visit Palestine, in order, as he expressed it, "To collect materials for a systematic work on the physical and historical geography of the Holy Land." The results of these labors were published under the title, "Biblical Researches." They at once were accepted as a standard authority, and as such were quoted by French, German, American, and English authors; of the last, Dean Stanley is the most prominent. The dean in his work on "Sinai," says that he found only two statements in the "Researches" which subsequent investigation proved to be somewhat inaccurate.

The first edition was published simultaneously in Boston, London, and Halle in 1841—Mrs. Robinson having translated the work into German as its writing was finished. In 1852 Dr. Robinson revisited Palestine, and was thus enabled to bring out a revised edition in 1856. The publication of the "Biblical Researches" took the intelligent religious world by surprise, and directed the attention of Biblical scholars to the importance of the subject, and also enlisted in the same cause numbers of well read Christian laymen. The "Biblical Researches" had influence in suggesting the formation of three associations for the purpose of exploring Palestine—one in England, one in Germany, and one in the United States—the expenses are borne by the subscriptions of those interested in the cause. These associations—except the American—are still (1899) engaged in the work, which has already thrown so much light on portions of the Bible in the identification of the sites of places mentioned, as well as on the general topography of the Holy Land, Says an eminent writer: "Edward Robinson created out of nothing the study of Biblical geography." More work has been done in Biblical history since 1835 than in all the previous centuries combined." (*Study of Holy Scripture, p. 508.*)

The manifold benefits conferred upon the church at large, and especially upon the Presbyterian branch, by Dr. Robinson, were in two forms of influence—the one by means of his lexicons, giving a new impulse to the study of the Old and New Testaments in their original tongues; the other, by his Biblical researches, to the study of Bible history, by ascertaining the conditions under which it was written, and thus aiding in the elucidation of its truths, historical statements, and allusions.

Incessant labor impaired Dr. Robinson's strong constitution. He once said to the writer, whose privilege it was to be one of his pupils, "The continual pressure of work for years is wearing me out." On January 27, 1863, the Master called him home, in his sixty-ninth year.

Rev. Dr. Philip Lindsley richly deserves mention among the worthies of the Presbyterian Church. A native of New Jersey, of English Presbyterian ancestry, born December 21, 1786; a graduate of Princeton, 1804; studied theology, meanwhile engaged in teaching; was licensed to preach in 1810 by the presbytery of New Brunswick, and in 1817 was ordained *sine titulo* by the same authority. His unusually fine scholarship and aptness in giving instruction were recognized and appreciated by his first being appointed tutor in his *Alma Mater*, and then promoted to the Professorship of Languages (1813), and soon after elected Vice-president of the college; a vacancy having occurred, he was acting President for one year (1822).

During these intervening years he was twice elected to the Presidency of Transylvania University, Kentucky, and also virtually to that of the University of Ohio at Athens; and twice to that of Cumberland College, at Nashville, Tennessee, and twice elected President of Princeton, and refused to consider overtures in respect to the Presidency of Dickinson College.

Dr. Lindsley declined these honorable positions, especially the Presidency of his *Alma Mater*, that he might enter upon a new and very important sphere of usefulness in the Southwest. In that region, unfortunately, the conditions in respect to classical and the higher grades of education were such as to call for the aid of a man of high standing, both as to scholarship and to experience as an instructor.

At this point (1823) was again presented the claims of Cumberland College as an important center of influence —the latter phase of the subject induced Dr. Lindsley to visit the city of Nashville. After surveying the field he consented to enter it by accepting the Presidency of Cumberland College, whose corporate name was changed the following year to Nashville University.

In entering upon this important field of usefulness Dr. Lindsley's "purpose was to build up a great university that should be to the South and West what Harvard, Yale, and Princeton were to the North and East. His plans were large, his conceptions were noble, and he did his part to realize them—that he partially failed was no fault of his." We cannot in this connection go into detail, only to state that the promise of an ample endowment was never realized; yet notwithstanding this drawback, Dr. Lindsley labored on assiduously, and under the circumstances accomplished an immense amount of good on the line of a generous and liberal education, whose benign influence is felt to-day in the Southwest.

Nashville was then quite a center of Presbyterian influence. The culture and refinement of its leading citizens were proverbial, numbers of whom were thrifty merchants and others owned plantations further South. It was the capital of the State, and was also noted for its seminaries for the education of young women.

Dr. Lindsley was inaugurated President of the college with imposing ceremonies on January 12, 1825. His brilliant address on that occasion was regarded as eminently replete with judicious ideas suitable to the occasion and to the educational conditions of the times and in that section of the Union. Here for twenty-five years his great influence was extended by means of his numerous addresses, and his well-trained students who went forth from year to year. The members of the scholarly faculty of the university were of his own choosing, and under his inspiration they acted in sympathy with him in zealously promoting the cause of education and good morals among the students. Thus in that region was given an impulse to classical learning by raising its standard, and also to that of other departments of knowledge. In due time these influences reached the intelligent and the younger portions of both sexes of the citizens of that beautiful city.

The General Assembly of the church when in session in Philadelphia in 1834 by a unanimous vote chose Dr. Lindsley its moderator.

Dr. Lindsley saw just cause in the financial troubles to which the university was subjected to present his resignation as its President in October, 1850. He was afterward for three years professor of "Ecclesiastical Polity and Biblical Archæology" in the Presbyterian Theological Seminary at New Albany, Indiana. After retiring from the latter institution "the remaining two years of his life were spent chiefly in study, devotion, and intercourse with friends." The Master called him home suddenly on May 23, 1855, in his beloved Nashville, whither he had come as a commissioner to the General Assembly.

Rev. Charles Hodge, D.D., LL.D., born in Philadelphia, December 28, 1797; graduate of Princeton, 1815; professor of Theology in Princeton Seminary in 1822. Author of "Commentaries on Romans, Corinthians, and Ephesians." Founder of the *Princeton Review,* through which he exerted a great influence for good; every important movement in the religious world he carefully noticed and fairly criticized, commending cordially when he approved and condemning conscientiously when he did not; but by no means in an arbitrary manner, always giving his reasons as drawn from the storehouse of his learning. His influence over his students was almost unbounded.

He wrote among a number of other works "A Constitutional History of the Presbyterian Church in the United States," but the crowning and most elaborately constructed of his writings is his "Systematic Theology." The latter, the outcome of more than a half century of careful study and teaching in the class-room. He died June 19, 1878, at the close of an unbroken professorship of fifty-six years.

Rev. William Adams, D.D., LL.D., born in Colchester, Connecticut, in 1807; a graduate of Yale, 1827, and of Andover Theological Seminary, 1830. His father, Dr. John Adams, was principal of Phillips Academy, Andover, thus his youthful surroundings were of educated persons. After being a pastor, elsewhere, for some years, he was invited to New York City in 1834 to take charge of a Presbyterian church in Broome street, and afterward in 1853 he became pastor of the then recently formed church on Madison Square, where at this writing it is a power for usefulness under the ministry of Rev. Charles H. Parkhurst.

For forty years he was a most efficient pastor, being reckoned among "the foremost preachers of his time;" of progressive instincts, he was an earnest advocate of every good work; broad in his views, he took an interest in the affairs of both church and state. In 1852 he was moderator of the General Assembly of the New School branch, and afterward an earnest advocate of the reunion of the church in 1870. Innately courteous, he took his congregation into his confidence, and always treated them, even when discussing an abstract question, as though they knew as much as himself, and he was merely reminding them of the different phases of the subject in hand.

He was chosen President of Union Seminary in New York, and also appointed to the chair of sacred rhetoric in that institution in 1873. In which office and professorship, by his magnetism and sympathy with young men, he exerted a most beneficent influence over the students, and thus indirectly in the church. Says Professor Roswell D. Hitchcock: "The administration of Dr. Adams came upon us like a burst of sunshine. . . . The whole institution was toned up. Professors and students, equally and all, felt the magnetism of his courtly and stimulating presence. On all public occasions he was our ornament and pride. In all the dry details of our daily, weekly, and monthly routine of work he was a model of punctuality, precision, and thoroughness. He possessed in an eminent degree what I will venture to call the institutional instinct and habit. Of fifty years of signal service, the last seven had been the golden autumn of his life." The Master released him from his earthly labors, August 31, 1880, in the seventy-third year of his age. (*The Union Theological Seminary, pp. 87, 88.*)

Rev. Henry Boynton Smith, D.D., LL.D., was born in Portland, Maine, in 1815; a graduate of Bowdoin College, 1834; studied theology in Andover, Halle, and Berlin. Honored in Germany as a man of superior intellect and scholarship. While pastor in the vicinity he was instructor in Hebrew in Andover Seminary; then professor of Mental and Moral Philosophy in Amherst College; then, 1850, of Church History in Union Seminary, and afterward, in 1853, of Systematic Theology in the same institution. In the latter professorship he remained till his resignation because of impaired health, January, 1874; he was, however, made Professor Emeritus, and Lecturer on Apologetics.

It is worthy of note that the experience and knowledge derived, personally, in giving instruction in the class of subjects pertaining, respectively, to his previous professorships, were available as a preparation for that of theology. He was the author of several monographs, all of which related to history in its moral aspects, as applied to church matters and theology. "The historic spirit which characterized him has ever since been characteristic of Union Seminary." Unfortunately, his impaired health, and, we may say, premature death, precluded a consecutive and perfect summary of his views on these varied and important subjects, as molded by himself into a uniform system, He has been characterized "the gifted, learned, and inspiring teacher," "he had brilliant scholarship, a fervid and deeply spiritual nature, a gentle and winning disposition." His students could preach the theology which they learned from him. The theological views of Professor H. B. Smith are more quoted with approbation by theologians and pastors in the different evangelical denominations than those of any recent theological writer. Professor Archibald A. Hodge of Princeton "declared Professor H. B. Smith to be the greatest theologian of the American Presbyterian Church." (*Vol. VI., Ch. Hist., p. 130.*) He was released from his earthly labors February, 1877, in the sixty-second year of his age.

Rev. Robert Jefferson Breckinridge, D.D., born in 1800 in Kentucky; studied and practised law for some years. Meanwhile, a ruling elder in the Presbyterian Church, he turned his attention to theology, which he studied privately. Afterward, for thirteen years was pastor of the First Presbyterian Church in Baltimore. He took a prominent part in the division of the Church in 1837. (*See pp. 374, 387.*) President of Jefferson College (1845-1847), but notwithstanding his great mental ability, it was a sphere of labor for which he was not perfectly

REV. HENRY BOYNTON SMITH, D.D., LL.D.
(501, 502.)

qualified, simply because of his lack of experience in teaching. Then Professor of Theology in Danville Seminary (1853).

Nearly thirty years before the Civil War, when it required sterling courage to oppose the system of slavery in his native State, Dr. Breckinridge ever stood firm in his convictions of its enormous injustice to the slave and its injurious influence on the slave-owner, characterizing it as "utterly indefensible on every correct human principle, and utterly abhorrent from the law of God."

A strong Union man during the Civil War, he exerted a determined and commanding influence to preserve the integrity of the Nation. In duty bound, he took an intense interest in the public affairs of that trying period, especially in his native State. He was an influential member of the Republican Convention which nominated Mr. Lincoln for a second term. His crowning efforts for good, however, were made after the close of the Rebellion, when he became a most energetic and efficient advocate in aiding the National government to introduce the common school system into his native Kentucky, which, like the other slave-labor States, never had public schools similar to those within the free-labor States, until thus established.

Rev. William Greenough Thayer Shedd, D.D., LL.D., was born in Massachusetts, 1820; a graduate of the University of Vermont and of Andover Seminary; professor of English literature in his *Alma Mater;* then of Rhetoric and Pastoral Theology in Auburn Seminary; then of Ecclesiastical History in Andover, and when collegiate pastor with Dr. Gardiner Spring, of the historic Brick Church in New York, was elected in 1863 professor of Biblical Literature in Union Seminary of that city, and afterward, in 1874, transferred to the chair of Systematic Theology. In consequence of impaired health he retired from active duty, but was retained by the directors in the service of the institution as Professor Emeritus. His earthly labors were finished in 1894.

Dr. Shedd was the author of a number of valuable works, one of which was very important, "The History of Christian Doctrine," and last of all, "Systematic Theology." Says a writer: "As a theologian, Dr. Shedd is regarded as developing the sterner elements of Calvinism more fully than is common in recent years."

Dr. Shedd was a Calvinist of the extreme type and held rigidly at all points to that system. He was greatly admired and beloved by his students, his high character and kindly spirit commanding their respect and esteem, and his clear-cut logical style making his lectures always intellectually attractive, but the majority of those under his instructions found themselves unable to accept all his conclusions, though they never ceased to prize the valuable philosophical training he gave them.

Another class of Presbyterian worthies deserve a passing notice, because of their influence on the *inner Christian life* of the church. They are termed evangelists. Pastors have sometimes resigned their charges in order to engage in that form of work as a sphere of greater usefulness. To perform that class of duties properly requires in those who thus labor special qualifications; such as fervid piety, a marked familiarity with the Scriptures, that on the occasion they may promptly and aptly apply their truths and illustrations; practical wisdom and tact in conducting the services, especially in connection with settled pastors. Their efforts are often confined to a single church or neighborhood, and only for a limited time. One drawback occurs to these efforts, when they are not supplemented after the evangelist has departed by the continuous exertions of the church members themselves, and of the pastor. The labors of this class of ministers are very often blessed in a remarkable manner in leading sinners to the Saviour, and in stimulating Christian professors to greater zeal for the salvation of men.

We have room for the notice of only one of this class of worthies. Rev. Daniel Baker, D.D., who was blessed with a pious parentage, which very likely were Puritan (*see p. 276*), was born in Midway, Georgia, August 17, 1791. An entire Puritan congregation in 1754 moved from near Charleston, S. C., to Midway. He became a Christian at the age of fifteen. Dr. Moses Hoge urged him to study for the ministry. He entered Hampden-Sidney College in 1811, but afterward went to Princeton, where he graduated in 1815. When he first entered the latter institution only six of his fellow-students—about one hundred and fifty in number—were professing Christians; two of these he persuaded to join him in a daily prayer-meeting. They for a time were subjects of ridicule by some of their fellow-students, but ere long their prayers were answered, and a gracious outpouring of the Holy Spirit came in such power that in a revival which followed, about fifty of the students were brought to Christ; *twenty* of whom were afterward preachers of the gospel.

Mr. Baker studied theology and when licensed, began to preach with great fervor and with corresponding success in securing conversions from the world. Thus he labored for three or four years, having in charge two congregations in Virginia, but in 1822 he was installed pastor of the Second Presbyterian Church in Washington City. Among the prominent men who attended his church were Presidents John Quincy Adams and Andrew Jackson; they both encouraged and cheered the young clergyman with many marks of their appreciation. Great pressure induced him to remove from Washington to Savannah, Georgia, and become pastor of an independent Presbyterian church in that city. Here his labors were marvelously blessed, his congregation, numbering about fifteen hundred, appeared to enjoy an almost continuous revival. Dr. Baker has been characterized as a "man of one book—the Bible; one idea, the salvation of souls, and one occupation, the proclamation of the gospel." Moved by the impression that it was his duty to give his services to the church at large, as an evangelist, he resigned his pastorate in 1826, in order to devote himself to that phase of Christian work.

Dr. Baker was remarkably judicious in his treatment of the non-professors as well of the professors of religion. Numerous instances are recorded of his tact in meeting questions that were sometimes put to him, perhaps, with a tinge of irony. Once a lady, a great favorite in society, because of her attractiveness and accomplishments, but not a Christian, *twitted* him with being partial in holding special meetings for his *dear members,* but not, said she, for us *poor sinners*. He promptly answered, "Suppose I call a meeting for you poor sinners; would you come?" "Yes I will," was the prompt reply. The following Sabbath he announced a meeting for the unconverted, *alone*. Having spent in prayer the forenoon of the day appointed for the meeting, what was his surprise when he reached the lecture-room to find it crowded! The outcome was many conversions, among whom was the lady who spoke to him on the subject. On another occasion, when making an appeal for missions in Texas, one man in his presence remarked, "I can give five dollars, and not feel it." Dr. Baker said to him: "Suppose, my brother, you give twenty dollars and feel it. Your Saviour felt what he did for you." The man was ever after a liberal giver.

In his preaching tours he traveled extensively in the Northern and also in the Western States, and was listened to by thousands upon thousands in the churches of all evangelical denominations, and his labors were wonderfully blessed. He labored specially for some years in Kentucky and in Mississippi; but his greatest work was done within the recently formed republic of Texas; thither he went in 1838, and therein he labored to the end. The peculiar circumstances under which that republic had originated attracted him thither as a very important field of usefulness. He assisted in constituting the Presbytery of Brazos (1840), the first in that region, and before Texas was annexed to the United States.

This presbytery, in the line of its traditions, resolved to found a college that should be under Presbyterian influence. It imposed upon Dr. Baker the labor of obtaining funds for that purpose, and the result was the founding of the present flourishing institution known as Austin College. He made six separate tours in portions of the Southern and of Northern States, appealing principally to Presbyterians for funds, but preaching whenever he had an opportunity. It is estimated that on his last tour which extended for eight months, *seven hundred* persons were led to accept the Saviour; their first convictions being induced by his eloquent presentation of the plan of salvation.

He had directed that his epitaph should be "A preacher of the gospel—a sinner saved by grace." The end came December, 1857. When the news of his death reached the State capital the Legislature was in session, and at once both branches adjourned out of respect to his memory, and to hear eulogies on his patriotic and Christian character, while the citizens of the capital exhibited equally their sympathy in the loss the people of the State had sustained.

Rev. Henry Little, D.D., takes rank, virtually as an evangelist, but also more especially as a superintendent of Home Missions. He was born March 30, 1800, in Boscawen, New Hampshire; the son of a farmer, he labored as such in his early life, but in his boyish days had a desire to become a minister. His religious life seems to have commenced when he was quite young, and during his youth and upward was remarkable for his active Christian work and the good influence which he exerted over his friends and college-mates. He inherited a vigorous constitution from his stalwart Puritan ancestry, and which was strengthened in his youth by healthful labor and exercise in a bracing climate amid the hills of his native State. An active and temperate mode of living in after years preserved his health and prolonged his life to beyond four score.

At the age of seventeen he began to teach school during the winter months, and at twenty commenced to prepare for college; graduated in 1826 at Dartmouth, the second in scholarship in a class of thirty-six; studied theology at Andover, was licensed to preach, and afterward ordained in 1829 in Park Street Church, Boston, with *fifteen* other young men, all of whom designed to become missionaries, either in their native land or in the foreign field.

Having spent one year as agent for the American Educational Society, we find him in 1831 pastor of the Presbyterian church in Oxford, Ohio, the seat of Miami University. Modest and unassuming, yet energetic in the performance of duty, his symmetrical character as preacher and pastor elicited the admiration of all, and the love of those who knew him more intimately. Says Rev. Dr. D. W. Fisher: "I doubt whether a more useful minister of the gospel has lived in our country during the period covered by his [ministerial] life, but of what he had done he seldom spoke, unless he was compelled to do so by some direct inquiry."

Dr. Little was most earnestly urged by the officers

and friends of the American Home Missionary Society to become their Western Secretary or agent. This position he accepted and entered upon its duties in April, 1833. To the labors of this office he devoted all his energies and with great success in that very important field of mission work. For twenty-eight years he thus labored, till 1869, when he became connected with the Presbyterian Board of Home Missions. With that organization he was connected for thirteen years, when the Master called him home on February 25, 1882, in his eighty-third year.

We of this day have only a faint conception of the difficulties which at that time had to be overcome in superintending a field of missions, so vast as to include the States in the peninsula between the rivers Ohio and Mississippi; Kentucky and Tennessee on the south and Missouri on the West. Dr. Little traveled from place to place, often preaching by the way, over this extensive territory wherever he was specially needed in directing the work.

Changes manifestly for the better in the material and moral condition of the inhabitants of these States had been going on for a generation or more (*pp. 377, 378*) when Dr. Little entered upon his life's work. Owing to better facilities for travel and transportation an unusual impulse had already been given to migrations of many thousands annually from the older States to the great Central valley. These energetic and progressive Americans, mostly young married people, had been accustomed in their native homes to churches and common schools, all of which they had left to found settlements and homes for themselves and their families in this land of promise. There were also others who came in untold multitudes from foreign lands; some ignorant of the Bible and priest-ridden, others speaking a different language, and with views more or less antagonistic, especially to the American mode of Sabbath observance, and indeed often to the Christian institutions of the land. His work, through the ministry of the gospel by means of home missions, was to mould this miscellaneous crowd of foreigners and native born into a homogeneous Christian civilization. As a collateral sphere of influence and usefulness, he was a sturdy friend of the common schools, which he also labored to introduce and to elevate their standard of scholarship.

For more than a half a century, even unto the end of his life, Dr. Little was blessed with a most devoted wife—Susan Norton Smith—who was finely educated and refined, and who entered heart and soul into all his plans and sustained him in his years of toil. At his death, of his eight children, he bequeathed to the church four of his sons as ministers and one daughter, the wife a clergyman.

LI.

THE TRIALS OF PROFESSOR CHARLES A. BRIGGS.

The author enters with many misgivings upon the narrative of the several ecclesiastical trials of Dr. Briggs; he realizes the unusual difficulties that present themselves in treating the subject and its several phases in such manner as to satisfy all parties. It is designed to give concisely the salient and essential points of the charges made and in a similar manner the replies thereto. The reader will please notice that when quotations are given, reference is made to the page whence taken, that their *accuracy* may be verified. The design has also been to make the narrative as concise as truth and justice would permit. The memory of these trials still lingers in the minds of those private members of the Presbyterian Church and likewise of many outsiders, who at the time took an intelligent interest in the several proceedings; scanned the charges and the arguments used to sustain them, and also the replies thereto, of the Professor, and thus they became able to form definite opinions on the subject.

In respect to the various charges and specifications connected therewith, and the discussions of the doctrines involved, and also Scriptural interpretation, the author has endeavored to be concise, though not at the expense of clearness. It is noteworthy that these trials, because of the questions thus brought into notice, elicited unusual attention in Christian circles, which continues at this writing, not merely among intelligent members of the Presbyterian Church, but likewise among the similar class in other denominations—all being equally and deeply interested in the interpretation of the Bible.

The Professorship Founded.—The late Charles Butler, LL.D., a highly respected and benevolent gentleman of New York City, and President of the Board of Directors of Union Theological Seminary, donated $100,000 to found a professorship of Biblical Theology in that institution. This was named the Edward Robinson professorship in honor of that eminent Biblical scholar.

The Outline of Study.—The course of studies to be pursued in that professorship was distinctive, and may be partially learned from the following brief outline. "Biblical theology takes a comprehensive grasp of the Bible as a whole in the unity and variety of the sum of its teachings . . . aiming to limit itself to the theology of the Bible itself—the only infallible authority." Again, "Biblical theology makes no selection of texts—it uses the entire Bible in all its passages, and in every single passage, giving each its place and importance in the unfolding of divine revelation. To Biblical theology the Bible is a mine of untold wealth; treasures new and old are in its storehouses; all its avenues lead in one way or another to the presence of the living God and the Divine Saviour." (*Professor Briggs' Inaugural, pp. 5, 6.*)

The future outcome on that line of study is summed up by the professor as follows: "The Apostolic theology will be traced from its origin at Pentecost in its subsequent division into the great types, the conservative Jewish Christian of Saint James and the advanced Jewish Christian of Saint Peter; the Gentile Christian of Saint Paul and the Hellenistic of the Epistle to the Hebrews; and, finally, the Johannine of the Gospel, Epistles, and Apocalypse of John; and the whole will be considered, in the unity of the New Testament. As the last thing the whole Bible will be considered showing not only the unity of the Theology of Christ and His apostles, but also the unity of the Theology of Moses and David and all the prophets with the Theology of Jesus and His apostles, as each distinct theology takes its place in the advancing system of divine revelation, all conspiring to the completion of a perfect, harmonious, symmetrical organism, the infallible expression of God's will, character, and being to His favored children." (*Study of Holy Scripture, p. 606.*) On this line of interpreting the teachings of the word of God, Professor Briggs had been giving instruction for a number of years, and he was accordingly *transferred* to the new professorship by the directors, November 11, 1890.

The Inaugural—Action Thereon.—On the occasion of his entering upon his assigned duties (January 20, 1891) Professor Briggs delivered an inaugural address, and to some of the expressions and sentiments contained therein certain parties took exceptions. In consequence, the Presbytery of New York, on motion (April 13, 1891) appointed a committee, "to which the said address (the inaugural) was referred for consideration, with instructions to report at the meeting in May, what action, if any, be appropriate thereto." This committee reported to the Presbytery, May 11, 1891, and thereupon it was "*Resolved,* that a committee be appointed to arrange and prepare the necessary proceedings appropriate in the case of Dr. Briggs." This committee, consisting of three ministers and two elders, then became the prosecuting committee. The hearing of the case, however, was postponed to the meeting of the presbytery in the autumn. The following ministers and elders constituted the prosecuting committee: Rev. Drs. George W. F. Birch, Joseph J. Lampe, and Robert F. Sample; Elders John J. Stevenson and John J. McCook. Dr. Sample took no part publicly in the action of the committee.

At this point in the proceedings of these trials it is due truth and justice that the reader's attention be directed to certain influences that had been operating within the church for two or three years. These influences were the legitimate outgrowth of a series of articles published in a certain newspaper and which were systematically sent *gratis* in untold numbers to the leading ministers and elders of the church, especially west of the Alleghanies. These articles were published previous to the meeting of the General Assembly at Detroit, in 1891, but after that body took action on the subject they virtually ceased.

In illustration we give the following extract from "The History of Union Theological Seminary," by Professor George L. Prentiss (*pp. 182, 183*).

"The leading secular journals of New York watched the case with the greatest interest and furnished the public with a vast amount of information on all its successive phases. . . . For the most part they were impartial and eager to get at and to tell the truth, the whole truth and, so far as the infirmities of human nature in the matter of news would permit, nothing but the truth. One of them, however, 'the leading evening paper,' was an exception. Its proprietor at that time, who was said to be also the author of some of its sharpest editorials on the subject, was one of the most estimable men in New York; kind-hearted, generous, and full of varied Christian activity; but his zeal for Presbyterian orthodoxy was not at all according to knowledge—Dr. Briggs was to him a *bête noire*, and 'higher criticism' another name for downright infidelity. The editorials on these subjects were laden with the wildest sort of personal abuse and denunciation. They were just what for the honor of fair and truthful journalism they should not have been. Dr. Briggs, his colleagues and friends, Union Seminary and its Board of Directors, day after day, and month after month, were stigmatized in frenzied assaults of blind passion and calumny. And yet this paper was sent far and wide to ministers and elders of the Presbyterian Church in countless numbers, renewing old theological prejudices and sowing the seeds of new ones. As a faithful historian of Union Seminary I have felt bound to refer to this painful instance and illustration of the kind of warfare which it had to endure."

In this connection the following incident may not be lacking in interest for the reader. It is a general rule that writers employed on newspapers are required to prepare articles which in their influence do not antagonize, but rather reflect the notions and wishes of the proprietor; to follow out his suggestions and conform to his directions. It was because of this rule that two of the journalists employed at that time on the newspaper mentioned above afterward came to Dr. Briggs and, explaining the circumstances in which they were placed, expressed their deep regret that they had been instrumental in thus inflicting upon him a great wrong.

The General Assembly of 1891 met at Detroit, Michigan, and to it came sixty-three overtures from presbyteries asking that action be taken in relation to the "utterances of Professor Charles A. Briggs." In accordance with the evident desire implied in these overtures, the assembly resolved: "That in the exercise of its rights to veto the appointments of professors in the seminaries, the General Assembly hereby disapproves of the appointment of Rev. Charles A. Briggs to the Edward Robinson professorship in Union Theological Seminary."

First Trial of Dr. Briggs.—Four months after this action of the assembly the matter came before the Presbytery of New York, October 15, 1891, when the prosecuting committee presented their charges in pamphlet form. In order to give Professor Briggs an opportunity "to plead to the charges and specification," thus placed in his hands, the hearing was postponed to a meeting of the presbytery to be held on November 4th. The presbytery at this meeting heard the case. In order that the members might follow the argument, they had in their hands printed copies of the charges and specifications of the prosecuting committee, and also copies of the inaugural, and of the response to the above charges made by Professor Briggs. The Professor was heard in his defense. The presbytery, however, thought proper after hearing the "response to the charges" to exercise its right, and in so doing it dismissed the case. The vote stood ninety-four to thirty-nine—in the affirmative, seventy-one ministers and twenty-three elders; in the negative, twenty-seven ministers and twelve elders.

The presbytery adopted the following: *"Resolved, that the Presbytery of New York, having listened to the paper of the Rev. Charles A. Briggs, D.D., in the case, etc., . . . and without approving of the positions stated in his inaugural address, at the same time desiring earnestly the peace and quiet of the church, and in view of the declarations made by Dr. Briggs touching his loyalty to the Holy Scriptures and the Westminster standards, and his disclaimers of interpretations put on some of his words, deems it best to dismiss the case, and hereby does so dismiss it."* (*Minutes of the Presbytery.*)

In consequence of this action of the presbytery the prosecuting committee appealed to the General Assembly which met the following May (1892) at Portland, Oregon. When the appeal came before the assembly it was sustained, and the decision of the Presbytery of New York, in dismissing the case, was reversed, and that judicatory was directed to prosecute the trial. This assembly took action only on the appeal, and did not enter upon the merits of the case, but directed a new trial.

The Second and Exhaustive Trial of Dr. Briggs.— This trial covers the entire ground, as in the one held afterward, before the General Assembly of 1893, the same arguments were virtually presented and replied to in like manner. In accordance with the direction of the assembly, as mentioned above, the Presbytery of New York at its regular session, October 3, 1892, took preliminary action in relation to a *second* trial of Dr. Briggs. The respective parties in the case were notified to be in readiness at a special meeting of the presbytery, on November 9, 1892.

This trial was exhaustive in its various details. It commenced on the day named, November 9, 1892, in conducting it the presbytery, as time and convenience permitted, occupied about *twenty* days, and sometimes two sessions a day. The final report was made on January 9, 1893.

That the reader may have an idea of the facilities for obtaining information on the subject in hand, by the presbytery, when sitting as a court, a few facts are adduced. In the hands of each member of the presbytery— one of the most scholarly in the church—when acting as a court on this occasion were printed copies of the inaugural address, on whose doctrine the charges were based. Dr. John J. McCook, in his argument in behalf of the prosecuting committee before the assembly of 1893, says: "The trial is based upon the doctrines of the inaugural address, and upon those doctrines of the inaugural address which are alleged to be offenses against Presbyterian doctrine. (*The Appeal in the Briggs Heresy Case, p. 372.*) This statement implied that criticisms should be confined to the inaugural alone.

In this, the most complete trial in the series, there were in the hands of each member of the presbytery printed copies of the inaugural, the charges themselves, the response of Dr. Briggs to the said charges, the committee's *second* pamphlet in reply to Dr. Briggs's criticisms on its *first*, and also its "amended charges and specifications, etc., and other documents bearing on the subject.

Reason as an Authority.—In the inaugural (*p. 24*) occurs the following: "There are historically three great fountains of divine authority—the Bible, the Church, and the Reason." The prosecuting committee inferred that the inaugural in this sentence: "Coördinated the Church and Reason with the Bible;" that is, to use their own words: "Making the Church and the Reason, each to be independent and sufficient fountain of divine authority." This assumption the Professor repudiated strenuously. *First,* because it was untrue; and *second,* because it was an inference of the committee. In respect to the latter, he cited as an authoritative precedent the ruling of the General Assembly of 1824 (*see p. 403*), in relation to admitting *inferences* as arguments. That ruling says: "No one can tell in what sense an ambiguous expression is used but the speaker or writer, and he has a right to explain himself. . . . Another principle is, that no man can rightly be convicted of heresy by inference or implication . . . it is not right to charge any man with an opinion which he disavows."

The Professor states that though the church and reason are fountains in the sense of *means or mediums* of divine authority, they both are fallible, but on the other hand, "the Scriptures of the Old and New Testaments are the only infallible rule of faith and practice." On the second page following the one from which the objectionable sentence is quoted, the inaugural has this passage which shows the sense in which he used the word "fountain." It seems strange that the gist of the following incidental and clear definition of the sense in which Dr.

Briggs used the above word was *unfortunately* overlooked by the committee. Thus he says: "Another *means* used by God to make himself known is the forms of the reason, using reason in a broad sense to embrace the metaphysical categories, the conscience and the religious feeling. Here in the Holy of Holies of human nature, God presents Himself to those who seek Him." (*Inaugural, p. 26.*) Again, "Unless God's authority is discerned in the forms of the reason there is no ground upon which any of the heathen could ever have been saved, for they knew nothing of Bible or Church. . . . Unless God's authority works in the forms of the reason we cannot explain 'the inward work of the Holy Spirit, bearing witness by and with the Word, in our hearts,' or 'the testimony of the spirit of adoption,' witnessing 'with our spirits that we are the children of God.' 'It is impossible that the Bible and the Church should ever exert their full power until the human reason, trained and strained to the utmost, rise to the heights of its energies and reach forth after God and His Christ with absolute devotion and self-renouncing love.'" These passages, quoted from the inaugural, were not *elicited* as explanatory in reply to a charge of the committee, but were used in an appropriate connection, and therefore the more significant. (*Inaugural, p. 66; App. thereto, 88, 89. Con. Faith, I., 5; XVIII., 2.*)

The reason used as a *means* can only be made available in its exercise, and that implies the freedom of choice. Our first parents in the Garden of Eden had that freedom, when they chose to disobey the command of God, and as such they were held responsible. The same principle is inherent in the souls of their descendants. Abraham reasoned when he chose to accept the call of God, or else he was a mental and moral machine, and thus devoid of responsibility. Joshua urged the Israelites, saying:

"Choose ye this day whom ye will serve." Could they thus choose without exercising their reason? The same principle runs through the New Testament from beginning to end; "whosoever *believeth* in him shall not perish but have everlasting life." Thus believing is choosing, and therefore exercising reason.

The Stress on Reason.—In these trials the prosecuting committee seemed to lay special stress upon the "utterances" of Professor Briggs in respect to the reason or the church as a *means or fountain* of divine authority. In more fully expressing his views on this subject Professor Briggs said: "I do not mean that there is any original divine authority in the human reason, or that there is any original divine authority in the Christian Church, but simply that they are channels, fountains, media, through which God's Holy Spirit speaks to men. . . . I use fountain not in the sense of the original source, because, as I have said, God alone is the original source." . . . The church and reason must yield to the Supreme Judge, the Holy Spirit, when speaking in Holy Scripture. I have not exalted the reason over the Bible. I am no rationalist." The charges were elaborately discussed by three members of the committee, to whose arguments, sometimes traversing the same charges, the Professor made answer *seriatim*. He contended that great numbers of the citations from the Scriptures made by the committee were irrelevant to the case, and that the others, when properly interpreted, did not invalidate his position. He also urged that the committee directed their objections specially against *their own interpretation* of words and phrases in isolated passages in the inaugural, and in consequence their arguments were defective, since they were leveled at illegitimate inferences rather than explicit statements. He likewise directed attention to the fact that the inaugural was very much condensed in its subject matter—which covered a large field—and that it was addressed to an audience of educated men, who were at once able to recognize the line of thought and illustration. Owing to these facts the inaugural was liable to be misinterpreted; and he complained of misleading statements in respect to its sentiments that had been sent broadcast throughout the church.

The Pentateuch and Isaiah.—We are much limited as to space, and in consequence we state concisely the charges, and in the same manner the replies thereto—but we hope clearly. That this should be done is due to truth and justice, and equally so to the private members of the church.

Some of the charges as presented may appear to the lay mind as involving veritable heresy. For instance, the opinion that Moses did not write the Pentateuch; and that Isaiah was not the author of more than half the book that bears his name. This was only a matter of opinion on the part of Dr. Briggs, and which he did not deem *an offense* against the standards of the church any more than the opinions held to-day by orthodox theologians as to who wrote the book of Job, or who was the author of the Epistle to the Hebrews. These opinions had, through certain of the press and otherwise, been so presented that great numbers of private members of the church were startled at a theory so contrary to their own notions on the subject that they received an impression that Dr. Briggs repudiated the Pentateuch, as if it were not Scripture given by inspiration. These are, however, the words of Professor Briggs: "Though Moses be not the author of the Pentateuch, yet Mosaic history, Mosaic institutions, and Mosaic legislation lie at the base of all the original documents, and the name of Moses pervades the Pentateuch as a sweet fragrance, and binds the whole together with irresistible attraction into an organism of divine law. . . . I firmly believe the Pentateuch one of the books of Holy Scripture, having divine authority, and as I have always taught, one of those Holy Scriptures which constitute 'the only infallible rule of Faith and Practice.'" Again: "Though Isaiah did not write half the book which bears his name, yet I firmly believe that holy prophets no less inspired than Isaiah wrote the greater half of the book under the guidance of the Divine Spirit, so that the book with different authors is as truly one of the books of Holy Scripture as if it were written by Isaiah alone." (*Response, p. 21.*)

"The great mass of the Old Testament was written by authors whose names or connection with their writings are lost in oblivion. . . . We desire to know whether the Bible came from God, and it is not of any great importance that we should know the names of those worthies chosen by God to mediate his revelation. It is possible that there is a providential purpose in the withholding of these names in order that men might have no excuse for building on human authority, and so should be forced to resort to divine authority." (*Inaugural, p. 33.*) In confirmation of his opinion he adduces the Confession of Faith, Chap. I., Sec. 4: "The authority of Holy Scripture, for which it ought to be believed and obeyed, dependeth not upon the testimony of any man or church, but wholly upon God (who is truth itself), the author thereof; and therefore it is to be received, because it is the word of God." Again: "All that we need to know, all that any Presbyterian ever subscribes to is that the Scriptures 'are the only infallible rule of faith and practice.'" (*Inaugural, p. 27, Third edition.*) "I affirm that I have never anywhere, or at any time, made any statements or taught any doctrines that in the slightest degree impair the above doctrine. . . . I yield to no one in reverence for the Bible. My life is devoted to the study of the Bible. Every word, every syllable, ever letter receives reverent and careful handling." (*Response, p. 20; Appendix, p. 91.*)

Progressive Sanctification after Death.—The intimations in the Scriptures that the redeemed in the Middle or Intermediate State take an interest in the spiritual affairs of the souls of men yet living on the earth, has directed especial attention to that subject, and also to the inference that such loving interest on the part of the saints in that state indicates progress in holiness and knowledge. Moses and Elijah manifested that interest when on the Mount of Transfiguration they "spake of His decease which he was about to accomplish at Jerusalem"—whereby an atonement was to be made for human sin. Our Lord said: "There shall be joy in heaven over one sinner that repenteth," and even Dives, in the parable, pleads in behalf of his brethren yet living.

The committee charged Professor Briggs "with teaching that sanctification is not complete at death"—that is it was not perfected—and it laid great stress on the charge "as contrary to the standards of the church." The committee cited as proof the answer to Question 37 of the Shorter Catechism, which says: "The souls of believers are at their death made perfect in holiness, and do immediately pass into glory." The question may be asked, Did the Westminster divines use the word *perfect* in this connection in an *absolute* sense, or intend it to be thus understood? Did they not use the term rather in the sense of a perfect *germ* of holiness; that is, as an element which is susceptible of being developed into a state of holiness that increases and becomes more and more assimilated to God in character. That they used the term in the latter sense is evident from their use of it in other connections. Such outcome would be consistent with the progressive nature of the soul itself, as an ever-active, spiritual, moral, and intellectual being; and more especially when freed from the infirmities of the body. On the contrary, if the souls of the redeemed are at death made *absolutely perfect* in holiness, in that respect they would remain stationary throughout the intermediate state, for being already *perfect* there could be no further progress.

"At their death," does not necessarily imply "in the very moment of the transition from life to death . . . but is in antithesis with, in this life," and means nothing more than "in the state of death." "Made perfect in holiness" does not necessarily imply "that sanctification of the soul is instantaneously perfected and completed, in the moment of time after it leaves the body," but is consistant with the belief that the soul is made perfect in holiness "in the state of death," in accordance with the answer to Question 86, L. C.: "The communion in glory with Christ, which the members of the invisible church enjoy immediately after death, is in that their souls are *then made perfect in holiness,* and received into the highest heavens, where they behold the face of God in light and glory." "Is that communion limited to the moment of time at death? Does it not rather continue during the whole time in that state, beginning immediately after death?" (*Condensed from Defense, pp. 151-153.*)

Professor Briggs holds the doctrine of the progress of the soul in holiness in this life, according to the Confession of Faith as presented in the answer to the thirty-fifth question of Shorter Catechism, which says: "Sanctification"—or making holy—"is a work of God's grace whereby we are renewed in the whole man after the image of God, and are enabled *more and more* to die unto sin and live unto righteousness."

Dr. Birch, in behalf of the committee, argued that "all

dead Christians are asleep. When we are asleep we show the rest which consists in the inaction of mind and body. But all the Christians, both dead and living, must be changed; and why the dead Christians should be compelled to go through the process of sanctification in the Middle State, while living Christians are the subjects of immediate sanctification, I cannot imagine. (*Argument, p. 62.*)

Dr. Briggs holds that this progress in sanctification or holiness *continues* in the Middle State, and contends that "the doctrine of immediate sanctification at death dishonors Jesus Christ, for it confines His heavenly reign and meditation to the Church in this world."

"Regeneration is an act of God, and from its very idea is instantaneous, for it is the production of a new life in man. Regeneration is one of the terms used in the New Testament to describe this beginning of Christian life. But sanctification is the growth of that life from birth to full manhood into the likeness of Christ. It is in this world a growth; it is incomplete with the best of men at death. . . . Believers who enter the Middle State, enter guiltless; they are pardoned and justified; they are mantled in the blood and righteousness of Christ; nothing will be able to separate them from His love. . . . But, above all, Christ is a king in the intermediate state. Here in this world His reign is only partial; there it is complete. Here His kingdom is interwoven with the kingdom of darkness; there it is apart from all evil and hindrance. His reign is entire over His saints, and they are being prepared by Him for the advent, in which they will come with Him to reign over the world." (*Inaugural Appendix, pp. 106, 107, 110.*)

The Soul in the Middle State.—In proof that his belief was in accordance with that taught in the standards of the church, Dr. Briggs cited what is said of the condition of the soul in the Middle State, when "in communion in glory with Christ." Question 86, Larger Catechism: "The communion in glory with Christ, which the members of the invisible church enjoy immediately after death, is in that their souls are then made perfect in holiness and received into the highest heavens, where they behold the face of God in light and glory, waiting for the full redemption of their bodies." The professor refers to the group of questions and answers in the Larger Catechism (82-90), which treat of the communion of saints in glory with Christ in the Middle State, and to Chapter XIII. of the Confession. He sums up by saying: "There is no authority in the Scriptures or in the creeds of Christendom for the doctrine of immediate and perfect sanctification at death. The only sanctification known to experience, to Christian orthodoxy, and the Bible is progressive sanctification. Progressive sanctification after death is the doctrine of the Bible and of the church, and it is of vast importance in our times that we should understand it and live in accordance with it." (*Inaugural, p. 54.*) "It is extremely improbable that the Westminster divines would limit the communion in the future state to two points of time—first, the moment of death, and *second,* the moment of resurrection, and leave entirely out of view the millenniums of the Middle State and the eternities of the Ultimate State. (*The Defense, p. 155.*) The human soul is a finite being and can never reach infinity; it, therefore, can ever increase in holiness, but never attain the infinite holiness of God. How could the redeemed, if no farther endowed in holiness than they are on earth or in the article of death, be able to enjoy or sympathize continuously with the communion of saints in heaven? In order to do so, must they not continually increase in holiness and knowledge?

A Future or Second Probation.—In relation to the

modern theory of a second probation after death the Professor says: "I do not find this doctrine in the Bible." In consequence, he repudiated the supposition that in the Middle State the training of redeemed souls *partook* of the nature of probation. He says: "I do find in the Bible the doctrine of the Middle State of conscious higher life in the communion with Christ and the multitudes of the departed of all ages (*II. Cor., v., 1-9, and Heb. xii., 21-24*), and of the necessity of entire sanctification in order that the work of redemption may be completed." (*Inaugural, p. 54.*)

The committee virtually argued that in respect to the redeemed souls' progress in sanctification or increase in holiness after death there was no explicit statement, either in the Scriptures or in the Confession; yet such progress is obviously implied in both, and is also consistent with the ever-active, moral, and intellectual nature of the soul itself. Is the aged and devout Christian no more Christlike in character than when in youth he or she set out to follow the Saviour "in the regeneration?" To reject such progress in sanctification or holiness, is to contravene the spiritual and glorious doctrine of the communion of saints in the Middle State, as set forth by the Apostle Paul with exstatic joy (*II. Cor. xii., 1-8*). Professor Farrand in his booklet, "The Other Side," on page 30, says: "The verdict of heresy on this charge is the most astonishing of all. . . . That judgment of the assembly would rule John Calvin out of the Presbyterian ministry." Calvin on Phil. 1-6, as quoted by Professor Briggs, says: "For although those who have been freed from the mortal body do no longer contend with the lusts of the flesh. . . . Yet there will be no absurdity in speaking of them as in the way of advancement." Still further, it is a marvel that a Christian scholar should be charged with heresy because he held this doctrine, so

528 A HISTORY OF THE PRESBYTERIAN CHURCH.

real and so comforting to God's people, so sublime in its spiritual and intellectual results, and universally recognized by the experience of all Christians as consistent with their longing desire to be more and more assimilated to God in holiness.

LII.

Briggs Trial Continued.

Errors or Rather Discrepancies in the Bible.—The prosecuting committee charged Dr. Briggs with holding there were errors in the Bible, and that therefore such teaching "was contrary to the standards of the church." Referring to the Confession, Chap. I., 1, the Professor says this teaches that God "committed wholly to writing that knowledge of God and of his will, which is necessary unto salvation. This statement I sincerely adopt." Note what was thus committed to writing: "Not the knowledge of geography, not the knowledge of chronology, not the knowledge of correct citations, not exactness in names of persons and things, unless you can prove that these are necessary unto salvation." (*Defense, p. 93.*)

Such errors or rather discrepancies have been recognized by theologians and Bible students from Augustine and Jerome to John Calvin, and from the latter to the present day. But what is wonderful, not one of them impairs or infringes upon the truths that pertain to the salvation of men. Professor Briggs says: "These errors are all in the circumstances, and not in the essentials; they are in the human setting, not in the precious jewel itself"—that is, the divine revelation. . . . "The only errors I have found or ever recognized in Holy Scripture have been beyond the range of faith and practice. . . . I have always refrained as far as possible from pointing to errors in the present text of the Scriptures. But every Biblical scholar admits them." (*Inaugural, p. 35, and Defense, pp. 89, 105.*) Intelligent lay members of the church have, unfortunately, been much disturbed on this point within recent years, in consequence of the frequent publication by portions of the religious press and otherwise of remarks made by Professor Briggs in relation to these discrepancies. These remarks were very often quoted by certain newspapers, without reference or explanation as to the connection in which they occur, but rather with unfriendly comments upon their own interpretation of the views of the professor, with the legitimate result that he came to be looked upon by great numbers of the private members of the church as an impugner of the integrity of the Bible.

The Two Citations.—Since the Reformation much study has been devoted by the theologians to reconcile these discrepancies. Elaborate investigations have been made into the original tongues in which these passages were written, together with the translations thereof, and into contemporary profane history. It is *due the reader* that we give an instance or two of these discrepancies from a number that might be adduced. John Calvin said, in respect to Matt. xxvii., 9: "How the name of Jeremiah crept in, I confess I know not, nor am I seriously troubled about it. That the name Jeremiah has been put for Zechaniah by an error, the fact itself shows, because there is no such statement in Jeremiah."

Take another instance which Calvin also noticed; one very simple in character and inoffensive in influence. Gen. xlvii., 31, reads: "And he said, swear unto me; and he swore unto him. And Isreal bowed himself upon the *bed's* head." In Heb. xi., 21, we read: "By faith Jacob, when he was a-dying, blest each of the sons of Joseph; and worshiped leaning upon the top of his *staff*." Calvin, in substance, explains; there are two Hebrew words alike in their consonant letters, but under one of the letters of one word, the vowel point is different from that under the same letter in the other word. In the Greek version of the Old Testament, which the Apostles used, and which was made at Alexandria in Egypt, about 250 B. C., the seventy Jews—uninspired men—the translators, instead of rendering the Hebrew word in question, by a Greek word, meaning *couch* or *bed*, by an oversight in respect to the vowel point, translated the word by one meaning a *staff*. "But what matters such an error as this? What difference does it make to our faith and practice, whether Jacob leaned on his staff or his bed's head?" (*Defense, pp. 106, 107.*)

Professor Briggs in the course of his argument directed attention to a number of discrepancies that may be more important in their influence than the two cited above, but none of them *impair divine revelation in respect to the salvation of men*. Is a scholar a heretic because he incidentally notices these discrepancies and points out their harmlessness? In truth, they ought to have a beneficial influence in directing judicious and reverent criticism, thus making known how wonderfully God has preserved the "precious jewel" of His revelation.

Dr. Briggs protested most earnestly against certain changes in phraseology made by the committee, and the arguments based thereon as misleading and giving an untrue impression. For instance in the inaugural (*p. 28, Third edition*) is the following: "Men are influenced by their temperaments and environments, which of the three ways"—alluding to the Bible, the Church, and the Reason—"of access to God they may pursue." This sentence the prosecuting committee in its charges (*p. 19*) for some reason changed to the active voice, and for the word "influenced" substituted the word "determine." Dr. Briggs, after referring to the false impression made by this change, said in reply: "It is the Spirit of God who alone determines in which of the ways they shall find the divine certainty of which they are in quest." (*Res., p. 28.*)

Race Redemption.—"The Bible tells us of a race origin, a race sin, a race ideal, a race Redeemer, and a race redemption (*Rom. v., 18; I. John ii., 2*). But Dr. Birch, in his argument (*p. 68*), says: "The assertion of a race redemption suggests Universalism." The inaugural, however (*pp. 55, 56*) had already said: "The Bible does not teach universal salvation, but does teach the salvation of the world . . . of the race of man . . . the salvation of the world as a whole, compared with which the unredeemed will be few and insignificant, and evidently beyond the reach of redemption by their own act of rejecting it."

The Prejudices Excited.—The committee charged that the "utterances" of Dr. Briggs—which it characterized as "erroneous and ill-advised"—"have seriously disturbed the peace of the church . . . and produced such widespread uneasiness and agitation, as to cause sixty-three presbyteries to overture the assembly [at Detroit] with reference to the same . . . yet we [the committee] have determined not to include this grave offense against the peace of the church in the list of formal charges." (*Report of Committee, pp. 4, 5.*) This proclamation of leniency had virtually the same effect upon the public mind as if such charges had been made; against that impression Professor Briggs earnestly protested.

The prejudice against Dr. Briggs, so notorious that it has been noticed adversely by writers in other denominations, can be explained in view of influences exerted for years through the press (*see page 514*). The persons thus influenced were of two classes—private members of the church and the ministry—though only a portion of either class. That which obtained, especially among the private members, was the outgrowth of two causes; the one, his notices of the errors or discrepancies in the Bible —as mentioned above—which occurred incidentally in his investigations; the other, his opinion that Moses did not write the Pentateuch and Isaiah did not write all the book that bears his name. Under the first head, some Christian people assumed that if the Bible contained errors or discrepancies it could not be an inspired book; and under the second head, that if Professor Briggs did not accept the *current opinion* as to the authorship of the Pentateuch and of the book of Isaiah, they took for granted he rejected their divine authority. For the most part, the private members, for obvious reasons, never took much intelligent interest in the ecclesiastical trials in the Presbyterian Church during the last half century or more, because in them were involved many metaphysical theories which are discussed only by theologians; for similar reason the same class took comparatively little interest in the present trial in regard to the "fountain of authority in the church and reason." They took, however, an interest in the discussion on progressive sanctification or increase in holiness, as it appealed to their own spiritual life or consciousness. It was different in respect to the authors or writers of the Bible, which they were accustomed to recognize as such—that they understood. They also could appreciate certain statements—though misleading—that were in the public prints in relation to discrepancies in the Bible, and concerning Moses and Isaiah. During a number of years previous to these trials unauthorized statements in relation to the professor's views in respect to these errors were spread broadcast throughout the church. Reference was scarcely ever made in these publications as to the unimportant character of the discrepancies, nor explanation given of the connections in which they occur, but on the contrary, they were usually accompanied by unfriendly comments. In consequence, great numbers of Christian people whose range of Biblical interpretation was somewhat limited, seeing these bald statements, inferred that if the Bible contained errors or discrepancies its divine character was impeached. If these Christian men and women had had the facts in the case fully presented to them, their faith in the Bible would have been not only unimpaired but strengthened.

Educated Bible scholars know well the *unimportant* character of these few discrepancies in the sacred volume, which, owing to misapprehensions, so sadly disturbed the minds of many of the Presbyterian laity. In respect to the ministry and their apparently unconscious prejudice, it seems to have been occasioned by an idiosyncrasy of Dr. Briggs himself—was this characteristic on trial? He was so confident of the correctness of his own position in relation to Biblical interpretations, that he was unable to understand why educated theologians could not see the same from their standpoint that he did from his. And sometimes he impulsively treated their opinions on such subjects with little respect, almost indeed with contempt. This was very unfortunate and perhaps even unreasonable, and meanwhile very irritating. But he earnestly and publicly asked pardon of both these parties when, in reply to the charge of the committee, he said: "If I have in any way, directly or indirectly, been the occasion of disturbing the peace of the church, I deeply regret it. If I have given pain and anxiety to my brethren in the ministry, or to the people of Christ's Church by any utterances in the inaugural address, I am very sorry." (*The Response, p. 6.*)

The Minute Adopted.—On the conclusion of the *second* trial of Dr. Briggs—January 9, 1893—the presbytery adopted the following from the report of the committee "appointed to bring in a minute to express its action . . . and final judgment in the case."

"In obedience to this mandate"—that of the General Assembly of 1892—"the Presbytery of New York has tried the case. It has listened to the evidence and argument of the committee of prosecution, acting in fidelity to the duty committed to them. It has heard the defense and evidence of the Rev. Charles A. Briggs, presented in accordance with the rights secured to every minister of the church.

"The presbytery has kept in mind these established principles of our polity, 'that no man can rightly be convicted of heresy by inference or implication,' that 'in the interpretation of ambiguous expressions candor requires that a court should favor the accused by putting upon his words the more favorable rather than the less favorable construction,' and 'there are truths and forms with respect to which men of good character may differ.'

"Giving due consideration to the defendant's explanation of the language used in his inaugural address, accepting his frank and full disclaimer of the interpretation which has been put upon some of its phrases and illustrations, crediting his affirmations of loyalty to the standards of the church and to the Holy Scriptures as the only infallible rule of faith and practice, the presbytery does not find that he has transgressed the limits of the liberty allowed under our constitution to scholarship and opinion.

"Therefore, without expressing approval of the critical or theological views embodied in the inaugural address or the manner in which they have been expressed and illustrated, the presbytery pronounces the Rev. Charles A. Briggs, D.D., fully acquitted of the offenses alleged against him, the several charges and specifications accepted for probation having been not sustained." (*The Briggs Heresy Case, p. 21.*)

We find that twenty-three regular pastors voted in the affirmative, and in connection with the churches of the latter ten chapel or assistant pastors; in the negative, regular pastors ten, chapel or assistant pastors two. That is, *thirty-three* of the regular pastors and their assistants voted to acquit, while *twelve* of the same class voted to condemn.

Thus ended the *second* trial of Professor Briggs before the Presbytery of New York. It was marked by a careful scrutiny of every point at issue, and for being conducted in a courteous manner. The physical and mental strain upon the moderator, Dr. John C. Bliss, was very great. He presided with courtesy and close attention to every speaker and phase of the trial; his rulings being well considered and impartial. In addition, to the mental strain during the day, at night, came the careful revision with the stenographer of the notes of the latter, in order to have them in readiness for the session on the following day. These labors were appreciated and recognized by a unanimous vote of thanks, most heartily given by the presbytery.

The General Assembly of May, 1893, met in Washington, D. C. Rev. Prof. Craig of McCormick Seminary was elected moderator. In order that the reader may have a clear conception of these trials, certain facts and influences ought to be considered. The members of the Presbytery of New York were the *same* during the two trials of Dr. Briggs which it held, and its members were thus familiar with all the phases connected therewith. The presbytery had for weeks the documents mentioned above (*pp. 516, 517*), and also heard the respective arguments presented on the occasion, and could compare their relevancy to the charges based on doctrines of the inaugural, which they had in their hands. The members of the General Assembly, according to conventional rule, are virtually changed from year to year; in consequence of the nearly 600 members of the assembly of 1893 at Washington, D. C., very few, comparatively, had been also members of the one of 1892, at Portland, Oregon, or, perhaps, at Detroit in 1891. Then, again, of the documents that were in the hands of the Presbytery of New York, how many copies of which were in use by the members of the assembly of 1893, when it sat as a court? Strange as it may seem, though all the charges against Dr. Briggs were based upon his inaugural address, not a copy of that document was the assembly of 1893 willing to adduce. A commissioner proposed to have copies of it introduced, "that the quotations [from it] might be read in their connections, but the assembly paid no heed to the proposal. (*A Calm Review. Dr. Laidlow, p. 29.*)

To be sure, the assembly of 1893 heard the arguments bearing on the merits of the case, which were in essential points the same as those presented by the committee to the presbytery, but previous to this it also heard at great length the elaborate speeches made by three members of the prosecuting committee in behalf of their *own appeal* from the decisions of the presbytery. These speeches contained adverse criticisms on the action of the latter court, in *first* dismissing the case, and *second* in its acquittal of Dr. Briggs.

These "adverse criticisms," which took so much time of the assembly, had really nothing to do whatever with the merits of the case, though their influence might incidentally prejudice the court against the professor, and also against the action of the Presbytery of New York. There were one or two influential considerations in contrast. The presbytery, in conducting the trials, was not distracted by outside matters, but was able to give its entire attention to the subject in hand. On the contrary, the attention of the members of the assembly must have been given, also, to the other numerous affairs of the church, such as to the reports of its many committees, and the discussions thereon. In consequence, instead of attending, uninterruptedly, to the trial as did the presbytery, the assembly, amid the pressure of other business and at different times as opportunity served, heard in turn the pleas of the contestants. That its members were, sometimes, weary is indicated by the following statement in Dr. Laidlaw's "Review," p. 28: "No wonder that at one stage of the proceedings, when Dr. Briggs was presenting some of his most important evidence, a commissioner should have moved that the assembly take an extended recess, as about half a dozen commissioners near him were fast asleep."

Inerrancy of the Bible—A New Phase.—The inerrancy of the Bible came up in a new phase, when the General Assembly of 1892 in session at Portland, Oregon, declared: "Our church holds that the inspired word, as it came from God, is without error." (*Minutes, p. 179.*) This deliverance is deemed to teach "the inerrancy of the original autographs of Scripture to be the faith of the church." In allusion to this deliverance Dr. Briggs (*App., p. 96*) says: "The Westminster Confession does not teach the modern dogmatic theory of inerrancy. Nothing is said of original autographs. The Westminister divines were concerned only with the purity and authenticity of the texts in their hands. . . . These divines knew as well as we do that the accents and vowel points of the Hebrew text then in their possession did not come down from the original autographs, pure and unchanged. They were not in the original autographs at all."

This deliverance attracted attention and numbers of pastors throughout the church protested in general terms against such declaration, which was introduced by a committee and hastily adopted by the assembly only a few hours before its final adjournment, when one hundred and seven members were not present. In consequence, there was not time to enter a dissent to the proceedings, but at the assembly of 1893, Washington, D. C., a protest was presented and signed by eighty-seven members, whose names are honored in the church, such as Rev. Drs. Herreck Johnson, S. J. Niccolls, Charles L. Thompson, George Alexander, Charles A. Dickey, Francis Brown, Ninian Beal Remick, and others.

The Protest, which in part said: "We protest, because it is insisting upon a certain theory of inspiration, when our standards have hitherto only emphasized the fact of inspiration. So far as the original manuscript came from God, undoubtedly it was without error . . . but we have no means of determining how far God controlled the penman in transcribing from documents purely circumstantial." Again, we protest: "Because it is dogmatizing on a matter of which, necessarily, we can have no positive knowledge. . . . Notwithstanding some apparent discrepancies in matters purely circumstantial, we earnestly protest against imposing this new interpretation of our standards upon the church to bind men's consciences by enforced subscription to its terms."

The committee appointed to answer the above protest closes their answer with the following conditional sentence: "If errors were found in the original autographs, they could not have proceeded from God, who is truth itself, the Author thereof." (*Minutes, 1893, pp. 167-169.*)

The Explanatory Resolution.—In order apparently to explain the feature objected to in the Portland deliverance the assembly of 1893, at the suggestion of Dr. William C. Young, resolved: *"That the Bible as we now have it, in its various translations and versions, when freed from all errors and mistakes of translators, copyists and printers, is the very word of God, and consequently without error."* (*Minutes, p. 169.*) The reader, perhaps, will ask wherein does the above deliverance differ in idea from the statement on the same subject, expressed by Dr. Briggs, when in his inaugural, page 35, he says: *"These errors are all in the circumstances and not in the essentials; they are in the human setting, not in the precious jewel itself"*— that is, in the divine revelation? The position of Dr. Briggs on the inerrancy of the Bible was the outgrowth of careful and reverent study, and in consequence he came to the same conclusion on the subject years before the General Assembly of 1893 unanimously made the above deliverance. The latter body in this "resolution" recognized, indirectly, the existing discrepancies in the Bible, and determined to put on record its decision in respect to them in terms clear and definite.

A protest was presented to the assembly by Dr. E. P. Sprague of Auburn, New York, and entered upon the Minutes (*pp. 772-3*) against the suspension of Dr. Briggs. It was signed by sixty-two members of that body; among other reasons given was that the action "seemed to abridge the liberty of opinion hitherto enjoyed under our standards . . . as tending to the discouragement of thorough study of the Bible and reverent advance in the apprehension of divine truth . . . as inflicting what we cannot but feel is an injustice to a Christian scholar of high character and learning, as well as to the Presbytery of New York, which had fully acquitted him of the charges alleged against him."

Misapprehensions.—Had the laity of the Presbyterian Church, as well as those of other denominations, known the fact that Dr. Briggs had for years been laboring to remove extraneous matter from the word of God, and present it pure in its sacred contents, which he characterized as the "precious jewel,"their minds on this subject would never have been disturbed as represented. Another phase of this subject ought to attract the attention of church members. In his instructions Dr. Briggs has ever, when occasion required, made prominent the essential and recognized doctrines of the standards of the church. On another phase of the subject he says: "I am assured by my pupils that I make the Bible to them more real, more powerful, more divine. I have never heard a single one of the thirteen hundred theological students I have trained in the last twenty-six years who has said that I impaired his faith in Holy Scripture."

A Review—Comments.—"It is beyond question that he [Professor Briggs] knew how to win the enthusiastic affection of his pupils, and that in some cases he had been the means of rescuing young men from a profound skepticism as regards the Bible, to a practical faith in its authority." (*Vol. VI., p. 265, Church Hist. Series.*) On the same lines of sentiment an earnest and successful Western Presbyterian pastor, though prejudiced by certain newspaper rumors, was heard to say: "Well, after all, there must be something in that man Briggs; I never met a student of his who was not an ardent student of the Bible."

"The prosecution was conducted with distinguished ability and legal acumen, though not with great exegetical learning." . . . In his reply Professor Briggs showed his superiority in a professional familiarity with the subjects under discussion, and was unhappy only in the tone which characterized every reference to the prosecution and the assembly.

"This decision"—the suspension of Dr. Briggs—"lacks the calm of the judicial temper. It is pervaded by a personal animus which finds an outlet in many of its phases, especially in the conversion of the charge of unsound teaching into one of personal immorality, and in making the restoration of the offender dependent, not upon his retraction of his alleged errors, but upon his 'repentance' for his 'sin.' It thus affixes a stigma to the accused, which was not warranted by any evidence before the assembly, nor embodied in any of the charges on which he was tried." (*Vol. VI., Church Hist. Series, pp. 266, 267, 269.*)

The Apparent Outcome.—The remembrance of these trials and many of the incidents connected therewith is fresh in the minds of those Presbyterians, and others, who keep themselves in touch with the movements within the church. As a portion of the latter's history worthy of being noticed, we cite two instances that may appear as the outcome of these trials. For illustration, the prosecuting committee took exception to "what is called Biblical theology," being used "to the disparagement of systematic theology," as formulated in the creeds and confessions of the church. It went so far as to characterize "Biblical theology as unscientific" (*The Argument of Dr. Birch, pp. 68, 69*). Prof. Briggs had published in the *Presbyterian Review* in 1870 and in 1872 his views in respect to the method of studying the word of God, which he characterized as *Biblical* theology.

It is noteworthy that this, in a measure, new departure in the curriculum of American theological seminaries was adopted by Princeton Seminary in establishing a professorship of "Biblical Theology" in 1893, as did also McCormick Seminary in 1894. These institutions thus recognized the importance of that scope of Biblical instruction by adopting the same name and, it is presumed, the same methods.

Union Seminary Independent of the General Assembly.—In consequence of the reunion of the church in 1870, after several preliminary adjustments, Union Seminary, on the basis of a certain compact, came into connection with the General Assembly.

The Board of Directors of the Seminary felt deeply wronged by the action of the assembly of 1891, at Detroit, in refusing to sanction the *transfer* of Professor Briggs to another chair in the seminary, contending that a transfer was not an *appointment* nor an election, and therefore they had a right to make such transfer as other seminaries were in the habit of doing and which they themselves had often done. We do not deem it expedient in this connection to trace the full history of the several conferences held by committees appointed by both parties to adjust the difficulties that arose between the General Assembly and the Directors of Union Seminary, in consequence of the above action of the former, but refer the reader to "Union Theo. Sem., p. 93, and Chap. V., pp. 255-280.

The Board of Directors, however, sent a memorial on the subject to the assembly of 1892 at Portland, Oregon. They gave their reasons in full pertaining to the case, and asked "that the *veto* power conceded to the General Assembly in 1870 should no longer reside in that body." In a courteous manner the memorial urged that by so doing the present assembly could "restore Union Seminary to its former relations to the General Assembly." To this memorial, without noticing the reasons stated therein, came the brief answer: "That the assembly declines to be a party to the breaking of the compact with Union Theological Seminary."

In reply to this answer the directors subsequently said: "There is no provision, whatever, in our charter or constitution for the principle of synodical or assembly supervision." "Again, after investigation, we find the legal consideration . . . leaves us no room to doubt that under the laws of the State of New York the attempted agreement of 1870 was beyond the powers of the Board of Directors of the Seminary." We "cannot abdicate any of our official duties in whole or in part." "The directors and faculty are personally bound by their official vow." We express "our earnest desire for the restoration of our former relations to the General Assembly." The outcome was that the Board of Directors, by a vote of nineteen to one, rescinded the resolution or compact of 1870. For this act on the part of the directors was found what might be termed a precedent in the abrogation in 1837, of the Plan of Union by the General Assembly, *alone,* without even consulting the other party to the compact—the General Association of Connecticut (*p. 389*).

The assembly of 1893 at Washington, D. C., indicated the relation of Union Seminary to that body as follows: "Because of the attempt by the Board [of Directors] and on its own motion and against the expressed desire of the assembly, to abrogate the compact of 1870, the assembly disavows all responsibility for the teaching of Union Seminary, and declines to receive any report from its board." Though thus cherishing a hope and promising a welcome, should the seminary return, yet afterward the assembly gave notice that it would not give aid to any students who may pursue their studies in a seminary under its ban. (*Minutes of 1890, pp. 157, 161.*) "Union Seminary was founded as an independent seminary upon its own charter, owing ecclesiastical allegiance as an institution to no body whatever. . . . There is no spirit of revolt or rebellion behind this action, but a serious, earnest, profound desire to be faithful to obligations assumed in the sight of God and men, and to do, without fear or favor, what conscience dictated in obedience to those obligations" (*Professor Francis Brown, on the floor of the assembly*).

LIII.

ASSEMBLIES, 1894-1897.

Assemblies, 1894-1897.—The General Assembly of 1894 met at Saratoga Springs on May 23d of that year. Rev. Dr. Samuel A. Mutchmore was elected moderator. In course of a correspondence since 1875 (*see p. 485*), overtures had been made in respect to organic union with the Presbyterian Church South. In answer to these overtures a telegram was received at Saratoga, which, after wishing the assembly "Godspeed," said: "We regard it unwise to reopen the question of organic union." In view of this statement, the assembly resolved: "That while this assembly accepts the action of the Presbyterian Church in the United States, of which it has been notified, as sufficiently indicating the wisdom of suspending for the present everything like overtures looking to a union with that body, it desires to put on record its expression of regret for such suspension." (*Minutes 1894, p. 140.*)

Case of Professor Smith.—Professor Henry Preserved Smith of Lane Theological Seminary published a pamphlet, entitled "Biblical Scholarship and Inspiration." Exception was taken by the Presbytery of Cincinnati to certain views expressed therein, and in consequence Professor Smith was brought to trial and suspended by a vote of *thirty-one to twenty-seven* from the ministry (August, 1892), "until he renounces his errors and promises no longer to teach or propagate them." The following July Professor Smith resigned his chair in the seminary and afterward, in the autumn of the same year, the Synod of

Ohio approved the decision of the presbytery, and the following year (1894) the General Assembly, in session at Saratoga, also approved the same sentence.

The General Assembly of 1895 met in Pittsburg. Dr. Robert Russell Booth of New York was elected moderator. The report of the Committee on Financial Affairs said: "We are sorry to note that the debt is larger than ever before. It has reached the portentious amount in round numbers of $365,000." The sessions of the assembly in discussing and acting upon the routine business of the church were remarkably harmonious. A spirit of hopefulness and trust seemed to pervade the entire assembly. All were anxious to promote the cause of religion by having the church, as soon as possible, relieved of the incubus of the oppressive debt.

Comparison of Statistics.—We may obtain a fair idea of the progress of the church by comparing its statistics at different periods. We here introduce a comparison in order to ascertain that progress during ten years. According to the minutes of the respective general assemblies we find in those of 1886 the number of synods was 26; presbyteries, 199; ministers, 5546; churches, 6281; admitted on examination, 51,177; communicants, 661,889; attendance of Sabbath-school scholars, 743,565; and total contributions, $10,502,331. In 1896, synods, 31; presbyteries, 224; ministers, 6942; churches, 7573; admitted on examination, 64,806; communicants, 943,716; attendance of Sabbath-school scholars, 1,006,391; and total contributions, $14,149,477. In this connection it is proper to note that in 1893 a universal depression in the industrial and financial affairs of the country began, and which had not come to an end in 1896.

The one hundred and ninth General Assembly, on May 20, 1897, met in the Winona Assembly Grounds, Eagle Lake, Indiana. Rev. Dr. Sheldon Jackson was elected moderator, and the Hon. John Wanamaker vice-moderator.

Increased Contributions.—During the previous ecclesiastical year a gradual improvement was made in the industrial and commercial interests of the Nation, and in consequence the private members were enabled to increase their contributions to the benevolent institutions of the church. The reports of the standing committees and of the secretaries showed, also, an increased progress in the operations of all the boards of the church. It was reported that during the past year (1896) 13,300 persons were received into its fellowship by our home missionaries.

The following is a summary of the condition of the church during the ecclesiastical year of 1896: Synods, 32; presbyteries, 229; ministers, 7129; churches, 7631; added on examination, 57,011; communicants, 990,911; Sunday-school members, 1,024,462; contributions, $13,298,151.

The Rule—Home Missions.—This assembly adopted the following rule, which is of special interest to the theological students of the church, and also indirectly to its private members: "Candidates for licensure in addition to the examination required by Chap XIV., Sec. 4, of the Form of Government shall be diligently examined in the English Bible and shall be required to exhibit a good knowledge of its contents and of the relation of its separate parts and portions to each other. The General Assembly further directed that this rule shall be known as Constitutional Rule No. 2, and shall be appended to the Constitution of the Church. (*Minutes, p. 119.*)

The General Assembly took action in respect to home missions in the following order: "That the Board of Home Missions be directed to reorganize its methods of administration that the executive work shall be placed in charge of one secretary, with whatever assistants may be necessary, and that he be accountable to the board for its faithful and efficient management." (*Min., p. 56.*)

Effect for Good on Two Lines.—The assembly made declaration that it had "learned with profound satisfaction" that a number of associations of the secular press had "expressed their sympathy with the women's movement for the promotion of purity in literature and art, as tending to maintain a Christian standard of morality in society;" and also that these associations, as "the best friends of humanity," had pledged themselves to exclude from their publications "all impure advertisements." (*Min., p. 84.*)

It will surely not be deemed out of place by the Christian patriot to notice that, while the General Assembly was in session, Congress at Washington was enacting, for the first time in our history, a financial measure in which "all persons were prohibited from importing into the United States from any foreign country, any obscene book, pamphlet, advertisement" [here follows a long enumeration of prohibited articles] "or anything of an immoral nature." (*Tariff of 1897, Schedule N, Sec. 10, under 672.*)

An Eventful Period.—During the three-fourths of the century just closing (1899) great advances were made by Christian scholars in the study of the Bible, while the religious knowledge of the church members themselves were meanwhile proportionately rising to a higher plane. The elaborate works in elucidation of the Bible, that were published in Europe and America, were in number beyond precedent. Explorations, meantime, were begun and are still in progress in the Holy Land, in Assyria, and in Egypt, whose findings have corroborated the historical statements of the Bible, wherever the latter have been touched upon. Within this period came the Civil War, with its demoralizing effects upon the spirituality of the churches, and which left to them as a legacy an enlarged field for domestic missions in the form of the religious wants of the freedmen. The division of the Presbyterian Church also took place, which lasted thirty-two years, when a reunion was welcomed by all its members. Within these years a revision of the English version of the Bible was made, on which learned theologians and linguists of England and the United States labored assiduously, and produced the most perfect translation from the original tongues of the Bible that was ever made into English or any modern language. This revision was the occasion of creating an unusual interest in the Bible in the Presbyterian Church, and also in the other Protestant denominations. Meantime, preliminary measures were introduced by the General Assembly in respect to a revision of the Confession of Faith. That purpose is still held in abeyance; the committee having reported progress from time to time.

It would seem as if designed as an antidote for the demoralizing influence of the Civil War, that within a few years after its close a new impulse for studying the Bible was given the children and youth of Protestant parents. This gift was the introduction of the International Sunday-school Lessons. This comprehensive system of Biblical instruction recognizes the Old Testament, and gives it due attention, as the forerunner of the New. The intimate connection with the contents of the latter of the Old Testament history, prophecies, and sublime truths are pointed out in such manner as to impress with their importance the minds of these youth.

How marvelous has been the blessed and stimulating influence of this uniform course of Bible study; beginning in the infant class and systematically carried on in varied stages, till all the youth are reached. One grand result is seen in the societies known as the "Christian Endeavor." These associations have been efficient instruments in harmonizing truly Christian sentiments and in uniting the youth of the several Protestant denominations in religious sympathy one with another throughout the land, and in promoting a spirit of a *Christianized patriotism* that aids in cementing a national friendship in all sections of the Union. This good influence will not be limited, alone, to the young people of this generation, for when they themselves become heads of families they will surely train their children up to a still higher plane of a *Christianized civilization.*

LIV.

Assemblies of 1898-1899.

The General Assembly met in its one hundred and tenth session on May 19, 1898, in the auditorium of the Winona Assembly Grounds, Winona Lake, Indiana.

It was opened by a sermon by the retiring moderator, Rev. Sheldon Jackson, D.D., LL.D., a veteran missionary of the Presbytery of Alaska. The Rev. Wallace Radcliffe of the Presbytery of Washington, D. C., was elected moderator. The Hon. James A. Mount, Governor of the State of Indiana, made an appropriate address of welcome to the assembly, which was replied to by the moderator in similar terms.

The assembly was cheered by the reports concerning the gradual diminution of the debt that had been retarding the progress of the church since 1894, and by the prospect that it would entirely disappear before the meeting of the assembly in 1899.

The reports of the respective standing committees on the numerous enterprises of the church were, upon the whole, encouraging. The sessions of the assembly were pervaded by a spirit of harmony among the members that was cheering to the heart of brotherly love. Two subjects that pertain, also, to the outside world were noticed. The cause of temperance received a hearty commendation, while the increasing desecration of the Sabbath in certain portions of the land was heartily condemned, and the members of the church were urged most earnestly to observe the sacredness of the day as a boon to man, since it was made for him.

Overtures on the subject of biennial or triennial meetings of the General Assembly have been presented occasionally to that body for a number of years, and after a brief discussion were answered in accordance with recommendation of the committee, that no action be taken. To this assembly came eight overtures on the subject, and it thought proper to give some reasons why the present custom of annual sessions should be continued. One reason was that "our system of administration in connection with the great causes of missions and benevolence has been organized upon the basis of the annual meetings of the assembly. To change our system in this respect would require a radical change in the plans of management of the several boards. . . . The assembly constitutes the bond of union, peace, correspondence, and mutual confidence among our churches. . . . Our system of government is intended among other things to conserve the rights and privileges of every minister and member of the church. . . . The proposed change—to a triennial meeting—would of necessity involve such a readjustment of our judicial system as would [virtually] deny to an appellant the right to be heard by the whole church . . . such a denial of right, when conjoined with a proposed grievous delay in reaching a decision, would be contrary to both justice and equity." (*Min., p. 131.*) The assembly might have added that coming together once a year of the representative men of the church—ministers and elders—would elicit the sympathy of the intelligent private members of the church throughout the Union and indirectly cherish a patriotism based on Christian and fraternal principles.

It is a sad feature of these minutes that the reports show so little gain to the membership from the world on examination; such increase was only *thirty* persons more than were recorded of 1897; while the increase in the number of adult baptisms was only *twenty-two*. The increase in Sunday-school attendance was nearly ten thousand, and that in contributions was $205,410; admitted on examination, 57,041; number of communicants, 975,877.

The General Assembly of 1899.—Met in its one hundred and eleventh year on the 18th of May, 1899, in the city of Minneapolis. It was opened in the usual manner by the retiring moderator, Rev. Wallace Radcliffe, D.D., of Washington, D. C. The Rev. Robert F. Sample, D.D., LL.D., of the Presbytery of New York was elected moderator. Dr. Sample appointed Dr. Loyal Y. Graham of the Presbytery of Philadelphia, vice-moderator.

The assembly entered upon its labors with hearts full of gratitude, that in the providence of God, the boards of the church were no longer trammeled in their work by a debt which had been an incumbrance since the session of 1894.

This assembly of 624 members in attendance was noted for being composed of an unusually large number of regular pastors and of elders who were deeply and intelligently interested in all the works of the church. The several discussions showed, incidentally, no lack of the power of debate and of comprehensive views on the various phases of the ecclesiastical matters that came before the assembly. The session was comparatively a short one, the members being remarkably harmonious in their action upon the measures that demanded their earnest attention. A hopeful missionary spirit seemed to pervade the entire body. It put on record its steadfast adherence to the fundamental and evangelical doctrines of the gospel as derived from Holy Scripture and embodied in the standards of the church.

A most cheering feature of the narrative of the state

of religion in the church presented to the assembly was the manifest increased interest in the systematic study of the Holy Scriptures, especially by the young people of the church in Bible classes and Sunday-schools. The good work of the women of the church was shown to be effective and followed by the blessing of the Master. The attention of pastors and sessions and presbyteries was directed to their respective duties to foster and encourage and keep in sympathy with the young people's organizations within their bounds.

When compared with the reports in the minutes of the previous year it found that the number admitted to the church on examination was 8782 less than in 1898—why this decrease the members of the whole church may well inquire. The number of communicants was increased by 8030, and the contributions by $274,156. The assembly dissolved to meet in St. Louis, Missouri, on the third Thursday of May, 1900.

Patriots—Both Citizen and Christian.—The progress of the church is indicated by its statistics. These include its appropriate religious work, the latter's success or otherwise, and as a means thereto its financial condition must be good. The last mentioned element of success is in this day essential, and how to secure it is well worthy the attention of church members of every denomination as Christian citizens as well as patriots, since monetary affairs are so liable to be affected by political measures. The financial and industrial policies of the general government extend their influence throughout the land, and are, therefore, a great power for evil or for good in respect to the support of the institutions of the church, thus indirectly promoting or retarding its legitimate operations. Unfortuntely, in our time, too many intelligent Christians of the different denominations are quite often derelict as citizens in not fully realizing that it is their duty to inform themselves in relation to the financial and kindred measures of the government, in order that they may vote intelligently should there be mismanagement in consequence of incompetent men being in control of public affairs. Much more is it incumbent upon all the citizens to rouse themselves to counteract the evil. Church members should recognize their obligations to the country, as citizens and patriots, and never *shirk* the responsibility which rests upon them in proportion to their influence—be it great or small.

It is an undeniable fact that the financial policy of the National Government always affects more or less the various industries of the people, thus indirectly retarding or promoting the progress of the church, especially in its benevolent operations. For illustration, the reports to the General Assembly in a certain year really contain the results of the one immediately preceding; thus the report of the total contributions credited to the year 1893, in truth, were those of 1892. The amount contributed, though credited to 1893, was the largest ever recorded in the annals of the Presbyterian Church. Strange to say, the following year (1893) the amount contributed fell off nearly one million dollars, as told in the reports of 1894, and in consequence all the boards of the church were overwhelmed with debt. The managers of the latter had based, and that reasonably, their financial estimates on the contributions of 1892, and in a proportionate ratio had extended their operations.

A similar result was produced in a greater or less degree in the contributions of the churches of all the other denominations in the Union. In this instance a depression in almost every industry prevailed, a lowering of wages, and likewise a lack of opportunity for employment, and in consequence an unusual diminution of incomes. Such facts indicate that it is the duty of the members of the churches of all denominations, as Christians and patriotic citizens, not to shirk their responsibility, but conscientiously make it an object to inform themselves in respect to what may be the present or prospective political and financial policies of the Nation, in order they may vote intelligently. Let all church members of the various denominations promote a *Christianized patriotism,* whose principles permeate the people at large.

INDEX.

Abbreviated Creeds, 457.
Adams, William, 500.
Accessions from Other Bodies, 301.
Act and Testimony, 420, 421, 424.
Adopting Act, 113, 114.
Allen William, 285, 286.
Alexander, Archibald, 129, 250, 337.
    " James W. and Addison, 251.
American B'd of Mes., 342, 343.
Andros, Gov., 75.
Apostolic Succession, 24-26, 52, 59, 64.
Assembly, Gen. (Scotland), 40.
    " Westminster, 50-58.
    " General Constituted, 207, 240.
Assembly, Ratio of Representatives, 351.
Assembly, Triennial, etc., 477, 478.
Association, Gen., of Conn., 237, 433, 435, 441, 442.
Association, Missionary Amer., 469.

Badger, Joseph, 232, 295, 297.
Balch, Hezekiah, 135, 216.
Baltimore, Lord, 78.
Baker, Daniel, 276, 277, 505, 507.
Baptists, 107, 177, 186, 187.
Barnes, Albert, 399.
    " Trials, 400-405, 406, 415.
Barr, Thomas, 294.
Beall, Ninian, Colonel (Elder), 80.
Beecher, Lyman, 244, 268, 320, 395, 415, 448.
Beliefs, Harmony of, 34.
Beman, N. S. S., 448, 451.
Berkeley, Sir Wm., 77, 169.
Bible, Translations of, 10, 45.
Bishops, 3, 17, 23, 40.
    " Romanizing, 33, 36, 64, 99.
    " Genuine, 60.
Blackburn, Gideon, 221, 327, 336, 363.
Booth, Robert R., 546.
Bray, Thomas, 94, 95.
Breckinridge, Robert J., 422, 436, 439, 502.
Bribery and Trickery, 101.
Brown, Prof. Francis, 544.
    " Matthew, 134, 324, 325.

Brigg, Charles Augustus, Trials of 511-542.

Caldwell, John, 137.
Calvin, John, 7, 16, 30, 32.
Campbell, Col. (Elder), 145.
Camp Meetings, 228, 347.
Carnahan, James, 282, 283.
Carrick, Samuel, 219, 221, 332.
Cavaliers, 77, 162, 196, 218.
Chamberlain, Jeremiah, 374.
Church, Rom. Catholic, 13, 213.
    " Gov. of, 15, 16, 63.
    " 1st in Cincinnati, 291.
    " 1st New Orleans, 315.
    " Culdee, The, 43-45.
    " Primitive, Self-Supporting, 28, 29.
Church, Migrating, A, 276, 334.
    " 1st Founded in Tenn., 220.
    " Separated from the State, Va., 159, 175-190.
Church, Freedom from Clannishness, 165.
Church and State, 6, 28, 30, 171.
    " Congregational, 70, 71, 89, 156, 240, 481, 483.
Church of Special Interest, 370.
    " of England, Established, 171.
    " Rates How Levied, 143, 164, 171.
Cincinnati Founded, 290.
Civil Court Trials, 454, 455.
Colleges (Log), 111, 117, 118, 127-136.
Colleges, Princeton, 118, 130; Jefferson, 133; Washington, 132, S. Hanover, 319; Maryville, 333; Center, 336; Blackburn Unv., 363.
Colony, Virginia, 68.
    " Plymouth, 68.
Commotions, Civil (in England), 59.
Committee, Ad Interim, 459, 466, 478.
Committee, Church Extension, 467.
    " Standing, 242.
    " Publication, Pres., 467.
    " on Reunion, 483.
Committeemen, 386, 388, 446.
Confessions of Faith, 31, 33-35.

Confessions, Westminster, 55-59.
" Revision Desired, 491.
Co-operation, Difficulties of, 467, 474.
Cornbury, Lord, 96, 100, 101.
Cornelius, Elias, 339, 341.
Contrast in Creeds and Discipline, 384, 385.
Conventions, Called, 422, 423, 431, 433, 436, 448.
Conventions, Congregational, 478, 481.
Cox, Samuel Hanson, 448.
Craig, John, 153.
" Prof., 536.
Craighead, Alexander, 144.
Cromwell, Oliver, 38, 61, 62, 64, 70.
Cummings, Charles, 216.
Cutler, Manassah, 289.

Davies, Samuel, 118, 140, 168, 171.
Dean, Milman (quoted), 26.
" Stanley (quoted), 26, 496.
Denton, Richard, 73.
Derrow, Nathan B., 356.
Despotism, Ecclesiastical, 213.
Detroit, Religions, etc., 375.
Dickey, J. M. (Father), 355, 356.
Dickinson, Baxter, 434, 457.
" Jonathan, 115, 117, 118.
Difficulties, Attending Assemblies, 443, 444.
Dissenters, 77, 99, 161, 179, 184, 185, 189, 191, 194.
Divine Right for Ch. Gov., 62, 63.
Doak, Samuel, 135.
Doughty, Francis, 72, 81.
Duelling, 268.
Duffield, George, 408.
Durand, Wm. (Elder), 80.
Dutch Liberality, 72, 74.

Education, Ministerial, 166, 172, 266, 303.
Education, Funds for, 119.
Edwards, Jonathan, 151, 160.
Elders, 2, 4, 12.
Eldership Introduced, 97.
Elective Affinity, 401, 424.
Elliott, David, 434, 450.
Ellis, J. M., 361, 362.
Ely, Ezra Stiles, 254, 366.
Emigrations to Colonies, 66.
Englishmen's Rights, 9, 11.
Episcopalians, 177, 183, 184.
Errors in Doctrine, 436.
" Acted Upon, 441.
Estimate, Appreciative, An, 263.
Evangelists, 504.
Exiles to Geneva, 16.
Ex-officio Members, 211.

Ex-officio, Action of, 343; the Effect 387.
" the Principal of, 237, 391, 424, 434, 441, 459.

Faith, Confessions of, 31, 34, 35.
" Westminster, 55-59.
" Guarding the, 112, 114, 210.
Finley, Robert, 251, 252, 281.
" James, 261.
Finney, Chas. S., 395, 417.
Fisher, Samuel, 451.
Fletcher, Gov., 104.
Flint, Timothy, 367, 371, 373.
Force, Religious, A, 27, 33.
Foreign Miss. Soc., Western, 389.
Fowler, Orin, 357.
Fraternal Intercourse, 108.
Frelinghugsen, Jacob, 150, 151.
Froude (quoted), 110.

Gelston, James, 139.
Giddings, Salmon, 367, 369, 370, 372.
Gillet, E. H., 153.
Gloucester, John, 336, 337.
Gooch, Gov., 125, 137, 142, 153.
Graham, Wm., 129.
Griffen, Edw. D., 234, 250.
Green, Ashbel, 250, 393, 399, 400, 409, 422.

Hall, Jas. W., 278.
Hamilton, Alexander, 268.
Harrison, Thomas, 79.
Henderson, Robert, 216, 221.
Henry VIII., 13, 14, 31.
Heroic Age, The, 33.
Herron, Francis, 271, 272.
Hill, Matt, 81.
Hodge, Charles, 165, 499.
Hoge, Moses, 257, 273, 407.
Holmes, Abiel, 276.
Hubbard, John, 100.
Hughes, Thomas E., 290.
Huntsville, Ch. of, 315.

Immigration, 287, 299.
" of Farmers, 356.
Immigrants, Character of, 384.
Independents, Unorganized, 37.
Indians Removed, 329.
" Missions to, 327, 328.
Influence, Leading Points of, 119.
" Retarding, 217.
Infidelity, Type of, 221.
Inglis, James, 281.
Injudicious ordinations, 397.
Instructions Transcended, 427.
Intolerance, 161.

INDEX.

James, King, 38, 39.
" His Motto, 41, 42.
Jacobus, M. W., 407.
Janeway, Jacob J., 252.
Jefferson, Thomas, 177, 181, 190, 191, 192, 225.
Junkin, George, 402-404, 422.
Jus Divinum, 29.

Knox, John, 17, 31, 40.

Laird, Robert M., 377.
Landholdings, 76.
Lamphier, Jeremiah, 470.
Larned, Silvester, 339.
Laud, Bishop, The, 51.
Law Misapplied, 104.
League and Covenant, 46, 51, 52.
Lindsley, Philip, 315, 497-499.
Little, Henry, 507-510.
Luther, Martin, 27.

Magna Charta, 9.
Magill, Daniel, 138.
Makemie, Francis, 82, 84.
" Trial, 86, 87, 93, 317.
Marietta Settled, 288, 289.
Marquis, Thomas, 233, 260, 261.
Mason, John M., 268, 389, 390.
Marion, Francis, Gen., 145.
Mary, Bloody, 32.
Matthews, John, 319, 373, 374.
Mechlenberg Declaration, 173.
Meetings, Camp, 228.
Memorial, Cincinnati, 398, 419, 420.
Methodism, 150, 177.
Monteith, John, 376.
Morals, Clerical, 169.
Moravians, 149.
Morgan, Daniel, Gen. (Elder), 145.
Morse, Jedekiah, 276, 377.
McCurdy, Elisha, 231, 232.
McCorcle, S. E., 278.
McGready, James, 224, 228.
McMillan, John, 133, 233, 258, 282, 324.
McLane, Wm. W., 336.
McNish, Geo., 93, 101.
McWhin, 316.
Migrations, Lines of, 256.
" on Reason for, 371.
Mills, Samuel J., 368.
Missions, Interest in, 237.
" Funds for, 107.
" Board of, 302, 387, 453.
" American B'd, 342, 380.
" Home, 353, 382.
Missionary Areas Compared, 383.

Names, Significant, 19.
Nevins, William, 280.
Nettleton, Asahel, 349, 395, 417.

New Measures, 394.

Old Side, New Side, 152, 153, 154, 156, 157.
Old School, New School, 458.
Opinions, Change of, 424.
Orders, Voting by, 212.

Parity of the Ministry, 18, 21, 23, 29, 51, 66.
Parties, The Two, 32.
Pastor, The Term, 19.
Patriotism, 192, 198, 214.
Patterson, James, 254, 255.
" Robert M., 154.
Patton, William, 450.
People, The, a Voice on Ch. Gov., 11.
Porrine, M. L. R., 247.
Persecutors, Non, The, 21.
Persecutions and Trials, 52.
Peters, Absalom, 437.
Pickens, Gen., 145.
Pietists, The, 149, 150.
Plan of Union, 238, 240, 424, 439.
" " Abrogated, 436, 481.
Plumer, Wm. S., 436, 437, 452.
Pope, The, A Presbyter, 24.
Population, Center of, 319, 320.
Porter, Samuel, 259.
Power, James, 260.
Prayer, Free, 33.
" Meetings, 272, 277, 300.
Prelatical Ch. Gov., 7, 15, 20.
Prelates, Why Feared, 50.
Presbytery, 1st (in England), 36, 37.
" Hanover, 175, 178, 182, 184, 188.
Presbytery, Redstone, 206; Transylvania, 206, 215; Abingdon, 214; S. Carolina, 88; Cumberland, 230; First Philadelphia, 91, 92, (in 1706), 98; New York, 72; The Third of, 410; Philadelphia, Second, 402; Ohio, 134; Erie, 297; Detroit, 378.
Presbyterians, Origin of, in Va., 121-126.
Presbyterians, The Name, 125.
" Why Liberal, 70.
" in Maine, 116.
" in N. J. and Del., 87.
Prime, Ebenezer, 157.
Principle, A Great, Established, 173, 174.
Principle, Voluntary, Influence of, 194.
Procter, David C., 358.
Puritanism, A Religious Force, 27, 33.
Puritans, 41.
" in Virginia, 66, 68.

Queen Elizabeth, 15, 30, 32.

Quakers, 177, 181, 186, 200.

Ralston, Samuel, 261.
Reading House, Morris', 122, 125.
Rector, The Term, 20, 21.
Reed, Isaac, 359, 360.
Religion, How Promoted, 274
" in Towns on the Mississippi, 340.
Reserve, Western, 283, 293.
Responsibility, Partial, 22, 159.
" Individual, 161, 180, 185, 193, 344, 380, 387, 459, 466.
Resumption of Specie Payments, 488.
Reunion, The, 155.
" (2nd), 480-485.
" Basis of, 484.
Revival, Great, The, 224-229.
" in Colleges, 305.
" Effects of, 242.
" in the South, 273.
" Numerous, 345-348.
" of 1857, 469.
Rice, David (Father), 214, 227, 291.
" John Holt, 257, 344, 394.
Richards, James, 318, 448.
Robinson, Edward, 493-497.
" William, 139.
Rodgers, John, 141, 208, 245.
Romeyn, John Broadhead, 247, 248.
Royce, Samuel, 340, 341.

Sabbath, Influence of, 46.
" Continental, 48.
" Desecration of, 218, 367.
" Mails (Sunday), 349, 350.
" Respected, 486.
Schools, Classical, 130, 131.
Secession of Synods, 469.
Sevier, Col. (Elder), 145, 146.
Seminaries, Theological, Auburn, 318; Lane, 328; Maryville, 322; Princeton, 250; S. Hanover, 319; Union, Virginia, 323; Union, N. Y. City, 428, 429; Western, 319.
Shedd, Wm. G. T., 503, 504.
Shelby, Col. (Elder), 145, 146.
Skinner, Thomas H., 253, 254.
Skelton, Samuel, 69.
Slavery, 444, 452, 466.
Smith, S. Stanhope, 128.
" John Blair, 238.
" Joseph, 132.
" Henry Boynton, 501, 502.
Society, Missionary, The First, 94.
" For P. G. F. Parts, 94.

Society, National, Formed, 265.
Society's Educational, 266, 341, 387.
Society, Irresponsibility of, 386, 433.
Spring, Gardiner, 248, 249, 472.
Sports, Book of, 40.
Statements, Misleading, 426.
Stephenson, Jas. W., 334, 335.
Stobo, Archibald, 89, 93.
Study on Two Lines, 134.
Subscription, Strict, 114, 116.
Succession, Apostolic, 24.
Sunday School Scholars, 488.
St. Louis, Religious Character, 367.
Synod, Constituted, 107.
Synods, Consolidated, 486.

Taggart, Samuel, 246.
Taylor, Nathaniel L. W., 393, 394.
Temperance, 244, 307.
Tennent, William, 110, 111.
" Gilbert, 118.
Toleration Act, 75, 124, 142, 167, 168.
Test and Schism Act, 109.
Thomson, John, 115.
Training a Household, 52.
" a Nation, 195.
Translations of the Bible, 10.
Trials and Persecutions, 52.
Tyndale, William, 10, 11.

Union of Church and State, 6, 28, 30.
" Separation of, 175-194.
" Meetings, 171, 277.

Vesey, William, 101, 102, 103.
Vagrants (Clerical), 162.

War (1812), Effects of, 300.
Washington, George, 204, 208.
Wesley, John and Charles, 35, 149.
Whitney, Eli, 140.
Whitefield, George, 149, 151.
Wick, William, 294.
Williams, Roger, 21, 22.
Witherspoon, John, 208.
Wilson, James P., 252.
" Joshua L., 292, 346, 409 412, 414, 422, 456.
Woman's Self-denying Labors, 297 378.
Woman's Work, 485.
Woods, Leonard, 393, 463.
Worthies, Presbyterian, Sec. XXVI. XXVII., and L.
Wyclif, John, 9, 34.

www.ingramcontent.com/pod-product-compliance
Lightning Source LLC
Chambersburg PA
CBHW010928180426
43194CB00045B/2833